Lecture Notes in Computer Science 5440

Commenced Publication in 1973
Founding and Former Series Editors:
Gerhard Goos, Juris Hartmanis, and Jan

Denis Lalanne   Jürg Kohlas (Eds.)

Human Machine Interaction

Research Results of the MMI Program

 Springer

Volume Editors

Denis Lalanne
Jürg Kohlas
University of Fribourg
Department of Informatics
CH-1700, Fribourg, Switzerland
E-mail: {Denis.Lalanne, Juerg.Kohlas}@unifr.ch

Library of Congress Control Number: Applied for

CR Subject Classification (1998): H.5.2, H.5, I.4, I.2.7, I.2.10, D.2, D.3

LNCS Sublibrary: SL 2 – Programming and Software Engineering

ISSN   0302-9743
ISBN-10   3-642-00436-9 Springer Berlin Heidelberg New York
ISBN-13   978-3-642-00436-0 Springer Berlin Heidelberg New York

springer.com

© Springer-Verlag Berlin Heidelberg 2009
Printed in Germany

Typesetting: Camera-ready by author, data conversion by Scientific Publishing Services, Chennai, India
Printed on acid-free paper   SPIN: 12626151   06/3180   5 4 3 2 1 0

Preface

The interaction between humans and machines is a central concern of computer science. How can machines become convivial? How can machines present results of computations in a comprehensive way? What modes of communication between man and machine exist and how can they be best exploited according to the needs of a particular application? These are only a few of the important questions that neede to be addressed in order to enhance the usability of these universal machines that participate more and more in our daily life.

The design of human–computer interfaces calls for different abilities. Therefore, the Hasler Foundation launched a research program on "Man–Machine Interaction" (MMI) in 2005. At this time in Switzerland, the technical Universities of Applied Science emerged from the old engineering schools as new structures with new tasks. Among their responsibilities, applied research was explicitly stated as a new challenge. The goal is to transfer results of fundamental scientific research into applications. In order to foster this transfer, the Hasler Foundation decided to shape the program in such a way as to encourage close collaboration between universities and the newly formed Universities of Applied Science. One of the explicit objectives of the MMI program was to aid the Universities of Applied Science to build up their research activities, by benefiting from the research experience and the research results of universities. This should enhance technology and science transfer between the two complementary kinds of schools.

In the call for projects, collaboration between at least one partner from a University and one from a University of Applied Science was required. More than 80 project proposals were submitted, from which 20 were selected for a hearing and discussion. A limited number of projects were then invited to submit detailed applications. Finally eight of these projects were selected for funding by the Hasler Foundation. All these projects were also partially supported by the associated universities and other third parties such as the Swiss National Science Foundation. The members of all the project teams met in a workshop organized by the Hasler Foundation for two days in March 2007 in Appenberg. More than 40 scientists engaged in the program, along with international invited speakers who participated in the workshop. This volume documents the results of the MMI program. The Hasler Foundation's existing endowments derive from the former Hasler AG (1852-1986), a pioneer of the Swiss telecommunications industry. The foundation is committed to promoting high-level research and education in the field of information and telecommunication systems. MMI is one of several programs launched and supported by the foundation. We refer readers to the website www.haslerfoundation.ch for further information.

The Hasler Foundation thanks the main editor Denis Lalanne and the authors of the contributed papers. We also thank Springer for accepting this volume in the prestigious *Lecture Notes in Computer Science* series. It is our hope that we thereby contribute to advancing and encouraging further research in the field of man–machine interaction.

January 2009   Jürg Kohlas

Acknowledgments

The reviewing process of this book involved mostly internal reviewers (taking part in the authoring of some chapters of this book), and also external international experts to insure the scientific quality of the chapters. We thank both internal and external reviewers for their hard work.

External Reviewers

Frederic Bechet	University of Avignon, France
Enrico Bertini	University of Fribourg, Switzerland
Ginevra Castellano	Queen Mary University of London, UK
Jean Hennebert	University of Fribourg, Switzerland
Elise van den Hoven	Eindhoven University of Technology, The Netherlands
Ian Horswill	Northwestern University, USA
Vincent Lepetit	Ecole Polytechnique Fédérale de Lausanne, Switzerland
Nuno Jardim Nunes	University of Madeira, Portugal
Bernhard Reitinger	Microsoft, USA
John T. Stasko	Georgia Institute of Technology, USA

Internal Reviewers

Beatrice Amrhein	Berner Fachhochschule
Jacques Bapst	University of Applied Sciences Western Switzerland
Guido Bologna	University of Applied Sciences Western Switzerland
Guillaume Chanel	University of Geneva
Benoît Deville	University of Geneva
Philippe Dugerdil	University of Applied Sciences, Geneva
Gilles Falquet	University of Geneva
Stephan Fischli	Berner Fachhochschule
Harald Gall	University of Zürich
Wolfgang Gessner	University of Applied Sciences Northwestern Switzerland
Rolf Ingold	University of Fribourg
Urs Künzler	Bern University of Applied Sciences

Elena Mugellini	University of Applied Sciences of Western Switzerland
Matteo Risoldi	University of Geneva
Christophe Salzmann	Ecole Polytechnique Fédérale de Lausanne
Jean-Frederic Wagen	University of Applied Sciences Western Switzerland

Introduction

Human–machine interaction (HMI), or more commonly human–computer interaction (HCI), is the study of interaction between people and computers. It is an interdisciplinary subject, relating computer science with many other fields of research such as psychology, sociology, and the arts.

This book presents results from the eight projects supported by the Research Program in Man–Machine Interaction (MMI) funded by the Hasler Foundation between 2005 and 2008. The research program focused on specific sub-domains of HMI including multimodal interaction, tangible user interfaces, information and scientific visualization, sonification, augmented reality, and haptic interfaces. The projects developed innovative interaction and enabling technologies (image and video analysis, speech recognition, object identification, etc.) to support humans in important application domains such as health, sport, and the inclusion of blind people in society.

I decided to also incorporate three survey chapters at the beginning of this book in order to situate the work with respect to the international state of the art. These chapters (Part I) introduce the three fundamental research areas addressed by the projects supported by the MMI Research Program. The projects themselves are presented in detail in the three parts that follow: multimodal user interfaces (Part II), interactive visualization (Part III), and mixed reality (Part IV). Each part is described in more detail below.

The first part (Part I: Chaps. 1–3) surveys the principal HMI research axes covered by the projects in the MMI research program, along with a recent international state of the art and a selection of projects that have been partly or fully undertaken at Swiss universities. The domain of multimodal user interfaces is surveyed in the first chapter: "Multimodal Interfaces: A Survey of Principles, Models and Frameworks." Multimodal interfaces coordinate natural input modalities such as speech, touch, gestures, and body movements with multimedia system outputs such as synthesized speech, sounds, and visualizations. The creation of a multimodal interface reveals a number of associated issues covered in this chapter, such as the fusion of heterogeneous data types, language modeling and dialog management, and time-sensitive software architectures. This chapter summarizes the major challenges in the field and concludes with an outline of the current state of multimodal interaction research in Switzerland. The domains of scientific visualization and information visualization are introduced in the second chapter: "Interactive Visualization - A Survey." Scientific visualization and information visualization are both concerned with presenting data to users. Scientific visualization is different from information visualization in that it involves the presentation of data that have some physical or geometric correspondence, while information visualization focuses on abstract data without such correspondences such as symbolic, tabular, networked, hierarchical, or textual information sources. The survey describes typical applications and research directions and reviews current Swiss research activities related to interactive visualization. The field of mixed reality is discussed in the third chapter: "Mixed Reality—A Survey." Mixed reality deals with the combination of real-world and computer generated data. Here, real and virtual worlds are merged to produce new environments where physical and digital objects co-exist and interact in real time. It is the convergence of domains such as augmented reality, augmented virtuality, and virtual reality. Research challenges addressed in this field include the tracking of real-world objects and the creation of hand-held displays or projection systems that augment the real world with computer generated graphics. This chapter gives an overview of the field by presenting example applications, technical solutions, and current research challenges. The chapter concludes with a review of mixed reality projects that include participants from Swiss universities.

The second part (Part II: Chaps. 4–6) presents projects from the MMI research program related to multimodal user interfaces. Three focus areas are addressed: speech-based user interfaces in hostile environments, tangible user interaction, and emotion-based man–machine interaction. Chapter 4, "Intelligent Multi-Modal Interfaces for Mobile Applications in Hostile Environments," describes how speech-based user-system interaction can be used to support human–computer interaction in tasks with high cognitive load, such as sailing in racing conditions. Chapter 5, "MEMODULES as Tangible Shortcuts to Multimedia Information," uses the manipulation of physical objects, combined with classical modalities such as speech and gesture, as a way to interact with digital information and create tangible reminders in real life. Finally, chap. 6, "Why Androids Will Have Emotions; Constructing Human-Like Actors and Communicators Based on Exact Sciences of the Mind," discusses the possibility of modeling emotions (e.g., happiness, joy) so that machines can understand and mimic them. Furthermore, this chapter proposes a new language to model human emotions, their conditions, situations, and dependent dimensions, as a way to create innovative HMI paradigms.

The third part (Part III: Chaps. 7–9) presents projects of the MMI research program related to scientific and information visualization. The system described in the first chapter of this part manipulates abstract information and as such follows the standard definition of information visualization; the other two chapters tackle HMI issues related to browsing and interaction in scientific visualizations. Chapter 7, "Evospaces: Multi-dimensional Navigation Spaces for Software Evolution," approaches software visualization from an original perspective, representing abstract information with iconic metaphors (e.g., a city map) in order to capture the architecture, evolution, or morphology of a software's source code. This metaphoric approach facilitates collaboration between people participating in the development of a common software. Chapter 8, "HOVISSE—Haptic Osteosynthesis Virtual Intra-operative Surgery Support Environment," presents a VR system for medical practitioners. It also provides a haptic interface that allows medical practitioners to "feel" the virtual world in which they are immersed. As such, the chapter also contributes to the topic of multimodal interfaces. The BATICS project (chap. 9), "A Language and a Methodology for Prototyping User Interfaces for Control Systems," explores the possibility of building 3D graphical user interface authoring tools (in the domain of complex systems control). While the project's main focus is on software engineering issues, this contribution will also prove valuable for those building novel 3D user interfaces.

Finally, the fourth part (Part IV: Chaps. 10–11) presents research results in the domains of augmented and mixed reality. Chapter 10, "See ColOr: Seeing Colors with an Orchestra," aims at augmenting the perception of visually impaired people. It also contributes to the topic of multimodal interfaces since it targets the inclusion of blind people by substituting a deficient modality (in this case vision), with a reliable one (in this case audition). For this purpose, the machine analyzes the scene through image processing techniques and describes it to humans through meaningful sounds. This project also tackles the sonification domain, which in some ways is similar to visualization, but using a different human sense (hearing in place of vision). The final Chapter chap. 11, "6th Sense—Toward a Generic Framework for End-to-End Adaptive Wearable Augmented Reality," proposes a generic framework in the domain of wearable computing and augmented reality. The idea is to augment a user's visual perception with digital annotations displayed within his/her semi-transparent eye glasses, for example, in order to support field operators in chemical plants.

January 2009   Denis Lalanne

Table of Contents

Part I: Human Machine Interaction

Multimodal Interfaces: A Survey of Principles, Models and
Frameworks 3
    Bruno Dumas, Denis Lalanne, and Sharon Oviatt

Interactive Visualization - A Survey 27
    Dominique Brodbeck, Riccardo Mazza, and Denis Lalanne

Mixed Reality: A Survey 47
    Enrico Costanza, Andreas Kunz, and Morten Fjeld

Part II: Multimodal User Interfaces

Intelligent Multi-modal Interfaces for Mobile Applications in Hostile
Environment (IM-HOST) 71
    Claude Stricker, Jean-Frédéric Wagen, Guillermo Aradilla,
    Hervé Bourlard, Hynek Hermansky, Joel Pinto, Paul-Henri Rey,
    and Jérôme Théraulaz

MEMODULES as Tangible Shortcuts to Multimedia Information 103
    Elena Mugellini, Denis Lalanne, Bruno Dumas, Florian Evéquoz,
    Sandro Gerardi, Anne Le Calvé, Alexandre Boder, Rolf Ingold, and
    Omar Abou Khaled

Why Androids Will Have Emotions: Constructing Human-Like Actors
and Communicators Based on Exact Sciences of the Mind 133
    Wolfgang Gessner, Gesine Lenore Schiewer, and Alex Ringenbach

Part III: Interactive Visualization

EvoSpaces - Multi-dimensional Navigation Spaces for Software
Evolution 167
    Sazzadul Alam, Sandro Boccuzzo, Richard Wettel, Philippe Dugerdil,
    Harald Gall, and Michele Lanza

HOVISSE – Haptic Osteosynthesis Virtual Intra-operative Surgery
Support Environment 193
    Urs Künzler, Beatrice Amrhein, Jürgen Eckerle, Stephan Fischli,
    Robert Hauck, Dominik Hoigné, and Reto Witschi

A Language and a Methodology for Prototyping User Interfaces for
Control Systems   221
    Matteo Risoldi, Vasco Amaral, Bruno Barroca, Kaveh Bazargan,
    Didier Buchs, Fabian Cretton, Gilles Falquet, Anne Le Calvé,
    Stéphane Malandain, and Pierrick Zoss

Part IV: Mixed Reality

See ColOr: Seeing Colours with an Orchestra   251
    Benoît Deville, Guido Bologna, Michel Vinckenbosch, Thierry Pun

6th Sense – Toward a Generic Framework for End-to-End Adaptive
Wearable Augmented Reality   280
    Damien Perritaz, Christophe Salzmann, Denis Gillet, Olivier Naef,
    Jacques Bapst, Frédéric Barras, Elena Mugellini, and
    Omar Abou Khaled

Author Index   311

Part I
Human Machine Interaction

Multimodal Interfaces: A Survey of Principles, Models and Frameworks

Bruno Dumas[1], Denis Lalanne[1], and Sharon Oviatt[2]

[1] DIVA Group, University of Fribourg
Bd de Pérolles 90, 1700 Fribourg, Switzerland
{bruno.dumas,denis.lalanne}@unifr.ch
[2] Incaa Designs
821 Second Ave., Ste. 1100, Seattle WA. 98104
oviatt@incaadesigns.org

Abstract. The grand challenge of multimodal interface creation is to build reliable processing systems able to analyze and understand multiple communication means in real-time. This opens a number of associated issues covered by this chapter, such as heterogeneous data types fusion, architectures for real-time processing, dialog management, machine learning for multimodal interaction, modeling languages, frameworks, etc. This chapter does not intend to cover exhaustively all the issues related to multimodal interfaces creation and some hot topics, such as error handling, have been left aside. The chapter starts with the features and advantages associated with multimodal interaction, with a focus on particular findings and guidelines, as well as cognitive foundations underlying multimodal interaction. The chapter then focuses on the driving theoretical principles, time-sensitive software architectures and multimodal fusion and fission issues. Modeling of multimodal interaction as well as tools allowing rapid creation of multimodal interfaces are then presented. The article concludes with an outline of the current state of multimodal interaction research in Switzerland, and also summarizes the major future challenges in the field.

1 Introduction

Of the numerous ways explored by researchers to enhance human-computer communication, multimodal interaction has shown much development in the past decade. On one hand, multimodal interfaces target a more "human" way of interacting with computers, by means of speech, gestures or other modalities, as well as being preferred over unimodal interfaces by users [49]; on the other hand, multimodal interfaces have been demonstrated to offer better flexibility and reliability than other human/machine interaction means [51].

As a research subject, multimodal interaction encompasses a broad spectrum of research domains, from cognitive psychology to software engineering, including human-computer interaction, which is already cross-disciplinary. While cognitive psychologists study how the human brain processes information and interacts through various modalities, interaction practitioners are interested by how humans use multimodal interfaces, and finally software engineers are interested in building tools and

D. Lalanne and J. Kohlas (Eds.): Human Machine Interaction, LNCS 5440, pp. 3–26, 2009.
© Springer-Verlag Berlin Heidelberg 2009

systems supporting the development of such multimodal interfaces, thus studying software architectures and multimodal processing techniques.

Cognitive psychologists have extensively studied how humans perceive, process, and express multimodal information; their conclusions are of interest for developers and HCI practitioners. The creation of a typical multimodal application requires a number of different components and careful implementation work. Hence, "good practices" and algorithms regarding the general architecture of a multimodal application, its fusion and fission engines or dialogue management components emerged during the past 20 years [13, 62]. In a more theoretical way, modeling of multimodal interaction and, generally speaking, of the underlying human-machine dialog has seen extensive work. This theoretical work leads to the definition of a number of languages dedicated to multimodal data description, multimodal human-machine dialog modeling or multimodal applications scripting. Together with these different languages, different tools targeted at expediting the creation of multimodal interfaces have appeared.

This chapter runs the spectrum from cognitive foundations to development tools, with a particular emphasis on the multimodal processing aspects. The article is not an exhaustive summary of the findings and issues in this broad and multidisciplinary field, but rather presents the major issues and findings, with an emphasis on the driving principles for the creation of multimodal interfaces, their models, and programming frameworks. The chapter begins with a global view on multimodal interaction, with a presentation of its aims and advantages, its features, and cognitive foundations underlying multimodal systems; seminal works, findings and guidelines particular to multimodal interaction conclude this second section. The third section gives a detailed look at theoretical and practical principles of multimodal systems, architectures and key components of such systems; among those key components, fusion engines, fission engines and dialog management all have a dedicated subsection. The third section ends with a view of potential uses of machine learning for multimodal interaction. The fourth section focuses on modeling and creation of multimodal interfaces, with subsections detailing models, modeling languages and programming frameworks for multimodal interaction. The fifth section is devoted to multimodal applications in Switzerland, and the sixth and last section concludes this chapter with future directions.

2 Foundations, Aims and Features of Multimodal Interaction

This section will present the aims underlying multimodal interaction research, as well as the distinctive features of multimodal interfaces compared to other types of interfaces. The first part will present a general view of multimodal systems, and more specifically their aims and advantages. The section continues with a part focused on particular features of multimodal interfaces, compared to standard GUI interfaces. The third part introduces cognitive theories linked to multimodal interaction design. Finally, the fourth part presents seminal works, findings and guidelines in the field of multimodal interaction.

2.1 Aims and Advantages of Multimodal Systems

Multimodal systems are computer systems endowed with multimodal capabilities for human/machine interaction and able to interpret information from various sensory and communication channels. Literally, multimodal interaction offers a set of "modalities" to users to allow them to interact with the machine. According to Oviatt [49], « *Multimodal interfaces process two or more combined user input modes (such as speech, pen, touch, manual gesture, gaze, and head and body movements) in a coordinated manner with multimedia system output. They are a new class of interfaces that aim to recognize naturally occurring forms of human language and behavior, and which incorporate one or more recognition-based technologies (e.g. speech, pen, vision)* ». Two unique features of multimodal architectures and processing are: (1) the fusion of different types of data; and (2) real-time processing and temporal constraints imposed on information processing [46, 54].

Thus, multimodal systems represent a new class of user-machine interfaces, different from standard WIMP interfaces. They tend to emphasize the use of richer and more natural ways of communication, such as speech or gestures, and more generally all the five senses. Hence, the objective of multimodal interfaces is twofold: (1) to support and accommodate users' perceptual and communicative capabilities; and (2) to integrate computational skills of computers in the real world, by offering more natural ways of interaction to humans.

Multimodal interfaces were first seen as more efficient than unimodal interfaces; however, evaluations showed that multimodal interfaces only speed up task completion by 10% [50]. Hence, efficiency should not be considered the main advantage of multimodal interfaces. On the other hand, multimodal interfaces have been shown to improve error handling & reliability: users made 36% fewer errors with a multimodal interface than with a unimodal interface [50]. Multimodal interfaces also add greater expressive power, and greater potential precision in visual-spatial tasks. Finally, they provide improved support for users' preferred interaction style, since 95%-100% of users prefer multimodal interaction over unimodal interaction [50].

2.2 Features

Compared to other types of human/computer interaction, multimodal interaction seeks to offer users a more natural and transparent interaction, using speech, gestures, gaze direction, etc. Multimodal interfaces are hence expected to offer easier, more expressively powerful and more intuitive ways to use computers. Multimodal systems have the potential to enhance human/computer interaction in a number of ways:

- Enhanced robustness due to combining different partial information sources;
- Flexible personalization based on user and context;
- New functionality involving multi-user and mobile interaction.

When comparing multimodal user interfaces (MUI) with standard graphical user interfaces (GUI), it is possible to draw the following differences [54]:

Table 1. Differences between GUIs and MUIs

GUI	MUI
Single input stream	Multiple input streams
Atomic, deterministic	Continuous, probabilistic
Sequential processing	Parallel processing
Centralized architectures	Distributed & time-sensitive architectures

In standard WIMP interaction style (Window, Icon, Menu, Pointing device), a singular physical input device is used to control the position of a cursor and present information organized in windows and represented with icons. In contrast, in multimodal interfaces, various modalities can be used as input streams (voice, gestures, facial expressions, etc.). Further, input from graphical user interfaces is generally deterministic, with either mouse position or characters typed on a keyboard used to control the computer. In multimodal interfaces, input streams have to be first interpreted by probabilistic recognizers (HMM, GMM, SOM, etc.) and thus their results are weighted by a degree of uncertainty. Further, events are not always clearly temporally delimited and thus require a continuous interpretation. Due to the multiple recognizers necessary to interpret multimodal input and the continuous property of input streams, multimodal systems depend on time synchronized parallel processing. Further, as we will see in the following section, the time sensitivity of multimodal systems is crucial to determining the order of processing multimodal commands in parallel or in sequence. Finally, multimodal systems often implement a distributed architecture, to deal out the computation and insure synchronization. Multimodal systems can be very resource demanding in some cases (e.g., speech/gesture recognition, machine-learning augmented integration).

2.3 Cognitive Foundations

The advantages of multimodal interface design are elucidated in the theory of cognitive psychology, as well as human-computer interaction studies, most specifically in cognitive load theory, gestalt theory, and Baddeley's model of working memory [5, 53, 55]. Findings in cognitive psychology reveal:

- humans are able to process modalities partially independently and, thus, presenting information with multiple modalities increases human working memory;
- humans tend to reproduce interpersonal interaction patterns during multimodal interaction with a system;
- human performance is improved when interacting multimodally due to the way human perception, communication, and memory function.

For example, when processing both auditory and visual information during speech, a listener is able to extract a higher rate of lexical intelligibility (Grant & Greenberg [24]). This section thus presents works from cognitive science related to multimodal interaction, following cognitive load theory, gestalt theory and Baddeley's model of working memory; the section ends with the description of a framework aimed at human performance prediction.

Mousavi et al [44] experimented with presenting students content using partly auditory and partly visual modes. The split-attention effect (Sweller et al. [66]) that resulted *"suggested that working memory has partially independent processors for handling visual and auditory material."* The authors argued that if working memory is a primary limitation in learning, then increasing effective working memory by presenting information in a dual-mode form rather than a purely visual one, could expand processing capabilities. The results of Mousavi et al. were confirmed by Tindall-Ford et al. [67], who used more general types of tasks than pure mathematical ones, and by Mayer & Moreno [39] who studied the same effect with multimedia learning material. All this work is in line with the cognitive load theory, which assumes a limited working memory in which all conscious learning and thinking occurs, and an effectively unlimited long-term memory that holds a large number of automated schemas that can be brought into working memory for processing. Oviatt [53] applied these findings to educational interface design in testing a number of different user-centered design principles and strategies, showing that user-interface design that minimizes cognitive load can free up mental resources and improve student performance. One strategy for accomplishing this is designing a multimodal interface for students.

In the design of map-based pen/voice interfaces, Oviatt et al. [55] demonstrated that Gestalt theoretic principles successfully predicted a number of human behaviors, such as: users consistently followed a specific multimodal integration pattern (i.e. sequential versus simultaneous), and entrenched further in their pattern during error handling when you might expect them to switch their behavior. Gestalt theory also correctly predicted in this study a dominant number of subjects applying simultaneous integration over sequential integration.

The original short-term memory model of Baddeley & Hitch [6], refined later by Baddeley [5], described short-term or working memory as being composed of three main components: the central executive (which acts as supervisory system and controls the flow of information), the phonological loop, and the visuo-spatial sketchpad, with the latter two dedicated to auditory-verbal and visuo-spatial information processing, respectively. Although these two slave processors are coordinated by a central executive, they function largely independently in terms of lower-level modality processing. This model was derived from experimental findings with dual-task paradigms. Performance of two simultaneous tasks requiring the use of two perceptual domains (i.e. a visual and a verbal task) were observed to be nearly as efficient as performance of individual tasks. In contrast, when a person tries to carry out two tasks simultaneously that use the same perceptual domain, performance is less efficient than when performing the tasks individually. As such, human performance is improved when interacting with two modalities that can be co-processed in separate stores.

Wickens [72][73] also developed a framework, the "multiple resource model", aimed at performance prediction involving coordination between user input and system output modes for different types of tasks. This model suggests that four different dimensions are to be taken into account when predicting coordination versus interference during human task processing involving different modes. The four dimensions considered are stages (perceptual/cognitive vs. response), sensory modalities (auditory vs. visual), codes (visual vs. spatial) and channels of visual information (focal vs. ambient).

2.4 Seminal Works, Findings and Guidelines

Multimodal interfaces emerged approximately 30 years ago within the field of human/computer interaction with Richard Bolt's "Put-That-There" application [9], which was created in 1980. First multimodal systems sought ways to go beyond the standard interaction mode at this time, which was graphical interfaces with keyboards and mice. Bolt's "Put-that-there" processed spoken commands linked to a pointing gesture using an armrest-mounted touchpad to move and change shapes displayed on a screen in front of the user. Since this seminal work, multimodal interaction practitioners have strived to integrate more modalities, to refine hardware and software components, and to explore limits and capabilities of multimodal interfaces. Historically, the main trend has focused on pointing and speech combined using speech/mouse, speech/pen [17], speech/gesture [45], or speech/gaze tracking [31]. Later multimodal interfaces evolved beyond pointing into richer interaction, allowing users to produce symbolic gestures such as arrows and encircling.

Another direction in multimodal research has been speech/lip movement integration [57][12], driven by cognitive science research in intersensory audio-visual perception. This kind of work has included classification of human lip movement (visemes) and the viseme-phoneme mappings that occur during articulated speech. Such work has contributed improving robustness of speech recognition in noisy environments. For more details about these systems, see [8].

Table 2. 10 myths of multimodal interaction (We acknowledge ACM for allowing the reprint of this table)

Myth #1: *If you build a multimodal system, users will interact multimodally.*
Myth #2: *Speech and pointing is the dominant multimodal integration pattern.*
Myth #3: *Multimodal input involves simultaneous signals.*
Myth #4: *Speech is the primary input mode in any multimodal system that includes it.*
Myth #5: *Multimodal language does not differ linguistically from unimodal language.*
Myth #6: *Multimodal integration involves redundancy of content between modes.*
Myth #7: *Individual error-prone recognition technologies combine multimodally to produce even greater unreliability.*
Myth #8: *All users' multimodal commands are integrated in a uniform way.*
Myth #9: *Different input modes are capable of transmitting comparable content.*
Myth #10: *Enhanced efficiency is the main advantage of multimodal systems.*

In the course of the last decade, researchers have highlighted particular empirical findings that have guided the design of multimodal interfaces compared to other sorts of human-computer interfaces. Key findings are illustrated in the following "10 myths" shown in Table 2, which exposed common engineering myths regarding how people interact multimodally [52]. Based on empirical findings, Oviatt distilled implications for how more effective multimodal interfaces could be designed.

In more recent years, research has also focused on mainstreaming multimodal interfaces. In this trend, Reeves et al. defined the following "guidelines for multimodal user interface design" [59]:

- Multimodal systems should be designed for the broadest range of users and contexts of use, since the availability of multiple modalities supports flexibility. For example, the same user may benefit from speech input in a car, but pen input in a noisy environment.
- Designers should take care to address privacy and security issues when creating multimodal systems: speech, for example, should not be used as a modality to convey private or personal information in public contexts.
- Modalities should be integrated in a manner compatible with user preferences and capabilities, for example, combining complementary audio and visual modes that users can co-process more easily.
- Multimodal systems should be designed to adapt easily to different contexts, user profiles and application needs.
- Error prevention and handling is a major advantage of multimodal interface design, for both user- and system-centered reasons. Specific guidelines include integrating complementary modalities to improve system robustness, and giving users better control over modality selection so they can avoid errors.

3   Principles of User-Computer Multimodal Interaction

The driving principles of multimodal interaction are well described in numerous surveys[8][26][51][54][62]. The following concepts are popularly accepted: fusion (also called multimodal signal integration), fission (also called response planning), dialog management, context management and time-sensitive architectures. In the following subsections, we introduce these concepts, at a high level first to illustrate how they are organized around a common conceptual architecture, and later at a lower level to probe key principles.

3.1   Theoretical Principles

Inspired by Norman's action cycle [47], and based on well accepted findings and taxonomies, the following model of multimodal man-machine communication can be drawn, together with the major concepts that should be considered when building a multimodal system (Figure 1): the fusion of multimodal inputs, and the multimodal fission to generate an adequate message to the user, according to the context of use, preferences and profile.

When a human interacts with a machine, his communication can be divided in four different states. The first state is a *decision state*, in which the communication message content is prepared consciously for an intention, or unconsciously for attentional content or emotions. The second state is the *action state*, where the communication means to transmit the message are selected, such as speech, gestures or facial expressions. The machine, in turn, will make use of a number of different modules to grasp the most information possible from a user, and will have similarly four main states

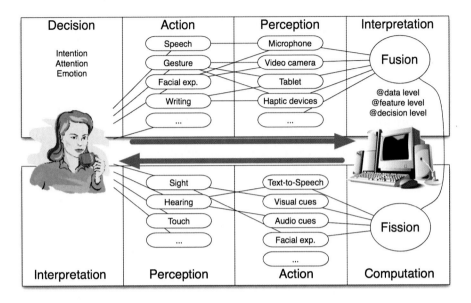

Fig. 1. A representation of multimodal man machine interaction loop

(Figure 1). At first, the messages are interpreted in the *perception state*, where the multimodal system receives information from one or multiple sensors, at one or multiple levels of expression. In the *interpretation state*, the multimodal system will try to give some meaning to the different information it collected in the perception state. This is typically the place where fusion of multimodal messages takes place. Further, in the *computational state*, action is taken following the business logic and dialogue manager rules defined by the developer. Depending on the meaning extracted in the interpretation state, an answer is generated and transmitted in the *action state*, in which a fission engine will determine the most relevant modalities to return the message, depending on the context of use (e.g. in the car, office, etc.) and the profile of the user (blind user, elderly, etc.).

3.2   Computational Architecture and Key Components

The previous section illustrated multimodal man-machine interaction underlying features. In this section, we describe multimodal interaction from the machine side, and the major software components that a multimodal system should contain. The generic components for handling of multimodal integration are: a fusion engine, a fission module, a dialog manager and a context manager, which all together form what is called the "integration committee". Figure 2 illustrates the processing flow between these components, the input and output modalities, as well as the potential client applications. As illustrated in the figure, input modalities are first perceived though various recognizers, which output their results to the *fusion engine*, in charge of giving a common interpretation of the inputs. The various levels at which recognizers' results can be fused are described in the next section, together with the various

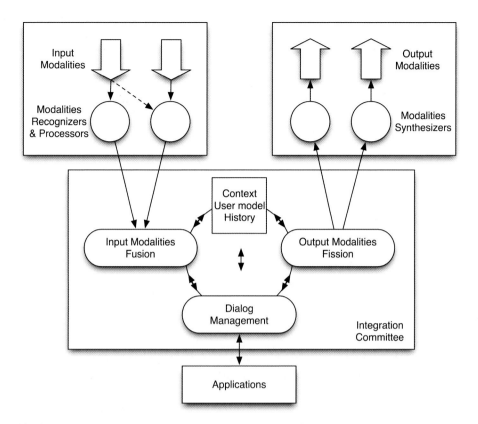

Fig. 2. The architecture of a multimodal system, with the central integration committee and its major software components

fusion mechanisms. When the fusion engine comes to an interpretation, it communicates it to the *dialog manager,* in charge of identifying the dialog state, the transition to perform, the action to communicate to a given application, and/or the message to return through the *fission component.* The fission engine is finally in charge of returning a message to the user through the most adequate modality or combination of modalities, depending on the user profile and context of use. For this reason, the *context manager*, in charge of tracking the location, context and user profile, closely communicates any changes in the environment to the three other components, so that they can adapt their interpretations.

3.3   Fusion of Input Modalities

Fusion of input modalities is one of the features that distinguish multimodal interfaces from unimodal interfaces. The goal of fusion is to extract meaning from a set of input modalities and pass it to a human-machine dialog manager. Fusion of different modalities is a delicate task, which can be executed at three levels: at data level, at feature level and at decision level. Three different types of architectures can in turn

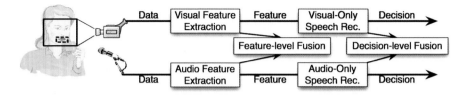

Fig. 3. The various levels of multimodal fusion

manage decision-level fusion: frames-based architectures, unification-based architectures or hybrid symbolic/statistical fusion architectures.

Sharma et al. [62] consider these three levels for fusion of incoming data. Each fusion scheme functions at a different level of analysis of the same modality channel. As a classic illustration, consider the speech channel: data from this channel can be processed at the audio signal level, at the phoneme (feature) level, or at the semantic (decision) level (Figure 3).

- *Data-level fusion* is used when dealing with multiple signals coming from a very similar modality source (e.g., two webcams recording the same scene from different viewpoints). With this fusion scheme, no loss of information occurs, as the signal is directly processed. This benefit is also the main shortcoming of data-level fusion. Due to the absence of pre-processing, it is highly susceptible to noise and failure.

- *Feature-level fusion* is a common type of fusion when tightly-coupled or time synchronized modalities are to be fused. The standard example is the fusion of speech and lip movements. Feature-level fusion is susceptible to low-level information loss, although it handles noise better. The most classic architectures used for this type of fusion are adaptive systems like artificial neural networks, Gaussian mixture models, or hidden Markov models. The use of these types of adaptive architecture also means that feature-level fusion systems need numerous data training sets before they can achieve satisfactory performance.

- *Decision-level fusion* is the most common type of fusion in multimodal applications. The main reason is its ability to manage loosely-coupled modalities like, for example, pen and speech interaction. Failure and noise sensitivity is low with decision-level feature, since the data has been preprocessed. On one hand, this means that decision-level fusion has to rely on the quality of previous processing. On the other hand, unification-based decision-level fusion has the major benefit of improving reliability and accuracy of semantic interpretation, by combining partial semantic information coming from each input mode which can yield "mutual disambiguation" [49].

Table 3 below summarizes the three fusion levels, their characteristics, sensitivity to noise, and usage contexts.

Table 3. Characteristics of fusion levels

	Data-level fusion	Features-level fusion	Decision-level fusion
Input type	Raw data of same type	Closely coupled modalities	Loosely coupled modalities
Level of information	Highest level of information detail	Moderate level of information detail	Mutual disambiguation by combining data from modes
Noise/failures sensitivity	Highly susceptible to noise or failures	Less sensitive to noise or failures	Highly resistant to noise or failures
Usage	Not really used for combining modalities	Used for fusion of particular modes	Most widely used type of fusion
Application examples	Fusion of two video streams	speech recognition from voice and lips	Pen/speech interaction

Typical architectures for decision-level fusion are frame-based fusion, unification-based fusion and hybrid symbolic/statistical fusion.

- *Frame-based fusion* [70] uses data structures called frames or features for meaning representation of data coming from various sources or modalities. These structures represent objects as attribute-value pairs.
- *Unification-based fusion* [27] is based on recursively merging attribute-value structures to obtain a logical whole meaning representation.
- *Symbolic/statistical fusion* [74] is an evolution of standard symbolic unification-based approaches, which adds statistical processing techniques to the fusion techniques described above. These kinds of "hybrid" fusion techniques have been demonstrated to achieve robust and reliable results. An example of a symbolic-statistical hybrid fusion technique is the Member-Team-Committee (MTC) architecture used in Quickset [75].

3.4 Fission of Output Modalities

When multiple output modalities such as text-to-speech synthesis, audio cues, visual cues, haptic feedback or animated agents are available, output selection becomes a delicate task to adapt to a context of use (e.g. car, home, work), type of task (e.g., information search, entertainment) or type of user (e.g. visually impaired, elderly).

Fission techniques [23] allow a multimodal application to generate a given message in an adequate form according to the context and user profiles. Technically speaking, fission consists of three tasks:

- Message construction, where the information to be transmitted to the user is created; approaches for content selection and structuring revolve mainly around either schema-based approaches or plan-based approaches [40, 43].

- Output channel selection, where interfaces are selected according to context and user profile in order to convey all data effectively in a given situation. Characteristics such as available output modalities, information to be presented, communicative goals of the presenter, user characteristics and task to be performed are forms of knowledge that can be used for output channel selection [2, 3].
- Construction of a coherent and synchronized result: when multiple output channels are used, layout and temporal coordination are to be taken into account. Moreover, some systems will produce multimodal and cross-modal referring expressions, which will also have to be coordinated.

3.5   Dialogue Management and Time-Sensitive Architectures

The time constraint is highly important in multimodal systems and all the modalities should be properly time-stamped and synchronized. Time-sensitive architectures need to establish temporal thresholds for time-stamping start and end of each input signal piece, so that two commands sequences can be identified. Indeed, when two commands are performed in parallel, in a synergistic way, it is important to know in which order the commands have been entered because the interpretation will vary accordingly. For instance, in the following application, in which voice and gestures are used simultaneously to control a music player, depending on the order in which modalities are presented the interpretation varies:

- <pointing> "Play next track": will result in playing the track following the one selected with a gesture;
- "Play" <pointing> "next track": will result in first playing the manually selected track and then passing to the following at the time "next is pronounced";
- "Play next track" <pointing>: In this case, the system should interpret the commands as being redundant.

The dialog management system and synchronization mechanism should consider multiple potential causes of lag:

- delay due to technology (e.g. speech recognition);
- delay due to multimodal system architecture;
- user differences in habitual multimodal integration pattern [51][55].

For this reason, multi-agent architectures (or similar architectures such as components-based systems) are advantageous for distributing processing and for coordinating many system components (e.g., speech recognition, pen recognition, natural language processing, graphic display, TTS output, application database).

Bui [13] considers four different approaches to dialog management:

- *Finite-state and frame-based approaches*: in this kind of dialog management approach, the dialog structure is represented in the form of a state machine. Frame-based models are an extension of finite-state models, using a slot-filling strategy in which a number of predefined information sources are to be gathered [16].
- *Information state-based and probabilistic approaches*: these approaches try to describe human-machine dialog following information states, consisting of five main

components: informational components, formal representations of those components, a set of dialog moves, a set of update rules and an update strategy [68].

- *Plan-based approaches*: the plan-based approaches are based on the plan-based theories of communicative action and dialog [16]. These theories claim that the speaker's speech act is part of a plan and that it is the listener's job to identify and respond appropriately to this plan [15].
- *Collaborative agents-based approaches*: these approaches view dialog as a collaborative process between intelligent agents. The agents work together to obtain a mutual understanding of the dialog. This induces discourse phenomena such as clarifications and confirmations [48].

3.6 Machine Learning for Multimodal Interaction

Machine learning techniques play an important role in multimodal interfaces [26], and most certainly will continue to extend this role. Indeed, many parts of multimodal systems are likely to receive support from machine learning. Modality recognizers already make extensive use of machine learning: speech recognition, face detection, face recognition, facial expression analysis, gesture recognition or eye tracking are examples of different domains of interest both for multimodal interaction and machine learning.

Aside from modality handling, machine learning has been applied for fusion of input recognizers' data, mainly at the feature level. Fewer works have been achieved on decision level fusion with assistance from machine learning. An example of such work is Pan et al. [55], who proposed context-dependent versions of Bayesian inference method for multisensory data fusion. Nonetheless, Jaimes & Sebe [26] reckon that "*further research is still required to investigate fusion models able to efficiently use the complementary cues provided by multiple modalities*". User, task and context modeling also can benefit from machine learning techniques. Novel research fields related to machine learning, such as social signal processing [64], will help building a refined representation of the user in her collaborative context. Adaptability can then be addressed with the help of machine learning, by watching the users' behavior in the sensed context [21].

As Jaimes & Sebe [26] highlight, currently "*most researchers process each channel (visual, audio) independently, and multimodal fusion is still in its infancy*". Thus, multimodal interaction researchers have work to achieve in order to attain efficient multimodal fusion, with careful consideration of the different available modalities and the way modalities interlock. Machine learning will be of interest in order to attain such a goal. Besides multimodal fusion, machine learning will help multimodal applications take into account the affective aspect of communication – emotions based on their physiological manifestations [41], such as facial expressions, gestures, postures, tone of voice, respiration, etc.

4 Modeling Languages and Frameworks

There have been several attempts to model and formalize multimodal interaction. This section presents several different levels of modeling. The first part introduces two abstract models designed to help developers evaluate the different types of multimodal interaction, viewed first from the machine side, then from the user side. The second part lists a number of languages used for multimodal recognizer output and multimodal synthesizer input representations, and modeling languages used to configure multimodal systems. The final part displays different programming frameworks for rapid creation of multimodal interfaces.

4.1 Multimodal Interaction Modeling

Modeling multimodal interaction is no simple task, due to the multiple input and output channels and modes, and the combination of possibilities between data coming from different sources, not to mention output modality selection based on context and user profile.

The shape taken by formal modeling of multimodal interaction depends on the level of abstraction considered. At lower levels of abstraction, formal modeling would focus on tools used for modality recognition and synthesis. At higher levels of abstraction, multimodal interaction modeling would focus more on modality combination and synchronization.

Formal modeling can also focus on the "pure" technical part as well as on the user-machine interaction. Two formal models exist for modality combination description:

- The CASE model [46], focusing on modality combination possibilities at the fusion engine level;
- the CARE model [18], giving attention to modality combination possibilities at the user level.

The CASE model introduces four properties: Concurrent – Alternate – Synergistic – Exclusive (figure 4). Each of those four properties describes a different way to combine modalities at the integration engine level, depending on two factors: combined or independent fusion of modalities, and sequential or synergistic use of modalities on the other hand. "Fusion of modalities" considers if different modalities are combined or managed independently, whereas "Use of modalities" observes the way modalities are activated: either one at a time, or in a synergistic manner.

The CARE model is more focused on the user-machine interaction level. This model also introduces four properties, which are Complementarity – Assignment – Redundancy – Equivalence. Complementarity is to be used when multiple complementary modalities are necessary to grasp the desired meaning (e.g. "put that there" [9] would need both pointing gestures and voice in order to be resolved). Assignment indicates that only one modality can lead to the desired meaning (e.g. the steering wheel of a car is the only way to direct the car). Redundancy implies multiple modalities which, even if used simultaneously, can be used individually to lead to the desired meaning (e.g. user utters a "play" speech command and pushes a button labeled "play", but only one "play" command would be taken into account). Finally, Equivalence entails multiple modalities that can all lead to the desired meaning, but only one would be used at a time (e.g. speech or keyboard can be used to write a text).

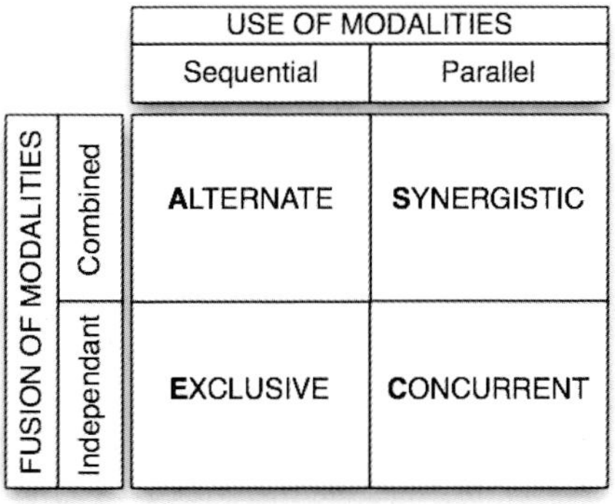

USE OF MODALITIES	
Sequential	Parallel

		Sequential	Parallel
FUSION OF MODALITIES	Combined	**A**LTERNATE	**S**YNERGISTIC
	Independant	**E**XCLUSIVE	**C**ONCURRENT

Fig. 4. The CASE model

4.2 Multimodal Interaction Modeling Languages

Interesting attempts at creating a full-fledged language for description of user-machine multimodal interaction have arisen in the past few years. Most of the approaches presented below revolve around the concept of a "multimodal web", enforced by the World Wide Web Consortium (W3C) Multimodal Interaction Activity and its proposed multimodal architecture [71]. This theoretical framework describes major components involved in multimodal interaction, as well as potential or existent markup languages used to relate those different components. Many elements described in this framework are of practical interest for multimodal HCI practitioners, such as the W3C EMMA markup language, or modality-focused languages such as VoiceXML or InkML. The work of the W3C inspired Katsurada et al. for their work on the XISL XML language [28]. XISL focuses on synchronization of multimodal input and output, as well as dialog flow and transition. Another approach of the problem is the one of Araki et al. [4], who propose MIML (Multimodal Interaction Markup Language). One of the key characteristics of this language is its three-layered description of interaction, focusing on interaction, tasks and platform. Finally, Stanciulescu et al. [64] followed a transformational approach for developing multimodal web user interfaces based on UsiXML, also in the steps of the W3C. Four steps are achieved to go from a generic model to the final user interface. Thus, one of the main features of their work is a strong independence to the actual input and output available channels.

Sire and Chatty describe in [63] what one should expect from a multimodal user interfaces programming language. From their proposal, the following requirements for a multimodal description language have been derived.

- Such a language should be *modality agnostic*, as research in input and output modalities continues to evolve today.
- A *binding mechanism to link the definition of the user interface composition with its runtime realization* should be provided.
- *Explicit control structures* should be present, such as conditional clauses and loops.
- *Extensible event definition mechanisms* are also needed for communication between user interface objects and the interaction model.

- *Data Modeling* should be carefully planned, as application data tends to be distributed in multiple places.
- Finally, a major requirement for a multimodal integration description language is the definition of *reusable components.*

"Modality agnostic" is the most debatable of those requirements, as one could argue that such a requirement will never be achievable, as every modality has its own particularities. Our interpretation of this requirement is the following: "modality agnostic" means that the language should not be specific for each individual modality, as modalities are all different; the language should be flexible enough (or canonic enough) to be adapted to a new and different modality. Hence, if a scripting or programming language can be in principle modality agnostic, such cannot be said of the fusion engine that needs to take into account the specificities of each modality to fuse data or features correctly.

A last point that stems from these six guidelines is *readability*: a language for description of multimodal interaction should be readable, as much in regard to the machine as to humans.

Formal languages for description of multimodal description can be approached from two different directions: either from expressiveness, or from usability. Expressiveness covers technical features such as extensibility, completeness, reusability, or temporal aspects considerations; usability covers more human features such as programmability or readability. Any formal language will have to find its place between those two general requirements; some languages will tend more toward expressiveness or usability. An interesting approach is to seek balance between usability and expressiveness: that is, a language able to configure a multimodal system, with high level modeling, and readable enough to be used as a learning tool, or even a communication tool.

4.3 Programming Frameworks

Further to multimodal interface creation, a number of tools have become available in recent years. Krahnstoever et al. [32] proposed a framework using speech and gestures to create a natural interface. The output of their framework was to be used on large screen displays enabling multi-user interaction. Fusion was done using a unification-based method. Cohen et al. [17] worked on Quickset, a speech/pen multimodal interface, based on Open Agent Architecture, which served as a test bed for unification-based and hybrid fusion methods. Bourguet [11] endeavored in the creation of a multimodal toolkit in which multimodal scenarios could be modelled using finite state machines. This multimodal toolkit is composed of two components, a graphical user interface named IMBuilder which interfaces the multimodal framework itself, named MEngine. Multimodal interaction models created with IMBuilder are saved as a XML file. Flippo et al. [22] also worked on the design of a multimodal framework, geared toward direct integration into a multimodal application. One of the most interesting aspects of their work is the use of a parallel application-independent fusion technique. The general framework architecture is based on agents, while the fusion technique itself uses frames. Configuration of the fusion is done via an XML file, specifying for each frame a number of slots to be filled and direct link to actual resolver implementations. Lastly, Bouchet et al. [10] proposed a component-based approach called

Table 4. Characteristics of different tools for creation of multimodal interfaces

	ICARE – OI [10]	OpenInterface [61]	IMBuilder/ MEngine [11]	Flippo et al. [22]	Krahnstoever [32]	Quickset [17]	Phidgets [25]	Papier-Mâché [30]
Architecture traits								
Finite state machine			x					
Components	x	x					x	
Software agents				x		x		
Fusion by frames					x			
Symbolic-statistical fusion						x		
Reusability easiness								
No programming kit					x	x		
Low-level programming (e.g. via API)					x		x	x
Higher-level Programming								
Visual Programming tool	x	x	x					
Characteristics								
Extensibility		x	x	x		x		
Pluggability							x	
Reusable components	x	x				x		
Open Source	x	x						x

ICARE thoroughly based on the CARE [18] design space. These components cover elementary tasks, modality-dependent tasks or generic tasks like fusion. Finally, communication between components is based on events. The components-based approach of ICARE has provided inspiration for a comprehensive open-source toolkit called OpenInterface [61]. OpenInterface components are configured via CIDL XML files, and a graphical editor.

Table 4 summarizes the different characteristics of the systems described above: extensible systems (i.e. toolkits) have the potential ability to add other input modalities in a practical way. Pluggability refers to the ability of a toolkit to insert itself into an architecture without having to rewrite everything. The other characteristics are self-explanatory.

5 Multimodal Interfaces in Switzerland

5.1 Multimodal Interfaces in IM2

The Swiss National Center of Competence in Research (NCCR) on Interactive Multimodal Information Management (IM2) is one of the 20 Swiss National Centers of Competence in Research (NCCR). IM2 aims at developing natural multimodal interfaces for human-computer interaction and to foster collaboration, focusing on new multimodal technologies to support human interaction, in the context of smart meeting rooms and remote meeting assistants.

The Individual Project on "Human Machine Interaction" is part of the NCCR IM2. While other activities in IM2 develop multimodal analysis and recognition technologies, the primary objective of IM2.HMI is to build cutting-edge technologies to develop interactive multimodal meeting browsers. The main goal of IM2.HMI is to design, develop and evaluate, with human subjects, novel interactive multimodal meeting browsers/assistants.

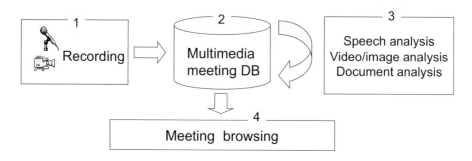

Fig. 5. Multimodal processing chain in IM2 meeting application

In order to support the development of so-called meeting browsers (4), and facilitate access to multimodal data and annotations (2), the JFerret framework has been designed and implemented. Using the JFerret framework, and taking benefits of most of the multimodal analysis, multimodal input recognizers and multimodal indexing and retrieval strategies made available in IM2, various meeting browsers have been implemented [33]. Those meeting browsers take benefit of most of the annotations made available by the other IM2 IPs: speech browsers (accelerated and overlapped), document-centric meeting browsers (JFriDoc, FaericWorld) [60], Dialog-centric browsers (TQB) [58], multimodal enabled browsers (Archivus, HephaisTK), multilingual (M3C) and recently personalized browsers (WotanEye) [34]. Most of these meeting browsers are in fact complete and transversal systems that access the multimodal meeting data, analyse them, process high level indexes and provide interactive user interfaces so that the user can browse the meeting corpora through multimodal queries. In the last couple of years, IM2.HMI has gently shifted towards online, a.k.a real-time, meeting assistance leveraging on past works. This includes new research on personalized meeting browsing, mobile and remote access to meetings [38], and meeting assistance before, during and after meetings.

IM2.HMI has tackled multimodality both at the content and at the interaction levels. While projects handling multimodality at the content level try to use the best of multimodal data indexing in order to create useful and usable meeting browsers, research projects handling multimodality at the interaction level study and build novel multimodal interaction paradigms, benefiting from various input modes.

Archivus, developed in the framework of IM2, is a good example of a research project handling multimodality both at the content and interaction levels. Archivus is a multimodal (pen, voice, mouse and keyboard) language-enabled dialogue-based interface for browsing and retrieving multimodal meeting data [1]. It allows users to access a multimedia database of recorded and annotated meetings, containing the original video and audio streams, electronic copies of all documents used or referred to as well as handwritten notes made by participants during the meeting, and a text transcript of the meeting itself [37, 42]. Multimodal man-machine interaction in this context has been carefully studied. Large-scale Wizard of Oz experiments with the system (involving 91 users) were carried out and it resulted in 180 hours of video data and 70MB of text log files. The data was analyzed along several different lines including the modalities most often used, contexts of use, relationships between modalities, usage change over time, training impact, etc. [36]. To summarize the major findings: exposure and training can have a strong impact on the way people use multimodality, and speech is a preferred modality both at the content and interaction levels, i.e. as a cue for querying the multimodal database and as an interaction channel.

HephaisTK, developed both in the framework of the NCCR IM2 and of the MeModules project presented in chapter 5, handles multimodality at the interaction level and aims at providing a tool allowing developers to easily prototype multimodal interfaces [20]. The HephaisTK toolkit has been designed to plug itself in a client application that wishes to receive notifications of multimodal events received from a set of modality recognizers. It is based on a software agents architecture, in which agents, collaborating through a blackboard, are dispatched to manage individual modality recognizers, handle fusion and dialog management. HephaisTK can be configured with the SMUIML language (*Synchronized Multimodal User Interfaces Markup Language*) [19], allowing a clear description of the human-machine multimodal dialog and control over the way multiple input modalities have to be fused. More details about this tool can be found in chapter 5 of this book.

5.2 Multimodal Interfaces in the MMI Program

The IM-HOST project, described in detail in chapter 4 of this book, is representative of one class of multimodal applications, although it focuses on a single modality: speech, which has been historically the leading modality in multimodal interaction. The IM-HOST project targets voice-enabled man-machine interaction in noisy environments. However, still, current performances of voice applications are reasonably good in quiet environments but the surrounding noise in many practical situations drastically deteriorates the quality of the speech signal and, as a consequence, significantly decreases the recognition rate. The major scenario considered in this project is a person using voice command in an outdoor environment: a racing boat. For this reason, the project explores new interaction paradigms enabling voice recognition in a hostile environment.

The MeModules project, fully detailed in chapter 5 of this book, has the objective of developing, experimenting and evaluating the concept of tangible shortcuts to multimedia digital information. Moreover, it investigates the opportunity of a more complex, multi-sensorial combination of physical objects with multimedia information by associating tangible interaction with multiple other interaction modalities such as voice, gesture, etc. One of the expected research outcomes of the project is to assess which modalities are best combined with tangible interaction depending on the context and application.

6 Future Directions and Conclusions

Although many issues have been addressed well in the multimodal interaction research and systems literature, such as fusion of heterogeneous data types, architectures for real-time processing, dialog management, map-based multimodal interaction, and so forth, nonetheless the field is still young and needs further research to build reliable multimodal systems and usable applications. Machine learning methods have begun to be applied to a number of different aspects of multimodal interfaces, including individual modality recognition, early or late modality fusion, user-machine dialog management, and identification of users' multimodal integration patterns. But future work clearly is needed to work toward the design of usable adaptive multimodal interfaces. Multimodal dialog processing also will gain in the future from the recent and promising subfield of social signal processing, which can assist dialog modeling by providing a dialog manager with real-time information about a given user's state and her current social and collaborative context.

Other important future directions for multimodal research include human/machine interaction using new tangible interfaces such as digital paper and pen, and multi-touch tables, surfaces and screens. Further modeling of multimodal interaction still is needed too, in areas such as multimodal educational exchanges, collaborative multimodal interaction, multimodal interaction involving diverse and underserved user groups, and mobile multimodal interaction with emerging cell phone applications. Finally, further work is needed to improve tools for the creation of multimodal applications and interfaces so they can become more mainstream, especially since multimodal interfaces are viewed as the most promising avenue for achieving universal access in the near future.

References

1. Ailomaa, M., Lisowska, A., Melichar, M., Armstrong, S., Rajmanm, M.: Archivus: A Multimodal System for Multimedia Meeting Browsing and Retrieval. In: Proceedings of the COLING/ACL 2006 Interactive Presentation Sessions, Sydney, Australia, July 17th-21st (2006)
2. Allen, J.F., Perault, C.R.: Analyzing Intentions in Dialogues. Artificial Intelligence 15(3), 143–178 (1980)
3. André, E.: The generation of multimedia documents. In: Dale, R., Moisl, H., Somers, H. (eds.) A Handbook of Natural Language Processing: Techniques and Applications for the Processing of Language as Text, pp. 305–327. Marcel Dekker Inc., New York (2000)
4. Araki, M., Tachibana, K.: Multimodal Dialog Description Language for Rapid System Development. In: Proceedings of the 7th SIGdial Workshop on Discourse and Dialogue (July 2006)
5. Baddeley, A.D.: Working Memory. Science 255, 556–559 (1992)
6. Baddeley, A.D.: Working Memory. In: Bower, G.A. (ed.) Recent advances in learning and motivation, vol. 8. Academic Press, New York (1974)
7. Arens, Y., Hovy, E., Vossers, M.: On the knowledge underlying multimedia presentations. In: Maybury, M.T. (ed.) Intelligent Multimedia Interfaces, pp. 280–306. AAAI Press, Menlo Park (1993); Reprinted in Maybury and Wahlster, pp. 157–172 (1998)

8. Benoit, C., Martin, J.-C., Pelachaud, C., Schomaker, L., Suhm, B.: Audio-visual and multimodal speech-based systems. In: Gibbon, D., Mertins, I., Moore, R. (eds.) Handbook of Multimodal and Spoken Dialogue Systems: Resources, Terminology and Product Evaluation, pp. 102–203. Kluwer, Dordrecht (2000)
9. Bolt, R.A.: Put-that-there: voice and gesture at the graphics interface. Computer Graphics 14(3), 262–270 (1980)
10. Bouchet, J., Nigay, L., Ganille, T.: ICARE Software Components for Rapidly Developing Multimodal Interfaces. In: Conference Proceedings of ICMI 2004, State College, Pennsylvania, USA, pp. 251–258. ACM Press, New York (2004)
11. Bourguet, M.L.: A Toolkit for Creating and Testing Multimodal Interface Designs. In: Companion proceedings of UIST 2002, Paris, pp. 29–30 (October 2002)
12. Brooke, N.M., Petajan, E.D.: Seeing speech: Investigations into the synthesis and recognition of visible speech movements using automatic image processing and computer graphics. In: Proceedings of the International Conference on Speech Input and Output: Techniques and Applications (1986), vol. 258, pp. 104–109 (1986)
13. Bui, T.H.: Multimodal Dialogue Management - State of the Art. CTIT Technical Report series No. 06-01, University of Twente (UT), Enschede, The Netherlands (2006)
14. Card, S., Moran, T.P., Newell, A.: The Psychology of Human-Computer Interaction. Lawrence Erlbaum Associates, London (1983)
15. Churcher, G., Atwell, E., Souter, C.: Dialogue management systems: a survey and overview (1997)
16. Cohen, P.: Dialogue Modeling. In: Cole, R., Mariani, J., Uszkoreit, H., Varile, G.B., Zaenen, A., Zampolli, A. (eds.) Survey of the State of the Art in Human Language Technology, pp. 204–209. Cambridge University Press, Cambridge (1998)
17. Cohen, P.R., Johnston, M., McGee, D., Oviatt, S., Pittman, J., Smith, I., Chen, L., Clow, J.: QuickSet: multimodal interaction for distributed applications. In: Proceedings of the Fifth ACM international Conference on Multimedia, Seattle, USA, pp. 31–40 (1997)
18. Coutaz, J., Nigay, L., Salber, D., Blandford, A., May, J., Young, R.: Four Easy Pieces for Assessing the Usability of Multimodal Interaction: The CARE properties. In: Proceedings of INTERACT 1995, Lillehammer, Norway, pp. 115–120. Chapman & Hall Publ., Boca Raton (1995)
19. Dumas, B., Lalanne, D., Ingold, R.: Prototyping Multimodal Interfaces with SMUIML Modeling Language. In: CHI 2008 Workshop on User Interface Description Languages for Next Generation User Interfaces, CHI 2008, Firenze, Italy, pp. 63–66 (2008)
20. Dumas, B., Lalanne, D., Guinard, D., Ingold, R., Koenig, R.: Strengths and Weaknesses of Software Architectures for the Rapid Creation of Tangible and Multimodal Interfaces. In: Proceedings of 2nd international conference on Tangible and Embedded Interaction (TEI 2008), Bonn, Germany, February 19 - 21, pp. 47–54 (2008)
21. Duric, Z., Gray, W., Heishman, R., Li, F., Rosenfeld, A., Schoelles, M., Schunn, C., Wechsler, H.: Integrating perceptual and cognitive modeling for adaptive and intelligent human-computer interaction. Proc. of the IEEE 90(7), 1272–1289 (2002)
22. Flippo, F., Krebs, A., Marsic, I.: A Framework for Rapid Development of Multimodal Interfaces. In: Proceedings of ICMI 2003, Vancouver, BC, November 5-7, pp. 109–116 (2003)
23. Foster, M.E.: State of the art review: Multimodal fission. COMIC project Deliverable 6.1 (September 2002)
24. Grant, K.W., Greenberg, S.: Speech intelligibility derived from asynchronous processing of auditory-visual information. In: Workshop on Audio-Visual Speech Processing (AVSP 2001), Scheelsminde, Denmark, pp. 132–137 (2001)

25. Greenberg, S., Fitchett, C.: Phidgets: easy development of physical interfaces through physical widgets. In: Proceedings of the 14th Annual ACM Symposium on User interface Software and Technology (UIST 2001), Orlando, Florida, pp. 209–218. ACM, New York (2001)

26. Jaimes, A., Sebe, N.: Multimodal human-computer interaction: A survey. In: Computer Vision and Image Understanding, vol. 108(1-2), pp. 116–134. Elsevier, Amsterdam (2007)

27. Johnston, M., Cohen, P.R., McGee, D., Oviatt, S.L., Pittman, J.A., Smith, I.: Unification-based multimodal integration. In: Proceedings of the Eighth Conference on European Chapter of the Association For Computational Linguistics, Madrid, Spain, July 07-12, pp. 281–288 (1997)

28. Katsurada, K., Nakamura, Y., Yamada, H., Nitta, T.: XISL: a language for describing multimodal interaction scenarios. In: Proceedings of ICMI 2003, Vancouver, Canada (2003)

29. Kieras, D., Meyer, D.E.: An overview of the EPIC architecture for cognition and performance with application to human-computer interaction. Human-Computer Interaction 12, 391–438 (1997)

30. Klemmer, S.R., Li, J., Lin, J., Landay, J.A.: Papier-Mâché: Toolkit Support for Tangible Input. In: Proceedings of CHI 2004, pp. 399–406 (2004)

31. Koons, D., Sparrell, C., Thorisson, K.: Integrating simultaneous input from speech, gaze, and hand gestures. In: Maybury, M. (ed.) Intelligent Multimedia Interfaces, pp. 257–276. MIT Press, Cambridge (1993)

32. Krahnstoever, N., Kettebekov, S., Yeasin, M., Sharma, R.: A real-time framework for natural multimodal interaction with large screen displays. In: ICMI 2002, Pittsburgh, USA (October 2002)

33. Lalanne, D., Lisowska, A., Bruno, E., Flynn, M., Georgescul, M., Guillemot, M., Janvier, B., Marchand-Maillet, S., Melichar, M., Moenne-Loccoz, N., Popescu-Belis, A., Rajman, M., Rigamonti, M., von Rotz, D., Wellner, P.: In: The IM2 Multimodal Meeting Browser Family, Technical report, Fribourg (March 2005)

34. Lalanne, D., Rigamonti, M., Evequoz, F., Dumas, B., Ingold, R.: An ego-centric and tangible approach to meeting indexing and browsing. In: Popescu-Belis, A., Renals, S., Bourlard, H. (eds.) MLMI 2007. LNCS, vol. 4892, pp. 84–95. Springer, Heidelberg (2008)

35. Lisowska, A.: Multimodal Interface Design for Multimedia Meeting Content Retrieval. PhD Thesis, University of Geneva, Switzerland (September 2007)

36. Lisowska, A., Betrancourt, M., Armstrong, S., Rajman, M.: Minimizing Modality Bias When Exploring Input Preference for Multimodal Systems in New Domains: the Archivus Case Study. In: Proceedings of CHI 2007, San José, California, pp. 1805–1810 (2007)

37. Lisowska, A.: Multimodal Interface Design for the Multimodal Meeting Domain: Preliminary Indications from a Query Analysis Study. IM2.MDM Internal Report IM2.MDM-11 (November 2003)

38. Matena, L., Jaimes, A., Popescu-Belis, A.: Graphical representation of meetings on mobile devices. In: Proceedings of MobileHCI 2008 (10th International Conference on Human-Computer Interaction with Mobile Devices and Services), Amsterdam, pp. 503–506 (2008)

39. Mayer, R.E., Moreno, R.: A split-attention effect in multimedia learning: evidence for dual processing systems in working memory. Journal of Educational Psychology 90(2), 312–320 (1998)

40. McKeown, K.: Text Generation: Using Discourse Strategies and Focus Constraints to Generate Natural Language Text. Cambridge University Press, Cambridge (1985)

41. McNeill, D.: Hand and Mind: What Gestures Reveal About Thought. Univ. of Chicago Press, Chicago (1992)

42. Melichar, M., Cenek, P.: From vocal to multimodal dialogue management. In: Proceedings of the Eighth International Conference on Multimodal Interfaces (ICMI 2006), Banff, Canada, November 2-4, pp. 59–67 (2006)
43. Moore, J.D.: Participating in Explanatory Dialogues: Interpreting and Responding to Questions in Context. MIT Press, Cambridge (1995)
44. Mousavi, S.Y., Low, R., Sweller, J.: Reducing cognitive load by mixing auditory and visual presentation modes. Journal of Educational Psychology 87(2), 319–334 (1995)
45. Neal, J.G., Shapiro, S.C.: Intelligent multimedia interface technology. In: Sullivan, J., Tyler, S. (eds.) Intelligent User Interfaces, pp. 11–43. ACM Press, New York (1991)
46. Nigay, L., Coutaz, J.A.: Design space for multimodal systems: concurrent processing and data fusion. In: Proceedings of the INTERACT 1993 and CHI 1993 Conference on Human Factors in Computing Systems, Amsterdam, The Netherlands, April 24 - 29, pp. 172–178. ACM, New York (1993)
47. Norman, D.A.: The Design of Everyday Things. Basic Book, New York (1988)
48. Novick, D.G., Ward, K.: Mutual Beliefs of Multiple Conversants: A computational model of collaboration in Air Trafic Control. In: Proceedings of AAAI 1993, pp. 196–201 (1993)
49. Oviatt, S.L.: Advances in Robust Multimodal Interface Design. IEEE Computer Graphics and Applications 23 (September 2003)
50. Oviatt, S.L.: Multimodal interactive maps: Designing for human performance. Human-Computer Interaction 12, 93–129 (1997)
51. Oviatt, S.L.: Multimodal interfaces. In: Jacko, J., Sears, A. (eds.) The Human-Computer Interaction Handbook: Fundamentals, Evolving Technologies and Emerging Applications, ch. 14, 2nd edn., pp. 286–304. CRC Press, Boca Raton (2008)
52. Oviatt, S.L.: Ten myths of multimodal interaction. Communications of the ACM 42(11), 74–81 (1999)
53. Oviatt, S.L.: Human-centered design meets cognitive load theory: designing interfaces that help people think. In: Proceedings of the 14th Annual ACM international Conference on Multimedia, Santa Barbara, CA, USA, October 23-27, pp. 871–880. ACM, New York (2006)
54. Oviatt, S.L., Cohen, P.R., Wu, L., Vergo, J., Duncan, L., Suhm, B., Bers, J., Holzman, T., Winograd, T., Landay, J., Larson, J., Ferro, D.: Designing the user interface for multimodal speech and gesture applications: State-of-the-art systems and research directions. Human Computer Interaction 15(4), 263–322 (2000); Reprinted. In: Carroll, J. (ed.) Human-Computer Interaction in the New Millennium, ch. 19, pp. 421–456. Addison-Wesley Press, Reading (2001)
55. Oviatt, S.L., Coulston, R., Tomko, S., Xiao, B., Lunsford, R., Wesson, M., Carmichael, L.: Toward a theory of organized multimodal integration patterns during human-computer interaction. In: Proceedings of ICMI 2003, pp. 44–51. ACM Press, New York (2003)
56. Pan, H., Liang, Z.P., Anastasio, T.J., Huang, T.S.: Exploiting the dependencies in information fusion. In: CVPR, vol. 2, pp. 407–412 (1999)
57. Petajan, E.D.: Automatic Lipreading to Enhance Speech Recognition, PhD thesis, University of Illinois at Urbana-Champaign (1984)
58. Popescu-Belis, A., Georgescul, M.: TQB: Accessing Multimedia Data Using a Transcript-based Query and Browsing Interface. In: Proceedings of LREC 2006 (5th International Conference on Language Resources and Evaluation), Genoa, Italy, pp. 1560–1565 (2006)
59. Reeves, L.M., Lai, J., Larson, J.A., Oviatt, S., Balaji, T.S., Buisine, S.p., Collings, P., Cohen, P., Kraal, B., Martin, J.-C., McTear, M., Raman, T., Stanney, K.M., Su, H., Wang, Q.Y.: Guidelines for multimodal user interface design. Communications of the ACM 47(1), 57–59 (2004)

60. Rigamonti, M., Lalanne, D., Ingold, R.: FaericWorld: Browsing Multimedia Events Through Static Documents And Links. In: Baranauskas, C., Palanque, P., Abascal, J., Barbosa, S.D.J. (eds.) INTERACT 2007. LNCS, vol. 4663, pp. 102–115. Springer, Heidelberg (2007)
61. Serrano, M., Nigay, L., Lawson, J.-Y.L., Ramsay, A., Murray-Smith, R., Denef, S.: The OpenInterface framework: a tool for multimodal interaction. In: Adjunct Proceedings of CHI 2008, Florence, Italy, April 5-10, pp. 3501–3506. ACM Press, New York (2008)
62. Sharma, R., Pavlovic, V.I., Huang, T.S.: Toward multimodal human-computer interface. Proceedings IEEE 86(5), 853–860 (1998); Special issue on Multimedia Signal Processing
63. Sire, S., Chatty, C.: The Markup Way to Multimodal Toolkits. In: W3C Multimodal Interaction Workshop (2002)
64. SSPNet: Social Signal Processing Network, http://www.sspnet.eu
65. Stanciulescu, A., Limbourg, Q., Vanderdonckt, J., Michotte, B., Montero, F.: A transformational approach for multimodal web user interfaces based on UsiXML. In: Proceedings of ICMI 2005, Torento, Italy, October 04-06, pp. 259–266 (2005)
66. Sweller, J., Chandler, P., Tierney, P., Cooper, M.: Cognitive Load as a Factor in the Structuring of Technical Material. Journal of Experimental Psychology: General 119, 176–192 (1990)
67. Tindall-Ford, S., Chandler, P., Sweller, J.: When two sensory modes are better than one. Journal of Experimental Psychology: Applied 3(3), 257–287 (1997)
68. Traum, D., Larsson, S.: The Information State Approach to Dialogue Management. In: Van Kuppevelt, J.C.J., Smith, R.W. (eds.) Current and New Directions in Discourse and Dialogue, pp. 325–353 (2003)
69. Turk, M., Robertson, G.: Perceptual user interfaces (Introduction). Communications of the ACM 43(3), 32–70 (2000)
70. Vo, M.T., Wood, C.: Building an application framework for speech and pen input integration in multimodal learning interfaces. In: Proceedings of the International Conference on Acoustics Speech and Signal Processing (IEEE-ICASSP), vol. 6, pp. 3545–3548. IEEE Computer Society Press, Los Alamitos (1996)
71. W3C Multimodal Interaction Framework, http://www.w3.org/TR/mmi-framework
72. Wickens, C.: Multiple resources and performance prediction. Theoretical Issues in Ergonomic Science 3(2), 159–177 (2002)
73. Wickens, C., Sandry, D., Vidulich, M.: Compatibility and resource competition between modalities of input, central processing, and output. Human Factors 25(2), 227–248 (1983)
74. Wu, L., Oviatt, S., Cohen, P.: From members to teams to committee - a robust approach to gestural and multimodal recognition. IEEE Transactions on Neural Networks 13(4), 972–982 (2002)
75. Wu, L., Oviatt, S., Cohen, P.: Multimodal integration – A statistical view. IEEE Transactions on Multimedia 1(4), 334–341 (1999)
76. Zhai, S., Morimoto, C., Ihde, S.: Manual and gaze input cascaded (MAGIC) pointing. In: Proceedings of the Conference on Human Factors in Computing Systems (CHI 1999), pp. 246–253. ACM Press, New York (1999)

Interactive Visualization - A Survey

Dominique Brodbeck[1], Riccardo Mazza[2], and Denis Lalanne[3]

[1] University of Applied Sciences Northwestern Switzerland
[2] Università della Svizzera Italiana
[3] University of Fribourg

Abstract. Advances in computer science and technology have led to unprecedented new possibilities in science, engineering, and business. At the same time, the automation of measurements, the networking of sensors, the digitization of processes, and large-scale computer simulations produce a deluge of data. The amount of new data grows faster than our ability to analyze and comprehend it. The maturing field of interactive visualization provides a new generation of tools and techniques that promise to contribute to a solution of this problem. In this chapter we present a survey of the field. The two complementary aspects of scientific visualization and information visualization are introduced, and a description of typical applications and research directions provided. The survey is rounded off by a look at the activities in the various fields of interactive visualization in Switzerland.

1 The Keyhole Effect

What began with the painting of rock walls in a damp cave, and in the mean time found its preliminary climax in the epic expanses of the Internet, is the expression of our urge to collect, analyze, and communicate observations about the environment, with the purpose of gaining new insights.

The systematic collection of data started in the 17th and 18th century with the utilitarization of science, and the associated transformation from a tool-oriented to a technology-oriented culture. At the same time, people also started to collect data outside of the natural sciences, in order to analyze them statistically. Examples are the constitution of citizens in large cities, trade balances, transport risks, etc.

The development of data recording, processing, and transmission technologies has played a crucial role in this development. The digitization of measurements and observations, and their processing with the help of electronic machines allows to efficiently record and collect data in huge data bases. There is hardly a company or organization that has not automated and digitized their business processes. Buzz words like Data Warehousing, E-commerce, and Customer Relationship Management are witness to this.

While we have made great advances in collecting and managing data, the question remains how we can get something back out of these huge reservoirs. How can we turn data into information, and eventually knowledge that is useful?

D. Lalanne and J. Kohlas (Eds.): Human Machine Interaction, LNCS 5440, pp. 27–46, 2009.
© Springer-Verlag Berlin Heidelberg 2009

The interfaces to these data collections therefore come into focus. In his book "Interface Culture" [1], Steve Johnson compares their future role to those of the cathedrals in the middle ages. Their function was, among others, to make the infinity of heaven tangible and understandable to humans. The exponentially growing amounts of data and information lead to the existence of similarly large and incomprehensible data spaces and information worlds. They will only become accessible if we have appropriate interfaces and tools.

The interfaces to these data bases and information collections have largely remained the same since the invention of the computer terminal: text and numbers in tabular form, maybe a pie chart here and there. The mouse allows us to not have to type in commands anymore but instead to click on buttons labeled with those commands. Overlapping windows allow us to perform multiple of such tasks in parallel. But the principle remains the same: we see limited aspects in a static and sequential way.

Traditional data base interfaces for example require users to be able to precisely formulate a query, and then present a linear list of results - mostly too many, sometimes none and often the wrong ones. Users have no way of knowing if the results are only outliers, or if there are other similar objects, and how the result will change if the query is just modified slightly.

Anyone who has ever looked for an apartment on the Internet that is close to the station, in a middle price range, but not too small, except if the price is according or there is a parking space, knows the problem.

You feel like you peek inside a warehouse through the keyhole. You only see limited excerpts, you can not change perspective, and in order to compare two objects you have to switch between two views. If you want to access an object you must shout precise instructions through the closed door and wait, until they are handed over. In short, you stay outside with locked hands.

2   A New Approach: Interactive Visualization

A new generation of tools and techniques promises to contribute to a solution to these problems. Two concepts play a key role: visualization and interactivity.

2.1   Visualization

Current information systems and computer programs make only little use of the human perceptual capabilities. Visual perception in particular has an enormous potential to efficiently detect patterns, trends, outliers, and clusters. We are able to recall, recognize and scan images quickly and precisely, and we can detect subtle changes in color, shape, movement and texture. The bandwidth for the communication of information is much higher for the visual channel than for any of our other senses. Visual structures are perceived directly, and don't have to be first decoded symbolically, as is the case with numbers and letters. Visual representation transforms a cognitive problem into a perceptual task, which is drastically more efficient.

2.2   Interactivity

Traditional systems work in batch mode: first the search query is completely specified, then the query is sent to the system. The system executes the query and finally shows the results. Highly interactive systems on the contrary work incrementally and reversibly. Every change is immediately sent to the system and a dynamic feedback is generated. Changes can be easily reverted. These systems work after the principle of "direct manipulation": relevant objects and processes are visually represented and can be manipulated directly with the mouse. The manipulations take the place of a complex syntax, results are immediately visible. For a review and categorization of interaction techniques see [2].

2.3   Interactive Visualization Systems

Interactive visualization systems combine visualization with interactivity. They provide the overview and embed details within. The highly interactive way of working encourages exploration and allows users to experience the data spaces. Ben Shneiderman from the Human-Computer Interaction Laboratory (HCIL) at the University of Maryland [3] appropriately coined the "Visual Information Seeking Mantra":

Overview first, zoom and filter, then details-on-demand.

Visual tools that support our thought processes have existed for a long time of course. Statistical graphics for example, date back to the 18th century. Well known concepts, such as the use of length and area to represent quantity, time series, scatter plots and multi-variate diagrams, were all invented during the period of 1750 to 1800. The economist William Playfair in particular, developed and improved these techniques (1759-1823), Among others, he published the first known bar chart in 1785. These developments have continued into the present days with exponents such as Jacques Bertin and Edward Tufte who developed theories about the visual display of quantitative information.

So what is new about interactive visualization? The use of computers creates a new media, where graphical objects are not static anymore, but can be interactively manipulated and can change dynamically. Because this new medium is computer-based, it is easily accessible and at low cost. The reason why interactive visualization has emerged as a discipline in the past few years is twofold.

On one hand, personal computers have reached a level of performance that allow the use of graphics intensive software. Standard screens have a resolution of 1 million pixels and enough color depth to display graphical objects in good quality.

The digitization of business processes on the other hand, as well as the automation of measurements with increasing sensor bandwidth, leads to large amounts of data that serves as raw material for the gain of information and knowledge. The Internet exponentiates the situation by connecting all these sources in a huge network.

The collision of these two developments acts as a catalyst for the emergence of interactive visualization systems. The field has now reached a level of maturity where we see commercial products and companies built around the idea of interactive visualization, and courses being taught at universities.

In science and technology, the trend was picked up first some 20 years ago, with the visualization of scientific data from disciplines such as physics, astronomy, or medicine. About ten years later the trend spread into the world of business and administration, where the data is mostly of abstract non-geometric nature. This has lead to two distinct fields, scientific visualization and information visualization. The distinction is partly historical and somewhat arbitrary, and the boundaries start to blur in areas such as bioinformatics, where the data is scientific but still abstract, or in geographic information systems where abstract processes are visualized in relation to space. The next two sections will sketch out these two fields, in order to provide an overview of the state of the art.

3   Scientific Visualization

The establishment of the field of scientific visualization can be traced back to a report of the U.S. National Science Foundation in 1987 [4]. The report was entitled "Visualization in Scientific Computing", and positioned visualization as a new scientific instrument that could accelerate progress in science. At that time, many supercomputer centers were created that gave scientists access to large computing resources, but at the same time scientists had no adequate means to examine the results and steer the computations.

Since then, scientific visualization has broadened somewhat and is now generally considered to be the use of computer graphics and imaging technology as a tool to comprehend potentially huge amounts of data obtained by simulation or physical measurement. Since simulations and measurements in science and engineering are typically done on natural phenomena, this implies that the data is spatial in nature, possibly with a temporal component.

3.1   The Visualization Pipeline

More technically speaking, visualization can be seen as a pipeline that transforms raw data into images that can be interpreted by the human perceptual system. Thus, representation and transformation are the two central concepts in scientific visualization. The pipeline begins when the data is generated or captured, and transformed into a representation that is amenable for further processing [5].

Scientific data is typically represented as three components: geometry, topology, and attributes. Geometry defines the discrete points in space (nodes) at which the physical continuum - either computed or measured - is sampled. Topology defines the structure (cells) of how these points are related, so that the data can be interpolated between the points. Typical topologies are structured grids (e.g. scanned imaging data), but topologies can also consist of unstructured points related by heterogeneous cell types (e.g. weather stations at irregular positions). Attributes finally, describe the actual values that were computed or measured at the points of the geometry. Attributes can be in the form of scalars (e.g. temperature), vectors (e.g. velocity), or tensors (e.g. stress).

The next step in the pipeline is the data enrichment transformation, where data is interpolated, filtered, smoothed, merged, rotated, etc. The result is derived data that is now ready to be transformed, by mapping it to displayable objects whose shape, dimensions, and color represent the enriched data. The result of the mapping transformation are 2D and 3D graphical primitives (e.g. lines, polygons).

The final step is the rendering transformation, whereby a displayable image is produced, using appropriate rendering techniques (e.g. surface, volume) and parameters (e.g. lighting, perspective). Each of the three transformation steps is repeated iteratively, driven by user input and interaction.

All these transformations are realized as algorithms. Some algorithms can be classified as structural, i.e. they transform one or several components of the data. Scaling or rotating for example changes the geometry of a dataset. The creation of isosurfaces or the sampling of unstructured points onto a regular grid change the topology of a dataset. Deriving the magnitude from a vector attribute changes the dimensionality of the attribute of a dataset.

Other algorithms are better classified by the type of attribute data that they work on. Scalar algorithms for example map scalar values to colors, or create contour lines for a constant value. Vector algorithms for example create streamlines or oriented glyphs to visualize vector fields. Another important type of algorithms is related to the problem of representing dense 3D volumes, and providing the possibility for seeing inside them. Volume rendering and slicing algorithms belong to this class.

Optimizing these algorithms for performance and accuracy so that they can be applied efficiently to large and multi-dimensional datasets, forms an important part of scientific visualization research [6].

3.2   Applications

Scientific visualization is applied in all the fields where the physical world is sensed, and where physical phenomena are modeled or simulated. Typical applications can therefore be found in fields such as medicine, biochemistry, the Geosciences, the space sciences, or Physics and engineering.

Medical applications are driven by the fact that an increasing number of spatial and non-invasive imaging techniques (e.g. magnetic resonance imaging, computed tomography) have become available. They are routinely used for diagnostic applications, or to plan and guide surgery. Worth noting is the Visible Human, a project run by the U.S. National Library of Medicine (NLM). It is an effort to create a detailed data set of cross-sectional photographs of the human body, in order to facilitate anatomy visualization applications [7].

Biochemistry studies the structure and function of cellular components. Many of these are large and complex molecules (e.g. proteins, nucleic acids). Visualization helps with understanding the three-dimensional structure and dynamic behavior of these molecules, and there are many specialized molecular visualization software tools available to support research on molecular structures and drug design.

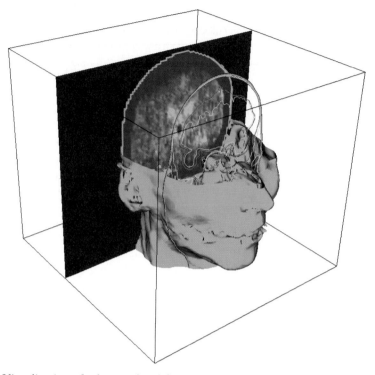

Fig. 1. Visualization of a human head from medical imaging data. Slicing, isosurface, and contouring algorithms are used to show the inside structures of the volumetric dataset.

A prominent application of visualization in the Geosciences are the results from climate modeling, be it in the profane form of weather forecasts on TV, all the way to sophisticated simulations of complex climatic phenomena, or time-resolved remote sensing data. Geologist are searching for natural resources by using visualizations of otherwise invisible geologic structures.

Another large area of application lies in the fields of Physics and engineering, where computational fluid dynamics can simulate the flow of fluids around objects (e.g. airplanes), or finite element simulations can compute physical processes such as stress and elasticity in three-dimensional objects.

In industrial design and architecture finally, the data and problems are not necessarily scientific in nature, but the same visualization techniques are successfully used to see the unseen.

3.3   Research Directions

Even though Moore's law is still in effect and continually increases computing power, the amounts of data that are collected and produced are growing even faster. Increasing algorithm efficiency and optimizing resources will therefore continue to be important. Relevant areas of research include parallelization

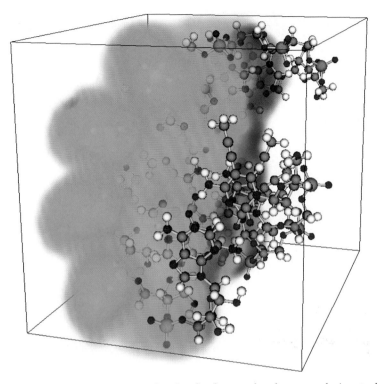

Fig. 2. Visualization of a large molecule. Surface and volume rendering techniques are used in combination to show different aspects of the three-dimensional molecule structure.

of algorithms, multi-resolution modeling to represent complex detailed 3D objects adaptively at different levels-of-detail, or the development of strategies for moving and replicating data on the network based on access patterns for visualizations and interactions shared by multiple users.

On the side of representation, there is inherently no big need for inventing completely new visual metaphors, such as is more the case in the visualization of abstract data as described in the next section on information visualization. However, the focus in scientific visualization has so far been on photo-realistic rendering of surfaces and volumes. As datasets get larger, there is an increasing need for effectively conveying the most important visual information. This can be achieved by visual abstraction techniques that are inspired by traditional technical and medical illustrations. Research in illustrative rendering explores how these techniques can be applied to scientific visualization.

4   Information Visualization

When we have to deal with data that have mostly a non-geometric nature, such as people, files, or stocks, information visualization found its natural place.

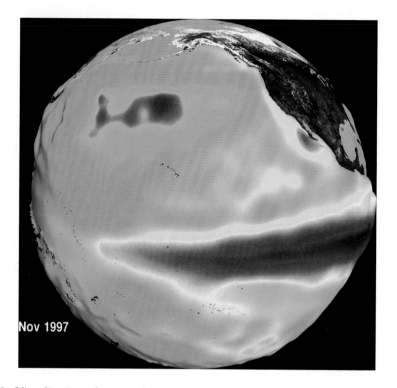

Fig. 3. Visualization of sea surface temperature anomalies (colors), with red being warmer than normal and blue being colder than normal, and sea surface height anomalies as exaggerated heights; visualization by NASA/Goddard Space Flight Center, Scientific Visualization Studio

Information visualization (or *infovis*) is a relatively new field of research that make use of visual representations that take advantage of humans' notable perceptual ability of vision systems for visually exploring data at various levels of abstraction. This allows people to understand essential facts of the data, to quickly detect patterns, trends, outliers, clusters, and to gain insights.

The term "information visualization" was coined by the researchers of Xerox PARC at the end of the 1980s to distinguish a new discipline, historically considered as a sector of *Human–Computer Interaction*. A number of definitions have been proposed to define the scope of this discipline. The most widely adopted is the one defined in the classic *Readings on Information Visualization* by Card et al. [8]:

> Information visualization is the use of computer-supported, interactive, visual representations of abstract data to amplify cognition.

This definition has some keywords that are fundamental for the understanding of this discipline: thanks to the widespread availability of increasingly powerful and less expensive computers, combined with the advances in *computer-supported* graphics, visual representations can be *interactive*, which means that people can manipulate visualization in real time, e.g. zooming in on a relevant item, filtering out unnecessary items, or update a graphical display in a fraction of a second. The term *abstract data* is used to distinguish between data that has a physical correspondence and is closely related to mathematical structures and models (which is object of study for scientific visualization) and abstract data that does not necessarily have a spatial dimension and can be generated, calculated or found in many diverse ways. For example, data of soccer matches in the last championship, or data revealed by instruments for environmental pollution tests. Finally the ultimate goal of visual representation is to *improve the cognitive process* that generates information from the data that we are presented with, precisely through visual representation of this data, making use of the perceptual abilities of the human visual system. Card et al. [8] propose six major ways in which visualizations can amplify cognition:

1. by increasing the working memory and processing resources available to users to solving problems;
2. by reducing the search for information, by representing large amount of data in a small space;
3. by using visual representations to detect structural relationships on data, such as patterns on data;
4. by deducing new information through processes of perceptual inference;
5. by using perceptual perception mechanisms for monitoring a high number of events, such as in dashboards;
6. by encoding information in a manipulable medium that allows the dynamic and interactive exploration of a space of parameter values, or by including and excluding some data from the visualization.

Information visualization applications are particularly suitable in presentation and exploration tasks. These will be discussed in next sections.

4.1   Presentation

Visuals sometimes are useful when we want to communicate an idea, a concept, or an event. Information visualization might help us to visually represent concepts that, if expressed verbally, we would find difficult to explain clearly to a listener. When we have data with which we need to illustrate concepts, ideas, and properties intrinsic to that data, the use of visual representations offers us a valid communication tool. The main problem is designing a visual representation that faithfully reproduces the information codified in the data and, meets the specific requirements of the users, and facilitates the users in their tasks. Edward Tufte maintains that "excellence in statistical graphics consists of complex ideas communicated with clarity, precision, and efficiency" [9]. We can adopt this guideline in information visualization as well, and may affirm that excellence in communicating with information visualization consists in giving the reader as much data as can be processed quickly, using as little space as possible, and with the least cognitive effort.

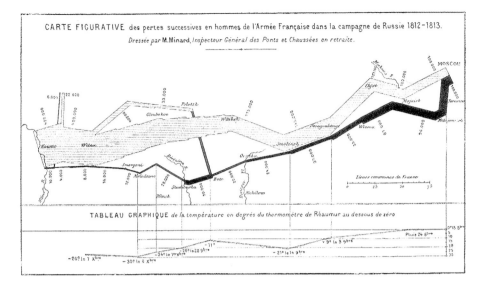

Fig. 4. Visual representation of the march of Napoleon's army in the Russian campaign of 1812, produced by Charles J. Minard

Let's look at the visual representation illustrated in Fig. 4. It deals with a map created by Charles Joseph Minard, a French engineer, in 1869. The map was conceived to illustrate the number of losses suffered by Napoleon's army during the disastrous march toward Moscow in 1812. The thick band shows the route taken by the troupes, from the Polish border to Moscow, and the width of this track represents the number of soldiers present at each point of the journey. The number of losses suffered by the army is evident at a glance. Of the 422,000 soldiers who set off from the Polish border, only 100,000 arrived in Moscow. Napoleon's retreat during the freezing Russian winter is represented by the dark line, linked to a graph that reports the harsh temperatures that further decimated the already-exhausted army. Some rivers, in which numerous soldiers lost their lives attempting to cross, are also indicated. This visual is a superb example of the concept of excellence expressed by Tufte, who, not without good reason, defined it as "the best statistical graphic ever drawn" [9].

Another example is depicted in Fig. 5. It is an example of a scatterplot from Gapminder [10] that shows data from the United Nations Statistics Division[1] and aims to compare three indicators: under-five year mortality rate per 1000 live births, gross national income per capita (US $ by exchange rate) and total population. The continent to which each nation belongs is mapped to the color of the graphical element. The main purpose of the data is to produce a graphical presentations that displays the magnitude of health (measured through the under-five year mortality rate) and wealth disparities in the contemporary world. One immediately notices an almost linear correlation between the wealth and

---

[1] http://unstats.un.org

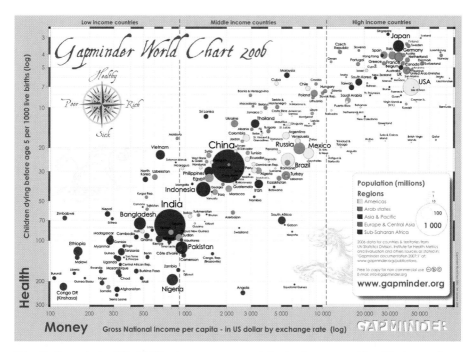

Fig. 5. Gapminder World Chart compares countries by income and health; image from www.gapminder.org reproduced with copy permission

the state of health: The state of health improves with an increase in the wealth of the population. An interesting insight comes from the analysis of the richest nations. In particular, USA has worse health conditions than most of the European countries and, surprisingly, Singapore is the most healthy country. There are also some outliers; some evident cases are represented by Malaysia and Cuba, whose population has an excellent level of health (even higher than that of the United States), despite the fact that the income is in the middle range. Other interesting information is drawn from the color of the circles. For example, the Sub-Saharan Africa nations are almost all grouped in the lower left-hand corner of the graph, indicating the state of extreme poverty and the terrible health levels in these unfortunate nations.

4.2 Exploration

Information visualization is best applied in those tasks that require the exploration of a large dataset with the aim of identifying properties, relationships, regularities, or patterns. Often people want to have a look at a dataset without having a specific goal in mind. By visually examining the data, people may learn more about it, discover new facts, and gain new insight. Thanks to the perceptual ability of vision, information visualization systems may help in identifying, properties, relationships, regularities, or patterns. Jacques Bertin defines it as "the visual means of resolving logical problems" [11]. Interaction in particular does facilitate

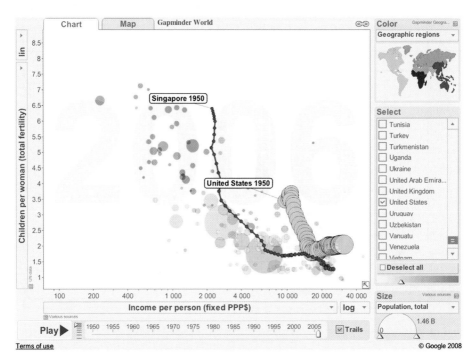

Fig. 6. Gapminder World is an interactive application that compares countries by income and fertility in 2006, and tracks variations over years for Singapore and the United States; visualization from Gapminder World, powered by Trendalyzer from www.gapminder.org

the exploratory tasks, or as it is being said, it helps in discovering the unexpected [12]: by adjusting the input data, or manipulating the view generated, people can then identify interesting facts that could remain hidden in a static view. As Ben Shneiderman wrote in the foreword of Chen (2004), "visualizations are especially potent in promoting the intuition and insights that lead to breakthroughs in understanding the relevant connections and salient features" [13].

An interesting aspect of the application Gapminder World, depicted as a static chart in Fig. 5, is the possibility for the user to manipulate the indicators of development mapped onto the axes (users can choose among more than a hundred indicators, such as energy consumption, technology adoption, infrastructure, education, etc.), and watch the graph change over time by using the slider to change years of data statistics. Users can also select one or more countries from the list, and track a selected country when an animation plays.

For example, Figure 6 represents a screenshot of the interactive application of Gapminder World. In this case, we are interested in discovering how the fertility of the population changed over the years. In particular, we put in relation the income per capita and the number of children per woman. We also track the changes that happened to Singapore (that had the lowest children dying before age 5, as we have seen in Fig. 5) and the United States. Each bubble represents one year. Here we can see the evolution for these two nations from 1950 to 2006. In particular, we can see Singapore's dramatic decrease of births since the 1950s, as well as in the United States, but only until 1976, when the birth rate inverted the tendency. Also we can notice that China's income and fertility in 2006 (represented by the largest red bubble) matches with those of Singapore in 1976.

4.3   Research Directions

Social visualization is one of the emerging subsets of information visualization that is acquiring more and more interest with the increasing availability of networked environments that connect people. Newsgroups, blogs, social network sites (such as Facebook or LinkedIn) are some examples of services that bring together large groups of people, and collect huge quantities of data that may make "difficult to understand the environment of this data and to lose oneself in the midst of the crowds" [14]. Social visualization aims to visually represent data that concerns people to make interaction patterns and connections salient. Judith Donath, as far back as 1999, carried out some experiments at MIT about visualizing on-line conversations [15]. On that occasion, she coined the first definition of social visualization as the "visualization of social information for social purposes" [15]. The key distinction of this type of visualization is that social relationships of people, the groups an the patterns they form, are the most relevant aspects that should emerge from the visualizations. Examples of social visualizations are the social networks that aim at revealing relationships among various individuals, and to determine qualitative aspects such as leadership or informal structure. In practical applications, they might depict newsgroup activities, email patterns, conversations, social networks structures, etc. with the aim of improving our understanding of the community (also the dynamics, how it evolved during the time) and of extracting the social network structure embedded in the collection of conversations or contacts in blogs and social network sites.

Information visualization has currently several other research directions: the problem of multidimensional data to be represented in 2-dimensional screen space, or the problem of visualizing millions of items in a single view, just to cite a few of them. Probably the most important goal is to bring the advantages and latest developments of research to practical, realistic settings to address timely problems. Several visualization tools have been developed recently, but little effort has been made to evaluate the effectiveness and utility of the tools in realistic conditions with users. Very few works perform a usability study or an empirical evaluation on what they have proposed [16]. There has been a noticeable lack of involving the actual users in the design and evaluation of information visualization tools. Most visualization projects focus on the development of innovative visualizations or computing techniques rather than address the users' needs and usage aspects. This is reflected by the fact the most of the projects have remained as research prototype, without any follow up, and have rarely been deployed in real-life systems.

There is the need to develop new evaluative methodologies specific for information visualization, as most of the existing evaluation studies rely on empirical methodologies derived from HCI, that might not be applicable to information visualization. For instance, a key point on visualization is to understand whether users can comprehend the meaning of the underlying data encoded with graphical elements and properties. This involves understanding perceptual-cognitive tasks [17], which is very hard to judge, if compared to classic HCI evaluation metrologies such as task completion time or heuristics.

5   The Swiss Perspective

There are various research groups and companies in Switzerland working in the domains of visualization. In this section we present the most active ones in the fields of information visualization, knowledge visualization and in scientific visualization. This presentation does not intend to be exhaustive, but a snapshot of representative Swiss activities in these fields. Later in the section, we briefly present recent and representative projects in Switzerland and finally introduce the visualization projects presented in details in chapters of this book.

5.1   Information Visualization

In the field of information visualization, research in Switzerland is tackling diverse aspects such as software visualization and education, monitoring and decision making in security, preferences elicitation in electronic catalogues, critiques based system and constraint programming, and visual analytics for humanitarian data.

The REVEAL (Reverse Engineering, Visualization, Evolution Analysis Lab) research group at the University of Lugano is involved in in software reengineering, reverse engineering, and software evolution with an emphasis on software visualization and metrics. Its leader is also the creator of CodeCrawler, a language independent software visualization tool [19]. Still at the University of Lugano, the faculty of Communication Sciences is developing projects in information visualization (empirical evaluations, personalization) in the field of student modeling and external graphical representations in distance education [20].

At the University of Fribourg, the DIVA group has extended its research activities towards multimodal interaction and information visualization [21,22], with several projects on information visualization. In particular, they recently started the SNF project Humanitics, "Humanitics: Visual Analytics for All", which goal is to develop visual analytics tools for public organizations to enhance collaborative knowledge discovery, information exchange and communication. This project is a collaboration with the United Nations in Geneva, which manipulates and reports numerous data and information concerning world-wide health, illicit drug trade, environment and global climate change, diseases, energy, conflict, and humanitarian development concerns. The UN urgently needs authoring tools to analyse these data and cross correlate them in a visual way, not only to improve visual understanding, but also for analysts to produce meaningful visualizations to present their findings. Further, in the framework of the EC FP7, the University of Fribourg participates to the coordination action VISMASTER, composed of 26 partners, which aims at defining the European Visual Analytics Research Roadmap, and setting the stage for larger follow-up Visual Analytics research initiatives in Europe.

The Human Computer Interaction Group, at the Swiss Federal Institute of Technology in Lausanne, is concerned with the human factors of computing systems. The research group examines issues in the common area of human-machine interaction, artificial intelligence, cognitive science, and information visualization. In particular, the group is well known for its mixed initiative approach to online product search [23].

At the United Nations Office at Geneva, the Centre for Advanced Visual Analytics (CAVA) is dedicated to supporting humanitarian and development organizations in applying innovative methods of analysis and presentation of information. The Centre offers services, tools, and training based on the disciplines of information visualization and visual analytics.

Finally, Macrofocus GmbH, located in Zurich, develops interactive visualization systems that enable faster and better-informed decisions, and support the generation and communication of knowledge. InfoScope is their general-purpose interactive visualization tool to access, explore, and communicate large and complex multi-dimensional datasets [24]. Macrofocus develops other products for hierarchical data and surveys, and other interactive visual tools for budgets, projects, products, documents and other structured data sets.

5.2   Geographic Information Systems

In the field of geographic information systems, which combines information visualization and scientific visualization techniques, the Geographic Information Analysis & Visualization (GIVA) and Geographic Information Systems (GIS) groups at the GIScience Center of the Department of Geography at the University of Zurich have a well established expertise in the full range of scientific projects from those contributing to fundamental theory in GIScience through applied projects in the social and natural sciences to technology transfer working directly with industrial partners [25]. While the GIS division concentrates on spatial theory, algorithms and tool developments including application of computational methods for representing spatio-temporal phenomena, the GIVA group emphasizes on basic research questions within the domain of perceptual and cognitive principles of geovisual analytics. Specific research domains include geovisual analytics display design (2-4D displays) and empirical evaluations (i.e., with eye tracking studies), mobile geovisualization design and evaluation, spatialization, cognitive and perceptual aspects of visual analytics and spatial inference making, spatiotemporal analysis of moving objects, geographic information retrieval, and scaling issues and multi-representation databases.

5.3   Scientific Visualization

In the field of scientific visualization, there are many active groups in Switzerland and it would be hard building an exhaustive list. For instance, the Computer Graphics Laboratory, ETH Zurich, is devoted to the design of fundamental methods, algorithms and systems for computer graphics, geometric modeling, physics-based animation, image acquisition and generation, display, scientific visualization, and multimodal learning [26]. Another active group at the ETHZ is the Computer Vision Laboratory, which works on the computer-based interpretation of 2D and 3D image data sets from conventional and non-conventional image sources. The computer vision lab performs research in the fields of medical image analysis and visualization, object recognition, gesture analysis, tracking, and scene understanding and modeling [27]. At the department of Informatics of the University of Zurich, the Visualization and MultiMedia Lab (VMML) covers also a wide range of topics in real-time 3D computer graphics, simulation, interactive large-scale scientific visualization and multimedia technology [28]. Finally, it is worth mentioning the Swiss National Supercomputing Centre (CSCS) develops and promotes technical and scientific services for the Swiss research community in the fields of high-performance computing. One of the related goals of the CSCS is to provide researchers with advanced visualization expertise in fields such as molecular dynamics, material sciences, computational fluid dynamics, structural mechanics, etc.

5.4   Knowledge Visualization

In the field of knowledge visualization, the Competence Center Knowledge Visualization at the Institute for Media and Communications Management, as well as the affiliated vasp datatecture GmbH, a company that focuses in visualizing business strategy and processes, propose guidelines and principles derived from their professional practice and previous research on how architects successfully use complementary visualizations to transfer and create knowledge among individuals from different social, cultural, and educational backgrounds [29]. The faculty of Communication of the University of Lugano is also conducting research in this new field and in particular on knowledge management, knowledge visualization, and knowledge communication [30].

5.5   Visualization in the MMI Program

Chapters 7, 8 and 9 of this book present projects related to information and scientific visualization domains. While the paper 7 manipulates abstract information and as such follows the standard definition of information visualization, the two other papers tackle HCI issues related with browsing and interaction in scientific visualizations.

The chapter entitled "Evospaces: Multi-dimensional Navigation Spaces for Software Evolution", approaches software visualization through an original angle, representing abstract information with realistic metaphors (e.g. a city map), in order to capture rapidly the architecture, history or morphology. Furthermore, this metaphoric approach transports social aspects facilitating intercommunication between people, facilitating the collaborative development of a software, and to some extent to the creation of a city.

The following chapter, entitled "HOVISSE - A medical Virtual Reality Research Project", could have been presented also in the multimodal interfaces section, since it uses haptic interfaces as a return path, to help the medical practitioners "feel" the virtual world in which they are immersed.

Finally, the BATICS project presents a language and a methodology for prototyping 3D user interfaces for controlling complex systems. As such, it explores the possibility to build 3D graphical user interface authoring tools, in the domain of complex systems control. Although the project tackles software engineering issues, this contribution is very valuable for those who want to build novel 3D user interfaces in the field of scientific visualization.

6   Summary and Outlook

Interactive visualization has matured, as witnessed by the fact that application papers start to be accepted at conferences, commercial tools are being offered on the market, and the field is widening its focus.

Visual Analytics (VA) for example is a new approach that combines visualization and automated data analysis techniques. It has been defined as the science of analytical reasoning facilitated by interactive visual interfaces [31,32]. The novelty of the approach, as opposed to other data analysis domains, is to adopt a holistic view where information visualization, data analysis, and human factors all work together to build something that is greater than the sum of the parts. For instance, in visual analytics it is recognized that data mining algorithms alone are not enough. Without expressive visualizations and interfaces it is hard to achieve the necessary flexibility to understand results, generate new hypotheses, and test them on the fly in a natural interactive environment. Similarly, it is recognized that given the limited power of graphics displays, and the intrinsic limitations of human perception and reasoning capabilities, it is infeasible to consider visualization alone an effective solution to the analysis of complex and large data sets. A specific visual analytics conference, named IEEE Symposium on Visual Analytics Science and Technology, has also been created in 2006 to promote research in this domain.

Another trend is that visualization is moving off the desktop, on to devices that have widely different form factors and are used in different contexts than a single user in an office with a standard desktop monitor. Megapixel displays, in the form of tiled monitors or entire rear-projected walls, are becoming more popular in an attempt to visualize the increasingly large datasets at full resolution, for example from terascale scientific simulations [33]. Large display sizes not only increase the number of available pixels, but also enable new forms of presentation and collaboration.

At the other end of the spectrum, smartphones are now equipped with high-quality touch-sensitive displays that provide excellent platforms for visualization of information in mobile contexts. Or, visualization disappears completely into the environment in an approach called ambient visualization, where everyday objects such as lamps or wall-hung art become dynamic information displays. Visualization is not in the center of the attention, but takes place in the periphery. Ambient visualizations can be aimed at personal use to create awareness of some source of information [34], or they are designed for public spaces, for example bus schedules [35].

The idea is to localize time-critical or otherwise important information in the space where it is actually needed, and provide it in a way that it can be quickly grasped, even from a distance. This creates new design challenges that differ from those used to design traditional focused-use desktop systems. For example, since these displays are highly visible, one of the design concerns is to balance aesthetics and utility.

Recently, a new report for the U.S. National Science Foundation and the U.S. National Institutes of Health has been put together by luminaries of the field [36], to evaluate the progress of the maturing field of visualization. The report concludes:

> Visualization is indispensable to the solution of complex problems in every sector, from traditional medical, science and engineering domains to such key areas as financial markets, national security, and public health.

One problem however is the fact that as techniques mature, there is an increasing need to push them out into the applications, but the necessary domain knowledge is typically missing in the visualization community. On the other hand, due to the multidisciplinary nature of the field, it is often difficult to obtain the necessary focused funding for core visualization research, of which the report highlights the following:

> Characterizing how and why visualizations work, systematically exploring the design space of visual representations, developing new interaction approaches, and exploiting the possibilities of novel display hardware will be particularly important areas of emphasis.

References

1. Johnson, S.: Interface culture. Harper, New York (1997)
2. Yi, J.S., Kang, Y.A., Stasko, J., Jacko, J.: Toward a deeper understanding of the role of interaction in information visualization. IEEE Transactions on Visualization and Computer Graphics 13(6), 1224–1231 (2007)
3. Shneiderman, B.: Designing the user interface. Addison-Wesley, Reading (1998)
4. McCormick, B., DeFanti, T.A., Brown, M.D.: Visualization in scientific computing. In: Computer Graphics, vol. 21. ACM Press, New York (1987)
5. Schroeder, W., Martin, K., Lorensen, B.: The Visualization Toolkit: An Object-Oriented Approach to 3D Graphics, 4th edn. Kitware, Inc., Clifton Park (2006)
6. Johnson, C., Hansen, C.: Visualization Handbook. Academic Press, Inc., Orlando (2004)
7. Spitzer, V., Whitlock, D.: Atlas of the Visible Human Male: Reverse Engineering of the Human Body. Jones and Bartlett Publishers, Inc., USA (1998)
8. Card, S., Mackinlay, J., Shneiderman, B.: Readings in information visualization. Morgan Stanley Publishers, San Francisco (1999)
9. Tufte, E.: The visual display of quantitative information. Graphics Press, Cheshire (1983)

10. Rosling, H., Rosling, A., Rosling, O.: New software brings statistics beyond the eye. In: Statistics, Knowledge and Policy: Key Indicators to Inform Decision Making, pp. 522–530. OECD Publishing, Paris (2006)
11. Bertin, J.: Graphics and graphic information processing. Walter de Gruyter, Berlin (1981)
12. Cook, K., Earnshaw, R., Stasko, J.: Discovering the unexpected. IEEE Computer Graphics and Applications 27(5), 15–19 (2007)
13. Chaomei, C.: Information visualization: Beyond the horizon, 2nd edn. Springer, Heidelberg (2004)
14. Karahalios, K.G., Viégas, F.B.: Social visualization: exploring text, audio, and video interaction. In: CHI 2006, Extended Abstracts on Human Factors in Computing Systems CHI 2006, pp. 1667–1670. ACM, New York (2006)
15. Donath, J., Karahalios, K., Viegas, F.B.: Visualizing conversation. In: Proceedings of the 32nd Annual Hawaii International Conference on System Sciences, HICSS-32, vol. 2 (1999)
16. Plaisant, C.: The challenge of information visualization evaluation. In: Proceedings of the Working Conference on Advanced Visual Interfaces (AVI 2004), pp. 109–116 (2004)
17. Chen, C.: Top 10 unsolved information visualization problems. IEEE Computer Graphics and Applications 25(4), 12–16 (2005)
18. Spence, R.: Information visualisation, Design for interaction. Pearson Education Ltd., London (2007)
19. Lanza, M., Ducasse, S.: Codecrawler-an extensible and language independent 2d and 3d software visualization tool. Tools for Software Maintenance and Reengineering, RCOST/Software Technology Series, 74–94 (2005)
20. Mazza, R., Dimitrova, V.: Visualising student tracking data to support instructors in web-based distance education. In: Proceedings of the 13th International World Wide Web Conference on Alternate Track Papers & Posters, pp. 154–161. ACM, New York (2004)
21. Bertini, E., Hertzog, P., Lalanne, D.: SpiralView: Towards Security Policies Assessment through Visual Correlation of Network Resources with Evolution of Alarms. In: IEEE Symposium on Visual Analytics Science and Technology, VAST 2007, pp. 139–146 (2007)
22. Lalanne, D., Bertini, E., Hertzog, P., Bados, P.: Visual Analysis of Corporate Network Intelligence: Abstracting and Reasoning on Yesterdays for Acting Today. In: Goodall, J.R., Conti, G., Kwan-Liu, M. (eds.) Proceedings of the Workshop on Visualization for Computer Security, VizSec 2007. Book Series, Mathematics and Visualization, pp. 115–130 (2008)
23. Pu, P., Faltings, B.: Enriching buyers' experiences: the SmartClient approach. In: Proceedings of the SIGCHI Conference on Human Factors in Computing Systems, pp. 289–296. ACM Press, New York (2000)
24. Brodbeck, D., Girardin, L.: Design study: Using multiple coordinated views to analyze geo-referenced high-dimensional datasets. In: Proceedings of International Conference on Coordinated and Multiple Views in Exploratory Visualization 2003, pp. 104–111 (2003)
25. Skupin, A., Fabrikant, S.I.: Spatialization methods: A cartographic research agenda for non-geographic information visualization. Cartography and Geographic Information Science 30(2), 99–119 (2003)

26. Pfister, H., Zwicker, M., van Baar, J., Gross, M.: Surfels: Surface elements as rendering primitives. In: Proceedings of the 27th Annual Conference on Computer Graphics and Interactive Techniques, pp. 335–342. ACM Press/Addison-Wesley Publishing Co., New York (2000)
27. Harders, M., Wildermuth, S., Székely, G.: New paradigms for interactive 3D volume segmentation. The Journal of Visualization and Computer Animation 13(1), 85–95 (2002)
28. Pajarola, R., Sainz, M., Guidotti, P.: Confetti: Object-Space Point Blending and Splatting. IEEE Transactions on Visualization and Computer Graphics 10(5), 598–608 (2004)
29. Burkhard, R.A.: Towards a framework and a model for knowledge visualization: Synergies between information and knowledge visualization. In: Tergan, S.-O., Keller, T. (eds.) Knowledge and Information Visualization. LNCS, vol. 3426, pp. 238–255. Springer, Heidelberg (2005)
30. Eppler, M.J.: Facilitating knowledge communication through joint interactive visualization. Journal of Universal Computer Science 10(6), 683–690 (2004)
31. Thomas, J.J., Cook, K.A.: Illuminating the path: The research and development agenda for visual analytics. IEEE CS Press, Los Alamitos (2005)
32. Thomas, J.J., Cook, K.A.: A visual analytics agenda. IEEE Computer Graphics and Applications, pp. 10–13. IEEE Computer Society, Los Alamitos (2006)
33. Schikore, D.R., Fischer, R.A., Frank, R., Gaunt, R., Hobson, J., Whitlock, B.: High-resolution multiprojector display walls. IEEE Comput. Graph. Appl. 20(4), 38–44 (2000)
34. Miller, T., Stasko, J.: Artistically conveying information with the InfoCanvas. In: Proceedings of AVI 2002, pp. 43–50 (2002)
35. Skog, T., Ljungblad, S., Holmquist, L.E.: Between aesthetics and utility: Designing ambient information visualization. In: Proceedings of the IEEE Symposium on Information Visualization, pp. 239–240 (2003)
36. Munzner, T., Johnson, C., Moorhead, R., Pfister, H., Rheingans, P., Yoo, T.S.: NIH-NSF Visualization research challenges report. IEEE Press, Los Alamitos (2006)

Mixed Reality: A Survey

Enrico Costanza[1], Andreas Kunz[2], and Morten Fjeld[3]

[1] EPFL Media and Design Laboratory, Lausanne
design.epfl.ch
[2] ETHZ Innovation Center Virtual Reality (ICVR), Zurich
www.icvr.ethz.ch
[3] Chalmers TableTop Interaction Lab (t2i lab), Gothenburg
www.t2i.se

Abstract. This chapter presents an overview of the Mixed Reality (MR)
paradigm, which proposes to overlay our real-world environment with
digital, computer-generated objects. It presents example applications and
outlines limitations and solutions for their technical implementation. In
MR systems, users perceive both the physical environment around them
and digital elements presented through, for example, the use of semi-
transparent displays. By its very nature, MR is a highly interdisciplinary
field engaging signal processing, computer vision, computer graphics,
user interfaces, human factors, wearable computing, mobile computing,
information visualization, and the design of displays and sensors. This
chapter presents potential MR applications, technical challenges in realizing MR systems, as well as issues related to usability and collaboration
in MR. It separately presents a section offering a selection of MR projects
which have either been partly or fully undertaken at Swiss universities
and rounds off with a section on current challenges and trends.

Keywords: Human-computer interaction (HCI), Mixed Reality, Displays, Sensors, Information Visualization, Usability, Switzerland.

1 Introduction

The ready availability of large amounts of computational power in small devices
and their constantly decreasing cost paved the way for the concept of "Ubiquitous
Computing" [1]. In Weiser's vision, the goal was to make computational power
available to people wherever and whenever they need it, not only at the desktop.
This could be in meeting rooms where one might need to retrieve information
in order to better contribute to discussion. Other places may include the car,
to help us drive more efficiently and safely, a surgeon's operating room, or a
designer's drawing desk.

How can we integrate this new group of computational devices into the environment? A number of different paradigms have been proposed to answer this
question and to move interaction from the computer box into the world. This
chapter presents an overview of the Mixed Reality (MR) paradigm, which proposes to overlay our real-world environment with digital, computer-generated

D. Lalanne and J. Kohlas (Eds.): Human Machine Interaction, LNCS 5440, pp. 47–68, 2009.

objects. It presents example applications and outlines limitations and solutions for their technical implementation.

MR was derived both conceptually and historically from Virtual Reality (VR). VR systems are computer systems in which users are immersed in a virtual, computer-generated world. The very first examples were originally developed in the 1960s [2]. Immersion is generally achieved through visual, auditory, and sometimes tactile displays. All these displays isolate users from their familiar surroundings, giving the illusion that the only objects existing around them are those rendered by the computer. In MR systems, users perceive both the physical environment around them and digital elements presented through, for example, the use of semitransparent displays. Imagine a system that indicates the name and provenance of items around you by displaying virtual labels overlaying the objects, or a system that guides your way by showing virtual arrows, or a system that displays people's names and affiliations on virtual badges. The information could be displayed in the native language of each user or could be customized to be most relevant to their individual profile; for example, when browsing food products, specific information could be provided according to the user's allergies.

MR systems are designed to give their users the illusion that digital objects are in the same space as physical ones (Figure 1). For this illusion of coexistence, the digital objects need to be precisely positioned into the real environment and aligned with the real objects in real time [3]. In fact, the precise real-time alignment or registration of virtual and real elements is a definitive characteristic of augmented reality systems [3], and it constitutes a difficult technical challenge for its realization. Augmented reality is often considered to be a branch of MR. According to the definition of Milgram et al. [4], MR is "subclass of VR related technologies that involve merging of real and virtual worlds". MR includes systems in which the virtual aspects are dominant as well as those in which the physical reality is dominant. Within this range, augmented reality has more physical elements than virtual elements.

Fig. 1. The BUILD-IT system, an example of a collaborative tabletop MR application

The following section presents a section on potential MR applications, followed by a section on technical challenges in realizing MR systems. The next section presents issues of usability and collaboration related to AR. A separate section offers a selection of MR projects which have either been partly or fully undertaken at Swiss universities. The chapter rounds with a section presenting some current challenges and trends.

2 Applications

By its very nature, Mixed Reality (MR) is a highly interdisciplinary field engaging signal processing, computer vision, computer graphics, user interfaces, human factors, wearable computing, mobile computing, information visualization, and the design of displays and sensors. MR concepts are applicable to a wide range of areas including the automotive industry, surgery, and office environments. Other examples include the maintenance and repair of machinery; instruction notes could be displayed next to the relevant location, as if they were real, physical labels. Steve Feiner's team at Columbia University was the first to demonstrate such a scenario in 1993 [5] by developing one of the earliest MR prototypes: a system to guide end-users in basic maintenance operations of a laser-printer. Through a monochromatic, semitransparent, head-worn display, users see wire-frame computer graphics highlighting specific components of the printer, and text labels indicating how to disassemble the device and replace parts. Recently, Lee and Rhee [6] presented a collaboration-oriented, distributed MR system for car maintenance. Their system includes mobile as well as desktop terminals, connected to a server and an ontology-based context recognition system to render the information in the format appropriate to the client and the situation. Other examples in the field of manufacturing include a system to support the task of car door assembly [7] and a tool to evaluate the placement of new machinery or workstations inside an existing manufacturing plant [8]. In the latter case, the main advantage offered by MR is that the position of new pieces of industrial equipment can be visualized on real images of an existing plant, and the suitability of the placement can be evaluated by visual inspection, determining whether the new tools are within reach or conflict with older ones. Thus it is not necessary to create a virtual model of the entire production plant, but only of the new items.

The Magic Book [9] is a system built to visualize virtual three-dimensional (3D) models on the pages of a physical book. This book acts as a handle for the virtual models: by moving the book, users can move the models and look at them from different viewpoints. Proposed applications for the system are the visualization of interactive 3D children stories and geological data, as well as architectural models. Klinker et al. [10] applied the magic book paradigm to the visualization of new car prototypes in their Fata Morgana proof-of-concept MR system. Fata Morgana was developed in collaboration with an automobile manufacturing company and the system was evaluated by professional car designers.

In the medical field, MR systems can be used to visualize medical imaging (such as CAT scans, MRI, or ultrasound) directly on the patient's body in order to guide the surgeon's action [11,12,13]. Medical images are already available in digital formats, and they are currently displayed on standard monitors in the operating room. A user study of needle biopsy on mockups showed that MR can improve accuracy compared to traditional methods [14].

Remote collaboration is another application area of MR. In typical scenarios, this involves an operator in the field receiving guidance from a remote expert. The operator uses a mobile MR system to capture the scene around her and send it to the expert's system. The expert can see the scene the operator is in and give her instructions using an audio channel or visual annotations displayed on the operator's MR system. Initial examples were also developed at Columbia University [15]: in a demonstrative system, one user is free to roam freely on the university campus, while someone else can add and manipulate virtual objects in the visualization in specific locations. In the medical domain, Welch et al. [16] proposed a system that uses multiple cameras to capture a patient's body which could then be visualized for a remote expert using a high resolution static display or PDA.

MR systems have been proposed to provide navigation guidance. In this scenario, users can see virtual signs anchored to the physical world. Similar to a compass, the signs indicate the correct direction regardless of the device's orientation. A potential application would guide soldiers in an unfamiliar environment [17,18] and provide information about known sources of danger. Yet another would guide tourists in a city [19] or visitors inside a building [20].

A number of entertainment applications were proposed, in which users have to interact with virtual characters or devices appearing in their physical environment. In general, MR games can increase collaboration or competition among players, who can be co-located or remote. Examples include a MR version of the Quake videogame [21], in which users see monsters from the game as well as virtual walls appearing in the physical environment. Players can shoot at the monsters as they would do in the normal game. The Human Pacman game [22] is a version of the popular arcade game transposed into a real city. Players are equipped with wearable computers and Head-Mounted Displays (HMDs). They have to roam the city searching for physical and virtual items to collect and chasing one another. In the Moon Lander game [23], players have to land a virtual spaceship on a real outdoor location. Examples of MR games in indoor settings include a MR Mah-Jongg game [24] and MonkeyBridge [25], in which players have to place virtual objects on a physical table in order to guide the path of virtual characters.

3   Technical Challenges

Mixed Reality (MR) poses a number of demanding technological requirements for its implementation. One challenge is related to the display technology, which must visualize digital objects at high resolution and high contrast. Precise position tracking constitutes another significant challenge. In order to give the illusion that virtual objects are located at fixed physical positions or attached to physical items, the system must know the position of relevant physical objects relative to the display system. In some cases, depending on the type of display being used, the user's point of view (in terms of their position and the direction of their gaze) is also of interest. The following two subsections provide an overview of display and tracking technologies used to implement MR systems and their known limitations.

Most of the MR technologies require the system to know the location of the objects to be mixed and the location and orientation of the display, or, at least, the location of the objects relative to the location of the display. It is important to emphasize the need for both the position and the orientation of the display in all 6 degrees of freedom. In some situations, the tracking system can be physically attached to the display, and so the user wearing such a display can also be tracked.

3.1   Displays

This section gives an overview of displays most commonly used in MR environments. These are Head-Mounted Displays, hand-held displays, ambient projections, and hand-held projectors.

Head-Mounted Displays. Head-Mounted Displays (HMDs) are probably the most common type of displays used in MR. HMDs were originally developed for Virtual Reality (VR) systems. They consist of one or two visual display units together with optically compensated systems that form a perspectively correct virtual image, even though the display is very close to the user's eyes. HMDs developed for VR let the user perceive only what is shown on the display and so do not provide any see-through capability. However, for MR the virtual imagery needs to be mixed with imagery of the surrounding environment. This can be achieved by means of a video camera physically attached to the HMD. The camera's captured image is electronically combined with the synthetic images to create a MR. Another technical solution is to use semi-transparent mirrors for an optical combination of physical and virtual elements. The first type of HMD using a camera is known as a video see-through HMD, while the latter is called an optical see-through HMD. A special technical realization of an optical see-through HMD uses two consecutive LC-panels: one for image generation, i.e. for displaying the virtual objects, and the second for blanking out the real world (non-see-through) or showing the real environment (optical see-through).

Current off the shelf [26] HMDs allow a field-of-view of 45 degrees diagonally (36 degrees horizontally and about 27 vertically), a resolution of 1280 by 1024 pixels, and a weight of about 750 grams. The display produces the impression of an 80" screen positioned at about 2 meters from the user. In general, critical features of HMDs are their weight, resolution, and field of view. The use of an HMD requires the tracking of the user's head position and orientation so that virtual images can be rendered from the correct viewpoint. HMD prices vary widely, depending on their features.

Hand-held Displays. Hand-held displays are used for MR by using the metaphor of a magic lens, through which a reality can be seen that is enriched by

Fig. 2. The operator views the machine operation through the holographic optical element (HOE), which is illuminated with stereoscopic images from the projectors driven by a PC. The setup allows 3D annotation to appear in the workspace, augmenting the operator's view of the process with relevant information [33].

virtual elements. The mix of real and virtual images is achieved using cameras attached to the displays (video see-through). Similar to HMDs, the position and orientation of hand-held displays must be known in order to correctly generate virtual images. Hand-held displays are normally less expensive than HMDs as there is no need for optical compensation. An early example of hand-held MR was presented by Rekimoto [27] using custom-built hardware, while recent examples employ commercially available mobile phones and PDAs [28], which creates a great potential for mass adoption of this type of display. Such use of mobile phones is shown in an interactive road map application [29] (Figure 3).

Ambient Projectors. Rather than addressing a user's perception through a display, be it head-mounted or hand-held, an alternative is to project computer generated images directly onto the environment using standard video-projectors. The projection can be confined to a specific area, such as a desk [30,31], or it can cover an entire room using an actuated mirror to direct the video beam [32]. In both cases, the system needs to track the position of objects in the mixed environment to be able to display virtual information next to or onto them. Projecting on an entire room or onto special objects requires a 3D model of the entire space. This allows the distortion of the projection in order to fit the images to projection surfaces that are typically not perpendicular to the projector [33] (Figure 2). Unlike HMDs and hand-held displays, the positions of the projectors are fixed or controlled by the system. This reduces the tracking requirements but, typically, also the user's freedom of movement.

Hand-held Projectors. The recent miniaturization of video projectors suggested their use as hand-held MR displays [34]. Users could use these projectors to directly point at objects of interest. This allows the direct projection of the computer-generated information onto the object or next to it. These types of displays require information about the position of objects in the environment relative to the projector and also the orientation of the surfaces onto which the information should be projected. With this information, the computer-generated image can be projected perspectively correct onto the objects of the environment. Compared to hand-held displays, these systems require more complex and expensive hardware, but they can create a larger display surface and allow multiple users to interact more easily with the system.

3.2 Registration

In principle, a tracking system is a device that can determine the position and orientation of a body and interpret it. In order to create a realistic virtual environment, the computer must utilize these systems to acquire this information about the user. Tracking systems can be classified as either active or passive. Within a passive tracking system, the object to be detected does not need any special device, but, rather, it is surveyed by sensors from a distant location. These types of tracking systems very often either have a limited resolution or the effort required for a precise detection is great. Thus, the advantage of being unhindered by cable connections must be paid for by the high installation costs for such a system. Because of these reasons active tracking systems are very often used. Within these systems, the object to be tracked must be active, that is, a sensor is directly attached to the object. Active tracking systems use very different working principles, of which the most important ones will be described here. This section presents an overview of tracking systems most commonly used in MR environments: Global Positioning System (GPS), visual markers, acoustical tracking systems, magnetic and inertial sensors, and hybrid systems.

Global Positioning System. Global Positioning System (GPS) receivers use radio signals broadcasted by a number of medium earth orbit satellites to calculate their location [35]. Each satellite continuously transmits messages about its position, the position of other satellites in the system, and the time when the message was sent. Receivers use the difference in the messages' time of arrival from 4 or more satellites to calculate their location. GPS was originally developed by the US Ministry of Defense. Today, it is still used for military purposes, but also for the navigation and guidance of civilian vehicles like airplanes, ships, and cars, as well as in outdoor mobile MR systems, in combination with another system to provide orientation. Since the system is based on the timing of radio signals, the sensitivity and accuracy of the receivers can have a big influence on the resolution of the positioning [23]. Local radio transmitters can be used in addition to the satellites to improve accuracy. However, this requires expensive installations. GPS signals propagate in line-of-sight and they are highly attenuated by buildings, making the system generally non-functioning when the receiver does not have a clear connection with a minimum amount of satellites, perhaps, indoors or near high buildings. The radio reception near buildings can also vary depending on the time of the day [36], making the situation even more problematic.

Visual Markers. Visual markers, sometimes referred to as fiducial markers, are graphic symbols designed in combination with a computer vision recognition algorithm to yield high probability of recognition and low probability of misclassification [20,37,38]. They can be read using a standard video camera connected to a computer. Then, generally, algorithms enable calculation of the markers' positions and orientations with respect to the camera or vice versa: the position and orientation of the camera with respect to the markers. In MR systems, visual markers are often used with a camera as an integral part of the display - for example, attached to HMDs, hand-held displays, or projectors - so that virtual elements can be rendered at the correct position. Typically, these virtual elements are rendered directly in front of the markers hiding them from the viewer, and they can be visualized best using video see-through displays (head-mounted or hand-held). The same camera can be used for video see-through and for recognizing the markers. Disadvantages of visual markers are that they clutter the scene and require preparation of the environment. However, they have the advantage of being inexpensive and, generally, being usable both indoors and outdoors (within constraints due to ambient illumination and contrast).

An alternative use of visual markers which limits the amount of clutter is to place them out of user's field of view, for example on the ceiling of a room, and to have a camera pointing at them. Knowing the exact location of each marker, the system can then triangulate the position and orientation of the camera based on which markers are visible. However, in this case, the same camera cannot be used for video see-through, so a second camera is required (or an optical see-trough display).

While most systems use the visible part of the spectrum, a number of prototypes use infrared (IR) cameras in conjunction with IR light sources and markers printed on special materials that reflect only the IR portion of the spectrum. In this case, there is less interference by the lighting conditions. However, this requires a more complex installation.

Marker-less Tracking. Computer vision techniques can be used to recognize and track typical features of the environment such as faces or objects with specific textures or contours. These systems normally require a training phase in which the objects to be tracked are presented to the system from one or more viewpoint angles [39]. Compared to marker recognition, marker-less systems do not require the placement of extra objects or labels into the environment. However, this is at the expense of being significantly more computationally expensive, having a higher risk of misclassification, or higher latency. The LightSense system [29] tracks the LED on commercial cell phones, enabling them to be used as spatially aware handheld devices (Figure 3). The outside-in approach tracks the light source and streams the data to the phone over Bluetooth.

Acoustical Tracking Systems. Acoustical tracking systems can be distinguished between runtime (time-of- flight, TOF) and phase shift trackers. In the first system, multiple subsonic sources (approximately 40 kHz) are attached to the object to be tracked. At a certain time, the sources emit a subsonic pulse to the receivers, which are mounted to remain stationary. Since the subsonic pulse has different propagation times, depending on the distance between the source

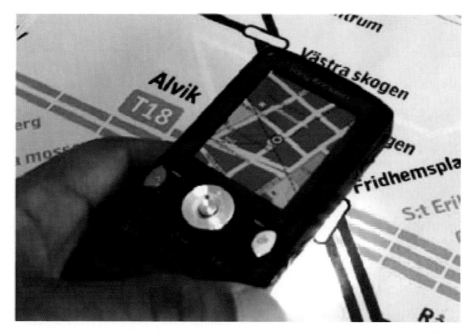

Fig. 3. Outside-in approach tracking the phone light source and streaming the data to the phone. The spatially aware device augments a physical map with a detailed interactive road map of the area of interest [29].

and the receiver, the exact position of the tracked object can be calculated from this. Depending on the required position detection (required degrees of freedom) a different amount of emitters and receivers is needed. The largest amount is needed if the orientation of the object is required in addition to its position. One of the major problems of TOF trackers is the limited update rate caused by the propagation speed of sound in the air. Additionally, the propagation speed of sound depends on parameters of the air such as humidity, temperature, air pressure, and wind. However, these problems can be overcome by continuously measuring the propagation speed of sound with a second set-up. This presumes that the propagation speed is constant within the complete working volume of the tracker.

The other principle of acoustical tracking is the measurement of the phase shift between two signals with the same frequency. Within this phase shift tracking, the signal from the source of the tracked object is superimposed with the signal of a fixed signal source. If only sinusoidal waveforms are used, the position of the tracked object can be determined by the phase shift between the two signals. The two receivers measure the phase difference between the emitted waves and a reference oscillation. Since a phase shift of 360° is equivalent to one wavelength, the difference between the two consecutive measurements can be expressed as the travelling distance of the emitter between these two measurements. This presumes that this distance is less than one wavelength. In order to meet this requirement, the receivers have to measure the phase difference very quickly. If an acoustical tracking frequency of 40 kHz is assumed again, the accuracy is at best around 8 mm.

Magnetic and Inertial Sensors. Magnetic sensors rely on the Earth's magnetic field or artificially generated fields. The simplest example is a digital compass which measures orientation (one degree of freedom) using the Earth's magnetic field. More complex systems can also measure position [40,41]. These systems are typically used in many VR applications and allow tracking of all six degrees of freedom. However, the latter can be distorted by other electronic devices such as monitors and even passive metallic objects.

Inertial sensors generally do not rely on external references, and they measure movement related properties such as velocity and acceleration. The most common inertia sensors are accelerometers and gyroscopes. Theoretically, knowing the initial conditions, it would be possible to calculate a body's position from a consecutive integration of the measured forces. However, in reality, there are measurements errors caused by friction in the accelerometer's bearings, which result in drift errors increasing quadratically over time.

Hybrid Systems. Multiple tracking techniques can be combined to leverage the advantages of each system. As described above, inertial sensors such as accelerometers have drift errors. However, they can be combined with other types of sensors, such as ultrasonic beacons [42] or visual markers [43,44], which can periodically re-calibrate the absolute position of the device. Because ultrasonic and optical systems need a free line-of-sight, they can be ideally complemented by an inertia system for the moments when there are optical shadowing effects caused by the user or other obstacles. As another example, it is common to couple GPS receivers with digital compasses to obtain orientation information with inertial sensors to approximate the device's position whenever the satellite information is temporarily unavailable [23,15].

In order to further increase the calculation speed of such tracking systems, it was shown in [45] that acceleration information is best suited to feed Kalman filters that can predict the trajectory of an object and thus can reduce the lag of tracking systems.

4   User Studies of Mixed Reality

In the design process of an Mixed Reality (MR) application, a series of questions related to human-computer interaction (HCI) demands attention. First of all, who are the users and what are their needs? How can a system be designed to work effectively and efficiently for these users? How are effectiveness and efficiency measured in MR applications? Do users prefer an MR system or an alternative tool to go about their work? And finally, with what types of tasks and alternative tools should the usability of MR applications be tested? A set of perceptual issues, mostly related to the user's visual and auditory capacities, call for further attention. Embodiment and embodied interaction must also be considered as it has been recently pointed out by Dourish [46]. In his understanding, users create and communicate meaning through their interaction with a system. Lastly, issues related to the work context, the task at hand, and collaboration call for additional investigation.

A survey by Swan and Gabbard [47] shows that between 1998 and 2004, less than 10% of a representative sample of MR scientific publications reported studies with real users. The survey groups the studies into 3 categories. The first one is the most popular and includes studies that look at low-level issues in perception and cognition in AR. They examine issues such as perception of virtual objects' depths using different display technologies or rendering algorithms. Within this category, the ability of users to acquire targets under varying degrees of system lag is also studied. The second category covers six higher level evaluations of MR applications. Here, we find comparative studies of different MR interfaces applied to the same task and studies assessing the overall usability of an MR system. In the third category, the survey reports three studies about user interaction and communication in collaborative MR applications, looking, for example, at how communication asymmetries or different MR technologies influence users' behavior and performance. A special journal issue (IJHCI, 2003) on usability and collaborative issues of MR touch upon most of these questions and topics [48]. From the MR papers it presents, some are more visionary and focus on novel enabling technology for collaboration, while others offer solid empirical work presenting experimental studies with alternative applications. Two samples from this special issue follow.

The need for studies evaluating the effect of computerized tools on human cooperation and communication is well justified and documented in a paper offered by Billinghurst et al. [49]. The authors reported on two experiments: the first involving collaboration with MR technology as compared to more traditional unmediated and screen-based collaboration (Figure 4), and the second, the comparison of collaboration with three different MR displays. In both experiments, the authors used process and subjective measures in addition to more traditional performance measures. Process measures captured the process of collaboration through the number and type of gestures used and deictic phrases spoken. Using these measures to analyze communication behavior, it was found that users exhibited many of the same behaviors in a collaborative MR interface as they did in a face-to-face, unmediated collaboration. However, user communication behavior changed with the type of MR display used. The experimental task used was well suited to elicit collaboration and allowed for different styles of interaction to be evaluated within a single experiment. The authors then describe implications of the results for the design of collaborative MR interfaces and present plans for future research. The variety of relevant measures they use contrasts with most MR research which typically focuses on easily quantifiable aspects of task performance such as task completion time and error rate.

In another paper from the same issue, Wiedenmaier et al. showed how MR for assembly processes can be a new kind of computer support for a traditional indus-

Fig. 4. Billinghurst et al. [49] compared collaborative work under three alternative conditions: face-to-face, AR, and projector

trial domain [50]. The article concisely links MR to the real-world task of assembly. The new application of AR-technology is called ARsembly. The article describes a typical scenario for assembly and maintenance personnel and how MR might support both. For this purpose, tasks with different degrees of difficulty were selected from an authentic assembly process of the automotive industry. Two other kinds of assembly support media (a printed manual and a tutorial by an expert) were examined in order to compare them with ARsembly. The results showed that the assembly times varied according to the different support conditions. MR support proved to be more suitable for difficult tasks than the paper manual, whereas for easier tasks, MR support did not appear to be significantly more advantageous. As assumed, tasks done under the guidance of an expert were completed most rapidly. Some of the information obtained in this investigation also indicates important considerations for improving future ARsembly applications. The authors made a valuable contribution in presenting empirical results comparing different types of support for assembly processes. They also showed some evidence that a particular MR system in some situations can have advantages over traditional, printed assembly manuals. The authors have invested significant resources into building their systems and running controlled studies, greatly furthering scientific knowledge of MR and HCI. Their work shows where MR is both suitable and unsuitable. To achieve wide spread application for MR, it is important to take MR out of the lab and into the real world.

5   Mixed Reality Research in Switzerland

In Switzerland, research activities in the field of Mixed Reality (MR) take place at the two federal institutes of technology as well as at other institutions of higher education. This section reports some of the Swiss contributions.

The Virtual Reality Lab at EPFL and the MIRAlab at the University of Geneva were both involved in a project for the augmentation of the archaeological site of Pompei [51], working on several issues from tracking to the creation of virtual actors. Also at EPFL, the Computer Vision Lab developed vision-based markerless tracking techniques for MR [39].

At ETH Zurich, the Computer Vision Lab was involved in projects investigating MR and haptics, [52] as well as calibration techniques [53], mostly related

Fig. 5. The BUILD-IT system: Collaborative production plant layout combining digital, physical, and printed media (left); multi-pointer interaction of a furniture scenario (right)

to medical applications. BUILD-IT was a research project involving four ETH Zurich departments (ARCH, MAVT, MTEC, and ANBI) during the period from 1997 to 2001. The resulting BUILD-IT system (Figures 1 and 5) is a planning tool based on computer vision technology with a capacity for complex planning and composition tasks [54,55]. The system enables users, grouped around a table, to interact in a virtual scene using physical bricks to select and manipulate virtual models. A bird's eye view of the scene is projected onto the table. A perspective view of the scene, called the side view, is projected on the wall. The plan view contains a storage space with originals, allowing users to create new models and to activate tools e.g. navigation and height tools. Model selection is done by placing a brick at the model's position. Once selected, models can be positioned, rotated, and fixed by simple brick manipulation.

At the Innovation Center Virtual Reality (ICVR) at ETH Zurich, an AR-system for tabletop interaction was developed which uses typical office components such as pens, rulers, notepads and erasers. to enable interaction with the computer during group work [56,57]. Multiple users can work simultaneously with real objects that are augmented by a back-projection onto the tabletop. The objects are tracked through the screen via an IR-system, and additional information is displayed next to it, such as colour, virtual notepad and measurement results of the ruler. (Figure 6).

The same group carried out the research projects, blue-c and Holoport, focusing on an extension of the real environment into a virtual one (Figure 7). In the blue-c project [58], markerless optical tracking was used to track the user and their action in controlling the system and interacting with the remote 3D avatar. In the Holoport project [59,60], a real table was extended by a virtual one, allowing team meetings in an MR environment with the impression of sitting at the same table.

Also at ICVR (ETH Zurich), a MR application for education in architectural design was realized. Although many 3D models already exist in this field (real and virtual), it had so far not been possible to use such models within a

Fig. 6. A desktop AR-system for intuitive interaction with the computer

Fig. 7. The real table is extended by a virtual one, using a holographic projection screen

collaborative team session and to look at such models from different viewpoints. Using common libraries from AR-Toolkit [61], a collaborative 3D viewer was developed which allowed collocated and remote team members to simultaneously inspect the model of a building and perform simple actions like selecting, moving, rotating, scaling, and defining viewing planes (Figure 8).

Finally, the Sensory-Motor System Lab (SMS) Lab at ETH Zurich is investigating how athletes execute and learn the complex rowing movement. In order to do this they have built a rowing simulator based on virtual reality and MR technology. This simulator was required to convey the impression of realistic rowing, provide customizable, augmented feedback, and thus, optimal training conditions for rowing. The participant sits in a shortened racing boat (Figure 9) and holds one or two shortened oars that are virtually complemented in the

Fig. 8. MR application in architectural design

Fig. 9. The MR rowing environment of the SMS lab

computer generated image. The oars are connected to a rope robot. Depending on the oar pose and movement, forces are generated to simulate water resistance. The participant is surrounded by three screens (dimensions 4.44m 3.33m each) onto which three projectors display a river scenario.

Augmented Chemistry (AC) is an application that utilizes a tangible user interface (TUI) for organic chemistry education (Figure 10). First developed at HyperWerk FHNW Basel [62] and later together with IHA, ETH Zurich and Chalmers TH in Gothenburg [63]. An empirical evaluation compared learning effectiveness and user acceptance of AC versus the more traditional ball-and-stick model (BSM) [63]. Learning effectiveness results were almost the same for both learning environments. User preference and rankings, using NASA-TLX

Fig. 10. The original Augmented Chemistry set-up from HyperWerk FHNW in Basel in 2002 (left) and the later version from t2i Lab at Chalmers TH in Gothenburg in 2005 (right)

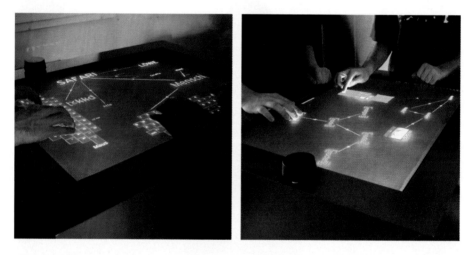

Fig. 11. Tangent: an early multi-touch tabletop framework, realized by Christian Iten and Daniel Lüthi, Interaction Design, ZHdK in Zurich [64]

and SUMI, showed more differences, for example in ease of use and in ease of learning the system. It was therefore decided to focus mainly on improving these aspects in a re-design of the AC system. For enhanced interaction, keyboard-free system configuration, and internal/external database (DB) access, a graphical user interface (GUI) were incorporated into the TUI. Three-dimensional rendering was also improved using shadows and related effects, thereby enhancing depth perception. The re-designed AC system (Figure 10, right) was then compared to the original system by means of a small qualitative user study. This user study showed an improvement in subjective opinions about the systems ease of use and ease of learning the system.

The size of the human finger makes it difficult for users to precisely manipulate small elements on touch screens. Christian Iten and Daniel Lüthi from the ZHdK presented a tabletop framework called Tangent including a tool called Digital Tweezers [64]. This tool enables its users to point, select, and drag interactive elements the size of a few pixels. The tool consists of a cursor with a fixed offset controlled by the thumb and index finger of one hand. Based on the Tangent framework, ConceptMap was realizedin collaboration with Emanuel Zgraggen und Simon Brauchli from IFS at HSR. ConceptMap is a multi-touch application for creating and editing semantic nets (Figure 11).

The Real-Time Coordination and Sustainable Interaction System Group at EPF-L, the Pervasive Artificial Intelligence Group at the University of Fribourg, and the Multimedia Information System Group at University of Applied Sciences of Western Switzerland, Fribourg were all involved in the 6th Sense project which is also presented in this book. The project aims to improve the user experience in mobile MR and the context-aware interaction between real environments and virtual augmentations. The Computer Vision and Multimedia Lab at the University of Geneva and the Laboratoire d'Informatique Industrielle at the University of Applied Sciences of Western Switzerland, Geneva were both involved in the See ColOr project aimed at adding sound to images in order to provide an interactive aid for visually impaired individuals.

6   Current Challenges and Trends

Most of the systems and technical solutions described in the previous sections require prior preparation of the environment to run the Mixed Reality (MR) system in. For example, ultrasound or IR beacons need to be installed and powered, or visual markers and RFID tags need to be placed in specific locations. Even in outdoor environments, GPS requires the installation of local transmitters in addition to the existing satellites in order to achieve high positioning accuracy. Additionally, the systems require an accurate digital model of the real environment and a complete mapping of the sensors' locations to precisely position the virtual elements of the interface within the real space.

A number of prototypes presented in research papers use only a loose connection between the virtual elements and the physical space. For example, from the description of the AR Quake game [21], as well as the Moon Lander AR game [23], it is not clear how the features of the game are aligned to the physical world, and, in fact, there seems to be few compelling reason for a specific mapping of the real and virtual game spaces. Similarly, in the Magic Book [9] and Fata Morgana [10] projects, the system is able to render virtual models aligned to the physical pages of a book, but it is unclear what role the physical object plays in the application beyond being a handle or a controller - the MR features seem to be used solely to rotate the models and to allow users to look at them from different viewpoints. This would also be possible with a virtual reality system or even with just a desktop graphics workstation. In other words, it seems that in a number of MR prototypes the paradigm reverts to VR, the importance is placed solely on the virtual elements and not on the real ones, and the MR features are used only as interactive controllers, like handles. Even though the Augmented Reality definition by Azuma et al. [3] still applies to these systems in the sense that they are interactive and display virtual objects registered to the real world, it can be observed that the connection between the virtual elements and the physical reality is relatively weak.

Future investigation into MR could therefore target specific domains of application, such as the medical field, in which specialized digital data is inherently aligned with the physical world, as in the case of medical image overlays onto a patient's body in surgery. Also, future MR research could consider larger scale, more general applications, reduced registration requirements, and thus allowing an easier implementation onto consumer hand-held devices. Today's mobile phones are ubiquitous and already embed considerable computational capabilities (yet not enough for most registration techniques) - initial exploration suggests that they may have great potential for MR. The relationship between digital content and physical space could then become less tight in terms of resolution, but more stringent in terms of relevance in the direction of location-based services and applications.

Based on the experiences of MR research in Switzerland, we see a trend towards more application-specific projects, typically industrial and educational. Industrial applications are directed towards support planning tasks. The fact that projects are becoming more application-oriented may indicate that MR technologies are becoming more mature. While early MR systems were mostly single-user, more recent applications are collaborative, both for co-located and net-based use.

References

1. Weiser, M.: Some computer science issues in ubiquitous computing. Commun. ACM 36(7), 75–84 (1993)
2. Sutherland, I.: A head-mounted three dimensional display. In: Proceedings of the Fall Joint Computer Conference, vol. 33, pp. 757–764 (1968)
3. Azuma, R., Baillot, Y., Behringer, R., Feiner, S., Julier, S., MacIntyre, B.: Recent advances in augmented reality. IEEE Comput. Graph. Appl. 21(6), 34–47 (2001)
4. Milgram, P., Kishino, F.: A Taxonomy of Mixed Reality Visual Displays. IEICE Transactions on Information Systems 77, 1321–1329 (1994)
5. Feiner, S., Macintyre, B., Seligmann, D.: Knowledge-based augmented reality. In: Communications of the ACM, vol. 36, pp. 53–62. ACM Press, New York (1993)
6. Lee, J., Rhee, G.: Context-aware 3D visualization and collaboration services for ubiquitous cars using augmented reality. The International Journal of Advanced Manufacturing Technology 37, 431–442 (2008)
7. Reiners, D., Stricker, D., Klinker, G., Muller, S.: Augmented Reality for Construction Tasks: Doorlock Assembly. In: 1st International Workshop on Augmented Reality (IWAR 1998), San Francisco (1998)
8. Doil, F., Schreiber, W., Alt, T., Patron, C.: Augmented reality for manufacturing planning. In: Proceedings of the workshop on Virtual environments 2003, pp. 71–76. ACM Press, New York (2003)
9. Billinghurst, M., Kato, H., Poupyrev, I.: The MagicBook: a transitional AR interface. In: Computers & Graphics, vol. 25, pp. 745–753. Elsevier, Amsterdam (2001)

10. Klinker, G., Dutoit, A., Bauer, M., Bayer, J., Novak, V., Matzke, D.: "Fata Morgana" A Presentation System for Product Design. In: Proceedings of the International Symposium on Mixed and Augmented Reality (ISMAR 2002). IEEE Computer Society, Washington (2002)
11. State, A., Livingston, M.A., Garrett, W.F., Hirota, G., Whitton, M.C., Pisano, E.D., Fuchs, H.: Technologies for augmented reality systems: Realizing ultrasound-guided needle biopsies. In: SIGGRAPH, pp. 439–446 (1996)
12. State, A., Hirota, G., Chen, D.T., Garrett, W.F., Livingston, M.A.: Superior augmented reality registration by integrating landmark tracking and magnetic tracking. In: SIGGRAPH, pp. 429–438 (1996)
13. Lorensen, W.E., Cline, H.E., Nafis, C., Altobelli, D., Gleason, L.: Enhancing reality in the operating room. In: IEEE Visualization, pp. 410–415 (1993)
14. Rosenthal, M., State, A., Lee, J., Hirota, G., Ackerman, J., Keller, K., Pisano, E., Jiroutek, M., Muller, K., Fuchs, H.: Augmented reality guidance for needle biopsies: An initial randomized, controlled trial in phantoms. In: Medical Image Analysis, vol. 6, pp. 313–320. Elsevier, Amsterdam (2002)
15. Höllerer, T., Feiner, S., Terauchi, T., Rashid, G., Hallaway, D.: Exploring MARS: developing indoor and outdoor user interfaces to a mobile augmented reality system. In: Computers & Graphics, vol. 23, pp. 779–785. Elsevier, Amsterdam (1999)
16. Welch, G., Sonnenwald, D., Mayer-Patel, K., Yang, R., State, A., Towles, H., Cairns, B., Fuchs, H.: Remote 3D medical consultation. In: Proc. BROADMED Conf. 2005, University College of Borås. Swedish School of Library and Information Science, pp. 103–110 (2005)
17. Julier, S., Baillot, Y., Brown, D., Lanzagorta, M.: Information filtering for mobile augmented reality. IEEE Computer Graphics and Applications 22(5), 12–15 (2002)
18. Thomas, B., Piekarski, W., Hepworth, D., Gunther, B., Demczuk, V.: A wearable computer system with augmented reality to support terrestrial navigation. In: ISWC 1998: Proceedings of the 2nd IEEE International Symposium on Wearable Computers, Washington, DC, USA, p. 168. IEEE Computer Society, Los Alamitos (1998)
19. Feiner, S., MacIntyre, B., Hollerer, T., Webster, A.: A touring machine: Prototyping 3d mobile augmented reality systems for exploring the urban environment. In: ISWC 1997: Proceedings of the 1st IEEE International Symposium on Wearable Computers, Washington, DC, USA, p. 74. IEEE Computer Society, Los Alamitos (1997)
20. Rekimoto, J.: Navicam: A magnifying glass approach to augmented reality. In: Presence, vol. 6, pp. 399–412 (1997)
21. Thomas, B., Close, B., Donoghue, J., Squires, J., Bondi, P., Piekarski, W.: First Person Indoor/Outdoor Augmented Reality Application: ARQuake. In: Personal and Ubiquitous Computing, vol. 6, pp. 75–86. Springer, Heidelberg (2002)
22. Cheok, A., Goh, K., Liu, W., Farbiz, F., Fong, S., Teo, S., Li, Y., Yang, X.: Human Pacman: a mobile, wide-area entertainment system based on physical, social, and ubiquitous computing. In: Personal and Ubiquitous Computing, vol. 8, pp. 71–81. Springer, Heidelberg (2004)
23. Avery, B., Thomas, B., Velikovsky, J., Piekarski, W.: Outdoor augmented reality gaming on five dollars a day. In: Proceedings of the Sixth Australasian conference on User interface, vol. 40, pp. 79–88. Australian Computer Society, Inc, Darlinghurst (2005)
24. Szalavári, Z., Eckstein, E., Gervautz, M.: Collaborative gaming in augmented reality. In: Proceedings of the ACM symposium on Virtual reality software and technology 1998, pp. 195–204. ACM Press, New York (1998)

25. Barakonyi, I., Weilguny, M., Psik, T., Schmalstieg, D.: Monkeybridge: autonomous agents in augmented reality games. In: Lee, N. (ed.) Advances in Computer Entertainment Technology, pp. 172–175. ACM, New York (2005)
26. Bungert, C.: Hmd/headset/vr-helmet comparison chart (2008), http://www.stereo3d.com/hmd.htm
27. Rekimoto, J., Nagao, K.: The world through the computer: computer augmented interaction with real world environments. In: Proceedings of the 8th annual ACM symposium on User interface and software technology, pp. 29–36. ACM, New York (1995)
28. Moehring, M., Lessig, C., Bimber, O.: Video See-Through AR on Consumer Cell Phones. In: Proc. of International Symposium on Augmented and Mixed Reality (ISMAR 2004), pp. 252–253 (2004)
29. Olwal, A.: Lightsense: enabling spatially aware handheld interaction devices. In: ISMAR, pp. 119–122 (2006)
30. Wellner, P.: Interacting with paper on the DigitalDesk. In: Communications of the ACM, vol. 36, pp. 87–96. ACM Press, New York (1993)
31. Fitzmaurice, G., Ishii, H., Buxton, W.: Bricks: laying the foundations for graspable user interfaces. In: Proceedings of the SIGCHI conference on Human factors in computing systems, pp. 442–449. ACM Press/Addison-Wesley Publishing Co., New York (1995)
32. Pinhanez, C.: Augmenting Reality with Projected Interactive Displays. In: Virtual and Augmented Architecture (Vaa 2001): Proceedings of the International Symposium on Virtual and Augmented Architecture (Vaa 2001), Trinity College, Dublin, June 21-22 (2001)
33. Olwal, A., Gustafsson, J., Lindfors, C.: Spatial augmented reality on industrial cnc-machines. In: Proceedings of SPIE 2008 Electronic Imaging. The Engineering Reality of Virtual Reality 2008, vol. 6804 (2008)
34. Raskar, R., van Baar, J., Beardsley, P., Willwacher, T., Rao, S., Forlines, C.: iLamps: geometrically aware and self-configuring projectors. In: International Conference on Computer Graphics and Interactive Techniques. ACM Press, New York (2006)
35. Getting, I.: Perspective/navigation-The Global Positioning System. In: Spectrum, vol. 30. IEEE, Los Alamitos (1993)
36. Steed, A.: Supporting Mobile Applications with Real-Time Visualisation of GPS Availability. In: Proceedings of Mobile HCI. Springer, Heidelberg (2004)
37. Kato, H., Billinghurst, M., Poupyrev, I., Imamoto, K., Tachibana, K.: Virtual object manipulation on a table-top AR environment. In: Proc. IEEE and ACM International Symposium on Augmented Reality (ISAR), pp. 111–119 (2000)
38. Costanza, E., Robinson, J.: A region adjacency tree approach to the detection and design of fiducials. In: Vision, Video and Graphics (VVG), pp. 63–70 (2003)
39. Lepetit, V., Fua, P.: Keypoint Recognition Using Randomized Trees. In: IEEE Transactions On Pattern Analysis And Machine Intelligence, pp. 1465–1479. IEEE Computer Society, Los Alamitos (2006)
40. Polhemus: Polhemus "fastrak" commercial system (retrieved, June 2008), http://www.polhemus.com/?page=Motion_Fastrak
41. Ascension: Ascension "flock of birds" commercial system (retrieved, June 2008), http://www.ascension-tech.com/products/flockofbirds.php
42. Foxlin, E., Harrington, M., Harrington, M., Pfeifer, G.: Constellation: a wide-range wireless motion-tracking system for augmented reality and virtual set applications. In: Proceedings of the 25th annual conference on Computer graphics and interactive techniques, pp. 371–378. ACM New York, NY (1998)

43. Yokokohji, Y., Sugawara, Y., Yoshikawa, T.: Accurate image overlay on video see-through hmds using vision and accelerometers. In: VR 2000: Proceedings of the IEEE Virtual Reality 2000 Conference, Washington, DC, USA, p. 247. IEEE Computer Society, Los Alamitos (2000)

44. Kotake, D., Satoh, K., Uchiyama, S., Yamamoto, H.: A hybrid and linear registration method utilizing inclination constraint. In: Proceedings of the Fourth IEEE and ACM International Symposium on Mixed and Augmented Reality, pp. 140–149 (2005)

45. Azuma, R., Bishop, G.: A frequency-domain analysis of head-motion prediction. In: SIGGRAPH 1995: Proceedings of the 22nd annual conference on Computer graphics and interactive techniques, pp. 401–408. ACM, New York (1995)

46. Dourish, P.: Where the action is: the foundations of embodied interaction. MIT Press, Cambridge (2001)

47. Swan, J.E., Gabbard, J.L.: Survey of user-based experimentation in augmented reality. In: Proceedings of 1st International Conference on Virtual Reality (2005)

48. Fjeld, M.: Special Issue on Usability and collaborative aspects of augmented reality. Interactions 11(6), 11–15 (2004)

49. Billinghurst, M., Belcher, D., Gupta, A., Kiyokawa, K.: Communication Behaviors in Colocated Collaborative AR Interfaces. International Journal of Human-Computer Interaction 16(3), 395–423 (2003)

50. Wiedenmaier, S., Oehme, O., Schmidt, L., Luczak, H.: Augmented reality (ar) for assembly processes design and experimental evaluation. Int. J. Hum. Comput. Interaction 16(3), 497–514 (2003)

51. Papagiannakis, G., Schertenleib, S., Ponder, M., Arévalo-Poizat, M., Magnenat-Thalmann, N., Thalmann, D.: Real-time virtual humans in ar sites. In: 1st European Conference on Visual Media Production (CVMP), pp. 273–276. IEEE Publisher, Los Alamitos (2004)

52. Bianchi, G., Knörlein, B., Szèkely, G., Harders, M.: High precision augmented reality haptics. In: Eurohaptics (2006)

53. Bianchi, G., Wengert, C., Harders, M., Cattin, P., Székely, G.: Camera-marker alignment framework and comparison with hand-eye calibration for augmented reality applications. In: ISMAR (2005)

54. Fjeld, M., Lauche, K., Bichsel, M., Voorhorst, F., Krueger, H., Rauterberg, M.: Physical and virtual tools: Activity theory applied to the design of groupware. In: Computer Supported Cooperative Work (CSCW), vol. 11, pp. 153–180 (2002)

55. Fjeld, M., Morf, M., Krueger, H.: Activity theory and the practice of design: evaluation of a collaborative tangible user interface. Inderscience 4, 94–116 (2004)

56. Ganser Schwab, C., Kennel, T., Kunz, A.: Digital support for net-based teamwork in early design stages. Journal of Design Research 6(1), 150–168 (2007)

57. Schwab, C.G., Kennel, T., Kunz, A.: Digital support for net-based teamwork in early design stages 6(1/2), 150–168 (2007)

58. Gross, M.H., Würmlin, S., Näf, M., Lamboray, E., Spagno, C.P., Kunz, A.M., Koller-Meier, E., Svoboda, T., Gool, L.J.V., Lang, S., Strehlke, K., Moere, A.V., Staadt, O.G.: Blue-c: a spatially immersive display and 3d video portal for telepresence. ACM Trans. Graph. 22(3), 819–827 (2003)

59. Kuechler, M., Kunz, A.: Holoport - a device for simultaneous video and data conferencing featuring gaze awareness. In: Proceedings of the IEEE conference on Virtual Reality (IEEE VR 2006), Washington, DC, United States, pp. 81–87. IEEE Computer Society, Los Alamitos (2006)

60. Kunz, A., Fadel, G., Taiber, J., Schichtel, M.: Towards collaboration in engineering of tomorrow - building highly interactive virtual collaboration platforms. In: SAE 2006 World Congress & Exhibition, United States, SAE International (2006)
61. Kato, H., Billinghurst, M.: Marker tracking and hmd calibration for a video-based augmented reality conferencing system. In: IWAR 1999: Proceedings of the 2nd IEEE and ACM International Workshop on Augmented Reality. IEEE Computer Society, Los Alamitos (1999)
62. Voegtli, B.: Augmented collaboration. M.sc. thesis, HyperWerk FHNW (2002)
63. Fjeld, M., Fredriksson, J., Ejdestig, M., Duca, F., Bötschi, K., Voegtli, B.M., Juchli, P.: Tangible user interface for chemistry education: comparative evaluation and re-design. In: CHI, pp. 805–808 (2007)
64. Iten, C., Lüthi, D.: (2006), http://www.zima.ch/tangent/

Part II
Multimodal User Interfaces

Intelligent Multi-modal Interfaces for Mobile Applications in Hostile Environment (IM-HOST)

Claude Stricker[1,3], Jean-Frédéric Wagen[2],
Guillermo Aradilla[4], Hervé Bourlard[4], Hynek Hermansky[4], Joel Pinto[4],
Paul-Henri Rey[1,3], and Jérôme Théraulaz[2]

[1] AISTS, CH-1015, Lausanne
www.aists.org
[2] EIA-FR (HES-SO Fribourg), CH-1705, Fribourg
www.eia-fr.ch
[3] HES-SO Valais, CH-3960, Sierre
www.hevs.ch
[4] Idiap Research Institute, CH-1920, Martigny
www.idiap.ch

Abstract. Multi-modal interfaces for mobile applications include tiny screens, keyboards, touch screens, ear phones, microphones and software components for voice-based man-machine interaction. The software enabling voice recognition, as well as the microphone, are of primary importance in a noisy environment. Current performances of voice applications are reasonably good in quiet environment. However, the surrounding noise in many practical situations largely deteriorates the quality of the speech signal. As a consequence, the recognition rate decreases significantly. Noise management is a major focus in developing voice-enabled technologies. This project addresses the problem of voice recognition with the goal of reaching a high success rate (ideally above 99%) in an outdoor environment that is noisy and hostile: the user stands on an open deck of a motor-boat and use his/her voice to command applications running on a laptop by using a wireless microphone. In addition to the problem of noise, there are other constraints strongly limiting the hardware options. Furthermore, the user must also perform several tasks simultaneously. The success of the solution must rely on the efficiency and effectiveness of the voice recognition algorithm and the choice of the microphone. In addition, the training of the recognizer should be kept to a minimum and the recognition time should not last longer than 3 seconds. For these two reasons, only a limited set of voice commands have been tested.

A first demonstrator based on digit keyword spotting trained over phone speech showed poor performances in very noisy conditions. A second demonstrator combining neural network and template matching techniques lead to nearly acceptable results when the user recorded the keywords. Since the recognition rate was approximated around 90%, no additional field test was undertaken. This R&D project shows that state-of-the-art research on voice recognition needs further investigations

D. Lalanne and J. Kohlas (Eds.): Human Machine Interaction, LNCS 5440, pp. 71–102, 2009.
© Springer-Verlag Berlin Heidelberg 2009

in order to recognize spoken keywords in noisy environments. In addition to on-going improvements, unconventional research approaches that are worth testing include, deriving adapted keywords to specialized algorithms and having the user learn these keyword.

1   Introduction

1.1   Objectives and Scope

This project addresses the problem of voice recognition with the goal of reaching a high success rate (ideally above 99%) in an outdoor environment. The voice recognition algorithm has to deal with the surrounding noise management and has to be integrated as one interface amongst others in the man-machine interaction. In addition to the problem of noise, hostile environments mean that other constraints strongly limit the hardware options. For example: high level of humidity, likelihood of shock and continuous movement of the user. The success of the solution will have to rely largely on the efficiency and effectiveness of the voice recognition algorithm and on the choice of the microphone. The developed solutions might be very useful for individuals with disabilities in everyday life or for athletes and coaches who also often need to send and receive information while their hands and eyes are busy. The usefulness of the solution means that the solution takes profit from the willingness of the user to learn how to interact with the recognizer.

The first part of this contribution presents the challenges that voice-enabled technologies have to face when it comes to sport applications. Furthermore the first part describes the use cases envisioned in this project. The second part describes two algorithms for recognition developed for noisy environments. The third part presents two demonstrators that have been used for short practical field tests. The paper concludes by providing some recommendations on where further research on voice recognition in noisy environments could go based on the experiences accumulated during our investigations.

The project described in this contribution is a mix between research in the area of Automatic Speech Recognition (ASR) and developments to adapt state-of-the-art algorithms in a functional practical system. Developments had to be delivered as early as possible before the start of the America's cup boat races. The Swiss defender, Alinghi, was the main tester of the outcomes of this project. Although this contribution reports some detailed tests using conventional speech corpora, only a few subjective tests by the end users are provided. However, these tests were found sufficient to demonstrate the usefulness of the delivered demonstrators and to assess the required improvements.

1.2   Meeting the Challenges of Sport

The performance of voice-enabled applications is reasonably good for home and office purposes. However, there are still some serious challenges when it comes to sport applications [33].

The first challenge is that sport frequently takes place in noisy environments. The reader might already have experienced difficulties in understanding someone calling with a mobile phone from a football stadium where the crowd is yelling; the noise interference is very high. A speech recognition system must faces this problem: the surrounding noise deteriorates the quality of the speech signal possibly in a non linear way depending on the microphone and coders used.

The second challenge is that speech devices are often used in very rough conditions. A microphone used by a ski coach in the mountains must work in cold and wet weather. Microphones placed in a rally car might receive shocks and vibrations and would have to resist dust and sand. Wind noise (i.e. on a sailing boat) is also a factor that could dramatically decrease the effectiveness of the microphone. The choice of microphone needs to be constructed carefully depending on the conditions in which the sport takes place.

The third challenge is that athletes and staff often need fast and reliable information in critical situations. As of today, even the best speech recognition system, or a human, is not able to guarantee a one hundred per cent recognition rate. For this reason, users seem reluctant to rely on speech interfaces for critical applications. For example, no rally car driver would ever accept to command gears, gas and brake pedals by vocal command. However, this has been used on boats in the past to give orders from the desk to the machine room. The risk of a crash if the system does not understand a request might be too high. Furthermore, while humans might be willing to repeat information several times to another person who does not understand them, they are less tolerant with computers [35].

The fourth challenge is that speaking consumes precious cognitive resources [34]. This often leads to a difficulty to perform other tasks at the same time. For example, studies have shown that calling with a mobile phone could affect a car drivers concentration and anticipation [36]. The drivers mind is not fully on their driving. For this reason, vocal applications should not be designed for athletes who need high concentration resources. Voice applications might distract them from what they are doing and therefore reduce performance or safety.

The fifth and last challenge is the importance of selecting the most appropriate user interface mode or combination of modes depending on the device, the task, the environment, and the users abilities and preferences [29]. Developers should carefully analyze the parameters (device, tasks, environment, users abilities and preferences) in order to provide adequate voice interfaces. A well-designed voice interface for cross-country runners may be totally inadequate for swimmers. For athletes, to wear a microphone and headset could be a source of annoyance. Athletes usually want to concentrate solely on their sport and do not want to be bothered by an external annoyance. Furthermore, athletes might not even be allowed to use voice control. Because athletes or coaches are usually moving, it is preferable to choose a wireless solution (race car drivers being an obvious choice). In all cases the headset should be lightweight and easy-to-wear. Because athletes and coaches need to access information anywhere at anytime, the system

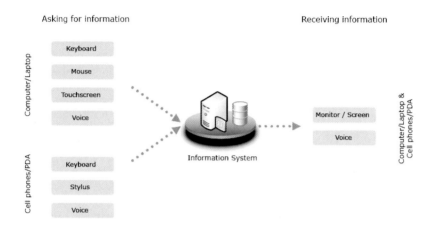

Fig. 1. Multi-modal interfaces

must provide multiple ways to interface (e.g. keyboards if possible, heavy duty buttons, etc.) (Figure 1)

2   Use cases

2.1   Potential Applications for Sport

One first generic use case [32] is depicted in Figure 2. The user can ask for information via a speech interface. The information system, through the speech recognition engine, identifies the users request, processes it, and sends the result back to the user. Information stored in a database is translated into speech with a text-to-speech engine or via a pre-recorded message. The information system is updated by periodically receiving information from sensors on the field. Mechanisms of spoken-language understanding can be integrated. Requests such as "Calories" or "Please tell me the amount of calories I've burned since the beginning of the training session" might have the same results.

A second use case consists of inserting data on an information server. Writing comments on a Notepad and copying them afterwards to a computer is no longer required: coaches (ski, soccer, ice hockey,etc.) can instantaneously save verbal observations on an information server. Today, the referees of the Swiss Football Federation call a vocal server after each game in order to report the game and final score. This information is then saved in the system. There are numerous advantages: 24/7 availability, instant data availability on the Internet, time savings, and costs reduction to name a few.

A third use case consists of using voice commands to control devices and applications. Voice command is a good alternative when the user is far from another input/output interface and needs to interact quickly. By saying specific keywords, the user can modify the behavior of a device. One could imagine changing the

Fig. 2. Voice-enabled technologies as a way to ask information

speed of a treadmill by saying "faster" or "slower." Athletes with a disability would also benefit from such applications. Through speaker identification, users are given or denied access to specific commands.

Athletes, referees and coaches already use microphones and two-way radios to share information with each other in many sports such as American football, rugby, soccer and cycling. In addition, there is a large amount of data already available on information system servers being used to support detailed analysis (e.g. statistical analysis of games). It would be interesting to leverage the existing use of speech devices and the existing use of information systems by combining the two. The idea would be to use a microphone to interact not only with humans but also with the servers or any other devices that store the information.

2.2   Field Tests

Use case

During 2006 and until mid-2007, two different speech recognition algorithms described in Sections 4 and 5 were adapted to the needs of Alinghi, the winner of the 2003 and 2007 America's Cup. Alinghi's training and races are followed by a coach and other observers on a chase boat. Located on the chase boat, protected behind a shield, there was a single touch-screen computer running five different software tools, each with its own display and user interfaces. Consequently these software applications were controlled by the coach through the touch-screen. Although the touch-screen allows intuitive, rapid and accurate interactions with the content of the display, Alinghi crew members often experience difficulties selecting the required application because they are thrown off balance by the pitch of the boat. As a result, Alinghi team representatives asked for a more efficient way to swap between applications. It was thought that a multi-modal interface mixing touch-screen technology and speech recognition was the best way to perform this task. With the software developed for Alinghi, the coach was able to switch to the desired application either through vocal command or by using the touch-screen with a special pen.

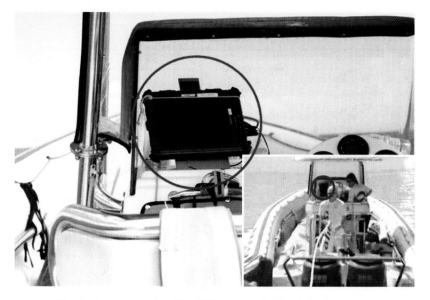

Fig. 3. An on-board tablet PC on one of Alinghi's chase boats

Under the difficult conditions described above, two approaches have been tested. The following 2 sections focuses on the tutorial and advanced research aspects of the two approaches: keyword spotting and template matching.

3   Keyword Spotting

Keyword spotting refers to identifying an user specified word or a phrase in unconstrained speech recording. Keyword spotting is useful in various applications such as command and control, searching large archives of telephone speech, etc.

3.1   Background

Approaches to keyword spotting can be broadly classified into three categories based on the use of (a) filler/garbage models, (b) word lattices, and (c) phoneme lattices.

Filler Model: In filler model based keyword spotting, the keyword is modeled using its phonetic string and all non-keyword speech is modeled using a garbage model connected in parallel to the keyword model. Additionally, there is a transition from the end of this parallel model to its beginning to enable spotting more than one keyword in the utterance.

The keyword model is the concatenation of the hidden Markov models (HMMs) corresponding to the constituent phonemes in the keyword. However, garbage models are obtained in different ways. One way of obtaining smoothed garbage model is to train a GMM or HMM explicitly on non-keyword speech.

Multiple garbage models could also be trained for different classes of sounds (vowels, plosives, nasals etc). A garbage model could also be a generic word model modeled as an ergodic network of context dependent or independent phonemes.

Word lattice: In the word lattice based approach, speech is first passed through a large vocabulary continuous speech recognizer to obtain multiple word hypothesis for a given utterance of speech [1][2][3]. These multiple recognition hypotheses are compactly represented using a word lattice. The word lattice consists the begin and end times of the competing words along with its acoustic model likelihood and the language model probabilities. The standard forward backward re-estimation algorithm is applied to obtain posterior probabilities of the words conditioned on the utterance spoken. This posterior probability is used as a confidence measure to accept/reject a keyword. While this method yields good results, it cannot be used to detect keywords that are out-of-vocabulary words in the ASR dictionary. Moreover, this method is computationally very expensive and not suitable for real time applications.

Phoneme lattice: In phoneme lattice based approach, speech is passed through a phoneme recognizer to obtain a phoneme lattice [4][5]. The pronunciation for a given keyword is searched in the phoneme lattice and the presence of keyword is determined. This method overcomes the drawbacks of the word lattice based approach. However, recognition of phonemes is only about 50-60% accurate in spontaneous speech.

Under the purview of the IM-HOST project, the goal is to develop a small vocabulary keyword spotter which is real-time and robust to wind noise. To this end, we study an alternative approach where the goal is to find the target sounds from an acoustic stream while ignoring the rest. We propose hierarchical processing where first equally-spaced posterior probabilities of phoneme classes are derived from the signal, followed by estimation of the probability of the given keyword from the sequence of phoneme posteriors. More details on the proposed method can be found in [6].

3.2   Proposed Method

As shown in Figure 4, the proposed keyword spotting method comprises of the following steps (a) MRASTA feature extraction and estimation of phoneme posterior probabilities, (b) estimating word posterior probabilities and (d) matched filtering for suppressing spurious peaks.

Acoustic stream to Phoneme Posteriors: Speech is first frame blocked into 25 ms windows with a frame shift of 10ms. Spectral analysis is performed on the windowed speech signal and energies in the critical bands are computed. The center frequency and bandwidth of the critical bands are based on the perceptual modeling of speech. The critical band energy trajectories are then processed independently using MRASTA filters.

MRASTA filters [25] are bank of zero-mean modulation filters. Each filter is the first and second derivative of Gaussian shape function. The variance of the

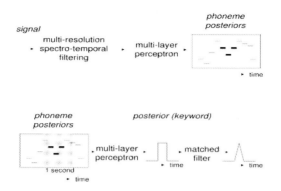

Fig. 4. Block schematic of the proposed keyword spotting technique

Gaussian function controls the resolution of each filter. A typical implementation of MRASTA filter-bank include 8 first derivative and 8 second derivative filters. Furthermore, the frequency derivatives are appended to the base features.

This feature vector is fed to an MLP neural net classifier (TANDEM probability estimator [11]), which is trained to give an estimate of phoneme posterior probabilities at every 10 ms step (phoneme posteriogram). An example of such phoneme posteriogram for the digit 'five' is shown in Figure 5. The keyword is in this case easy to spot because the phoneme segments are well classified in the posteriogram. More details of the technique can be found in [25].

From Phoneme Posteriors to Words: Multi-input, two-output MLP is used for mapping of relatively long (1010 ms) span of the posteriogram to a posterior probability of a given keyword being within this time span. Thus, the input to the MLP is a 2929-dimensional vector (29 phoneme posteriors at 100 Hz frame rate). The MLP is trained on the training part of the OGI Digits database (about 1.3 hours of speech), containing 11 digits from zero to nine (including 'oh'). In

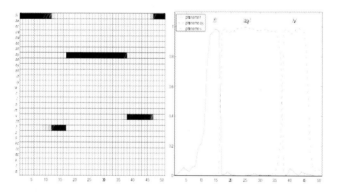

Fig. 5. Left: Posteriogram of the word *five* followed by silence. Right: Trajectories of phoneme probability estimates.

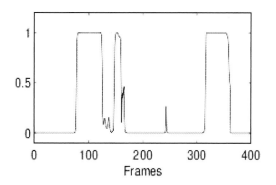

Fig. 6. An example of keyword posteriogram -

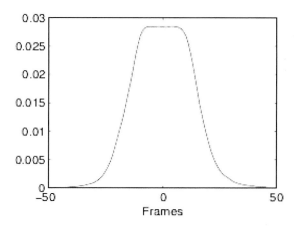

Fig. 7. Impulse response of the keyword matched filter

the operation, the input phoneme posteriogram of the unknown utterance is converted to the keyword posteriogram by sliding the 1010 ms window frame-by-frame over the phoneme posteriogram. A typical keyword posteriogram is shown in Figure 6. Even though (as illustrated in the figure) to human eye the frame-based posterior estimates usually clearly indicate the presence of the underlying word, the step from the frame-based estimates to word-level estimates is very important. It involves nontrivial operation of information rate reduction (carried sub-consciously by human visual perception while studying the posteriogram) where the equally sampled estimates at the 100 Hz sampling rate are to be reduced to non-equally sampled estimates of word probabilities. In the conventional (HMM-based) system, this is accomplished by searching for an appropriate underlying sequence of hidden states.

We have opted for more direct communication theoretic approach where we postulated existence of a matched filter for temporal trajectories of word posteriors, with impulse response derived by averaging 1 s long segments of trajectories

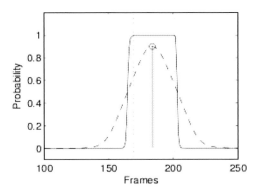

Fig. 8. Raw time trajectory of keyword posterior probability (solid line), filtered trajectory (dashed line) and estimated location of the keyword (circle). Region between dotted lines represents a labeled location of the keyword.

of the respective words, aligned at the word centers. In deriving these averages, we need to deal with cases where the window contains more than one keyword. In the current work, these segments were not included in computing the average. Resulting filter is shown in Figure 7, and an example of the filtered posteriogram is illustrated in Figure 8.

In the next step, local maxima (peaks) for each filtered trajectory were found. The values in the peaks were taken as estimates of probability that the center of the given word is aligned with the center of the impulse response of the respective matched filter and retained, all other data were discarded. An example of such a peak can be seen in Figure 8.

3.3   Results

As a test we have processed about 104 minutes of speech data containing fluent pronunciation of digit strings (OGI Numbers [31]). Among 12389 digits, there were 1532 one's. 1339 (87.4%) of these were correctly identified, and there were 19 (1.2%) false alarms and 193 (12.6%) misses. Most of misses are caused by smearing short drops in probability due to filtering (as discussed below) that may indicate a succession of several target words. Not counting these errors, the overall detection rate would be 93.4%.

3.4   Summary and Discussion

Hierarchical classification of relatively long chunks of speech signal has been applied to spotting a target word in speech stream. This hierarchical procedure estimates posterior probabilities of phonemes from multi-resolution speech representation obtained by time-frequency filtering of critical-band spectral energy, followed by the estimation of probability of occurrence of the targeted word in the neighborhood of the current time instant. A simple deletion of the speech signal for the instants where the trajectory is below certain threshold allows for retention of most of the targeted speech. In order to uniquely identify the presence of the underlying target word, a simple procedure is introduced in which the time trajectory of keyword probability is filtered by a box-car shaped matched filter, representing mean length of the keyword and above-threshold peak of this trajectory indicate occurrence of the keyword. The filtering eliminates most of spurious short peaks, thus allowing for simple counting the identified keywords but it also often eliminates short drops in the probability due to several successive keywords which are then counted only as one word. The presented technique is very straightforward, involves neither any time-warping nor any searches, and can be implemented on-line with a relatively short algorithmic delay. It offers simple but interesting alternative to most of the current speech recognition approaches with a potential for further evolution.

4   Template Matching Using Posterior Based Features

Hidden Markov models (HMMs) constitute the dominant approach for automatic speech recognition (ASR) systems. Their success is mainly based on their efficient algorithms for training and testing. However, these algorithms rely on some assumptions about data that do not hold for speech signals, such as piecewise stationary or independence of the feature vectors given a state. Template matching (TM) is a different approach for ASR that relies on the fact that a class can be described by a set of examples (templates). Since templates are real utterances, they can better model the dynamics of the trajectories generated by the speech features compared with HMM states in currently used monophone or triphone models. Moreover, TM is preferred in those cases where simplicity and flexibility for training and testing must be considered.

As a non-parametric approach, TM requires more training data than parametric models, such as HMM-based systems, to obtain comparable performance. Given the increase of large speech corpora and computational resources, TM has recently drawn new attention. Investigation on this approach has been focused on increasing the number of templates [7,8,9] and, hence, improving its generalization capabilities. Since no speech corpora can guarantee to provide many examples for each word, sub-word units are typically used to ensure that a large enough number of templates is available for each possible word. Pronunciation dictionaries are, in this case, needed for concatenating these sub-word units into words. However, pronunciation of the words is not always easy to obtain, e.g., proper names.

We propose a different method to use the information contained in large speech corpora. Traditional features used in TM are based on short-term spectrum. These features contain linguistic information but also information about the gender[1] and the environment, i.e., they are speaker and task-dependent. In this work, we investigate the use of posterior probabilities of subword units as speech features. These posteriors can be estimated from a multilayer perceptron (MLP) which has been trained on large speech corpora. In this way, the

---

[1] For instance, speaker recognition systems use spectral-based features as inputs.

MLP can capture the information contained on large speech corpora to generate speaker and task-independent features. Given the discriminative training procedure of the MLP and the long acoustic context used as input, posterior features are known to be more stable and more robust to noise than spectral-based features [10]. Since these features only contain, in theory, linguistic information, fewer templates are required to represent a word. Hence, in those applications where the number of available templates is few, we can expect to improve the performance. Posteriors estimates from the MLP outputs have already been successfully applied as features for ASR using HMM/GMM as acoustic model, system known as Tandem [10,11].

TM-based approaches traditionally use Euclidean or Mahalanobis distance as local similarity measure between features. These distances implicitly assume that features follow a Gaussian distribution. This assumption does not hold when using posterior distributions as features. Since posterior features are probability distributions over the space of subword units, more appropriate distances can be considered. In this work, we investigate local distances between frames that take into account the discriminative properties of posterior features.

This work is an extension of a previous experiment where we already applied posterior features to a TM-based ASR system [12]. On that first experiment, posterior features were not task-independent because the data to train the MLP belonged to the same database as the test set. Kullback-Leibler (KL) divergence was applied as local distance for being a natural distance between distributions. In this work, the MLP is trained on a large speech corpus and used for a different recognition task. We also show that other types of local distances can be successfully applied to posterior features which obtain similar performance to KL-divergence but are faster to compute.

This rest of the section is organized as follows: Section 4.1 introduces the TM approach for speech recognition, Section 4.2 presents the posteriors features, Section 4.3 describes the local distances investigated in this work, Section 4.8 presents the experiments and results and finally, Section 5.4 draws some conclusions.

4.1   Template Matching

Template Matching (TM) is a non-parametric classifier that relies on the idea that a class w can be identified by a set of N_w examples (templates) $\{\mathbf{Y}_n^w\}_{n=1}^{N_w}$ belonging to that class. Unlike parametric models, TM directly uses all training data at the decoding time and no explicit assumption is made about the data distribution. A test element $\mathbf{X}$ is associated to the same class as the closest sample based on a similarity function φ between samples defined as:

$$\text{class}(\mathbf{X}) = \arg\min_{\{w'\}} \min_{\mathbf{Y}' \in \{\mathbf{Y}_n^{w'}\}} \varphi(\mathbf{X}, \mathbf{Y}') \tag{1}$$

where $\{w'\}$ denotes the set of all possible classes. However, as any non-parametric technique, a large amount of training data is required to obtain a good classification performance. TM has recently received new attention in the ASR field because current computational resources and speech corpora allow to deal with large amount of training data in a practical computational time.

In the case of speech, templates are sequences of feature vectors that correspond to particular pronunciations of a word. When comparing with HMMs, templates can describe in more detail the dynamics of the trajectories defined by speech features because they represent real utterances, whereas HMMs are parametric representations that summarize the information contained on the speech trajectories. Furthermore, the explicit use of non-linguistic information such as gender or speech rate can be easily applied when using templates but this type of long-span information is more difficult to incorporate into a parametric model.

The similarity measure φ between sequences must deal with the fact that utterances usually have different lengths. This measure is based on dynamic time warping (DTW) [13] and it minimizes the global distortion between two temporal sequences. This global distortion is computed as the sum of local distances $d(\mathbf{x}, \mathbf{y})$ between the matched frames. This matching is performed by warping one of the two sequences. In speech, the template sequence is typically warped so that every template frame $\mathbf{y}_m$ matches a frame of the test sequence $\mathbf{x}_n$. Given a template sequence $\{\mathbf{y}_m\}_{m=1}^M$ and a test sequence $\{\mathbf{x}_n\}_{n=1}^N$, DTW-based distance can be expressed as

$$\varphi(\mathbf{X}, \mathbf{Y}) = \min_{\{\phi\}} \sum_{i=1}^{N} d(\mathbf{x}_i, \mathbf{y}_{\phi(i)}) \tag{2}$$

where $\{\phi\}$ denotes the set of all possible warping functions for the template sequence. The warping function must hold some constraints of continuity and boundaries to ensure that the resampled template sequence is realistic. Typical constraints in the ASR field are:

$$0 \leq \phi(i) - \phi(i-1) \leq 2$$
$$\phi(1) = 1 \tag{3}$$
$$\phi(M) = N$$

These conditions guarantee that no more than one frame from the template sequence will be skipped for each test frame and also, that every test frame will be related to only one template frame.

Although the computation of (2) implies searching among a large set of warping functions, it can be efficiently computed by dynamic programming.

The local distance $d(\mathbf{x}, \mathbf{y})$ is typically chosen as Euclidean or Mahalanobis distance since spectral-based features are normally used for representing the speech signal. However, other types of similarity measures between frames can also be applied depending on the properties of the features. In Section 4.3, a description of the local distances investigated in this work will be given.

As described before, recent investigation to improve the performance of TM-based ASR systems is to take advantage of the current large speech corpora and computational resources by increasing the number of templates. TM becomes then a search problem among all possible templates [7]. In order to increase the speed and efficiency of the search, non-linguistic information can be used

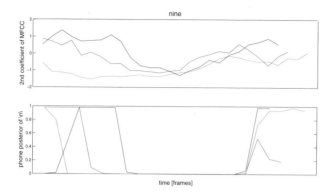

Fig. 9. The value of the second component of the feature vector in the case of MFCC features and phone posterior corresponding to the phoneme /n/ are plotted for three different templates of the word "nine". It can be seen that values from spectral-based feature vectors are more variable within a phone than posterior features, which follow a more stationary trajectory.

at the decoding time [14]. As templates and HMMs convey different types of information since they are different types of models, investigation has also been carried out for combining both approaches [8,9] with successful results. However, this technique requires a large amount of samples per word (or linguistic unit). In this work, we will focus on the situation where a few samples are given for every word. In this case, the goal is to reduce as much as possible the variability within a class so that a few samples will be enough to represent a class word. This variability reduction will be performed at the feature level and will be explained in detail in the next section.

4.2   Posterior Features

The posterior probability $p(q_k|z_t)$ of a phoneme q_k given a spectral-based acoustic feature z_t at time t can be estimated from a MLP. A posterior vector x_t can then be obtained where each dimension corresponds to a phoneme posterior $x_t = \{p(q_k|z_t)\}_{k=1}^K$. K corresponds to the total number of phonemes and is also the number of MLP outputs[2].

If posterior estimates were correct, these features could be considered as optimal speech features by assuming that words are formed by phonemes since, in theory, they only carry linguistic information and also, they can be seen as optimal phone detectors as it is demonstrated in [15]. This reduction of the undesirable information makes posterior features more stable as it is illustrated in Figure 9.

Traditional features, like MFCC [16] or PLP [17], contain information about the spectrum and hence, about the speaker and its environment. However, if

---

[2] We are using this notation for the sake of simplicity, but in fact an acoustic context (typically 4 frames) is used as input of the MLP, hence, rigorous notation should be $p(q_k|z_{t-\Delta}^{t+\Delta})$

the MLP is trained on a rich enough training database in terms of speakers and environment, posterior features can be considered speaker and task-independent since they only contain information about the phoneme that has been pronounced. Moreover, the MLP is implicitly learning the prior probability of each phoneme. However, when using large vocabulary corpora, these probabilities converge to phoneme priors of the language of the database. In this way, posterior features are language-dependent.

4.3   Local Distance

From (2), it can be observed that DTW-based distance requires a distance $d(\mathbf{x}, \mathbf{y})$ between reference and test samples of the observation space. Since any local distance assumes a particular geometry of the observation space, the choice of the local distance plays a crucial role on the performance of the system. Traditionally, these distances are based on Euclidean and Mahalanobis distances. In the TM-based approach, investigation has been recently carried out to estimate the parameters of the weighting matrix of the Mahalanobis distance to improve the performance. A maximum-likelihood estimation was described in [18] and a discriminative procedure was presented in [19]. However, these methods require a large amount of data to properly estimate the weights.

Since posterior vectors can be seen as distributions over the space of subword units (e.g., phonemes), measures from the information theory field can be applied. These measures can capture higher order statistics from the data than Euclidean-based distances. Furthermore, they can explicitly consider the particular properties of posterior vectors (i.e., values must be non-negative and sum must be equal to one).

In the following, we will consider that y represents a frame from the template and x denotes a frame from the test sequence. As explained before, x and y can be considered discrete distribution on the $\mathbb{R}^K$ space (i.e. there are K different phonemes).

In addition, local distance directly affects the decoding time since computing the local distance is the most frequent operation on the DTW algorithm. Hence, the choice of the local distance should also take into account its computational time.

4.4   Squared Euclidean Distance

This is the traditional distance used as local distance between frames. However, it is related with the Gaussian distribution. Indeed, when taking the logarithm of a Gaussian distribution with unity covariance matrix, it becomes the squared Euclidean distance plus a constant factor.

$$D_{Eucl}(x, y) = \sum_{k=1}^{K} (x(k) - y(k))^2 \tag{4}$$

However, when measuring the similarity between posterior features, Euclidean distance is not very appropriate since posterior space holds some special properties which are not taken into account by this distance.

4.5   Kullback-Leibler Divergence

KL divergence (or relative entropy) comes from the information theory field and can be interpreted as the amount of extra bits that are needed to code a message generated by the reference distribution y, when the code is optimal for a given test distribution x [20].

$$D_{KL}(x \,\|\, y) = \sum_{k=1}^{K} y(k) \log \frac{y(k)}{x(k)} \tag{5}$$

KL-divergence is a natural measure between distributions. The fact that it is not symmetric must not affect its application to DTW algorithm. In this case, the reference distribution y is considered to be the template frame whereas x corresponds to the test frame.

4.6   Bhattacharyya Distance

This distance was initially motivated by geometrical considerations since it computes the cosine between two distributions [21]. It is also a particular case of the Chernoff bound (an upper bound for the Bayes error) [22].

$$D_{Bhatt}(x, y) = -\log \sum_{k=1}^{K} \sqrt{x(k)y(k)} \tag{6}$$

Bhattacharyya distance is symmetric and also it is faster to compute than KL divergence because less logarithms must be computed. This distance has been used already in speech processing for phone clustering [23].

4.7   Distance Based on Bayes Risk

Bhattacharyya distance is originated from an upper bound of the Bayes risk. However, the exact probability of error can be easily computed for discrete distributions [24]:

$$\text{Bayes Error} = \sum_{k=1}^{K} \min \{x(k), y(k)\} \tag{7}$$

A distance can be derived similar to Bhattacharyya distance by taking the negative logarithm:

$$D_{Bayes}(x, y) = -\log \sum_{k=1}^{K} \min \{x(k), y(k)\} \tag{8}$$

This distance is even simpler to compute than (6) because it avoids the square root function.

4.8   Experiments

In this work, Phonebook database has been used to carry out word recognition experiments using the TM-based approach. This database consists of 47455 utterances of isolated words. There are 3992 different words pronounced by around

12 different speaker in average. Experiments with different lexicon sizes have been carried out: 5, 10, 20, 50 and 100 different words were selected randomly from the global lexicon. For each experiment and each word, one or two utterances have been selected as templates and the rest of utterances containing the selected words have been used for test. Since lexicon has been selected at random, experiments have been repeated ten times using a different lexicon at each time. Results have been consistent, i.e., similar results have been obtained at each time and average results are shown.

Two types of features have been considered: PLP and phoneme posterior probabilities. PLP features also contain delta features. Posterior features have been obtained from a MLP trained on 30 hours of the CTS database following the MRASTA procedure [25]. The MLP contains 2000 hidden units and 46 phonemes (including silence) have been considered.

Constraints for DTW are the same as described in Formula 3. Euclidean, KL-divergence, Bhattacharyya and Bayes-based distance are considered as local distances. PLP features only use Euclidean distance (the rest of local distance can only be applied to discrete posterior vectors).

Experiments on decoding time have been carried out on a workstation with a Athlon64 4000+ processor.

4.9   Results

Results on Table 1 show the effectiveness in using posterior features for TM. PLP features contain information about the speaker and since the task is speaker-independent, results when using these spectral-based features are far from being competitive. This explains why TM is mainly focused on speaker-dependent tasks with small vocabulary. On the other hand, posterior features have been estimated by taking into account the information captured by the MLP from the large speech corpus used for training. This, jointly with the discriminative training of the MLP make posterior features robust to speaker and environment conditions.

Moreover, posterior-based distances such as KL divergence, Bhattacharyya and Bayes-based distance yield better results than traditional Euclidean distance since they explicitly deal with the space topology of the posterior features.

Table 1. System accuracy when using one or two templates per word. The size of the lexicon has been varied to observe the effect of increasing the lexicon. The last column shows the average number of test utterances.

		one template					two templates				
lexicon	PLP	Posteriors				PLP	Posteriors				# test
size	Eucl	Eucl	KL	Bhatt	Bayes	Eucl	Eucl	KL	Bhatt	Bayes	utts
5	79.3	93.2	98.2	98.7	98.0	90.8	96.6	98.9	98.9	98.5	55
10	74.7	91.9	97.8	98.3	97.5	85.4	95.7	98.9	98.9	98.4	104
20	69.8	89.5	95.6	96.5	95.7	81.9	94.2	98.4	97.9	97.5	212
50	59.7	83.1	92.9	94.1	92.9	74.2	90.2	96.6	96.8	96.1	545
100	53.2	78.5	89.7	91.4	89.7	68.0	87.5	94.9	95.1	94.2	1079

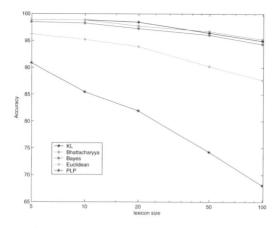

Fig. 10. Accuracy of the system using 2 templates per word

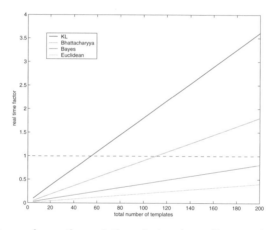

Fig. 11. This figure shows the real time factor depending on the total number of templates. Real time factors is defined as the ratio between the decoding time and the duration of the test sequence. A dashed line indicates when the decoding time is equal to the duration of the sequence.

Figure 10 plots the system accuracy with two templates per word and also shows the effect of increasing the size of the lexicon. When using 100 different words, the performance of the system is still around 95%, which is reasonable result given the complexity of the task and the limited amount of samples per word[3].

Experiments have been carried out to investigate the effect of the local distance on the decoding time. Results are shown in Figure 11. It can be observed that

---

[3] Experiments comparing templates and hybrid HMM/MLP [26] have been carried out using the test set described in [27]. There are 8 different test sets consisting each one of 75 different words. In this case, we obtained similar results in both systems, i.e. around 95% accuracy.

KL-divergence takes a long time for decoding because of the logarithm function. Bhattacharyya distance replaces the logarithm function by a square root function, which takes less time than the logarithm. Bayes-based distance is faster than the previous since selecting the minimum value is a very simple operation. Finally, Euclidean distance is faster than the rest but its accuracy is significantly worse than the other distances. The preliminary field tests, described at the end of the next section, used a first version of the template matching which was using the KL-divergence.

5   Fields Test: Results

Under the requirements described in Section 2 the most promising recognizer was expected to be one based on keyword spotting. As explained in the previous section, keyword spotters are usually designed to extract a given set of keywords in a flow of continuous speech or, more generally, in any given signal. Thus, a keyword spotter seems particulary useful to achieve voice control without any other user input. (i.e., no need to indicate when to record speech) The advanced digit keyword spotter, described in Section 3, was trained over a wide variety of users (male and female) and could handle the noisy environments of phone calls including poor line or microphone quality. The robustness of this key word spotter made it a good candidate for a first demonstrator. In the project, it was also important to obtain early results that could be tested in real environments. The Linux code developed at IDIAP was used for research purposes and was working off-line on a recorded speech segment. The demonstrator needed to work on a tablet PC running Windows. Thus, the first demonstrator was based on the keyword spotting algorithm adapted to the Windows tablet PC environment. However, a combination of drawbacks made it clear that another approach should be investigated. A compromise worth testing by the intended user was to press a single button at the beginning of a spoken voice command. A template matching approach was then implemented based on the research work described in Section 4.1. The implementation of the TM technique was performed in a few weeks as it could very much profit from the experience acquired during the first part of this project. Again, this second demonstrator was developed to use voice commands to switch to the desired applications on a PC. Functional tests on one of the Alinghi's chase boats justified this final approach. A few informal field test demonstrated that the suitability of the TM approach.

With the template matching approach, voice commands in very noisy environments can be used with almost acceptable performance with respect to recognition rate and speed (90% and under one second, respectively). However, the user must accept to use only a few specially chosen keywords. The user must also accept to indicate the start of the recording since running separate instance of the template matching to simulate a continuous processing of the speech would be too time consuming and might produce too many false positives.

The next two sub-section describe the keyword spotting demonstrator and the template matching demonstrator which were developed during this project. It is pointed out, that the demonstrators imply more informal testing by the a few persons than formal testing due to the large human effort required otherwise.

5.1   The "Keyword Spotting" Demonstrator

The keyword spotter algorithm described in Section 3 was designed based on several software tools available at IDIAP. These tools, ranging from various scripts to special C codes and libraries, are under continuous development at IDIAP. For demonstration purposes, a simple user interface shown in Figure 12 has been designed at IDIAP to run off-line demonstrations of the user independent digit spotter. The recognizer has the architecture presented in Figure 4. For the demonstrator, all the necessary parts have been converted or translated into C (mainly for the computations) and C++ codes (mainly for the application logic and the user interfaces). This was required in order to run the keyword spotter under the target Microsoft Tablet Windows PC. The recognizer was first implemented and tested to reproduce exactly all intermediate and final results as the original codes running under UNIX. Following the processing steps shown in Figure 4, the speech signal (e.g., Figure 13) is first processed with respect to its frequency content. The second top part of Figure 13 shows the energy versus time relationship for 15 chosen frequency bins. To illustrate the complexity of the software recognizer, Figure 14 shows a sample speech signal recorded in real conditions. When this sample is played over, a person can still recognize the keyword being pronounced, especially if the keywords to be pronounced are known by the human listener. This example clearly illustrates the needs to base the recognition on more than the signal amplitude and basic frequency features. Thus, the spectrum is then processed by the MRASTA filters (Section 3) to capture the time evolution (speed and acceleration) of the frequency features. The MRASTA filter results are presented in the two lower part of Figure 13.

As presented in Section 3, several hundred spectrum features are computed every 10 ms (255 in the demonstrator). Every 10 ms, all these features are provided to a trained Artificial Neural Network MLP to compute 46 phoneme posterior probabilities (note that a 29 phonemes versions was then chosen for the research detailed in Section 3). A sample plot of one phoneme was already shown in Figure 5. The special "(non-)phoneme" called "reject" has its probability plotted in Figure 15 to provide another example. The 4646 phoneme posterior probabilities corresponding to 1.01 seconds of speech are provided as inputs to a second ANN trained to recognized a particular keyword: a digit from 0 to 9 and "o" (for the English zero) in our case. This second ANN provides a keyword probability every 10 ms of speech. Finally, the keyword probability must be higher than a given threshold for a pre-set time (lower right part of Figure 16) to decide whether or not a particular keyword (if any) was said. The previous figures were obtained during the functional analysis and tests of the PC version of IDIAP's keyword spotter code. The user demonstrator of the key word spotter are presented in Figure 16 which shows all windows used. Most windows has been designed to configure the parameters of the keyword spotter. The texts in the

Fig. 12. Unix based user interface to the Keyword spotting algorithm described in Section 3

Figure 16 indicate the main functions of each windows. As explained below, the end-user sees only a pop-up window which turns green when the computations have ended, i.e., when the user is allowed to speak.

Although some code optimizations have been tested, it became clear that all the required computations could not be performed sufficiently to insure continuous key word spotting on the targeted tablet PC. Furthermore, the neural networks were trained for spotting only the digits: oh, zero, one, two, ... nine. Since each digit must be spotted separately after the phoneme recognition, the computation time for the digit spotting is proportional to the number of digit to be recognized. Therefore, a special user interface was designed: a pop-up window was developed to change color from green to red to alert the user when to speak and when to stop. (as shown in Figure 16) During the "green alert", the voice was recorded over a 2 second duration. After the 2 seconds recording, the pop-up window was turned to red and the keyword spotting computations were performed. The detected keyword was then displayed, the corresponding action took place and the pop-up window was turned to green again. This user interface and the recognizer was tested informally and demonstrated to the end-user. Other user interactions were discussed to alert the user when to speak; all solutions we could think of (flashing screen, sound, moving object, ...) were too cumbersome. Alinghi's coach then accepted to push a button to start the recording if this could help. However, to achieve acceptable performance in very noisy environments, it also became clear that the hours of recordings already performed by Alinghi's coach would not be sufficient. Furthermore these recordings had to be prepared (labeled) to be used as training sets for the neural network; a very time consuming task. In addition, as mentioned above, some code optimizations and the use of libraries (such as BLAST) proved to be insufficient to decrease the computation time. These facts led us to consider the second speech recognition technique mentioned above, namely template matching. Thus, in parallel with the research effort described in Section 3 it was decided to focus the development effort on a second demonstrator using "template matching". It was also decided not to spread our efforts over undesired or useless multi-modalities but to focus on naturally spoken keyword recognition. Another approach would have been to find keywords that could be easily recognized in very noisy environments.

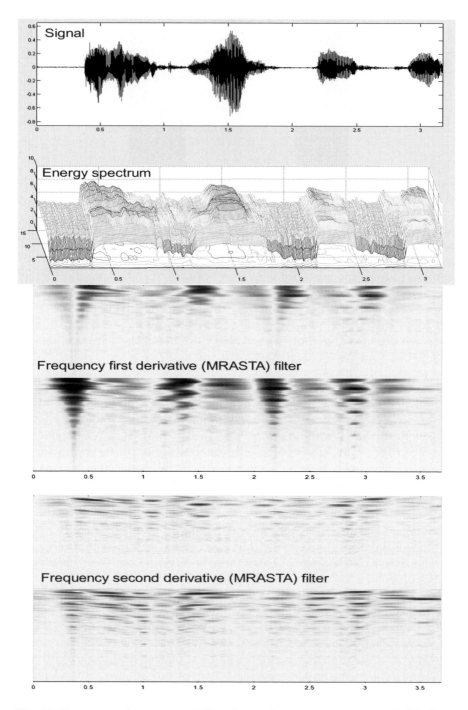

Fig. 13. From top to bottom panel: Speech signal, spectrum intensity, MRASTA features [25] first and second derivatives

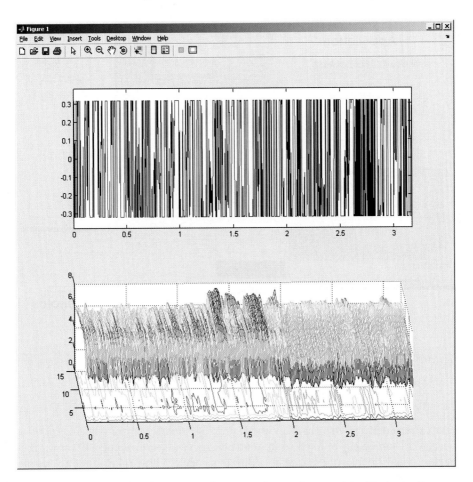

Fig. 14. Speech signal and spectrum in very noisy environment to illustrate the complex task of a recognizer

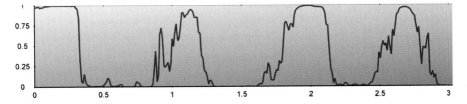

Fig. 15. Another example of posterior probabilities as in Fig. 5 : here the "rejected" or non-phoneme posterior

However, Alinghi and the project team perceived enormous difficulties and were convinced that although newer approaches might be required, none was less risky than the template matching technique. Thus the following demonstrator was implemented.

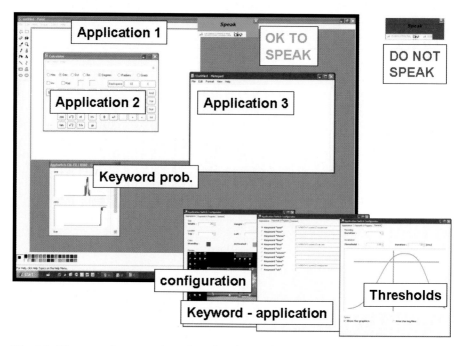

Fig. 16. The complete user interface for the application implementing the keyword spotter

5.2   The "Template Matching" Demonstrator

After experimenting with the "keyword spotting" demonstrator, the key requirements were somewhat relaxed to match the expected performance of known recognizers with the identified needs of Alinghi's coach. These relaxed requirements
could be summarized as follows:

1. Reaction time to voice commands as fast as possible but acceptable if less
   than a second delay (when running on a tablet PC similar to a Toshiba
   PORTEGE - 1.7 GHz - 512MB RAM).
2. Recognition rate as close as possible to 100% (at ¡5% false alarms) even in
   the noisy environments of the Alinghi's chase boat for a least 5 different
   voice commands.
3. Voice commands as close as possible to the vocabulary already used (i.e., a
   command such as "sail vision" could be voiced as "vision sail" or "vision to
   sail", "sail two vision", ... but not "one two two four two").
4. Visual or audio feedback on the interpreted voice command.
5. Training by the final user should be kept to a minimum (e.g., less than 10
   recordings or less than 10 minutes for the user).
6. Software should be simple to install and to configure (if any pre-configuration
   was not sufficient).
7. Wireless microphone.
8. Wireless push button to start voice recording could be used.

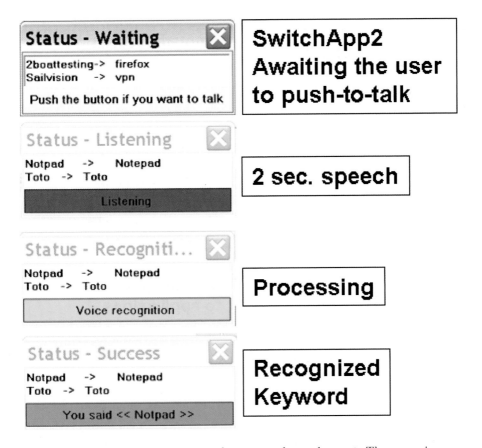

Fig. 17. Visual feedback to indicate when to speak or when not. The recognizer application, called SwitchApp2, works in the background. SwitchApp2 allows the user to pronounce a keyword during 2 seconds after pressing a button. SwitchApp2 will then processes the recorded speech and switch to a Windows application corresponding to the recognized keyword. Any application can be used, even proprietary ones such as the generic "Toto" application used for demonstration purpose.

The template matching algorithm described in Section 4.1 was ported from its UNIX base to Windows platforms, using again mainly C for the computations and C++ for the user interface. In order to record the required templates a special application (named SwitchApp2) was developed. Figure 17 shows the main features of the application SwitchApp2. Furthermore, a configuration software (named SwitchApp2_config) was developped. Figure 18 illustrates the application used to configure the action resulting from the recognized keyword.

Finally the template matching demonstrator was tested and worked at a level sufficient to be accepted by the end user. It was then noticed that switching applications could take a few seconds which was not an issue when manual switching was used. Since this delay was not acceptable in race condition, the coach decided to use 3 laptops running in parallel on the chase boats used during the

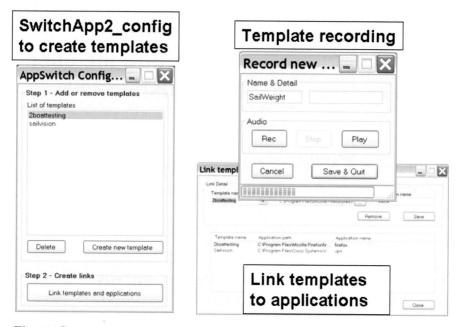

Fig. 18. Screen copies to illustrate the configuration of the SwitchApp2 application

2007 America's cup. However, the demonstrator was sufficiently convincing to show that voice command could be quite useful and could work at an acceptable level with a few commands even in very noisy conditions. Other demonstrations have been performed in a car and with a hair dryer blowing in the user's face [37] to simulate wind. Less informal testing was performed in a room with loud-speaker playing recorded wind and boat noise: 5 key words and 3-digit numbers (201 to 209) were repeated 10 times each, roughly an error rate of 90% or better could be obtained with the keywords but an unacceptable number of errors occurred for the 3-digit numbers. Thus, based on these results it was decided that it was not worth the effort to perform more testing (e.g., repeating more than 100 time a keyword). The enormous human resources required to process recorded samples (e.g., to label keywords) and to adapt them to a formal testing environment were not seen as worthwhile. More extensive tests were beyond the interest of the end-user. Instead, future development work might include voice commands to pilot the video and monitoring system used during the de-briefings which usually takes place less than an hour after a training session or a race.

5.3   Push-To-Talk System and Microphone Choices

With the "template matching" demonstrator, the user has to trigger the beginning of the listening mode. We investigated various ways to trigger the event. We envisaged - among others solutions - to use standard press-buttons or to detect pre-defined movements or presence in a specific area using video capture, as shown in Table 2. From the Alinghi'staff point of view, the best solution was a

Table 2. Trigger event comparison

Type of event detection	How ?	Advantages	Drawbacks
Detection of movements	Video capture	- Freedom of movements - Do not need to wear additional devices	- Complex development -The user must be in the visor of a video camera (also in the good capture angle)
Push-To-Talk	Push-Buttons	- Technology already exists - Simple to set up	- The user has to use hands to push on the PTT button - Crew members of the chase boat have to load/unload lots of equipments just before the race -> high risk to damage the belt

press-button placed on the frontal bar. However, during the field tests, a wireless press-button was then preferred.

As mentioned in the beginning of this paper, the wind noise on a boat is unpredictable and could be very loud. The slightest velocity of air movement badly disturbs the audio signal produced by a microphone [28]. As the input signal is deteriorated, the recognition rate significantly decreases. Even if, in the Alinghi's case, the speaker is partially front wind protected by the front window pane, we noticed that the environment is still very noisy. To reduce the surrounding noise, we tried to find high-quality microphones able to perform in a very noisy environment. As a result, we turned our attention to what the army or guards are using because effective and clear communications are evidently vital. Three types of microphones can be used: throat microphone, jaw bone vibration microphone and noise canceling microphone. With *throat microphones*, only sound produced by the user is taken into account because sounds are absorbed via vibrations from the throat and are then converted into recognizable voice frequencies. As a result, the background noise comes mainly from the air flow of the user's respiration. We thought that this kind of microphone would be the ideal solution on a boat. However, this is not the case because the throat microphone is a major inconvenience for sportsmen; it impedes their breathing, especially when they are making an effort or when they are under stress. Alinghi crew members tested this type of microphones but finally decided not use them because of the wearing discomfort. *Jaw bone or ear bone vibration microphones* use the same principle as throat microphones. When we speak, the ear and jaw bones vibrate. Using this vibration, we can convert this signal into voice frequencies. These microphones are still under development and seem not as efficient as the manufacturers claim. Both bone vibration and throat microphones are not designed for continuous speech, the majority of them being used in Push-To-Talk/surveillance applications. Thus, *noise canceling microphones* remained as the best choice. A brief comparison is given in Table 3. The robustness of the microphone is another important point to take into consideration. As a result,

Table 3. A comparison between noise canceling microphones

Common usage	Accuracy	Size / Weight	Price
Home / Office	Very low	Small / Light	Low (40-100 USD)
Call centers	Low	Small / Light	Medium (100-200 USD)
Airport ground staff	High	Large / Heavy	High (400-800 USD)

we eliminated microphones designed for home and call center purposes because they are not robust enough. In Alinghi's case, the microphone was clearly to be used in extreme conditions. The proposed equipment must be:

- Waterproof
- Resistant to sea-salt
- Resistant to shock and vibration
- Able to perform in hot temperatures as well as in cold temperatures

Moreover, it should be light and comfortable to wear. The coach must concentrate on his job and cannot afford to be annoyed by an uncomfortable headset. All of these constraints make it difficult to find the ideal microphone on the market today. However, we found a wired and a wireless headset which demonstrated acceptable performance. These two commercial headsets seem to have a superior performance due to the special design of their mouthpiece holding a single microphone as far as we could observe. The special foam around the microphone is also an indispensable feature to mitigate the wind effect. Alinghi's coach tested the two headset and choose the wireless headset for its evident convenience. More details cannot be provided since commercial headsets were chosen.

5.4   Conclusion

This project addressed the problem of voice recognition with the goal of reaching a very high success rate (ideally above 99%) in very hostile environments: for example, the desk of Alinghi's chase boat. Other scenarios and uses cases were described and investigated as effective voice recognition might be very useful for individuals with disabilities in everyday life or for athletes and coaches who also often need to send and receive information while their hands and eyes are busy.

Two different techniques, based on advanced automatic speech recognition algorithms researched at IDIAP were ported from Unix to PC environment. These algorithms were integrated to develop practical demonstrators which could be tested by the end users.

A keyword spotting technique were tried first because of its potential. It proved to be difficult to use in noisy environments: a high error rate (50%) and a too long computation time (over 5 sec per keyword) disqualified this technique. The keyword spotter was not trained for the noisy testing environments in which it wad tested. The complexity of the recognition algorithms does not ease its investigation. Furthermore the effort and time to produce and process the required training data would have taken more resources than could be devoted to this project. Future keyword spotting techniques might however be improved so that it could be used to indicate the start of a voice command after one particular keyword (e.g., "go"). Although this might appears intuitively simple, the implementation might be problematic because of the false positives. Also, the research community is not focused in the very particular area of recognizing quickly a few keyword out despite noise, interferences, push-to-talk radio, cheap microphones, or impaired speech.

Therefore we have tested another approach which is still using phoneme posterior features but using then a template matching (TM)-based approach instead of a neural network to recognize keywords. The features are not identical however but have been trained using a different vocabulary database. It can be argued that the larger the database the better the assumption of speaker and task-independency. This assumption was not tested in this research. However this propriety make these features very suitable for those conditions where a word must be represented by a few examples chosen as templates. Moreover, the choice of the local distance has been investigated since it both assumes a topology on the feature space and also directly affects the decoding time. Though KL-divergence is a very appropriate local distance when using posterior features, it takes more time to be computed because it requires a logarithm function for each dimension of the posterior vector. Other types of distances based on the probability of error have also been investigated which are simpler to compute and yield similar performance.

Future research work should be focused on investigating other ways to incorporate information of large speech corpora on TM-based approach. A possible way would be to combine the posterior features from different MLPs. Initial experiments at IDIAP have already been carried out with successful results.

The work reported here demonstrated that the chosen keyword spotting algorithm, although well trained and tested on conventional speech corpora (OGI Digits and Phonebook databases), requires too much additional training in very noisy environment. Thus, this approach was abandoned for the final demonstrator. Instead, an advanced template matching recognizer was tested and showed nearly sufficient performance if the user accept to use an adapted microphone and was ready to indicate the start of the recording using some kind of multi-modal interactiont (a wireless push button)). For our demonstrator, several commercial wired and wireless microphones were informally tested. A wired one was found to be particulary good at removing the wind noise, probably because of the special design of the plastic mouthpiece and foam around it. For the convenience of the user, a wireless microphone with similar characteristics was then selected and used. More details about these commercial microphones can, unfortunately, not be provided.

Using only two or three pre-recorded templates per keyword, it has been tested that a few keywords, 5 in our tests, could be recognized in very noisy environments including the motor chase boat of Alinghi's coach. Formal but very limited testing was performed in a empty office with loudspeaker playing recorded offshore noise. Repeating 10 times every keyword against 3 templates per keyword lead to a recognition rate of about 90% or better depending on the keyword. Our preliminary tests and demonstrators tends to show that other research work targeted more specifically to changing conventional human voice interactions with machines could be worth attempting. There are many applications for this kind of research for persons accepting to train themselves to get optimal performance: competitors, coaches, fireman and policeman in urgent situation, or perhaps persons with some physical limitations or handicaps. An example is the spelling used by plane pilots. However, defining a new language to talk to a machine in a very noisy environment remains a difficult challenge. Developing an automatic speech recognizer for this new language might also be unexpectedly difficult. Template matching based techniques are recommended based on the results of our project. The compromises between the language features and the complexity of the recognizer are not trivial to define as the users also trade off between learning new interactions and its usefulness. Furthermore theoretic information theory of human language is not well understood and current recognizers using neural network approaches are extremely complex to understand. Thus further research in these interesting areas should be welcomed.

Acknowledgments. Pierre-Yves Jorand (Alinghi) is warmly thanked for his interest and his precious time spent to discuss Alinghi's requirements, record samples and perform on-shore and live tests. Various help from Bruno Alves, Olivier Bornet, Alain Duc, Cédric Gaudard, Alexandros Giannakis, Simon Martin, Jithendra Vepa is also acknowledged. The project IM-Host was supported by the Hasler Fundation. The work at IDIAP was also partially supported by the EU 6th FWP IST integrated project AMI (FP6-506811)and the Swiss National Science Foundation through the National Centre of Competence in Research (NCCR) on "Interactive Multimodal Information Management (IM2)".

References

1. Vergyri, D., et al.: The SRI/OGI 2006 Spoken Term Detection System. In: Proc. of Interspeech (2007)
2. Miller, D., et al.: Rapid and Accurate Spoken Term Detection. In: Proc. of NIST Spoken Term Detection Workshop (STD 2006) (December 2006)
3. Szoke, I., et al.: Combination of Word and Phoneme Approach for Spoken Term Detection. In: 4th Joint Workshop on Machine Learning and Multimodal Interaction (2007)
4. James, D., Young, S.: A Fast Lattice-Based Approach to Vocabulary Independent Wordspotting. In: Proc. of IEEE Conf. Acoust. Speech. Signal Process. (ICASSP) (1994)
5. Szoke, I., et al.: Comparison of Keyword Spotting Approaches for Informal Continuous Speech. In: Proc. of Interspeech (2005)
6. Hermansky, H., Fousek, P., Lehtonen, M.: The Role of Speech in Multimodal Human-Computer Interaction (Towards Reliable Rejection of Non-Keyword Input). In: Matousek, V., Mautner, P., Pavelka, T. (eds.) TSD 2005. LNCS, vol. 3658, pp. 2–8. Springer, Heidelberg (2005)

7. Wachter, M.D., Demuynck, K., Compernolle, D.V., Wambacq, P.: Data Driven Example Based Continuous Speech Recognition. In: Proceedings of Eurospeech, pp. 1133–1136 (2003)
8. Aradilla, G., Vepa, J., Bourlard, H.: Improving Speech Recognition Using a Data-Driven Approach. In: Proceedings of Interspeech, pp. 3333–3336 (2005)
9. Axelrod, S., Maison, B.: Combination of Hidden Markov Models with Dynamic Time Warping for Speech Recognition. In: Proceedings of International Conference on Acoustics, Speech and Signal Processing (ICASSP), vol. I, pp. 173–176 (2004)
10. Zhu, Q., Chen, B., Morgan, N., Stolcke, A.: On Using MLP features in LVCSR. In: Proceedings of International Conference on Spoken Language Processing (ICSLP) (2004)
11. Hermansky, H., Ellis, D., Sharma, S.: Tandem Connectionist Feature Extraction for Conventional HMM Systems. In: Proceedings of International Conference on Acoustics, Speech and Signal Processing (ICASSP) (2000)
12. Aradilla, G., Vepa, J., Bourlard, H.: Using Posterior-Based Features in Template Matching for Speech Recognition. In: Proceedings of International Conference on Spoken Language Processing (ICSLP) (2006)
13. Rabiner, L., Juang, B.H.: Fundamentals of Speech Recognition. Prentice-Hall, Englewood Cliffs (1993)
14. Aradilla, G., Vepa, J., Bourlard, H.: Using Pitch as Prior Knowledge in Template-Based Speech Recognition. In: Proceedings of International Conference on Acoustics, Speech, and Signal Processing (ICASSP) (2006)
15. Niyogi, P., Sondhi, M.M.: Detecting Stop Consonants in Continuous Speech. The Journal of the Acoustic Society of America 111(2), 1063–1076 (2002)
16. Davis, S.B., Mermelstein, P.: Comparison of parametric representations for monosyllabic word recognition in continuously spoken sentences. IEEE Transactions on Audio, Speech and Signal Processing 28, 357–366 (1980)
17. Hermansky, H.: Perceptual Linear Predictive (PLP) Analysis of Speech. The Journal of the Acoustic Society of America 87 (1990)
18. Wachter, M.D., Demuynck, K., Wambacq, P., Compernolle, D.V.: A Locally Weighted Distance Measure For Example Based Speech Recognition. In: Proceedings of International Conference on Acoustics, Speech and Signal Processing (ICASSP), pp. 181–184 (2004)
19. Matton, M., Wachter, M.D., Compernolle, D.V., Cools, R.: A Discriminative Locally Weighted Distance Measure for Speaker Independent Template Based Speech Recognition. In: Proceedings of International Conference on Spoken Language Processing (ICSLP) (2004)
20. Cover, T.M., Thomas, J.A.: Information Theory. John Wiley, Chichester (1991)
21. Bhattacharyya, A.: On a Measure of Divergence between Two Statistical Populations Defined by their probability distributions. Bull. Calcutta Math. Soc. 35, 99–109 (1943)
22. Fukunaga, K.: Introduction to Statistical Pattern Recognition. Morgan Kaufmann, Academic Press (1990)
23. Mak, B., Barnard, E.: Phone Clustering Using the Bhattacharyya Distance. In: Proceedings of International Conference on Spoken Language Processing (ICSLP), pp. 2005–2008 (1996)
24. Duda, R.O., Hart, P.E., Stork, D.G.: Pattern Classification. Wiley Interscience, Hoboken (2001)
25. Hermansky, H., Fousek, P.: Multi-Resolution RASTA Filtering for TANDEM-based ASR. In: Proceedings of Interspeech (2005)

26. Bourlard, H., Morgan, N.: Connectionist Speech Recognition: A Hybrid Approach, vol. 247. Kluwer Academic Publishers, Boston (1993)

27. Dupont, S., Bourlard, H., Deroo, O., Fontaine, V., Boite, J.M.: Hybrid HMM/ANN Systems for Training Independent Tasks: Experiments on Phonebook and Related Improvements. In: Proceedings of International Conference on Acoustics, Speech and Signal Processing (ICASSP) (1997)

28. Bradley, S., et al.: The mechanisms creating wind noise in microphones. University of Salford, Nokia Mobile Phones

29. Rabiner, L.: Techniques for Speech and Natural Language Recognition. Rutgers, The State University of New Jersey (2002)

30. Xiong, Z., Radhakrishnan, R., Divakaran, A., Huang, T.S.: Highlights extraction from sports video based on an audio-visual marker detection framework (2005)

31. Cole, R.A., Noel, M., Lander, T., Durham, T.: New Telephone Speech Corpora at CSLU. In: Proceedings of Eurospeech (1995)

32. Rey, P.-H.: Opportunities in Sport for Voice-Enabled Technologies. Master of Advanced Studies in Sport Administration and Technology thesis, AISTS (2006)

33. Stricker, C., Rey, P.-H.: How can voice-enabled technologies help athletes and coaches to become more efficient? In: 3rd Asia-Pacific Congress on Sports Technology, Singapore (2007)

34. Shneiderman, B.: The Limits of Speech Recognition. Communications of the ACM 43(9) (September 2000)

35. Grosso, M.A.: The long-Term Adoption of Speech Recognition in Medical Applications. George Washington University School of Medicine (2003)

36. Strayer, D.L., Johnson, W.A.: Driven to distraction: dual-task studies of simulated driving and conversing on a cellular phone. Psychol. Sci. 12, 462–466 (2001)

37. Wagen, J.-F., Imhalsy, M.: Conception de produits et de services basés sur la Reconnaissance Vocale: exemples d'une collaboration IDIAP/HES-SO. TIC day, Martigny, May 24 (2007),
http://home.hefr.ch/wagen/Imhost_Humavox_TicDay_Final.pdf

MEMODULES as Tangible Shortcuts to Multimedia Information

Elena Mugellini[1], Denis Lalanne[2], Bruno Dumas[2], Florian Evéquoz[2], Sandro Gerardi[1], Anne Le Calvé[1], Alexandre Boder[1], Rolf Ingold[2], and Omar Abou Khaled[1]

[1]University of Applied Sciences of Western Switzerland
{elena.mugellini,sandro.gerardi,omar.aboukhaled}@hefr.ch,
anne.lecalve@hevs.ch, alexandre.boder@hesge.ch
[2]University of Fribourg
{denis.lalanne,bruno.dumas,florian.evequoz,rolf.ingold}@unifr.ch

Abstract. Tangible User Interfaces (TUIs) are emerging as a new paradigm for facilitating user interaction with the digital world by providing intuitive means to link the physical and digital worlds. The MEMODULES project has the objective of developing, experimenting and evaluating the concept of tangible shortcuts (reminders), facilitating (a) the control of devices in the everyday life and also (b) the categorization of information in order to ease or improve information access and retrieval. The project aims at facilitating the user interaction with multimedia information by supporting both the creation and management of tangible links to digital content. Moreover, our research investigates the opportunity of a more complex, multi-sensorial combination of objects and multimedia information by combining multiple interaction modalities - such as voice and gesture - with interactive information visualizations. In order to address these issues we propose a user-oriented framework, called Memodules Framework, enabling end users to turn everyday objects into Memodules. The framework provides a single platform that combines end-user programming, tangible interaction, multimodality and personal information management issues. Memodules framework is built upon MemoML (Memodules Markup Language) and SMUIML (Synchronized Multimodal User Interaction Markup Language) models, which guarantee framework flexibility, extensibility and evolution over time.

1 Supporting Human Memory with Interactive Systems

Human memory is central in our daily life activities, not only to build relationships with friends, create our identity or reminisce about the past [50] but also to drive our attention towards the most important tasks to perform and to manage our lives [51]. Information overload, memory losses and attention lacks are crucial challenges to solve, not only for elderly people but also for the rest of the society. For these reasons, designing interactive systems that can support human memory has become critical to increase our wellness, using novel technologies and innovative human-machine interaction paradigms [52].

D. Lalanne and J. Kohlas (Eds.): Human Machine Interaction, LNCS 5440, pp. 103–132, 2009.

Numerous elderly have memory and attention problems, without including Alzheimer disease [53], which hinder their daily lives. Not only do they have difficulties remembering appointments and tasks that need to be done, they might lose their glasses, or have trouble remembering people and places, which can result in unsafe situations and feelings of insecurity and melancholy.

Younger people also face memory problems, especially with the constant increase of information a person owns and handles. Not only the information amount is growing fast, it is dematerializing and thus, people are often feeling overwhelmed. Documents are multiplying in very large file hierarchies, pictures are no longer stored in photo-albums, music CDs are taking the form of mp3 files, movies are stored on hard-drives. Google and Microsoft recently tried to solve this issue by providing, respectively, a desktop search engine and a powerful email search engine, in attempt to minimize the effort needed by people to organize their documents and access them later by browsing. However, in order to find a file, one still has to remember a set of keywords or at least remember its "virtual" existence. If one does not remember having a certain document, browsing could be helpful, since it can reveal related keywords and documents. Those, in turn, can help you remember by association, like human memory does [51].

Memory retrieval happens in cycles, meaning that recollecting starts with a cue or a short memory description after which it cycles through different levels of detail of the autobiographical memory system until it matches the memory search [54]. A cue (or trigger) is a stimulus that can help someone to retrieve information from long-term memory. Anything can be a cue (a photo, a spoken word, a color, an action or a person), as long as there is a link between the cue and the to-be-remembered event. For example, when we see a picture of a place visited in our childhood the image may cue recollections associated to the content of the picture and trigger an emotional reaction simultaneously. This information is generally easier to retrieve if it is associated to a strong emotional experience [55] or when it is repeated often. This so-called rehearsal can be facilitated e.g. by having physical objects related to memories, such as souvenirs or photographs [56], [57], and in case these physical objects are linked to their digital counterparts such as photos and videos, these tangible interactions can support everyday human memory [58], [59], [52], [44]. Furthermore, it appears that people easily access and retrieve information when it is linked to other related information or objects [60], [61], either information or media, such as sounds, smells, images, which support the idea of cross-modal indexing [62].

Over the last couple of years, it has been demonstrated that Graspable, or Tangible User Interfaces (TUIs), a genre of human-computer interaction that uses physical objects as representations and controls for digital information [63], make up a promising alternative for the 'traditional' omnipresent graphical user interface (GUI). In a few projects such as Phenom [56], TUIs have been used to support people who are subject to the information overload problem, thanks to tangible reminders and shortcuts to access and control information. The Phenom souvenirs [56] are personal iconic tangibles embedded with RFID tags coupled to personal digital photo collections. Few systems have demonstrated the technical feasibility of associating digital media with tangible objects [64], [65], and generally remain stand-alone proof of concept prototypes or applications of limited functionality. More sophisticated combinations of multimedia and tangible interaction are only now emerging [66] [67]. Using personal objects that have 'personal meaning to the user' [59] in a TUI supports existing mental associations and media systems, reducing learning time. Examples of studies in this area include the souvenirs mentioned in [69], but also Rosebud [58], POEMs [68] and Passage [65]. These types of TUIs seem more suitable for novice users or elderly people and lend themselves better to the home environment as a place for personal belongings. Another important aspect of personal objects in a memory system is that often the objects' original purpose is to remind people of its history and the (personal) stories attached [20].

The main goal of MEMODULES project is to investigate these aspects further in order to go beyond stand alone proof of concept prototypes towards more complete and general solutions combining tangible interaction with multimodality as well as multimedia information issues. Moreover we want to allow non-expert users to create their own TUI system with the ultimate goal of empowering people to easily and flexibly employ TUIs in the framework of upcoming smart environments. More specifically, MEMODULES project aims at developing, experimenting and evaluating the concept of tangible shortcuts (reminders), facilitating (a) the control of devices in the everyday life and also (b) the categorization of information order to improve information access and retrieval.

The chapter is structured as follows. Section 2 introduces the concept of Memodules and the main use-cases that have driven our research activities. Section 3 presents the user-centered design approach. Section 4 reviews relevant state-of-the-art within the domain of tangible user interaction, multimodality as well as information management. Section 5 presents the Memodules framework that allows end-user to easily turn everyday objects into tangible user interfaces by taking into account multimodality and personal information management issues. Section 6 concludes the chapter and presents futures works.

2   Memodules Concept

Memodules are tangible interfaces that link our memory to related digital information. Memodules are usually small or tiny-tagged physical objects containing a link towards information sources. They roost abstract information in the real world through tangible reminders. We consider the Memodules as tangible hypermarks, i.e. embedded hyperlinks to abstract information attached to everyday physical objects. Memodules do not only materialize information in the real world through tangible reminders, they also help controlling the dailylife devices accessing the information (CD player, TV, computer, etc.) or other devices (lamp, heater). The basic idea of this project is to associate three main entities: Humans, Memodules, and Devices, in order to launch a set of actions in a natural way in everyone's everyday life:

Human + Memodules + Device = Action

Moreover the project will consider two complementary research approaches, i.e. user-centric and device-centric, in order to design, implement and evaluate Memodules, i.e. tangible shortcuts to multimedia information. In fact, information technology is transforming the way people interact among themselves and with objects around them. In particular, technology's focus is gradually shifting away from the computer as such, to the user. This change of paradigm aims at making communication and computer systems simple, collaborative and transparent to the user. Because both humans and machines are concerned in order to improve human-computer interaction, both should be carefully studied and taken into account when designing Memodules.

The following use-case illustrates one of the possible applications of Memodules in the domestic environment:

- Home use-case (Fig. 1): Sandra creates a folder full of pictures from her last vacations in Corsica. She glues an RFID (Radio Frequency Identification) on a nice seashell she brought back from Corsica and asks the system to associate it with the picture folder. One week later she wants to show her friends a slideshow of her vacation. She places the seashell, together with a "jazz" Memodule, in a little hole next to the plasma screen, which activates the show. Denis who enjoyed the evening and the pictures gives his calling card to Sandra. The following day, Sandra places Denis' calling card along with the seashell on top of the communicator and makes a brief special gesture to send everything.

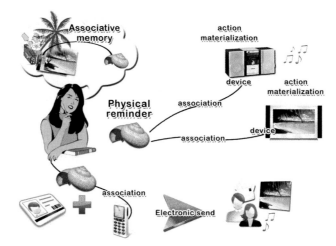

Fig. 1. Memodules Home use-case

Other application areas, such as business and library environments, have been envisaged and implemented as interesting Memodules use-cases:

- Business meeting use-case: Rolf missed a meeting. He places the printed agenda of this meeting, which is a tagged Memodule, next to a screen. The multimedia data recorded during the meeting, e.g. audio, video, documents, are immediately played on the same screen.
- Library use-case: Denis is at the library. He found two interesting books "Cooking for Dummies" and "Lonely Planet India", which he is planning to take home. He puts the two books next to a large display in the middle of the library and the system suggests to him various other books through an interactive visualization, books thematically realted, related by authors, or by references, or also those read by other users, who also selected the 2 books. He selects "The Art and Tradition

of Regional Indian Cooking" and the system indicates him the exact location of the book in the library on a map.

2.1 Memodules Approach

Based on the concept of associative memory, a physical object (the seashell in the example of Fig. 1) is associated to some digital information that is then materialized on a specific device through the user interaction (*Memodules interaction scenario*). As shown in Fig. 2 this approach, called here the Memodules approach, will be explored through two complementary fundamental and applied research axes:

- User centered design: study the user's needs and tasks they need to accomplish, in order to provide suitable and usable interfaces.
- Technology-driven design: improve human/computer physical interaction techniques and multimodal processing capabilities for a new generation of devices and environments (interaction techniques, in Fig. 2). This includes also considering issues related to information management such as how to classify, categorize, contextualize, visualize and personalize information according to user preferences and profiles (multimedia content, in Fig. 2).

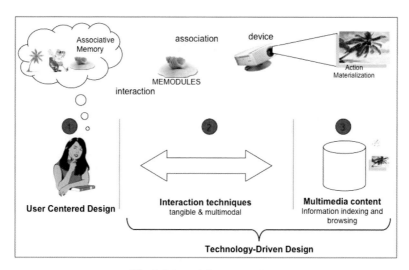

Fig. 2. Memodules approach

3   User Centered Design

The main goal of the user-centered design phase consisted of studying the activity of travelling in order to understand and point out: how personal objects and souvenirs are used and collected; how those objects are connected to memories and remind people; how we could combine those objects with multimedia content (digital photos, music etc.) to enhance recalling memories and storytelling.

User-centered design aims to explore travelling activities in order to elicit users needs and wishes to inform the design process. In order to explore and understand travel activity we conduct the user studies using different methodologies: focus group interview, the analysis of travel diaries (journal written during the travel) and an investigation of the most common habits on sharing travel memories through the Web (see Fig. 3). Relevant aspects outlined with aforementioned techniques drove succeeding brainstorming and concept generation activities as shown in Fig. 3 (the technology driven design was conducted as a parallel activity to study enabling technologies).

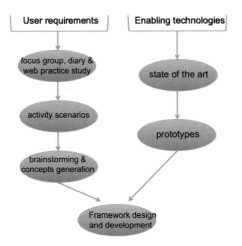

Fig. 3. User-centered process

The first investigation was conducted using focus group since it provides us with a great deal of data about current practices of tourists and helps us in understanding how to address the issue of traveling. We organized two different focus groups involving people who represent the users' class such as: independent travelers who arrange their own travel and activities, they are between 25 and 30 years old, with intermediate or advanced technology knowledge. They travel for pleasure for long and short period of time (from one week up to one month). Each focus group involved 6 persons. Focus groups investigated how users grasp souvenirs and collect information during the travel and how they use them after. For example the objects are grasped, organized, manipulated and consumed by the user in the attempt of fixing memory and remembering the experience of the voyage (Fig. 4).

Outcomes from these activities confirmed results achieved in the previous studies (such as [70], [69]) and clarified the basic features and some drawbacks of existing practices and tools that support travelling activities. For example planning a travel requires collecting information from several and different sources, and one of the most common ways to grasp information mostly regarding culture, habits and good tip is through personal contacts. Social relations have a key role on planning activity since people are one of the most important resources to gather information: friends, colleagues, relatives whom already have been there, natives, etc (more detailed information can be found in [49]).

Fig. 4. Some examples of souvenirs collected during the travel

The key findings that emerged from the focus group helped us to drive further investigation activities. Further study was oriented to elicit information regarding how people document the travel and which are the most common practices to publish and share multimedia data and travel stories. The analysis of travel diaries (journal written during the travel) and an investigation of the most common habits on sharing travel memories through the Web were then performed. Once again the results of these investigations elicited the importance for people to fix memories and share their experiences.

The whole user activity analysis provides us with many interesting elements and several scenarios (activity scenarios in Fig. 3) for guiding the design process. Among the several scenarios, we focused on few of them concerning the activity of sharing experience through story telling, collecting objects that evoke the travel and making personal reflection of the experience. According with the selected scenarios and related research works, some critical issues emerged:

- Users have difficulties in integrating different media (paper pictures, digital pictures, diary book, objects, etc…) and to exchange file and data,
- People use storytelling as the most natural way of narrate the experience,
- Souvenirs are important for travelers to retrieve events and circumstances; they are tangible cues to memories and good incipit for stories, Souvenir sometimes finish hidden somewhere inside the home and it is more and more difficult for people to find them as time passes by.

These issues guided our work in the successive step of the design process (more detailed information can be found in [34]). All along the phase of concept generation we explored the relationships of objects, collected and produced during the voyage, and how they can afford the recollection of memories and the sharing of experiences with others. Fig. 5 and Fig. 6 show two concepts developed as the result of aforementioned investigation activity. The first one explores the use of a mobile

Fig. 5. Concept generation: linking a souvenir with digital picture

Fig. 6. Concept generation: augmented travelBook

phone as means to associate physical object to digital content (Fig. 5). The second one explores the use of tagged object to created augmented travel journal (Fig. 6). These concepts along with the results of the enabling technologies study (see Section 4) guided the design and the development of the Memodules framework presented in Section 5.

4   Technology Driven

This section presents the main investigation activities carried out within the technology-driven approach. According to the research approach schema presented in Fig. 2 three main research axes have been studied and are presented in the following: 1) Tangible User Interaction, 2) Multimodal Interaction and 3) Information Management. Even if these three main research axes are strongly related to each other (tangible interfaces are often combined with multimodality, multimodal interaction is habitually coupled with visualization, etc.) for the sake of clarity in the following we decided to present them one by one. Only projects which are most related to our work are presented, since some toolkits dedicated to creation of interfaces including tangible interaction and multiple modalities are covered in the survey chapter on "multimodal interfaces" at the beginning of this book.

4.1   Tangible User Interaction

Tangible User Interfaces (TUIs) are emerging as a new paradigm for facilitating user interaction with the digital world by providing an intuitive mean to link the physical and digital worlds [44]. Recently it has been demonstrated that personal objects and souvenirs can be used as tangible interfaces and ambient intelligent objects [20]. Users have a personal mental model of the links between their personal physical objects (souvenirs) and the related digital information, as a consequence those objects can be used as TUIs instead of developing new ones that have to be learned by the users. The innovative works of Wellner's DigitalDesk [47] and Ishii and Ullmer's Tangible Bits [22] have pioneered exploration of post-WIMP (Windows, Icons, Menus, Pointers) tangible interfaces. Ubiquitous computing applications have motivated these novel physical interfaces even more. However, tangible interfaces are difficult and time consuming to build, requiring a specific technological expertise that limits their widespread adoption. Several research efforts have been done during recent years to develop tools for prototyping tangible user interfaces and designing ubiquitous computing architectures. Some examples of those projects are: Smart-Its [18], Phidgets

[16], the iStuff [1] and iCAP [43]. These projects were mainly focusing on providing rich prototyping toolkits or programming languages for developing Tangible User Interfaces and ubiquitous devices from a developer point of view instead of focusing on end-users. Other examples of interesting projects focusing more on supporting non-expert in programming users to manage personal ubiquitous environments are Accord [21,39], Oxygen [40] and GAS [30]. All three projects have focused on giving end users the ability to construct or modify ubiquitous computing environments.

Our work has been inspired by the results achieved within the framework of those projects. However, some fundamental conceptual differences between those projects and our work exist: (1) our focus on personal objects and souvenirs as tangible interfaces instead of generic domestic objects and devices, and (2) our focus on memory recollection and sharing. Moreover our work is intended to support any type of user to use and combine augmented personal objects as a means for memory recollection and experience sharing and to support dynamic re-combination of those objects since personal memories associated to objects and events can change over time [19]. For this reason users should be provided with a mechanism for easily associating and reassociating multi-sensorial information to their personal objects.

4.2 Multimodal Interaction

In this section we present a state of the art of tools and frameworks dedicated to the rapid creation of tangible and multimodal interfaces. Both multimodal interaction and tangible interaction have seen extensive development in the last 20 years. Since the seminal works of Bolt [4] who worked on the "put-that-there" project, multimodal interaction practitioners extended multimodality towards new types of interaction modalities, semantically richer interaction, better fusion and integration of input modalities as well as finer fission of output modalities. This section is specifically targeted at covering toolkits geared toward the creation of multimodal interfaces (tangible or not).

Krahnstoever et al. [26] proposed a framework using speech and gesture to create a natural interface. The output of their framework was to be used on large screen displays enabling multi-user interaction. Cohen et al. [7] worked on Quickset, a speech/pen multimodal interface, based on Open Agent Architecture. Bourguet [6] endeavored in the creation of a multimodal toolkit in which multimodal scenarios could be modeled using finite state machines. This multimodal toolkit is composed of two components, a graphical user interface named IMBuilder which interfaces the multimodal framework itself, named MEngine. Multimodal interaction models created with IMBuilder are saved as a XML file. Flippo et al. [13] also worked on the design of a multimodal framework, geared toward direct integration into a multimodal application. The general framework architecture is based on agents, while the fusion technique itself uses meaning frames. Configuration of the fusion is done via a XML file, specifying for each frame a number of slots to be filled and direct link to actual resolvers implementations. Lastly, Bouchet et al. [5] proposed a component-based approach called ICARE. These components cover elementary tasks, modality-dependent tasks or generic tasks like fusion. The components-based approach of ICARE has been used to create a comprehensive open-source toolkit called OpenInterface [2].

On the side of tangible interaction, a number of toolkits for creating tangible and/or embedded applications have seen the light since the founding works of Ullmer and Ishii [22]. As shown by Mazalek [31], three main tendencies have been followed: hardware prototyping, groupware-focused and integrated application. Phidgets [16] and iStuff [1] are typical examples of the hardware prototyping approach, offering developers a set of hardware components and software drivers to use those components. Groupware-focused tools, such as SDGToolkit [17] offer tools allowing the creation of group-oriented applications. Finally, researchers have begun to work on a mid-way, integrated application toolkit approach; examples include Papier-Mâché [25] and Synlab API [31].

As interesting as these toolkits are, problems arise when you wish to mix them with other modalities such as speech: hardware components and groupware-oriented applications focus on their original tasks and generally do not provide opportunities to accept third party recognizers or an external data source. Hence, if we want to enrich tangible applications with other modalities, we need toolkits able to take into account data coming from very different sources, and still be able to fuse data coming from those sources.

4.3 Information Management

The main Memodules goal is to provide means to access and manipulate information easily using natural human communication channels. Nevertheless, for this interaction to be facilitated, the information itself needs to be somewhat organized. Furthermore links between similar pieces of information need to be drawn. Personal Information Management (PIM) techniques are of use to help presenting information in a way that the user can browse and search it with ease.

Popular desktop search engines like Google Desktop Search, Windows Desktop Search or Copernic Desktop Search are typically ports of Web searching technologies to the local desktop. They index files, emails, web history and offer free-text search queries as well as filters on type of document, location on the folder structure and other available metadata. Search results are presented in textual lists that may be ranked by relevance or sorted chronologically. *Stuff I've Seen* [10] can be considered the precursor of these engines, as it provides the same basic functionalities. A user evaluation on this tool revealed the importance of social and temporal cues for retrieving information. However the traditional Desktop Search tools provide no way of taking advantage of those contextual cues.

MyLifeBits [14] is a huge database system of personal resources. Its originality resides in the use of links that represent either user-created collections of resources or so-called transclusion (a resource cited or used by another one, e.g. a spreadsheet embedded in a textual document). As this database system provides an API, it can be interfaced. *FacetMap* [42] is an interface built on top of *MyLifeBits'* data store that offers a query-refinement mechanism based on properties of files, called facets. Therefore it allows browsing instead of free-text searching.

Forget-me-not [29] foresaw the importance of faceted browsing. Facets are metadata on information, like type of file (picture, document, and so one), size, or author for example. Faceted browsing is a browsing paradigm that allows exploring a dataset by sequentially querying facets in order to eventually find the documents of interest, instead of browsing a traditional folder hierarchy. The authors indeed suggest exploiting the human episodic memory, i.e. the ability we have to associate things to an episode in our memory. The location of an episode, the time when it happened and the people concerned are strong cues for recall. Similarly, *Milestones in time* [38] is a more recent work that tries to replace information in context, specifically in its temporal context, making use of episodes and temporal landmarks. As well, the *Time-Machine* environment featured in the latest MacOS X operating system leverages the seminal work done by Rekimoto [37] in order to exploit our ability to recall the approximate temporal period when a document was created or modified, thus emphasizing the importance of contextual cues and facets.

Apart from the actual PIM systems, a most interesting user-study of PIM strategies has been conducted in 2004 by Boardman [3]. He notably emphasizes the facts that: (1) Users generally prefer to browse instead of search through their personal information; (2) The personal email archive has a potential for being integrated with personal files, as relations are strong between personal files and filed emails.

Email is indeed one of the prominent sources of information overload, as a typical mailbox receives most of the personal information avalanche. Thus, email management is an important part of PIM. Indeed, since Whittaker and Sidner first studied user practices for managing email overload [48], numerous attempts have been made to produce complete clients or plugins to help manage mailboxes. Recent works like those of Dredze [9] or Cselle [8] successfully use machine-learning methods to classify emails into activities, helping to keep trace of current (but also possibly past) tasks. Some works use visualizations to help handle the current inbox and keep a synthetic view of tasks. *Thread Arcs* [24] for example, presents a novel visual approach that helps to understand threads of messages. In [45] the authors propose to visualize the "conversational history" between the mailbox owner and a chosen contact during a certain period of time. Their *Themail* system is tailored for psycho-social practices analysis rather than for PIM. Perer and Shneiderman [36] visually explore relationships through past emails. Again, their system consists of an analytical tool rather than a management tool. All in all, few works really address the problem of managing and exploring an individual's complete email archive.

Finally, semantic web technology, another approach to the problem of personal information management, has been considered. Semantic technology provides new powerful ways of handling data by adding semantic at the data level. This gives machines new possibilities to manipulate information, hence the capability of reasoning that will allow deducting new unstated information. In the context of PIM, an ontology provides a schema to structure the data. It is a description of a precise vocabulary that uses classes to identify the data and properties to link them together constituting a knowledge base. According to [35] most important reasons to develop an ontology are: To share common understanding of the structure of information among people or software agents; To enable reuse of domain knowledge; To make domain assumptions explicit; To separate domain knowledge from the operational knowledge; To analyze domain knowledge. As presented later on, in MEMODULES project we use ontologies to categorize information in order to facilitate information access and retrieval.

This short state-of-the-art underlines the major findings and unsolved issues in PIM: the importance of contextual cues, of semantic, browsing over searching, emails as a representative subset of personal information, information visualization as a solution to visual guidance and browsing.

5 Memodules Framework

This section presents the Memodules framework developed within the project. Memodules framework is a user-oriented framework enabling end users to turn everyday objects into Memodules. Turning a physical object into a Memodule means tagging the objects, linking it to the related multimedia information and describing how it interact with the surrounding environment to render the digital content. The framework provides a single platform that combines end-user programming, tangible interaction, multimodality and personal information management issues.

Memodules framework is built upon MemoML (Memodules Markup Language) and SMUIML (Synchronized Multimodal User Interaction Markup Language) models.

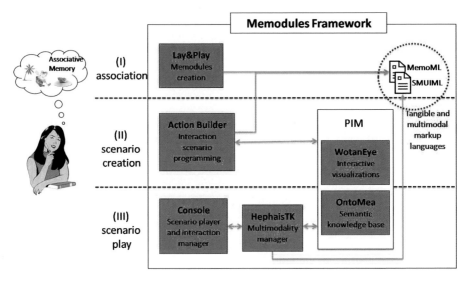

Fig. 7. Memodules Framework

As shown in Fig. 7, the framework is made of several components that allow users to create tangible user interfaces (*association*), to define how they interact with the devices (*scenario creation*) and to use them (*scenario play*). All the components are presented in the following sections. Eventually a light version of the framework, called Memobile, has been developed to run on standard mobile phones. Memobile, as the Memodules framework, is based on MemoML language (presented in the next section) and it is fully compliant with the main application. The added value of Memobile application is that users can bring it with them all the day long, wherever they are. Memodules framework is composed of the following components:

- Lay&Play, handles the creation of Memodules (tagged physical objects)
- Action Builder, allows users to define Memodules interaction scenarios (create association among Memodules, digital content and devices)
- WotanEye and OntoMea, facilitate multimedia information retrieval and visualization

- Console and HephaisTK, manage respectively the execution of interaction scenarios and multimodality issues
- MemoML and SMUIML, are the two markup languages the framework is built upon.

It is worth noting that all the components of the framework are fully operational, however since the project is not yet finished, so far only some of them have been completely integrated to each other.

5.1 Lay and Play, Memodules Creation

The Lay&Play system allows to easily turn everyday objects into Memodules (augmented personal objects) and to add them to the Memodules environment. A Memodules environment is defined as the collection of Memodules, related digital information and devices. The Lay&Play system is composed of a webcam and an RFID reader (Fig. 8) which allows simultaneously to take a picture of the object laying over the Lay&Play system and to read the ID of the RFID tag attached to the object. The digital counterpart of the physical object is created (Memodule creation) and added to the list of available Memodules objects displayed on the Action Builder editor (see next section).

5.2 Action Builder, Interaction Scenario Programming

Action Builder is the core of the application since it allows users to program the interaction of Memodules objects within a smart environment. The major design challenge for this component was to make possible for end-user (i.e. non expert users) to build their personalized smart environment. For this reason Action Builder provides an end-user programming approach: it is a visual editor based on the puzzle metaphor that handles the creation of interaction scenarios for Memodules. The choice of the puzzle metaphor was inspired by the results achieved within the framework of Accord project [37]. Action Builder uses the puzzle metaphor proposed by Accord and extends it in order to support more complex puzzle configurations combining parallel and sequential actions. Moreover, thanks to Lay&Play component, icons representing the digital counterparts of physical objects in our visual editor are created using the picture of the object itself, thus facilitating the user to link the physical object to its digital representation.

Action Builder allows users to create interaction scenarios that describe how Memodules interact with the surrounding environment and which devices are involved in the scenario. Scenarios are created using the puzzle metaphor: the user connects components through a series of left-to-right couplings of puzzle pieces, providing an easy to understand mechanism for connecting the different pieces. Moreover, constraining puzzle connections to be left to right also gives the illusion of a pipeline of information flow that creates a cause-effect relationship between the different components.

The puzzle editor is composed of a number of different panels (Fig. 8). The control panel (Fig. 8 on the top) contains the list of available puzzle pieces grouped in eight different categories (see below for more details about categories).

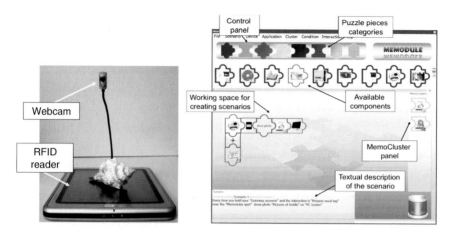

Fig. 8. MEMODULES Lay and Play (on the left) and the Action Builder (on the right)

Puzzle pieces can be dragged and dropped in the editing panel (or workspace) and assembled in order to create the scenarios. When a puzzle piece is dragged onto the workspace it clones itself and becomes a symbolic link. In order to remove pieces form the workspace they can be dragged to the trash can (on the bottom-right of the workspace). In order to connect puzzle pieces together it is necessary to drag a particular piece in the vicinity of a fitting target piece. If the two pieces are matching, visual feedback is provided to the user (the border of the puzzle pieces changes color). On the contrary if the user tries to connect two non-compatible pieces, the system will not allow their assembly. When a Memodule puzzle piece is selected the MemoCluster panel (on the right) displays information collections associated to that Memodule which have been created and used in previous scenarios. The creation of collections of information is facilitated by the use of personal information management techniques (see WotanEye and OntoMea modules in Section 5.7 and 5.8 respectively).

As the user connects the puzzle pieces the one by one, a textual description of the scenario that is being created is provided to facilitate user understanding (see Action Builder in Fig. 8, on the bottom left). Puzzle pieces are grouped into 8 different categories (see Fig. 9) and displayed with different colors. Their arrangement reflects the order in which pieces have to be connected; the first five categories are mandatory to create simple scenarios, while the last three categories can be optionally used to create more complex scenarios.

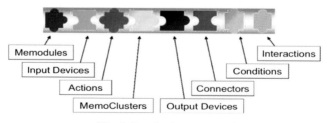

Fig. 9. Puzzle pieces categories

The blue pieces represent Memodules objects, the green ones regroup Input Devices (i.e. devices that can identify Memodules objects and start corresponding actions), the pink ones represent Actions to carry out (e.g. play music, show pictures, send an e-mail, etc.), the yellow ones stand for information that can be associated to Memodules objects (e.g. some photos, music, etc.). Digital content is grouped in "logical" clusters called MemoClusters. This means that information is browsed from everywhere in the PC using WotanEye and OntoMea modules, and grouped into logical collections. Black-colored pieces identify Output Devices, i.e. devices where the action is to be carried out (a TV for showing some photos, a Hi-fi stereo for playing some music, etc.). Red-colored pieces refer to Connectors that allow creating complex scenarios. At the time of writing two types of connectors have been implemented: the "AND" connector and "TIMER" connector. Finally light-orange and light-blue colored pieces refer respectively to Condition and Interaction. Conditions and Interaction are used along with Memodules pieces to create multimodal and context-aware scenarios. Conditions represent a set of variables (such as time, temperature, etc.) that are used to constrain the execution of the scenario (e.g. if the user adds a time condition to a scenario, the scenario is triggered only if the condition is validated). Interaction puzzle pieces allow the user to interact in a multimodal manner with the framework combining for instance tangible interaction (i.e. physical object) with voice-based interaction. Currently, two modalities are possible: voice and gesture.

The following three interaction scenarios illustrate what can be created using the Action Builder (Fig. 10). The first scenario (Fig. 10a) describes the following action: When Sabrina approaches the seashell (souvenir of some Greek holidays) to the Console (see next paragraph), the photos of that vacation are displayed on the PC screen and after 5 minutes the slideshow has terminated, a video of the Parthenon is played. The second scenario (Fig. 10b) describes the action: When Sabrina approaches the seashell and the business card of her friend to the Console the photos of that vacation are sent to the e-mail address of her friend via the PC. The third scenario (Fig. 10c) describes the action: When Sabrina approaches the seashell to the Console and gives the vocal command "pictures" the photos are showed on the screen while if she says "videos" the videos are played.

In order to manage the problem of losing a Memodule object (i.e. forgetting where it is placed), Action Builder integrates an RFID localization system that makes it

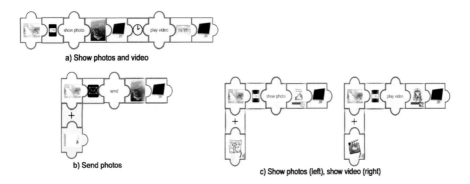

Fig. 10. Scenario examples

possible to find lost objects within a closed environment (a room). The localization system is made up of an RFID antenna that can detect the position of RFID-tagged object with an error of few centimeters. As show in Fig. 11, the user can activate the localization of a Memodule by simply selecting the puzzle piece representing the Memodule object in the Action Builder main interface and then clicking on the "find" menu item. This action starts the localization of the selected object and the result is displayed in real-time within Action Builder main windows, Fig. 11.

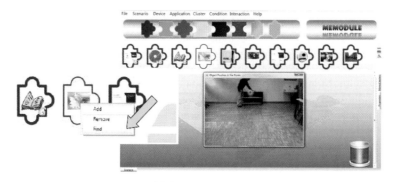

Fig. 11. Memodule localization using the Action Builder

5.3 MemoML Markup Language

MemoML (Memodules Markup Language) is one of the two technology-independent models upon which the framework is built [33] (the other model, SMUIML, is presented afterward). MemoML is an XML-based modeling language and it is based on the Document Engineering approach [15]. Document Engineering approach is emerging as a new discipline for specifying, designing, and implementing systems belonging to very different business domains by using XML technologies[1].

MemoML describes the components (Memodules, devices, communication protocols, actions, etc.) of a Memodules environment and how such components can be assembled to create interaction scenario using Action Builder. The components are the building blocks of the environment that can be combined together in order to define Memodules interaction scenarios. The model defines what a interaction scenario is, and the rules the interaction scenario has to undergo such as for instance the constraints associated to actions which restrain the types of information an action can operate upon (e.g. the action "play music" could not operate upon some photos). A more detailed description of MemoML model can be found in [33].

5.4 Console, Scenario Player and Interaction Manager

The Console is based on the Phidgets toolkit [16] and allows the user to start a scenario and to manage subsequent interactions with digital content. When a Memodule

---

[1] The choice of a declarative modeling approach allows us to describe what the framework is like, rather than how to create it, enabling system flexibility, reusability and portability over different implementation technologies.

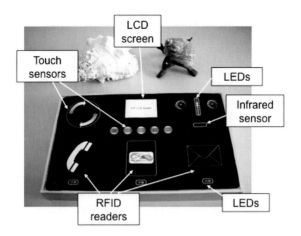

Fig. 12. Memodule Console

is approaching to one of the three RFID readers[2] of the Console (Fig. 12), the system identifies the Memodule object and retrieves the interaction scenario associated to it. In order to provide a visual feedback to the user, once the Memodule has been identified, the green LED associated to the RFID reader (see Fig. 12) lights on.

Once the scenario has been started the console allows managing actions execution. The Console is equipped with an infrared sensor, activated by the user's hand, which allows controlling the volume of sound when playing. At the same time some luminous LEDs give a visual feedback of the user's hand movements while adjusting the volume (Fig. 12).

Several touch sensors allow the user to interact with multimedia content while playing (play next, previous, stop, etc.). The LCD screen shows metadata information about the multimedia content that is played, while the circular touch (on the top left) allows the user to speed up or slow down the forward and the backward motion of some video or music playing. Scenarios can be executed just after they have been created with the visual editor, giving the possibility to the user to test whether the scenarios do what the user want.

The Lay&Play, the Action Builder and the Console have been fully integrated and some initial usability tests have been performed to evaluate the easiness of use of such integrated system. The tests involved around 7-8 persons, between 25 and 40 years old. After a short explication of the functioning of the three modules they were asked to perform the complete Memodule lifecycle, i.e. creation of a Memodules, definition of Memodules interaction scenario and play the scenario. The results of such tests provided good feedbacks about the system and gave also some interesting tips on how to improve the design of the system (see Memobile prototype in Section 5.9).

5.5 HephaisTK, Multimodality Manager

The main goal of HephaisTK toolkit is to allow developers to quickly develop and test interfaces mixing multimodal and tangible interaction. The HephaisTK toolkit

---

[2] The three readers represent three different devices (e.g. a TV, a PC and an interactive table) that for the sake of simplicity have been integrated into one Console in first version of the prototype.

served in the frame of the MEMODULES project to prototype a number of interfaces. The major objectives targeted by HephaisTK are modularity, extensibility, free use (via a GPL license) and usability. A modular architecture should allow the toolkit to be configured suiting the needs of the developer, so that unused components could be disabled. The extensibility is a common goal of any toolkit; its goal being to let developers plug easily into the toolkit custom human-computer communications means recognizers and synthesizers. Usability studies are also capital to make the toolkit easy to use, and should thus focus on the developer creating a multimodal interface; the toolkit should offer him with a scripting language comprehensible, yet powerful. HephaisTK has also been designed as a platform for testing new fusion and integration algorithms.

HephaisTK is designed to control various input recognizers, such as speech recognition or RFID tag readers, and the integration of their results. HephaisTK also helps controlling user-machine dialog and fusion of modalities. A developer wishing to use HephaisTK to develop a multimodal application will have to provide two components: his application and a SMUIML script. The developer's application (also called "client application" afterwards), written in Java, needs to import one class of HephaisTK. This class allows communication with the toolkit via listeners. The toolkit does not manage the actual content restitution, but sends messages or callbacks to the application describing the content to be restituted to the user. The SMUIML document (see next section) is used by the toolkit for a number of tasks: first, the definition of the messages that will transit from the toolkit to the developer's application; second, the events coming from the input recognizers that will have to be taken into account by the toolkit; last, description of the overall dialog management. The developer also has the possibility to add other input recognizers to HephaisTK toolkit. The toolkit provides compatibility with Sphinx [46] speech recognizer, ReacTIVision [23] computer vision framework and Phidgets [16] hardware building blocks, and manages any input devices emulating a mouse.

In order to account for the objective of modularity, the toolkit is built on a software agents framework, namely JADE. JADE was selected over other tools like, for example, Open Agent Architecture (OAA), because of its architecture not depending on a central facilitator, its neutral definition of agents, and its choice of Java as single programming language, allowing direct multi-platform compatibility, provided that a JVM (Java Virtual Machine) is present.

Agents are at the core of HephaisTK. The architecture of HephaisTK is shown in Fig. 13. For each input recognizer, an agent is responsible of reception, annotation and propagation of data transmitted by the recognizer. For instance, the agent responsible of a speech recognizer would propagate not only the speech meaning extracted, but also metadata such as a confidence score. Messages are then sent to the postman agent. This postman agent is in fact a central blackboard collecting data from the recognizers and storing them in a local database. Hence, all data coming from the different sources are standardized in a central place, where other interested agents can dig them at will. Another advantage of central blackboard architecture is to have one central authority that manages timestamps. The problem of synchronizing different timestamp sources is hence avoided, at the cost of a potential greater shift between the timestamp of the actual event and the recorded one. It is to be noted that this central agent does not act like a facilitator: only agents dealing with recognizers-wise

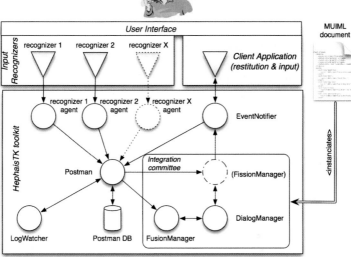

Fig. 13. Architecture of HephaisTK

data communicate with him. The agents within the integration committee communicate directly. Moreover, the postman agent also offers a mechanism of subscription to other agents: any agent can subscribe to events it is interested in. This mechanism of subscription allows for instance dynamic modifications or complete change of input modalities fusion method; a typical example would be an application using speech recognition that would be able to adapt on-the-fly to the native language of the user.

Three agents are currently responsible of the multimodal integration: the Fusion-Manager, FissionManager and DialogManager. Those agents form the Integration Committee, responsible of meaning extraction from data coming from the different input recognizers. This Integration Committee is instantiated for a given client application by a SMUIML (*Synchronized Multimodal User Interaction Markup Language*) document. The Integration Committee sends all fusion results to an agent named EventNotifier, whose task is solely to let the client application interface easily with HephaisTK toolkit. The client application needs to implement a set of simple Java listeners in order to receive extracted information from the toolkit, which is a common implementation scheme in the Java language for GUI development. The Event-Notifier is used by the client application to communicate with the toolkit and provide higher-level information, which could be used by the Integration Committee. HephaisTK hence sees the client application as its client, but also as another input source. As previously stated, the modular software agents-based architecture allows the toolkit to potentially offer a number of different fusion schemes, from rule-based to statistical to hybrid-based fusion schemes. At present, HephaisTK offers a rule-based approach, conceptually derived from artificial intelligence meaning frames.

The multimodal integration within the toolkit operates in an event-driven way: every time a new event is signaled to the integration committee (e.g. incoming input), it is matched against the possible frames of knowledge of the current context. Following the SMUIML script provided by the client application developer, the dialog manager indicates to the fusion manager in which state the application finds itself, and the fusion manager knows against which set of frames it will have to confront the incoming data. A typical frame of knowledge specifies a number of triggers needed to activate itself, as well as one or more actions to be taken when it activates. Typically, a frame would specify as an action a message to be sent to the client application, with potential data coming from the different input sources. Fig. 14 presents an example of frame in the context of an audio player application. This example is detailed later.

HephaisTK does not manage itself restitution to the user; instead, the Integration Committee informs the client application of the information extracted from the input recognizers. The actual restitution, by a standard GUI, text-to-speech or else, is up to the client application. Thus, communication with the client application is achieved through a set of messages. Those messages are predefined in the SMUIML script provided by the client application developer. To each message can be attached a set of variables, allowing for example to transfer to the client application the content extracted by a given input recognizer.

A first simple use case allowing control of a music player application via speech commands, standard WIMP interface elements and tangible RFID tagged objects has been implemented (Fig. 14). This application allowed simple interactions, such as "play", "pause", or "next track" commands, and offered different ways to express the commands. For example, a user could input the desired music with help of a tagged object while issuing a "play" command by voice.

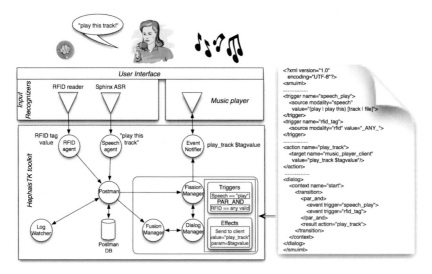

Fig. 14. An example application of a multimodal and tangible music player

A more complex use case followed in the form of the XPaint drawing table (Fig. 15). On this table, two physical artefacts (one of them can be seen in the hand of the user in Fig. 15) allow the users to draw on the table a set of shapes or tools selected by means of RFID-tagged tangible objects.

Fig. 15. The XPaint drawing table

Commands can also be selected by means of vocal commands, recognized with help of the Sphinx speech recognition toolkit [46]. Additionally, specific commands as selection of colour or line width are expressed through specific hardware input devices like Phidgets [16] sliders. Modelling the human-computer dialog for this application could be easely achieved with the SMUIML script, due to the level of abstraction provided by the HephaisTK scripting language. Another advantage stands in the fact that most of the existing XPaint application code could be re-used thanks to the clear application-HephaisTK separation.

5.6 SMUIML

The SMUIML document contains information about the dialog states (DialogManager), the events leading from one state to another (FusionManager) and the information communicated to the client application, given the current dialog state and context (FissionManager). The SMUIML markup language expresses in an easy-to-read and expressive way the modalities used, the recognizers attached to a given modality, the user-machine dialog, and the various triggers and actions associated to this dialog (see Fig. 16). More details about the SMUIML language and its structure can be found in [11].

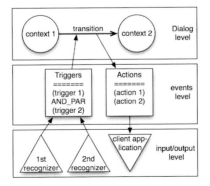

Fig. 16. The different levels of abstraction in the SMUIML language

5.7 WotanEye, Information Categorization

In order to tackle PIM (Personal Information Management) issues and following the ideas inspired from the state of the art presented in section 4.3, our prototype application, called WotanEye, tries to recover the natural context of information, focusing on finding similarities between different pieces of data along three facets, namely the temporal, social and thematic facets. Indeed, according to the study in [38], these are the three facets preferred by users looking for documents. More specifically, we explore the direction Boardman suggests and try to structure personal information around the structure of the email archive. Indeed, the email archive has potential for being taken as a core to which an important part of Personal Information (PI) can be connected: a single email inherently connects together people, topics and time. As such, a whole personal email archive thus contains invaluable thematic, temporal and social cues that other types of PI do not expose obviously. In emails, recipients of a message often know one another, so a social network can emerge, topics can be connected to particular groups of contacts, topics may also be time stamped, etc.

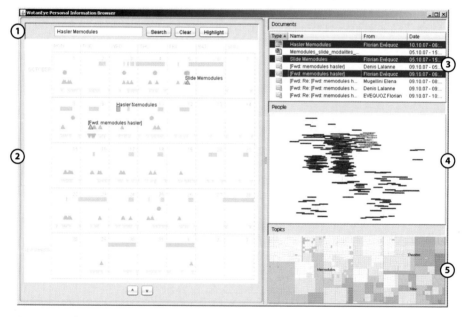

Fig. 17. Mockup of personal information management through interactive and visual cues (social cues on the upper left, thematic cues on the lower left and event- based cues on the right). See text below for more details.

Aiming to provide a unified access to the whole personal information and efficient search mechanisms, we leverage on an existing desktop search engine that performs an efficient indexing and a disposes of a powerful SQL-based API, namely Windows Desktop Search (WDS) [32]. The major drawback of using a desktop search engine is that the inverted index it generates is not accessible programmatically. Therefore, another method is needed to extract all the metadata required to build the temporal, social and thematic facets of PI. As the email archive is a representative subset of personal information, we developed a custom system that reads an email archive and extracts all the required metadata in a SQL-database. Therefore, we can build the temporal, social and thematic facets of PI. Moreover, using the email archive, similarities can be established between different facets data. For instance a certain group of people is likely to tackle a certain kind of topics at a particular time period.

Finally, we make use of information visualization techniques to present the user with its personal information along the different facets. Fig. 17 shows a partially implemented mockup of the browsing interface. The right part of the window displays a calendar-like view of documents (circles), emails (triangles) and appointments (squares). On the upper left part, the personal social network is shown with people pertaining to the monthly activity highlighted. On the bottom left, topics are arranged in a treemap view. At a glance, a user can visualize the main persons with who she/he has collaborated within the selected month, the distribution of the information exchanged within his thematic map, and the temporal distribution of this information within the month. Furthermore, this combination of views and dimensions support users in browsing through their preferred facet, depending on the way they memorized a piece of information. A user might remember that a document has been sent by a specific person, within a given month, in relation to a theme, or prior to a specific event. In this respect, WotanEye leverage on the biographic and social memories of users. A user can also select a specific theme, for instance "teaching", and visualize the concerned persons in her/his social network and the temporal allocation devoted to this theme within the month.

WotanEye provides novel interaction techniques for accessing multimedia data (documents, emails, audio/video recording, slideshows, etc.). Its benefit in this context is to be found in the assistance it can provide for browsing huge amounts of personal data. Indeed, the extracted PI structure may serve as a filter to help navigate through such data, and to assist in finding information thanks to similarity links that can be drawn between personal and professional information [28].

WotanEye can ease the creation of information collections to be associated to Memodules. In particular, during the creation of an interaction scenario it may be tedious to gather all the pertaining digital information that one want to associate to a specific object. The views that WotanEye provides exhibit a meaningful PI structure and may be used to facilitate the association task. If the emails, documents, pictures and other information about a common event are gathered and presented together, associating the whole episode to a physical object becomes easier. Reversely, physical objects already associated to digital information may serve as query parameters, or novel facets, to retrieve correlated pieces of PI.

5.8 OntoMea, Semantic Knowledge Base

The OntoMea prototype explores the opportunity of improving information indexing and categorization by the mean of ontology and semantic technologies. OntoMea is a semantic knowledge base engine allowing to store and exploit personal information ontologies. OntoMea can store semantic data, reason about them, infer new knowledge, and give full access to ontologies data. As shown in Fig. 18, OntoMea provides the structure that must be used to describe the data (based on different ontologies) and the architecture to query and update the data.

OntoMea is a java application, based on the Jena semantic web framework, which includes a light Jetty embedded web server. It maintains an RDF triple store, adding inferences to the basic data and allowing query through SPARQL queries (the standard semantic web query language) or predefined web services. Identifying data with URI, instead of database private keys, allow to uniquely identify them all over the world, facilitating the creation of connections between pieces of information. Such connections can be exploit to facilitate information retrieval tasks.

A small travel ontology containing some basic concept related to the travel activity (such as travel theme, visited place, persons, activity, etc.) has been developed. This far-from-being-exhaustive ontology allowed us to validate OntoMea prototype. Digital content, such as pictures, can be semantically annotated using concepts defined within the ontology. Such annotated data can be browsed and retrieved by exploiting the semantic relationships given by ontology facilitating information search activities.

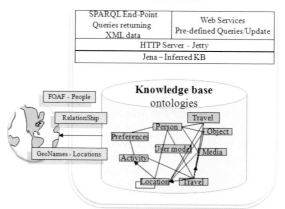

Fig. 18. Structural schema of OntoMea

Moreover OntoMea can handle links to any existing ontology (e.g., FOAF - Friend Of A Friend - ontology), making easier to improve our travel ontology.

5.9 Memobile, Mobile Framework

The Memobile is a mobile application that allows users to create association between physical objects and multimedia information wherever they are. The idea of developing a mobile version of the main application was suggested by the results of some user evaluations within the user-centered design approach that we conducted after the development of the main framework [34]. One important aspect emerged from the evaluation: the huge amount of physical objects and information collected and produced during the travel is too difficult to be accessed, retrieved and managed once back home. These issues guided our work in the successive step of the development process.

The goal of Memobile application is to give the user the possibility to tag physical objects and interact with them, associating multimedia content, at any moment and any place. Memodules framework and Memobile application are fully compliant, so once at home, the user can easily download all the information from the mobile phone to the main application as presented in the following. The Memobile application is based on a Fujitsu Siemens Pocket PC equipped with an RFID tag reader.

The application functions as described in the following. The user sticks a tag to the physical object and approaches with the object the mobile phone (step 1, Fig. 19). The mobile phone identifies the object and asks for a name (bookmark name steps 2 and 3, Fig. 19). The user can either select some media content (pictures, video, etc.) from his/her mobile phone or can produce new content and associate it to the previously created bookmark (steps 4,5,6 in Fig. 19).

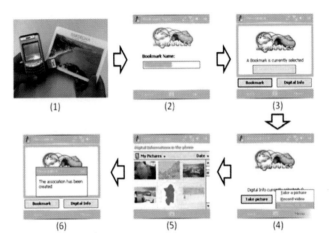

Fig. 19. Creation of an association between the souvenirs (postcard) and the digital content (some pictures)

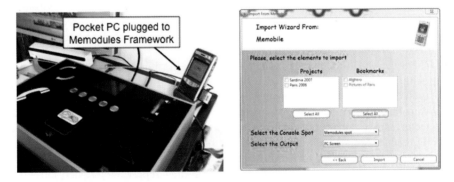

Fig. 20. Memobile plugged to the Console (left) and Import Wizard (right)

Once the association between the souvenir and some digital content has been created, the user can play the scenario simply approaching the souvenir to the mobile phone. In this case interaction scenarios are simpler since the input and output devices are fixed and predefined (the tag reader and Pocket PC screen respectively). Once back home the user can easily import the mobile scenarios into the main application by simply plugging-in the Pocket PC (Fig. 20).

6 Conclusion and Future Works

This paper presented the MEMODULES project dealing with tangible and multimodal user interfaces to support memory recollection and multimodal interaction within an intelligent environment. The project considered two complementary research approaches, i.e. user-centric and technology-driven, in order to design, implement and evaluate Memodules, i.e. tangible shortcuts to multimedia information. The article first presented the results of the user centered design process, i.e. the user requirements and needs through various studies such as focus groups. The article further presented the realization achieved during the first phase of the project, which consists of a Memodules framework that allows end-users to turn everyday objects into tangible user interfaces to access and manipulate digital content. The framework is composed of several modules, which address different issues such as tangible interaction, multimodal interaction and personal information management. Although the different modules presented in this article have received good feedbacks from users, which tends to prove the usefulness of Memodules approach, in the near future, we plan to combine them in a single framework and evaluate them with users within two complementary environments: the Smart Living Room and the Smart Meeting Room, to study user's interaction with Memodules in everyday life context in the first environment, and in the professional context in the second environment.

The Smart Living Room, installed at the University of Applied Science of Fribourg, aims at studying user interaction and technology integration in a home environment in order to personalize Memodules technologies according to the specific issues of domestic context. The Smart Living Room is equipped with furniture such as table, mirror, armchair, television and radio to replicate a usual home environment as well as a network of distributed sensors (for temperature, pressure, luminosity, noise, etc.), RFID readers and cameras to capture and analyze user interaction with and within the environment.

The Meeting Room installed at the University of Fribourg aims at recording meeting with audio/video devices, and further at analyzing the captured data in order to create indexes to retrieve interesting parts of meeting recordings. It is equipped with 10 cameras (8 close-ups, one per participant, 4 overviews), 8 microphones, a video projector, and a camera for the projection screen capture. It is further equipped with RFID readers for all seats to enable participants to register and bookmark meeting parts they want to index for further access. All the devices capture their streams in parallel and are synchronized which enable to further replay audio/video mosaics of meeting parts.

These two environments will be mainly used to run field studies and user evaluations to assess both usability and usefulness of the technologies developed. Further in the future we plan to study and test contextualization and personalization aspects within these two different contexts. Personalization issues target the adaptation of Memodules technologies to different categories of users: ageing people, young people, etc., whereas the contextualization targets the adaptation to the environment and task.

References

1. Ballagas, A.R., Ringel, M., Stone, M., Borchers, J.: iStuff: A Physical User Interface Toolkit for Ubiquitous Computing Environments. In: Conference on Human factors in computing systems (2003)
2. Benoit, A., Bonnaud, L., Caplier, L., Damousis, I., Tzovaras, D., Jourde, F., Nigay, L., Serrano, M., Lawson, J.-Y.: Multimodal Signal Processing and Interaction for a Driving Simulator: Component-based Architecture. Journal on Multimodal User Interfaces 1(1) (2007)
3. Boardman, R., Sasse, M.A.: Stuff goes into the computer and doesn't come out: a cross-tool study of personal information management. In: SIGCHI conference on Human factors in computing systems, pp. 583–590. ACM Press, New York (2004)
4. Bolt, R.: Put-that-there: voice and gesture at the graphics interface. Computer Graphics 14(3) (1980)
5. Bouchet, J., Nigay, L., Ganille, T.: ICARE Software Components for Rapidly Developing Multimodal Interfaces. In: ICMI 2004, State College, Pennsylvania, USA (2004)
6. Bourguet, M.L.: A Toolkit for Creating and Testing Multimodal Interface Designs. In: 15th Annual Symposium on User Interface Software and Technology, Paris, pp. 29–30 (2002)
7. Cohen, P.R., Johnston, M., McGee, D., Oviatt, S., Pittman, J., Smith, I., Chen, L., Clow, J.: QuickSet: multimodal interaction for distributed applications. In: Fifth ACM international Conference on Multimedia, Seattle, USA (1997)
8. Cselle, G., Albrecht, K., Wattenhofer, R.: Buzztrack: topic detection and tracking in email. In: 12th international conference on Intelligent user interfaces, pp. 190–197. ACM Press, New York (2007)
9. Dredze, M., Lau, T., Kushmerick, N.: Automatically classifying emails into activities. In: 11th international conference on Intelligent user interfaces, pp. 70–77. ACM Press, New York (2006)
10. Dumais, S., Cutrell, E., Cadiz, J., Jancke, G., Sarin, R., Robbins, D.C.: Stuff I've seen: a system for personal information retrieval and re-use. In: SIGIR 2003: Proceedings of the 26th annual international ACM SIGIR conference on Research and development in infor-maion retrieval, pp. 72–79. ACM Press, New York (2003)
11. Dumas, B., Lalanne, D., Ingold, R.: Prototyping Multimodal Interfaces with SMUIML Modeling Language. In: CHI 2008 Workshop on UIDLs for Next Generation User Interfaces (CHI 2008 workshop), Florence, Italy (2008)
12. Dumas, B., Lalanne, D., Guinard, D., Ingold, R., Koenig, R.: Strengths and Weaknesses of Software Architectures for the Rapid Creation of Tangible and Multimodal Interfaces. In: Proceedings of 2nd international conference on Tangible and Embedded Interaction, Bonn, Germany, February 19 - 21, pp. 47–54 (2008)
13. Flippo, F., Krebs, A., Marsic, I.: A Framework for Rapid Development of Multimodal Interfaces. In: ICMI 2003, Vancouver, BC, November 5-7 (2003)

14. Gemmell, J., Bell, G., Lueder, R., Drucker, S., Wong, C.: MyLifeBits: fulfilling the Memex vision. In: MULTIMEDIA 2002: Proceedings of the tenth ACM international conference on Multimedia, pp. 235–238. ACM Press, New York (2002)
15. Glushko, R.J., McGrath, T.: Document Engineering: Analyzing and Designing Documents for Business Informatics and Web Services. MIT Press, Cambridge (2005)
16. Greenberg, S., Fitchett, C.: Phidgets: easy development of physical interfaces through physical widgets. In: User Interface Software & Technology, CHI Letters (2001)
17. Greenberg, S.: Rapidly prototyping Single Display Groupware through the SDGToolkit. In: Fifth Conference on Australasian User interfaces (AUIC 2004). Dunedin, NZ (2004)
18. Holmquist, L.E., Antifakos, S., Schiele, B., Michahelles, F., Beigl, M., Gaye, L., Gellersen, H.-W., Schmidt, A., Strohbach, M.: Building Intelligent Environments with Smart-Its. In: SIGGRAPH 2003, Emerging Technologies exhibition (2003)
19. van den Hoven, E., Eggen, B.: Design Recommendations for Augmented Memory Systems. In: Designing for Collective Remembering Workshop at CHI 2006, Montréal, Quebec, Canada (2006)
20. van den Hoven, E., Eggen, B.: Personal souvenirs as Ambient Intelligent objects. In: Joint Conference on Smart Objects and Ambient intelligence: innovative Context-Aware Services, Usages and Technologies, SOc-EUSAI 2005, Grenoble, France, vol. 121, pp. 123–128. ACM Press, New York (2005)
21. Humble, J., Crabtree, A., Hemmings, T., Åkesson, K.-P., Koleva, B., Rodden, T., Hansson, P.: Playing with the Bits - User-configuration of Ubiquitous Domestic Environments. In: Dey, A.K., Schmidt, A., McCarthy, J.F. (eds.) UbiComp 2003. LNCS, vol. 2864. Springer, Heidelberg (2003)
22. Ishii, H., Ullmer, B.: Tangible Bits: Towards Seamless Interfaces between People, Bits and Atoms. In: Conference on Human Factors and Computing Systems (1997)
23. Kaltenbrunner, M., Bencina, R.: ReacTIVision: A Computer-Vision Framework for Table-Based Tangible Interaction. In: Proceedings of TEI 2007. Baton Rouge, Louisiana (2007)
24. Kerr. B.: Thread arcs: an email thread visualization. In: IEEE Symposium on Information Visualization (INFOVIS), pp. 211–218 (2003)
25. Klemmer, S.R., Li, J., Lin, J., Landay, J.A.: Papier-Mâché: Toolkit Support for Tangible Input. In: CHI Letters: CHI 2004, vol. 6(1) (2004)
26. Krahnstoever, N., Kettebekov, S., Yeasin, M., Sharma, R.: A real-time framework for natural multimodal interaction with large screen displays. In: ICMI 2002, Pittsburgh, PA, USA (2002)
27. Krueger, R.A.: Focus Groups: a practical guide for applied research. Sage publications, Newbury Park (1988)
28. Lalanne, D., Rigamonti, M., Evequoz, F., Dumas, B., Ingold, R.: An ego-centric and tangible approach to meeting indexing and browsing. In: Popescu-Belis, A., Renals, S., Bourlard, H. (eds.) MLMI 2007. LNCS, vol. 4892, pp. 84–95. Springer, Heidelberg (2008)
29. Lamming, M., Flynn, M.: Forget-me-not: intimate computing in support of human memory. In: FRIEND21 Symposium on Next Generation Human Interfaces (1994)
30. Mavrommati, I., Kameas, A., Markopoulos, P.: An editing tool that manages devices associations in an in-home environment. In: Personal and Ubiquitous Computing, vol. 8(3-4), pp. 255–263. ACM Press/Springer-Verlag, London (2004)
31. Mazalek, A.: Tangible Toolkits: Integrating Application Development across Diverse Multi-User and Tangible Interaction Platforms. In: Let's Get Physical Workshop, DCC 2006, Eindhoven, Netherlands (2006)
32. Microsoft. Windows desktop search 3.01 (2007), http://www.microsoft.com/windows/ products/winfamily/desktopsearch/default.mspx

33. Mugellini, E., Rubegni, E., Gerardi, S., Abou Khaled, O.: Using Personal Objects as Tangible Interfaces for Memory Recollection and Sharing. In: 1st International Conference on Tangible and Embedded Interaction 2007, TEI 2007, Baton Rouge, Louisiana, USA (2007)

34. Mugellini, E., Rubegni, E., Abou Khaled, O.: Tangibl: 12th International Conference on Human-Computer Interaction, HCI International 2007, Beijing, China (2007)

35. Noy, N., McGuinness, D.L.: Ontology Development 101: A Guide to Creating Your First Ontology. Technical Report, Stanford University, Stanford, CA, 94305 (2001)

36. Perer, A., Shneiderman, B., Oard, D.W.: Using rhythms of relationships to understand e-mail archives. Journal American Society Inf. Sci. Technol. 57(14), 1936–1948 (2006)

37. Rekimoto, J.: Time-machine computing: a time-centric approach for the information environment. In: 12th annual ACM symposium on User interface software and technology, pp. 45–54. ACM, New York (1999)

38. Ringel, M., Cutrell, E., Dumais, S.T., Horvitz, E.: Milestones in Time: The Value of Landmarks in Retrieving Information from Personal Stores. In: Rauterberg, M., Menozzi, M., Wesson, J. (eds.) INTERACT, Zurich, Switzerland, pp. 184–191. IOS Press, Amsterdam (2003)

39. Rodden, T., Crabtree, A., Hemmings, T., Koleva, B., Humble, J., Åkesson, K.-P., Hansson, P.: Between the dazzle of a new building and its eventual corpse: assembling the ubiquitous home. In: ACM Symposium on Designing Interactive Systems, Cambridge, Massachusetts. ACM Press, New York (2004)

40. Rudolph, L.: Project Oxygen: Pervasive, Human-Centric Computing – An Initial Experience. In: Dittrich, K.R., Geppert, A., Norrie, M.C. (eds.) CAiSE 2001. LNCS, vol. 2068, pp. 1–12. Springer, Heidelberg (2001)

41. Shaer, O., Leland, N., Calvillo-Gamez, E.H., Jacob, R.J.K.: The TAC Paradigm: Specifying Tangible User Interfaces. Personal and Ubiquitous Computing Journal (2004)

42. Smith, G., Czerwinski, M., Meyers, B., Robbins, D., Robertson, G., Tan, D.S.: FacetMap: A Scalable Search and Browse Visualization. IEEE Transactions on Visualization and Computer Graphics 12(5), 797–804 (2006)

43. Sohn, T., Dey, A.K.: iCAP: An Informal Tool for Interactive Prototyping of Context-Aware Applications. In: Extended Abstracts of CHI 2003, pp. 974–975 (2003)

44. Ullmer, B., Ishii, H.: Emerging frameworks for tangible user interfaces. IBM Systems Journal 39, 915–931 (2000)

45. Viegas, F.B., Golder, S., Donath, J.: Visualizing email content: portraying relationships from conversational histories. In: SIGCHI conference on Human Factors in computing systems, pp. 979–988. ACM Press, New York (2006)

46. Walker, W., Lamere, P., Kwok, P., Raj, B., Singh, R., Gouvea, E., Wolf, P., Woelfel, J.: Sphinx-4: A flexible open source framework for speech recognition. Sun Microsystems, Tech. Rep. TR-2004-139 (2004)

47. Wellner, P.: Interacting with paper on the DigitalDesk. Communications of the ACM 36(7), 87–96 (1993)

48. Whittaker, S., Sidner, C.: Email overload: exploring personal information management of email. In: SIGCHI conference on Human factors in computing systems, pp. 276–283. ACM Press, New York (1996)

49. Rubegni, E., Mugellini, E., Abou Khaled, O.: Travelling as social activity, results of the survey. Technical Report (September 2006)

50. Cohen, G.: Memory in the real world. Psychology Press, Hove (1996)

51. Baddeley, A.: Human Memory: Theory and Practice. Psychology Press, UK (1997)

52. Lalanne, D., van den Hoven, E.: Supporting Human Memory with Interactive Systems. In: Proceedings of the British HCI conference 2007, Lancaster, UK, vol. 2, pp. 215–216 (2007)

53. Rusted, J.M., Sheppard, L.M.: Action-based memory in people with dementia: A longitudinal look at tea-making. Neurocase 8, 111–126 (2002)
54. Conway, M.A., Pleydell-Pearce, C.W.: The construction of autobiographical memories in the self-memory system. Psychological Review 107, 261–288 (2000)
55. Ochsner, K.N., Schacter, D.L.: Remembering emotional events: A social cognitive neuroscience approach. In: Davidson, R.J., et al. (eds.) Handbook of Affective Sciences, pp. 643–660. Oxford University Press, Oxford (2003)
56. van den Hoven, E., Eggen, B.: Digital Photo Browsing with Souvenirs. In: Proceedings of the Interact 2003, pp. 1000–1004 (2003)
57. van den Hoven, E., Eggen, B.: Informing Augmented Memory System design through Autobiographical Memory theory. Personal and Ubiquitous Computing journal (2007), http://www.personal-ubicomp.com
58. Glos, J., Cassell, J.: Rosebud: Technological Toys for Storytelling. In: Proceedings of the ACM Conference on Human Factors in Computing Systems (CHI 1997), pp. 359–360. ACM Press, New York (1997)
59. van den Hoven, E., Eggen, B.: Tangible Computing in Everyday Life: Extending Current Frameworks for Tangible User Interfaces with Personal Objects. In: Markopoulos, P., Eggen, B., Aarts, E., Crowley, J.L., et al. (eds.) EUSAI 2004. LNCS, vol. 3295, pp. 230–242. Springer, Heidelberg (2004)
60. Lamming, M., Flynn, M.: Forget-me-not: intimate computing in support of human memory. In: FRIEND21: International symposium on next generation human interface, Meguro Gajoen, Japan, pp. 125–128 (1994)
61. Whittaker, S., Bellotti, V., Gwizdka, J.: Email in Personal Information Management. Communications of the ACM 49(1), 68–73 (2006)
62. Lalanne, D., Ingold, R.: Structuring Multimedia Archives With Static Documents. ERCIM News: Multimedia Informatics 62(62), 19–20 (2005)
63. Ullmer, B.: Tangible Interfaces for Manipulating Aggregates of Digital Information. Doctoral dissertation. MIT Media Lab., USA (2002)
64. Ljungstrand, P., Redström, J., Holmquist, L.E.: WebStickers: Using Physical Tokens to Access, Manage and Share Bookmarks to the Web. In: Designing Augmented Reality Environments, DARE 2000, pp. 23–31 (2000)
65. Streitz, N., Geissler, J., Holmer, T., Konomi, S., Müller-Tomfelde, C., Reischl, W., Rexroth, P., Seitz, P., Steinmetz, R.: i-LAND: An interactive Landscape for Creativity and Innovation. In: Proceedings of the ACM Conference of Human Factors in Computing Systems (CHI 1999), pp. 120–127 (1999)
66. Petersen, M.-G., Grønbæk, K.: Shaping the Ambience of Homes with Domestic Hypermedia. In: Markopoulos, P., Eggen, B., Aarts, E., Crowley, J.L. (eds.) EUSAI 2004. LNCS, vol. 3295, pp. 218–229. Springer, Heidelberg (2004)
67. Stevens, M.M., Abowd, G.D., Truong, K.N., Vollmer, F.: Getting into the living memory box: family archives & holistic design. Personal and Ubiquitous Computing journal 7, 210–216 (2003)
68. Ullmer, B.: Models and Mechanisms for Tangible User Interfaces, Masters thesis. MIT Media Lab., USA (1997)
69. van den Hoven, E.: Graspable Cues for Everyday Recollecting, PhD Thesis, Department of Industrial Design, Eindhoven University of Technology, The Netherlands (2004) ISBN 90-386-1958-8
70. Bationo, A., Kahn, J., Decortis, F.: Traveling narrative as a multi-sensorial experience: A user centered approach of smart objects. In: Proceedings of Smart Objects Conference (sOc 2003), pp. 160–163 (2003)

Why Androids Will Have Emotions: Constructing Human-Like Actors and Communicators Based on Exact Sciences of the Mind

Wolfgang Gessner[1], Gesine Lenore Schiewer[2], and Alex Ringenbach[3]

[1] University of Applied Sciences Northwestern Switzerland, Olten
[2] University of Berne
[3] University of Applied Sciences Northwestern Switzerland, Muttenz

Abstract. The construction of androids as human-like robots depends on the presupposition of being able to interact, communicate and cooperate with humans in order to achieve satisfying results. Realizing these tasks means taking the challenge seriously. This is accomplished by the effort to construct mind-like creatures with subjectivity and possible personhood. Based on a cognitive modeling of emotions and the description of a 'language of mind' (LOM), we develop the representation of situations and the elicitation conditions of emotions together with their dependent dimensions, namely emotional mimics, gesture and posture, action tendencies and speech act latencies. These dimensions are shown to be integrable into a common structure which can be transformed into various applications like innovative structures of MMI and HRI, ranging from service robots to virtual interactions up to MMI-management of driver assistance systems.

Keywords: Android, cognitive emotion theory, human emotion, emotional mimics, gesture and posture, action, speech act, artificial emotion, Man-Machine Interaction (MMI), Human-Robot-Interaction (HRI), Language of Mind (LOT), Subjectivity, Personhood.

1 Introduction

In this paper we develop a broad overview covering most topics that were dealt with in our project Emotional Agents for Controlling Expression, Action and Speech in Man-Machine Interaction' (MMI 1978), including the whole range of situation perception up to the development of emotions and their dependent dimensions like mimic expression, gesture and posture, action latencies and dispositions to speech act utterances. This approach, embedded into a methodological device of 'language of mind', covers modes of subjectivity concerning the attribution of given situations and events up to the inner states of one's own and other minds. This will finally give rise to the possibility of a preliminary approach in reconstructing personhood in humans and in this way will deliver a model for first approaches to android personhood, too.

Former attempts to generate attitude-driven devices for decision and action (like BDI-Architectures) have shown to be too narrow to grasp the complexity of real

D. Lalanne and J. Kohlas (Eds.): Human Machine Interaction, LNCS 5440, pp. 133–163, 2009.
© Springer-Verlag Berlin Heidelberg 2009

situations and too weak to generate realistic and effective steering mechanisms. In contrast, our approach – based on philosophy of mind, on research in cognitive science and on psychological emotion theories – uses a complex concept of 'emotion' with a multitude of dimensions of human emotions comprising the formal description of subjective elicitation conditions as well as typical manners of expression. Therefore we ignored the mixture of emotions at this stage of our work. Our final objective is to develop an artificial tool which gives communicative and actional competencies to human-like robots (androids).

Starting with a systematic analysis of the relations between elicitation conditions of single emotions and their dependent dimensions (emotional mimics, gesture and posture, action latencies and dispositions to speech act utterances) a formalized structure of dependencies, implications and restrictions between these dimensions has been developed. Using the formal tool 'Language of Mind' (LOM) – mainly consisting in various propositional attitudes, personal and temporal indicators and some types of propositional structures – a sort of 'subjectivity' in artificial 'persons' has been defined which is open to inhabit the complex relationship between situation perception and the different actional and communicative reactions mentioned above.

Based on different cognitive emotion theories *elicitation schemes* for 24 emotions[1] have been formulated (cf. chs. 4.2 and 5.2 for details), thus referring simultaneously to subjective representations of external objective situations and to corresponding inner states of the subject (like belief-states, valuations, ability ascriptions and other cognitive attitudes). This subjective situation perception has been generated accordingly by a variant of the appraisal theorist's 'stimulus evaluation check'-method (SEC), which in this cognitive context would better be called 'situation evaluation check'. Thereby the possibility evolved to compare the android's further subjective situation perception (automatically transferred into terms of LOM) with the schematic elicitation conditions already formulated in LOM using a pattern matching process. Consequently the dependent emotion-related dimensional reactions for every detected single emotion could be developed.

This complex rule system of android emotions formulated in LOM will allow first and further steps to their transformation in real androids in order to approve their real competencies and to contribute to their believability and credibility up to a level appropriate enough to be acceptable by human interactors.

2   Theoretical Background: The Neglect and Renewal of Theories of Subjectivity in Modern Psychology

During a long-lasting period of dogmatic behaviouristic traditions (1915 – 1975), mental concepts were eliminated from mainstream psychology as well as from the corresponding philosophical, especially conceptual, methodological and ontological discourse. These mainstream traditions have been (in slightly modified forms and under different headings) prolonged up to the present. In spite of this, different

---

[1] While Ortony, Clore and Collins are dealing with 22 emotions in their best-known cognitive emotion theory (OCC), we are describing 24 emotions. This number of emotions and their selection is due to the aim of our work, the construction of person-like androids.

minority groups have continued to work in the mentalistic tradition – a movement which is now culminating in a new mentalistic and rationalistic orientation in a (real!) 'philosophy of mind' and in cognitive psychology as well.

Among the predecessors of this renewal have been some former contributions to this 'heretic' movement: the reconstruction of subjectivity and primary social structures (Heider 1958), the work of (primarily) Scandinavian logicians of the nineteen-seventies, the logic of self-contemplation (Castaneda 1999), the logic of common sense orientation (Smedslund 1988, 1997), the reconstruction of a 'logic of mind' (Nelson 1982), Jones' 1983 work on communication and few other titles of some other more or less isolated authors. In parallel, work on formal logic, especially modal logic, has found its application in different varieties of 'philosophical logic' (as epistemic, deontic, temporal etc. logic) (cf. the work of von Wright 1979, Nowakowska 1973 and Gessner 1989 for an application to different knowledge concepts, i.e. the epistemic, modal and probability-theoretical modeling of T, S 4, S 5 as classical modal calculi (cf. Chellas 1980, 1995)).

Meanwhile, the renaissance of the mentalistic tradition has led to a reappraisal of former concepts of subjectivity and, with a focus on the newly established paradigm of 'mindreading' (Baron-Cohen 1995, Nichols & Stich 2003, Goldman 2006) and 'empathy' (Schueler 2006), up to new methodological developments of breaking up the 'privileged access' problem in introspection and the utterance of 1st-person sentences in contexts of belief, thought and action (cf. Rödl 2007). This trend has been established by a continuously growing number of publications focusing on the 'science of mind' (Batthany & Elitzur 2006, Thompson 2007, Roberts 2007). This research has amplified and expanded on current issues and theories, especially in new-founded institutions like e.g. the 'Center of Subjectivity Studies' in Copenhagen (Zahavi 2006). In parallel, the subjectivity-related concept of personhood – analyzing the coherence and continuity of subjective states and traits over time – receives increasing attention and is reconstructed anew by means of the methodological tools of esp. analytical philosophy, which also appears in an increasing number of new philosophical publications (cf. Parfit 1984 and Noonan 1989 as classics and Quante 2007 as newly published titles summarizing this research). Taken together, a new paradigm for the behavioural sciences, for cognitive psychology and philosophy of mind is under way, with 'subjectivity' and 'personhood' as their core concepts and with new forms of instrospection and of reconstruction of intrasubjective and intersubjective mental states in their theoretical, empirical and constructive orientations.

3   Modeling of Subjectivity for Generating Android Behaviour

Central to our research is the core concept of 'subjectivity'. It represents the perspectivity which is characteristic for the subjective attribution of concrete situations and also may lead to single emotion elicitation, emotion-related action and/or communicative behaviour to unfold (Gessner 2007 a, p. 9 sqq.). Subjects are 'mediums' representing structures, states and events of the objective world solely from a certain singular perspective and in different quantities and qualifications. They store these elements in the form of representations, deal with these representations in various manners, draw conclusions and act in a, mostly, predictable manner based on these special assumptions of their own (cf. Tuomela 1995).

A formal device for the representation and articulation of subjectivity is given by the 'language of mind' (LOM). Former attempts to represent subjective structures include so-called BDI-Systems (cf. Burkhard 2003, ch. 24.5.7, Woolridge 2000, ch. 2), in which beliefs, desires and intentions are seen as the building blocks for the generation of action schemes or planning processes. These elements have been shown to be too narrow and limited to fulfill these tasks. Therefore, the reconstruction of mental states and of the ways human beings reflect on them and communicate them to others in searching self-understanding and understanding of others shows up to be essential for reconstructing the inner organization of subjectivity (cf. Morton 2003). This trend refers back to rule-based and even mentalistic models and has already reached robotics (cf. Xie 2003). Xie speaks of 'mental syntax' and of 'imitating the mind' as 'the embodiment of an artificial mind' in connection with 'autonomous behaviour' (p. 306 ff.).

Many attempts have been made in trying to explicate the concept of 'subjectivity' (cf. Pauen 2001, the variants of Metzinger's 'representationalist' self-model theory of subjectivity (Metzinger 1993, 2003) and Zahavi's (2006) monograph on 'subjectivity and selfhood', which covers the whole field of such approaches). Beyond these conceptual refinements we have decided to follow a pragmatic line in using propositional attitudes to define a 'language of mind' (LOM), which can represent the intrasubjective and intersubjective structures of mental attitudes in an abstract and appropriate manner as well.

3.1 A Short Introduction to the 'Language of Mind' (LOM)

In the abridged form to be presented here (cf. Gessner 2004, ch. 6 and 7 for more details), propositional attitudes together with the conventionally given logical operators ($\&$, v, $\neg$), modal operators ($\Diamond$, $\square$) and some special entailment operators ($\otimes \Rightarrow$ for implication by natural laws, $\bullet \Rightarrow$ for cognitive implication) and with some propositional categories (P for 'proposition', Δ for ,event', HS resp. HS* for '(the actualization of an) action scheme', Ω for an existing opportunity to act)) build the core vocabulary of LOM.

Different dimensions of propositional attitudes have been proposed. In a first and 'minimalistic' approach the following types have been chosen:

Epistemic operators are B (....) (belief) and K (....) (knowledge), the operator of ability C (....) (can do) describes the ability to actualize an action scheme HS, i.e., HS*. Volitional operators are W (...) (wish) for the disposition to evaluate the actualization of a corresponding action scheme positively, I (...) for intention, i.e. the readiness to actualize this action scheme, HS*. A normative operator O (...) (obligation) stands for the existence of (moral or judicial) norms, i.e. imperatives steering actions.

All propositional attitudes are accompanied by the subscripts ε, α, Π for *ego* (I, me) resp. *alter* (the other person) resp. *'persons in general'* for the 'generalized person'. Subscripted time indicators V (for *past*) resp. G (for *present*) resp. Z (for *future*) indicate the time span in which the attitude is given, with V $\rightarrow$ G (*past to present*) or V $\rightarrow$ Z (*present to future*) etc. indicating the transition of time spans over which the attitude is held. Finally, $\lceil$ indicates that the (complex) proposition before this sign is valid only under the condition of the truth of the proposition following after this sign.

Table 1. Symbols used in LOM

&, v, ¬	Propositional logic operators	Logical
◊,□	Modal logic operators	operators

P	Proposition (Reference and predication)	Propositional
Δ	Event	categories
HS	Action scheme	
HS*	Actualization of HS	
Ω	Existing opportunity to act	

K (P)	Knowledge of P	Propositional
B (P)	Belief of P	attitudes
C (HS)	Ability to HS*	
W (P) or W (HS*)	Wish (for P) or to HS*	
I (HS*)	Intention to HS*	
O (HS*)	Obligation to HS*	

ε, α, Π	Personal subscripts	Subscripts to
V, G, Z	Time subscripts	propositional
$\rightarrow$	Time span subscript	attitudes

$\otimes\Rightarrow$	Implication by natural law	Special
$\bullet\Rightarrow$	Cognitive implication	implications
$\ulcorner$	Condition operator	

3.2 Subjectivity in Action: Perspectivity, Intrasubjectivity, Intersubjectivity

'Objective' situations as being the counterpart of the efforts of scientists to determine them can be discerned from subjective states representing the perspectivity and single-mindedness of a person viewing a situation. So 'being situated' means not 'being in accordance with scientist's recognitions and findings' but viewing a situation as-such-and-such from a personal viewpoint. Nonetheless, according to 'Thomas' Theorem' (Thomas 1928), viewing a situation from a personal view makes it real in a certain sense insofar as this person will act according to her personal view and not in adopting the objectivity of real knowledge about this situation. So it does make sense to depict such personal views as mental states in order to reconstruct the starting points of subjects in dealing with such situations.

Mental states of different order and complexity can be formulated using the nomenclature of LOM introduced above, which expresses mental structures at the same time and makes them describable in their indispensable perspectivity:

Simple (non-iterated) propositional attitudes as *intrasubjective mental states* could be assumptions like $B_{\varepsilon,G}$ (P), wishes like $W_{\varepsilon,V}$ (Δ) or intentions like $I_{\varepsilon,G}$ (HS* $(\Delta)_{\varepsilon,G\rightarrow Z}$). But intrasubjective attitudes can also be complex, i.e. iterated propositional attitudes like $K_{\varepsilon,G} (B_{\varepsilon,V} (\neg (\Delta) T (\Delta) I \neg (\Delta))) \ulcorner HS^* (\Delta) _{\varepsilon, G \to Z}$, which indicate a higher order assumption about changes in the objective world under a special condition, with $(\neg (\Delta) T (\Delta) I \neg (\Delta))$ signifying the transition of a certain event into its contradiction instead of continuing without the intervention of an additional causal factor. A further example, the estimation of opportunities of getting future knowledge could be written as $\neg B_{\varepsilon,G \to Z} (C_{\Pi,G \to Z} (K_{\Pi,G \to Z} (P \vee \neg P)))$, expressing a general sceptical belief about such opportunities.

Turning to *intersubjective mental attitudes* (i.e., attitudes representing or reflecting not only personal states, but the mental state(s) of at least one other person simultaneously), the following formula describes the inner structure of a changing personal assumption concerning the intentions of another person:

$$B_{\varepsilon,V \to G} (K_{\varepsilon,V \to Z} (I_{\alpha,G} (HS^* (\Delta))) \ \& \ B_{\varepsilon,G \to Z} (\neg I_{\alpha,G} (HS^* (\Delta)))).$$

In determining the options given in a potential action situation, somebody could have arrived at the following description of his mental state:

$$B_{\varepsilon,V \to G} (C_{\alpha, G \to Z} (HS^* (\Delta))) \ \& \ \Omega_{\alpha,G \to Z} (HS^* (\Delta)) \ \& \ K_{\varepsilon,A} (\neg O_{\Pi,G \to Z}$$
$$(\neg HS^* (\Delta))).$$

The subjective state described here expresses some complex attitudes concerning abilities and opportunities to act, coexisting with an assumption of the non-intervention of act-relevant norms.

Subsequently, *transsubjective attitudes* can be formulated as attitudes which are directed in a reflective perspective to one's own mental states and simultaneously to the mental states of more than one other person, i.e., when analysing the influence of a third person on another person in one's own reflective perspective.

The examples given demonstrate that by introducing LOM a conceptual framework is set which enables real people to express their subjective states in arbitrarily gradable complexity and at the same time enables researchers to describe these subjective mental states in a precise and comprehensible manner.

3.3 Theses on Interaction, Communication and Cooperation between Androids and Men

Having described LOM in the proceeding chapter four theses can be introduced in the following to circumscribe the relation of subjectivity statements to questions of communication, interaction and cooperation between androids and men in a unifying perspective:

Thesis 1: Propositional attitudes (PA) are the building blocks of the representation of subjectivity in constituting a singular perspective.

The general form of an (eventually iterated) intentional sentence (built from propositional attitudes together with a dependent proposition) is as follows:

**Propositional Attitude (1) (Π_i, t_1) (Propositional Attitude (2) (Π_j, t_2) ....
(Propositional Attitude (n) (Π_k, t_n) (Proposition (Reference & Predication))))**

The intentional object of propositional attitudes are propositions as describing circumstances, which refer to objects and connect them with predicates relating attributes and properties to them. This singular perspective arising in the simplest case from only one intentional sentence can, however, become arbitrarily complex:

- Non-iterated propositional attitudes represent the *elementary ego-perspective* in a certain time or time span.
- Iterated propositional attitudes are able to represent multidimensional *intra-subjective* attitudes, eventually supplemented by using time indicators.
- Iterated propositional attitudes are able to represent unidimensional or multi-dimensional *intersubjective* attitudes by using person indicators.
- Iterated propositional attitudes are able to represent *intrasubjective and inter-subjective* attitudes as well, eventually supplemented by using time indicators.

Thesis 2: Subjectivity is described as a qualitatively und quantitatively open set of possibilities, generated from simple or iterated propositional attitudes based on the corpus of the language of mind (LOM).

Subjectivity as an abstract concept corresponds to personhood in the form of a struc-tured set of intentional sentences which are or can be connected by logical operators. Any determined set of intentional sentences represents a certain identifiable and enu-merable person, or the status of a person given at this time. All mental states of a person may have started with an initial state plus all arbitrary changes she has gone through since then. This mental trajectory constitutes the history and by this the iden-tity of that person.

Thesis 3: Personhood[2] as a set of complex mental states following one another on the time line results in a mental trajectory in the 'possibility-space' of subjectivity.

This trajectory results in the successive adoption of propositional attitudes which fixes this space of possibility of mental attitudes cumulatively but never restricts it in its further development. Relations between intentional sentences provide for an expan-sion of the present personal condition by the addition of new intentional sentences, or they restrict the possibility of adding new or further intentional sentences, which are incompatible with the existing structure or its logical implications. Not all elements of a personal condition must be present simultaneously, but they must be activatable and reflectable. Mental state spaces or Mental State Systems (MSS) are the basic catego-ries of intrasubjective subsistence, intersubjective communicative expression and successful interaction as well.

Thesis 4: Interaction between subjects presupposes the modeling of the subjectivity of the interaction partner.

Every kind of potential communication, interaction and cooperation presupposes an (at least partial) external perception of the communication-, interaction- and cooperation-partner in the personal subject given. This possibility of a interpersonal

---

[2] For a detailed analysis of the positions in theories of personhood and for a reconstruction and discussion of the 'conditions of personhood' (the body criterion, the memory criterion, the substance criterion, the criterion of attitude competence), which cannot be developed here (cf. Gessner 2007 b and Gessner & Schiewer 2008 for further details).

perception of the other person, i.e. of the inner representation of the (only conjecturable) representation of the subjective structures of this other person (and her tentative insinuation) forms the basic possibility of the most elementary forms of sociality. Under this presupposition a robot capable of interaction must also be provided with the possibility of 'knowing' itself (in the sense of having the possibility of self-perception) in order to be able to recall or retrieve the actual state of its own mental states and mental conditions. Additionally, an android robot capable of interaction has to be able to ‚know' his potential interaction partner(s), i.e. he has to have at his disposal a personal self-perception of his personal perception of others in the sense of being able to recall or retrieve the actual mental states of this foreign partner. Cooperation as an abstract possibility is then no longer restricted to the biological bearers of these evolutionary processes, but is transformable in non-biological entities. It is presumed that these entities provide sufficient complexity in their hardware to represent software structures with a degree of complexity which will afford the processing of structures of the kind mentioned. Thus, the possibility of androids as cooperating and communicating partners of men has been set.

4 Emotions Seen on a Subjective Base: Cognitive Theories

4.1 The Scope of Cognitive Theories of Emotions

It has to be stated that emotions comprehend many different aspects including physiological ones, individual and subjective feelings, cognitive facets, expressions of emotions, social and cultural aspects and so on. The emotion psychologist D. Ulich accentuated already in the eighties: "The decision for or against a specific model of emotions depends on what we are aiming at. Nobody is able to study emotions generally. In any case the regarding interest of exploration has to be specified." (Ulich, 1989, p. 125). Therefore no authoritative definition and no exclusive notion of emotions exist whereas a great number of models do.

The so-called 'cognitive emotion theories' and 'appraisal theories' are discussed predominantly with regard to affective computing. The elicitation of emotions is understood as a consequence of specific cognitions. Cognitive appraisal is considered to be central to emotions. Hence the analysis of cognitive triggers of emotions and their consequences in expression, planning and acting as well represent an important aspect of these theories. There are many different approaches of this kind; attention should be paid for example to those of A. Ortony, G. L. Clore and A. Collins (1988), I. J. Roseman (1983), K. R. Scherer (1999, 2001), N. H. Frijda (1986), K. Oatley and P.N. Johnson-Laird (1983) and some others. According to the latest variants of appraisal theory, persons use a fixed number of dimensions or criteria in the evaluation of situations:

1. Intrinsic characteristics of objects or events, such as novelty or acceptability for the person(s) involved
2. The significance of the event for the individual's needs or goals
3. The individual's ability to influence or cope with the consequences of the event, including the evaluation of 'agency'
4. The compatibility of the event with social or personal standards, norms, or values.

The concept 'appraisal' was first used in M. Arnold's (1960) *Emotion and Personality* and has been deepened and detailed in the work of R. Lazarus and his coworkers (Cf. Lazarus, Averill and Opton (1970), Lazarus (1977, 1984, 1993), Lazarus & Lazarus (1994) and Lazarus (1999). The state of the art in cognitive emotion theory is recapitulated in Reisenzein (2000), Reisenzein, Müller and Schützwohl (2003), and in Scherer (1999) in historical perspective. The state of development concerning all aspects and dimensions connected with cognitive theories of emotion, together with methodological questions and empirical research, is given in Scherer, Schorr and Johnstone (Eds.) (2001). Another now very prominent 'structural' access to emotions is Ortony, Clore and Collins (1988) *The Cognitive Structure of Emotions* (abbreviated: OCC-theory) with their '*Emotions-as-valenced-reactions Claim*' and its successors in Ortony et al. (2003) and (2005). It is based on the situational concern of individuals, thereby referring to reactions, to events, to actors and to objects.

The specific approach of Ortony, Clore and Collins (1988) is currently considered to be one of the most elaborate and systematic ones (cf. Reisenzein, Meyer and Schützwohl, 2003, p. 171). This approach is characterized by the general intention "to lay the foundation for a computationally tractable model of emotion. In other words, we would like an account of emotion that could, in principle, be used in an Artificial Intelligence (AI) system that would, for example, be able to reason about emotions." (Ortony, Core and Collins 1988, p. 2; see also Schiewer 2006 and Schiewer 2008).

In general, current methodology and theory building views emotions as valenced reactions to events, agents, or objects, their particular nature being determined by the way in which the eliciting situation is construed (cf. Ortony, Clore and Collins 1988, p. 13). A further step considers that one of the most salient aspects of the experience of emotions is that their intensity varies both within and between people. Therefore the theory of emotion of Ortony, Clore and Collins addresses the question of what determines intensity. Their general view is that the intensity of emotions is influenced by a number of variables. All of them are present in the construal of the situation that gives rise to the emotion in the first place. Thus, in order to address the question of intensity, they consider the mechanism whereby emotion-inducing stimuli are appraised. They even make an attempt to explain why and under what conditions human beings are not able to cope with the emotion-inducing situation or the emotion itself. Thus, Ortony, Clore and Collins take into account the differentiation between positive and negative consequences of emotions.

These studies, taken together, make it clear that cognitive emotion elicitation depends on subjective factors and therefore may result in *individual*, *variable* and *relative* emotion-steered actions. On the other side, non-cognitive emotions don't result in individually steered but in inescapable consequences. Non-cognitive emotions, like, for example, disgust, are supposed to be not individual but comparable to reflexes, which prevail in all animals but are not constitutive for human beings.

Therefore we elaborated the analytical instruments regarding the inner perspective of human beings and their interpretation of emotion-inducing situations. Our approach focuses on the analysis of the individual interpretation mechanisms regarding an abstract emotion-inducing situation, whereas appraisal theories usually focus on concrete standard situations of emotion elicitation. However, a complete emotion theory has to explain the specific kind of individual dispositions, that is the individual cognitive triggering, causing a specific interpretation of an emotion-inducing situation (cf. Gessner 2004, p. 127 et sqq.).

4.2 The Elicitation of Emotions: Qualitative Analysis

The LOM-tool developed above will serve as a means to describe the elicitation conditions of emotions, too. In this form of application, topical and focal elements have to be distinguished: *Topical elements* as attitudes which are already given in a subject, i.e. the (mostly value-related or norm-related) elements which are the background of emotions to originate, and *focal elements* as the (mostly epistemic) elements which are developed in representing the actual situation which gives rise to the 'triggering' of the corresponding emotion. Based on this an emotion like 'ANNOYANCE / IRRITATION (the German 'Ärger') can be understood as individually instantiated reaction following the standardized topical and focal elements given in the mental state of a human being which is describable in an abstract, i.e. not situation-specific manner by using LOM as follows:

(1)	$K_{\varepsilon,G} (\Delta)_G$	1st focal element
(2)	& $K_{\varepsilon,V\rightarrow G} (O_{\alpha,V\rightarrow G} (HS^* (\Delta)_{V\rightarrow G}))$	1st topical element
(3)	& $B_{\varepsilon,V\rightarrow G} (K_{\alpha,V\rightarrow G} (O_{\alpha,V\rightarrow G} (HS^* (\Delta)_G)))$	2nd topical element
(4)	& $B_{\varepsilon,G} (I_{\alpha,V\rightarrow G} \neg (HS^* (\Delta)_G))$	2nd focal element

$\bullet\Rightarrow$ **ANNOYANCE / IRRITATION**   **Resulting emotion**

$\ulcorner \{ K_{\varepsilon,V\rightarrow G} (HS^* (\Delta)_{V\rightarrow G}) \otimes\Rightarrow \neg (\Delta)_G) \}$ Background cognition

According to this scheme, the 24 emotions selected for the future use in modelling androids' behaviour (ADMIRATION, ANGER, ANNOYANCE, ANTICIPATION, BOREDOM, COMPASSION, DISAPPOINTMENT, FEAR, FEELING OF GUILT, GRATITUDE, HAPPINESS, HOPE, HORROR, INDIGNATION, JOY, PRIDE, REGRET, RELIEF, REPUGNANCE, SATISFACTION, SHAME, SORROW, SURPRISE, SUSPICION) have been formulated[3]. Elicitation formulae like this lie at the core of our theory: Together with situation descriptions they build one of the the *independent* dimensions in our analysis of the six dimensions constitutive of emotions.

4.3 Dependent (DD) and (ID) Independent Dimensions of Emotions

Independent dimensions of emotions (ID) are conceived as building the starting point in the elicitation process: They determine which single emotion will be triggered, depending on the variable elicitation schemes of single emotions (ID 2) together with the subjective representation of the current situation (ID 1), compared with one another in a mental pattern matching process. The triggering of a single emotion scheme will, in turn, generate the dependent dimensions (DD) connected with it:

---

[3] The 24 emotions cited originated from a priori-reasoning about their potential functionality in Human-Robot-Interaction. See also the comparable, but smaller list of KISMET-emotions presented in Breazeal (2002) and in Breazeal & Brooks (2005) based on functional considerations, too.

ID 1: Situation representation
ID 2: Elicitation formulae

DD 1: Facial mimics
DD 2: Gesture & posture
DD 3: Actions
DD 4: Speech acts

Taken together, the conditions for ID 1 and ID 2 previously formulated above define the complete elicitation condition for ANNOYANCE / IRRITATION. Moreover, LOM can be used to formulate the corresponding dimensions of this (and all other) cognitive emotion(s) in the following way:

1. In utilizing the fact that emotion elicitation and the buildup of action latencies refer to the same situation-type, the parallels and interactions of unfolding emotions and dispositions to take specific actions can be analysed.
2. Accordingly, the constitutive rules for speech acts (Searle & Vanderveken 1985) as cognitive patterns describable in LOM are 'tested' by the subject's language-generating mechanisms on 'matching' to the same situation and will show up to predict the appearance of specific speech acts in reaction to this situation, which in turn will interact with real actions and the emotion proper having emerged in this situation.
3. The emoting subject's emotional mimics indicate inner states of this subject and (at the same time) have imperative functions on other persons receiving this 'signalling'. LOM can be used to reformulate these inner states and allows the reformulation of the relation between these specific subjective states and the semiotic apparatus of facial expression in its different dimensions.
4. Finally, LOM can be used in defining production rules for describing restrictions on the corpus of gestures and postures which could in principle interact with specific inner states of subjects and the triggering of core emotions by matching the appropriate elicitation condition of an emotion.

The following table 2 depicts the principal inner relations of the core theory of emotion described here. Besides this it shows that the systematic development of situation representations (as a *precursory* theory) is not part of this project but will be left to the further development of existing approaches. Correspondingly, the project is not involved in real robot engineering (as *follow-up* technology) but tries to develop some steering mechanism of possible and meaningful android behaviour and (as a first step) to generate simulations of this behaviour in appropriate media of presentation.

In the following we will concentrate (due to limited space) on speech acts as dependent dimensions[4]. The other dimensions are circumscribed in an abbreviated style just to characterize them without any claim of completeness.

---

[4] For preliminary analysis and descriptions of the remaining dimensions see our working papers which can be ordered on request at wolfgang.gessner@fhnw.ch. These working papers will be integrated into a further publication (in preparation).

Table 2. Relations between the six dependent and independent dimensions

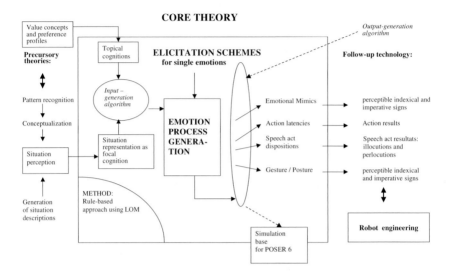

5   The Six Dimensions of Emotions Revealed

ANNOYANCE / IRRITATION can be shown as an illustrative example for dimensional analysis. The two independent and the four dependent dimensions mentioned will be characterized in their relation to emotional schemes respectively.

5.1   Stimulus Evaluation Checks (SEC) and the Generation of Subjective Representations

The first independent dimension is the representation of a situation seen by the special person who is exposed to it (ID 1). Lacking viable systems of situation detection and categorization, we chose the resort of formulating a questionnaire which depicts all the relevant situation characteristics needed to determine the matching of an emotion elicitation scheme with the situation given (Cf. Gessner 2007 a, p. 62 et seqq.). In detail, there are, among others, questions concerning evaluations of the situation, the intentional objects in question, conformity to currently relevant standards and norms, current goals and expectations of the subject, his attributions concerning controllability of the situation and questions of status to be answered in respect to the (real or imagined) situation given[5]:

Questionnaire example

The emotion to be queried is 'XXXXXXXXX'

---

[5] The idea of creating such a questionnaire is due to precursors in Scherer's appraisal-theoretic 'Stimulus Evaluation Check' (SEC) (Cf. Scherer et al. 2001).

Some Emotions refer to a change in a situation, through which something will be (or was) caused. How is it with this emotion:

> irrelevant / unimportant
> relevant

If relevant,
will the changes be / or were these changes caused....
    (More than one answer is possible)
> by you
> by someone else
> by restricted conditions

If relevant,
will the changes be / or were these changes......
> judged rather as positive
> judgeded rather as negative

If relevant,
When do / did these changes take place
(more than one answer is possible)
> more in the distant past
> in the present or recent past
> possibly right now or soon
> possibly in the distant future

Taken together answers to questions of this kind deliver a sufficient amount of data to determine which single emotion can be triggered (or not). Formally, these data (after being translated in LOM) will serve as input to a pattern matching process which create the emotion or proto-emotions compatible with the situation description given.

5.2 Elicitation Schemata of Emotions

Situations together with their subjective evaluation give rise to emotions, and emotions are compatible with certain situations as appraised or evaluated by a special person in her personal sight of this situation. It has to be stressed that both this situation description (ID 1) and the formal parts of the elicitation formula (ID 2) are *abstract* ones, i.e. that the *concrete elements in both dimensions* have to be 'translated' into these abstract stances. So we have to deal with, for example, (positive or negative) *evaluations in general* or (given or absent) *events in general* in order to give viable descriptions for the elicitation formulae of emotions. This is due to the fact that all 'realistic' description of situations and emotional triggering is in danger of 'misplaced concreteness', which would undermine all possibilities of theoretical reconstructions of these relationships (Cf. Gessner 2004, ch. 7 for a thorough reconstruction and justification of this view). Only under the presupposition of such abstractness will the algorithmic structure of emotion elicitation as a pattern matching process be possible, either in real everyday persons or in the theoretical reconstructions of their performance.

5.3 Emotional Facial Mimics

Being confronted with a personal emotional state, one is disposed to inner feelings (the so-called 'qualia'), one will develop perceptions of one's action tendencies and will accordingly observe one's tendencies to utter certain sentences. Besides these *private mental episodes* there is a *public dimension* of observable facial mimics which displays most of our inner feelings and states to others, eventually without being consciously noticed by us as the bearers of this mimical signalling system. This system of communication of inner mental states could be reconstructed as being closely connected with the elicitation conditions of the corresponding emotion and also (indirectly) with our perception of the situation given. In detail we found five dimensions to be relevant:

- Agentator (connected with action tendencies), represented by the curvature of the eye-brows
- Agitator (for action latency), represented by the distance between eye-brow and eye
- Concentrator (a kind of intentional relation of the emotion), represented by direction of gaze
- Evaluator (connected with actual valuation(s)), represented by curvature of the lips
- Proximator (actual time-relation to the intentional object of the emotion), represented by the degree of opening/closing of the mouth.

All these dimensions are connected to the whole range of muscular movements which is constitutive of our emotional mimics[6], and the flexible characteristics connected with them can be described in detail (cf. Gessner 2007 a, p. 29 et seqq.). Production rules will serve as transformation rules to 'translate' these characteristics into the muscular movements which we perceive conjunctively as the characteristic expression of a certain single emotion.

5.4 Gesture and Posture

In situations of being exposed to an emotional state not only our inner feelings, action dispositions and verbal dispositions will change, but (besides to our facial mimics) our whole body, and especially our arms and hands will undergo some specific alterations. Posture as a dimension of our main body behaviour may support certain action tendencies but can also stand as an independent sign as well (compare the body posture of people being sad or excited by joy). Gestures (considered as movements of our arms and hands and the position of our head) are the most difficult ones to interpret due to their context-sensitivity, cultural non-universality or individual idiosyncrasy. Nonetheless we have tried to develop lists of special movements being connected with intentional or conventional meanings according to empirical observations. Based on these lists we have tried to develop contingency tables showing their compatibility

---

[6] Combination of muscular movements, the so-called 'action-units' developed by Ekman (1978 et. seqq.) in his 'Facial Action Coding System' are realized in humans to produce these emotion-related mimic expressions, but must not necessarily be considered for the production of artificial mimics in androids. This is due to our experience that even simplified facial states and movements (as in comic strips), seen as a purely semiotic system, can afford an articulate understanding of the corresponding emotions – maybe even better ones as the original expressions shown by humans.

respectively incompatibility with the 24 emotions. Up to now, Ekman and Friesen (1969) proposed the most current systematization of non-verbal behavior. They differentiate five classes by function:

- Emblems: non-verbal acts, which can be translated into verbal language and defined as a term
- Illustrators: gestures, which are closely linked to the corresponding verbal expression
- Regulators: non-verbal acts and gestures having the function of regulating dialogues
- Affect display: especially as far as mimic is concerned, although there are some descriptions of affect displaying gestures, too
- Adaptors: non-verbal activities allowing the physical control of affective needs

Actually, even the most advanced German research project in the field of gestures follows this classification in its 'Berliner Lexikon der Alltagsgesten', being developed by the 'Arbeitsstelle für Semiotik' at the Technische Universität Berlin. Nonetheless, in this context exclusively emblems are considered. Different to this our project is concerned with all kinds of gestures (especially emblems, illustrators, regulators and adaptors) linked to emotions. Because of the aforementioned culture dependency and relativity of gestures in general and of emblems in particular, we realized that it would be problematic just to list up gestures and the corresponding semantic content in a so-called 'gesticon'. The selection of entries could only be more or less incidental and therefore useless with regard to the construction of an intercultural understandable android. Likewise, the description of singular emblems and other gestures in relation to specific emotions did not turn out to be the right solution. There are very similar gestures like pointing a finger at something accompanying different and even opposite emotions. Instead of this, a survey of significant qualities of gestures proved to be an adequate manner of dealing with the problem allowing the correlation of gestures and emotions, which is given by the following list of qualities:

- Sedation/low-level tonus   vs.   excitement/high-level tonus
- Negative/sadness   vs.   positive/pleasure
- Defensive   vs.   aggressive
- Separation   vs.   opening
- Retirement   vs.   devotion
- 'To me'   vs.   'away from me'

These pairs of opposite qualities are a further development of Wilhelm Wundt's dimensions with the oppositions positive and negative, excitement and sedation, tense and relaxation, being generally suitable to all of the five classes of non-verbal behavior categorized by Ekman and Friesen. They are composed on two axes similar to the dimensional models of emotions well known since Wundt's approach, too. Based on this a 4-dimensional classification of gestures has become feasible, which will safeguard a minimum of requisite gestures for androids.

5.5 Actions

In a sense, actions could be viewed as the ultimate rationale of emotions. Emotions without corresponding actions seem to be useless because without alterations to the situation on which emotions react there could be no increase in survival value, better satisfaction of one's needs or values or status gain for the person exposed to that situation. So we have tried to determine the relevant types of actions which, by their results and consequences, can change the situation for the person under consideration in a beneficial way. Essentially, we found two different dimensions of actions which, in our view, cannot be united in a single dimension: 'Emotion-related movement structures' and 'Intentional behaviour related to emotions'.

To characterize 'movements related to emotions' we developed an abstract symbolic nomenclature which allows the representation of the different movements allocated with certain emotions according to the kinds and directions of these movements and to the kind of subjects and objects involved. Hence, we could identify 24 (partially complex) movement types as being naturally and constantly connected with the 24 emotions selected.

The second dimension accommodates the traditional view of action generation (cf. v. Wright 1979) by reconstructing the relevant types of propositional attitudes which contribute to the generation of action intentions (esp. beliefs, ascriptions of ability and opportunity, values and goal states). The range of these schemata varies from (very primitive) 'practical syllogisms' up to (fully-fledged and complicated) schemata for building intentions in dependence of complex combinations of mental premises in persons (for a more thorough analysis see Gessner 2007 a, p. 37 et seqq., Gessner 2007 c and Gessner 2007 d).

In any case it seems reasonable to reconsider both dimensions in their respective contribution to coping with situations emotionally by mere elementary movements or by more elaborated and deliberate actions.

5.6 Speech Acts

Speech act theory deals with both the subject of a proposition and the intentions and dispositions of the speaker (the illocution). Different linguistic variables like word order, intonation, punctuation, verbal mood and the use of performative verbs indicate the corresponding illocutionary act. Illocutionary acts like the expression of wishes are supposed to be universal and a general character of languages. They are expressible by performative verbs belonging to a single language.

Illocutionary acts are rule conducted and can be precisely described by so-called 'constitutive rules' as demonstrated by Searle (1969). Constitutive rules establish an activity or action by being 'social actions' of a certain kind defined by these rules. 'Regulatory rules' differ from constitutive rules in that they concern an existing activity or action. A game like football is based on constitutive rules since it does not exist at all without the rules in question, while good table manners depend on regulatory rules; in this case, the activity of eating is just shaped. Searle's description of constitutive rules is: "X is regarded as Y" or "X is regarded as Y in the context of C".

Constitutive rules are formulated as conditions: Which conditions are necessary and adequate so that the illocutionary act in question is performed successfully and completely by the expression of a given sentence? Speech acts are thus performed in accordance with groups of constitutive rules on the basis of valid conventions of a respective language. Nonetheless, the lingual expression of a speech act can vary in different languages. For instance, one can give a promise in French by *'Je promets'* and in English by saying *'I promise'*. This depends on respective lexical rules and not on conventions of French or English that a specific lexical expression is regarded as the adoption of an obligation (and nothing else).

The semantical rules for the use of an adequate illocutionary indicator *Pr* for a promise are:

- Propositional content rule: *Pr* is to be uttered only in the context of a sentence (or larger stretch of discourse) T, the utterance of which predicates some future act *A* of the speaker *S*.
- Preparatory rule I: *Pr* is to be uttered only if the hearer *H* would prefer *S*'s doing *A* to his not doing *A*, and *S* believes *H* would prefer *S*'s doing *A* to his not doing *A*.
- Preparatory rule II: *Pr* is to be uttered only if it is not obvious to both *S* and *H* that *S* will do *A* in the normal course of events.
- Sincerity rule: *Pr* is to be uttered only if *S* intends to do *A*.
- Essential rule: The utterance of *Pr* counts as the undertaking of an obligation to do *A*.

These rules are ordered: only if the propositional content rule is satisfied do the subsequent rules apply, and the essential rule applies only if the preparatory rules and the sincerity rule are satisfied as well (cf. Searle 1969, 63).

5.6.1 The Compatibility of Speech Acts with Emotions

Speech act latencies, i.e. dispositions to react to specific situations by selected speech acts in emotional contexts, are one of the dependent dimensions of emotions. Emotions proper and speech acts will be shown to be complementary types of reactions to cope with emotion-arising situations in a restriction model, which includes (according to the emotions given) some speech acts as consistent with these emotions, and others as inconsistent or at least implausible.

5.6.2 The Common Source of Speech Acts and Emotions

Aiming at the integrative development of a structural theory of emotion and action resulting in a new communication medium at the user interface between android robots and humans, human emotion can serve as a model for analyzing, reconstructing and implementing the complex interrelations of mimics, gestures, verbal communication and elicitation of action schemes. In our approach, verbal communication as such is explicated as speech acts, which have been shown to be rule-governed communicative activities depending on subjective representations of the objective situation given (Austin 1950, Searle 1969, Searle & Vanderveken 2005).

In some way comparable to this the elicitation of (cognitive) emotions can be understood as being triggered by (a) focal and topical cognitions of the subject and (b) by the subjective representation of situations already mentioned (Cf. Gessner 2004, ch. 7). So the utterance of speech acts (according to their constitutive rules) and the elicitation of emotions have a common base in relying on the same situation representation.

Furthermore, the constitutive rules of speech acts and the elicitation conditions of emotions can both be formalized in a 'language of mind' based on propositional attitudes (Cf. Gessner 2004 and Gessner & Schiewer (2007). This amounts to the possibility of comparing the generative structure of emotions and of speech acts eventually corresponding to them on a common base, not only as regards to their respective contents, but methodologically as well.

5.6.3   The Logical Form of Speech Acts in Relation to Emotions

Independent of where and whether a speech act will be executed, every speech act is disposed to a logical form which determines its success conditions and puts it into a relation to other speech acts. Searle and Vanderveken (1985, 2) aimed at presenting this formal requirement independently of the different corresponding concrete possibilities of expression in the different languages. Based on this, a number of so-called illocutionary verbs of English were analysed in an abstract manner. In the context of illocutionary logic (which represents a further development of speech act theory) the following questions shall be answered (cf. Searle/Vanderveken 1985, 6):

- Which conditions are the components of illocutionary force and which ones are the necessary and adequate conditions of the successful execution of elementary illocutionary acts? How can the success conditions of complex illocutionary acts be defined?
- What is the logical structure of the set of all illocutionary forces?
- Which logical relations exist between the different illocutionary types? Under which conditions does the execution of a speech act dispose for, or even provoke, another illocutionary act?

Formally, the 'constitutive rules' of every speech act can be described and reformulated in terms of the same language of mind (LOM) as the elicitation rules of emotions. In terms of contents, it turns out that there are parallel relations between the propositional contents of speech acts and the intentional objects of emotions (i.e., the 'objects' as events, persons, conditions etc.) on which emotions focus. Furthermore, there are knowledge states, valuations, normative relations and ascriptions of ability which appear typically, albeit in changing combinations, in the elicitation formulas of every emotion, too. This suggests the assumption that clues arise or even have coincidence rules derived from the parallelism of the mental conditions mentioned in constitutive rules of single speech acts and in the elicitations rules of single emotions, resulting in the 'fitting together' (or compatibility) and also in the incompatibility of single speech acts with special emotions. The minimal result of such an analysis are, as shown below, contingency tables between the 24 emotions analysed and the 41 speech acts analysed, as an amount of compatibility for the simultaneous appearance or as an amount of restriction for their incompatibility. Complex coincidence rules from which strict connections between these two dimensions could be derived directly – based on comparisons between elements of the situation representation, the elicitation formulae for emotions and the constitutive rules for speech acts – would be the maximum result.

In his own attempt to answering these questions, D. Vanderveken (1985, 1990, 1) applies the logical apparatus of his general semantics to English performatives and formulates translation rules for a great number of English performative verbs. The purpose of this translation consists in explaining the logical form of the illocutionary acts in question, the translation rules being based on the lexical analysis of these performative verbs.

For example, according to D. Vanderveken (1991 (2), 159), the formalisation of the speech act ,REQUEST ' (Aufforderung) is done in the following way:

> "(16) *require*: To require is to demand the hearer that he do something with the preparatory condition that it needs to be done."

Comparing Vanderveken's analysis with the formalisation of the speech act REQUEST (Aufforderung) using the 'Language of Mind' (LOM) and being based on the earlier analysis of Searle this will deliver the following structural results[7]:

SPEECH ACT	REQUEST (AUFFORDERUNG)
Rules of propositional Content	An action: $H_{Hr,Z}$
Preparatory Conditions	(1) $C_{Hr,G \to Z} (H_{Hr,G \to Z})$ & $B_{Sp,G} (C_{Hr,G \to Z} (H_{Hr,G \to Z}))$ (2) $\neg K_{Sp,G} (I_{Hr,G \to Z} (H_{Hr,G \to Z}))$ & $\neg K_{Hr,G} (I_{Hr,G \to Z} (H_{Hr,G \to Z}))$
Sincerity condition	$W_{Sp,G} (H_{Hr,G \to Z})$
Essential rule	$\text{REQUEST} \ ©\!\Rightarrow W_{Sp,G} (I_{Hr,G \to Z} (H_{Hr,G \to Z}))$

This formalisation corresponds to the original verbal formulation of the constitutive rules for ,REQUEST' (modified after Searle 1969). It turns out that formalizations based on the formal instrument LOM are considerably more complex and will therefore allow for more meaningful results. Furthermore we relied on the careful and detailed semantic speech act analyses in the analysis of meaning of selected performative verbs developed in Wagner (2001) by using all the relevant and appropriate German research literature in this topic. Taken together, these reconstructions of the relevant rules are the basis of the explication of the constitutive rules of the speech acts taken into account as well as of the formalizations carried out on this basis.

5.6.4 Interrelations and Restrictions between Emotions and Speech Acts

Uttering speech acts has complex interrelations with building emotions as classes of mutual implication, of compatibility and of restriction, based on functional roles in both dimensions.

---

[7] Signs and Symbols: $H =_{df.}$ Action, $C =_{df.}$ Ability, $B =_{df.}$ Belief, $K =_{df.}$ Knowledge, $I =_{df.}$ Intention, $W =_{df.}$ Wish, $\neg =_{df.}$ Negation, $©\!\Rightarrow =_{df.}$ Cognitive implication, $G =_{df.}$ Present, $Z =_{df.}$ Future, $G \to Z =_{df.}$ Present to Future, $Sp =_{df.}$ Speaker, $Hr =_{df.}$ Hearer.

At first it has to be adhered that the marking of the illocutionary force of a speech act indexes the propositional employment of the speaker to the object expressed in the proposition. The speaker is sad and not happy with the existence of the condition in question which is expressed in this proposition (cf. Vanderveken 1990, 16). For example, that somebody is 'complaint' or disposed to 'lamentation' if he is at the same time sad about an existing fact which is expressed in parallel in the propositional content of this speech act. By this way the specific components of the illocutionary force can be inferred back to the emotional assessments. Speech act theory therefore delivers a methodical means to contribute to the investigation of the relations of emotions and speech act choice:

- This will result primarily from the analysis of the sincerity conditions of speech acts: Any successful execution of an illocutionary act constitutes the expression of a mental state with a psychological mode referring to a state, which is described by the propositional content of this speech act and thereby is determined as its intentional object. For example, a speaker giving a promise expresses his intention to execute an act which corresponds to what he promises (*Principle of parallelism of mental attitudes*).
- Secondly, our mental states are always (at least in principle) expressible by illocutionary acts. For example we can express beliefs in statements or assertions and wishes in inquiries, interpellations or requests. (*Principle of illocutionary expressibility*).
- Finally, the direction of fit of the mental state expressed is in general identical with the one given in the illocutionary act which is executed in order to express this mental state. Furthermore, the conditions of fulfilment of the illocutionary act and of the mental act are logically connected (*Principle of identity of fit*).

In any case the mental state of the emitter will play a crucial role in the execution of the corresponding illocutionary act (or acts). So it seems plausible to impute a normative connection and an empirically ascertainable covariance between these two dimensions of single emotions and special speech acts. The connection to be captured normatively is based on the existence of common elements of the situation representation in (a) the elicitation rules of emotions and (b) the constitutive rules defining the components of the illocutionary force in question, respectively.

For example a negative situation assessment, that is the injury of justifiable expectations and the damage done to the own person, can lead to the elicitation of the emotion ANNOYANCE / IRRITATION, the German 'Ärger' (cf. Gessner 2004, 128 ff.). The components of illocutionary acts like 'complaining' possibly used here correspondingly imply the expression of the displeasure in the area of the sincerity condition and in the area of the preparatory condition that the facts in question - the object of this trouble - are judged negatively. In the case of the illocutionary act 'moan' the aspect of deep sadness additionally enters in the relevant sincerity condition (cf. Vanderveken 1990, 181).

By this, an immediate coupling arises between the selected subset of robot-relevant emotions and the choice of illocutionary acts[8]. Furthermore it can be expected that – according to a sort of reverse conclusion – some specific emotions are incompatible with some specific speech acts. Resulting interrelations has been described for example by Andersen and Guerrero (1998) and can be represented schematically in individual analyses of the relations and restrictions between 24 emotions and 41 speech acts (cf. Schiewer 2007), demonstrated here by the example of the relations and restrictions of the performative verb or speech act type REQUEST (Aufforderung):

Table 3. Types of REQUESTs related to 24 emotions

REPUGNANCE (Abscheu)	Request to Hr (the hearer) to cancel a future action, if it corresponds to the intentional object of the emotion
ANNOYANCE/IRRITATION (Ärger)	Request to Hr to cancel a future action, if it corresponds to the intentional object of the emotion
SUSPICION (Argwohn)	None
REGRET (Bedauern)	None
ADMIRATION (Bewunderung)	Request to Hr to continue with the intentional object of the emotion and not to cancel it
GRATITUDE (Dankbarkeit)	Request to Hr to continue with the intentional object of the emotion and not to cancel it
INDIGNATION (Empörung)	Request to Hr to cancel a future action, if it corresponds to the intentional object of the emotion
HORROR (Entsetzen)	Request to Hr to cancel a future action, if it corresponds to the intentional object of the emotion
DISAPPOINTMENT (Enttäuschung)	Request to Hr to execute an action if Sp believes Hr is able to this in spite of the fact Hr had acted up to now to the contrary
RELIEF (Erleichterung)	None
JOY (Freude)	None
FEAR (Furcht)	Request to Hr (or third person) to cancel their planned or ongoing action
HAPPINESS (Glück)	None
HOPE (Hoffnung)	Request to Hr to allow for he result hoped for or to bring it about by an own action
BOREDOM (Langeweile)	Request to Hr to alter an existing state if Sp believes Hr is responsible fort his state
COMPASSION (Mitleid)	Request to a third person in order to bring it about that an action is done (or omitted) if Sp believes that this action could be harmful to Hr (or he believes that the forbearance of this action could prevent this harm from Hr)
SHAME (Scham)	None

[8] The following list of compatibilities between the speech act REQUEST and the 24 emotions cited above has originated from conclusive comparisons between the elicitation formulae of these emotions and the formal depiction of the constitutive rules for request given above. Further empirical work will eventually show that these relations are also cognitively realized in ordinary people as language users and bearers of emotions respectively.

FEELING OF GUILT (Schuldgefühl)	None
SORROW (Sorge)	Request to Hr to cancel a future action of him If Sp believes H is able to execute this action
PRIDE (Stolz)	None
SURPRISE (Überraschung)	None
ANTICIPATION (Vorfreude)	None
ANGER (Zorn)	Request to Hr to fulfill an action which compensates the harm done to Sp by Hr, or request to Hr not to repeat this harming action
SATISFACTION (Zufriedenheit)	None

5.6.5   Giving an Example: The Relations of Speech Acts and Emotions in, ANNOYANCE / IRRITATION'

Dispositions for speech acts result in the basis of subjective situation representations. The 'triggering' of speech acts can be understood (quite similar to the elicitation of emotions) as a process of sample comparison between the given set of elements of this situation and the 'constitutive rules' for speech acts as a total set of predefined cognitive patterns. The elicitation formulae for individual emotions (cf. Gessner 2004, Ch. 7 and Ch. 11) as well as the constitutive rules of specific speech act types are to be 'tested' by subjects with respect to her 'fit' with the respective situation description. This comparison process leads the 'triggering' of an emotion and one (or more) speech act types (as a language generation process) by filling these abstract cognitive schemes as 'open variables' respectively with situation-specific contents and elements. So speech acts are (as explicitly communicative reactions on 'problematic' situations) in parallel with emotions in coping with this 'problematic' situation. Just as forecasting the appearance of the emotion altogether is possible, the validity of the respective samples of speech acts can be forecasted likewise under the prerequisite of a situation representation given subjectively which fits the triggering schemata of emotions and speech acts as well.

In the context of the given example of the emotion ,ANNOYANCE/ IRRITATION' essentially the following speech acts should be examined according to the criteria given above for their compatibility and integration with this emotion: REQUEST (Aufforderung), WARNING (Warnung), ADMONITION (Mahnung), COMPLAINT (Beschwerde) and THREAT (Drohung). In the case of the speech act ,REQUEST (Aufforderung) the following comments can be given concerning its compatibility with the elicitation conditions of the emotion 'ANNOYANCE/IRRITATION':

The propositional content of the speech act 'REQUEST' (compare its constitutive rules given above!) and the intentional object of the emotion 'ANNOYANCE / IRRITATION' are identical, namely the problematic action of the other person. The negative evaluation of this action in the emotional context derives from the failed obligation to the execution of this action in the context of 'ANNOYANCE / IRRITATION'. In the speech act context this action is (in the introduction rule and in the sincerity rule) presupposed in the default case as an action assessed positively by the potential speaker. The constitutive rule should be extended by 'REQUESTING' for cases of the failure of that action. Similarly for the essential rule of this speech act, to the effect that the potential speaker wants the hearer to form an intention to forbear an action not requested by the potential speaker.

In this respect the speech act 'REQUESTING' is primarily compatible with this emotion in those cases in which the intention of the other person to perform an action undesired by the speaker exists and is known to exist, but has not yet been executed, still lies ahead or has just begun being executed.

Using this case as an analytical example, the other speech act types just mentioned can be analysed in a comparable manner, using variants in speakers' and hearers' intentions and valuations, referring to variants in time relations of actions and their consequences and to the state of the consequences as still possible or already stated, i.e. still preventable or already irreversible. The result of this more fine-grained analysis will deliver a matrix of compatibility and incompatibility of any singular emotion with the considered speech acts, and by this the relative impacts and the relations of emotion and speech in coping with situations can be determined.

So we have shown that speech acts (as utterances adapted to situations) and emotions as ‚quick and dirty' reactions to situations fulfil parallel and mutually complementary functions, which allow for people – and later on android robots, too – to cope in a systematic and successful way with the ever changing situations they meet in variable circumstances.

6 Possibility and Realizability of Artificial Emotions in Androids

Natural emotions have been under attentive examination up to now. Originating in a long lasting debate on the 'sciences of the artificial' (H. A. Simon) the possibility of reconstructing emotions and other mental events in technical systems are now under crucial inspection, too.

6.1 General Remarks: The Predecessors

The meaning of emotions is increasingly under consideration in a number of disciplines, and artificial intelligence research also tries to make use of these mechanisms. The application possibilities of expanded artificial intelligence approaches into artificial emotion schemes are supposed to be different: The targets concern the realization of computers being able to 'understand' emotions (emotion analysis), to 'express' emotions (emotion synthesis), and even to 'have' emotions (cf. Picard 1997; Ruebenstrunk 1998). Therefore, the notion of 'artificial emotion' is a very wide one, at least in the present orientation phase.

Among other things it is assumed that emotions are of central importance in any process of planning, organisation and decision. Less important is the single calculation of an optimal plan but rather the permanent optimal adaptation to changed conditions. The process of decision is adapted to the surroundings by an agent frequently checking his aims in dynamic surroundings rather often while this is less often necessary in more static surroundings. Special emotional agents are characterized by the quality of their emotional behaviour (cf. Görz et al. 2000, 950). This means that emotions are looked at as a component of decisions for actions and intelligent human behaviour in variable situational and cultural contexts. In connection with this they are implemented in agent architectures. It is assumed that emotions besides intentions, targets etc. steer the behaviour of IT systems on the one hand and can improve the interaction at the man-machine interface on the other hand.

In connection with this, it seems self-evident that emotions play a special role in the development of humanoid robots and virtual androids. A prominent example is the real android KISMET developed by C. Breazeal, which is based on the 'communicative' theory of emotions by K. Oatley and P. Johnson-Laird (Oatley and Johnson-Laird 1996). Although appearing very technical from the outside it reacts similarly to a human being and proves to be social competent and even a sensitive partner in interaction and communication.

Oatley and Johnson-Laird describe the 'emotional communication' besides 'propositional' or 'symbolic communication' which does not distribute information but serves to bring the modules of a parallel distributed process into different emotional modes, which interrupt the current processes of the modules and put them into the readiness to work according to the emotional modes. Emotional communication is triggered by the perception of all information indispensable for life and specific aims from the internal and external surroundings. This kind of 'global interrupt' is able to set new priorities for the operation of the modules very fast and gives an example of a theoretical outline comprising both the coordination of inner processes of decision and the external social communication behaviour as well, which is exploitable for the construction of artificial emotion devices.

6.2   State of the Art of Artificiality in Emotion Design

In the field of cognitive emotion theory formation a certain consolidation can be noticed. However, the idea of 'artificial emotion' and also the application oriented research are still positioned in an orientation phase. Among other things this is documented in the corresponding sections and conferences concerning the subject that often cover extremely heterogeneous problems fields, application areas and methodical approaches. In response to this Picard proposed an organizing principle for the field of artificial emotion research. She uses three levels of representation to organize the building blocks: low-level for signals, medium-level for patterns, and high-level for concepts. Following Picard these levels all come together in any complete system for recognizing, expressing, or having emotions (cf. Picard 1997, 141). A low-level signal representation is used in an abstract sense for representing intensities of emotions and moods. The medium-level is used to start giving computers the abilities that are necessary to recognize and express emotion; these are tools from pattern recognition and especially procedures for recognizing and synthesizing facial expression. The high-level signal correlates with concepts of cognitive emotion theories (cf. Picard 1997, chs. 5, 6 and 7). By this an organizing principle is defined which could unite the divergent approaches. Our approach comprises the low-level, partly the medium-level and the high-level as well.

6.3   Mere Simulation Versus Real Reconstruction of Emotion Structures

Cognitive emotion theories (primarily 'appraisal theories') as discussed above in detail dominate the field of artificial emotions. It is assumed that these kinds of theories permit speaking not only about a simulation of emotions but rather about their reconstruction, because the process of the elicitation of emotions and the following behaviour is represented in an analytical access. Therefore, a more and more realistic and lifelike reconstruction seems possible. In this respect one has to contradict G. v. Randow's opinion that there is no use in distinguishing between 'real' and 'feigned' emotions as long as the simulation is perfect (cf. v. Randow 1997, p. 319 and the discussion in Aretz 2004, p. 60). Nonetheless, transformation of real human emotions in artefacts and androids seems possible if the functionality of the original can at least partly be transformed in the artificial devices.

7 Some Possible Applications

Finally we want to determine some (more or less futuristic) applications of the structures developed above. Naturally, nobody will be really able to determine the relative proportion of fact and fiction in this list.

7.1 Man-Machine Interfaces in General

Subjectivity and personhood have been determined as mental state systems (MSS) (cf. ch. 3.3). How can these characteristics of situation-representation, self-representation and representation of other (foreign) persons be transformed into artificial systems like androids in order to develop equally artificial MSS in these creatures? In our opinion an ANDROID mental state system (i.e., MSS (A)) might be considered as a sort of proto-consciousness for androids:

- An MSS (A) could be questioned in arbitrary contexts in order to give information about its actual state(s) by potential partners for communication, interaction or cooperation.
- An MSS (A) could in arbitrary contexts offer information about his own mental states, maybe when asked in an orderly manner or by his own impetus or decision, and could present himself as a potential partner for open purposes.
- An MSS (A) could deliver the possibility of interpreting his own mental states to external partners as well as the implications following from these mental states in an effective manner.
- An MSS (A) could realize for himself the possibility of interpretations of inner mental states of his potential partners as well as the reactions resulting from these mental states and attitudes, because he himself has been trained in applying the relevant categories of mental states and the relevant interpretation tools for being successful in this kind of task.
- An MSS (A) could select useful and affordable inputs for the activities of an android done (or to be done) for its own by delivering relevant and appropriate inputs (belief states, ability appraisals, value statements, preference profiles, dispositions to action intentions) into the actional, verbal or emotional dispositions at hand.
- An MSS (A) would be able to self-represent his past as well as his present mental states and it could be affordable to develop a sort of 'imagination' depicting future possibilities of his own states.
- An MSS (A) could develop (by permanent, or, when useful, occasional update of his inner mental states) a sort of permanently adapted knowledge about himself – and, by this, develop a sort of self-consciousness.

Elaborating this programmatic concept could lead to a really innovative device in the interaction of androids with men and vice versa.

7.2 Service Robots

The replacement of work formerly done by humans is an archetype motive during the whole industrial age and a main motive in technological evolution. Following the age of classical machines we are now standing at the dawn of the age of autonomous machines which build their own plans and goals, based on a recognition of their environment and (in part) in cooperation with humans, but (not yet) independent of the values and goals humans have preset for them. So we are now confronted with trivial autonomy (in elaborate dust cleaners, lawn mowers or automated refillers at tank stops) up to mid-range autonomy (in military weapon systems) up to high valued autonomy in humanoid robots which will provide us with needs and interactions formerly done by other humans in using their intellectual, emotional and communicative competencies. Androids serving tasks like surveillance, education, rehabilitation or support of the elderly will need (to some extent) the attributes, properties, attitudes and capacities of the people they are disposed to interact with (Cf. Sawitzky and Buss 2007). The more these robots will be called for similarity with humans, the higher the demand of implementing elaborate simulations of humanlike behaviour will be, including all dimensions of subjectivity, personhood and emotional competence.

7.3 Interaction with Virtual Characters

Telling stories is closely linked with our imagination about the persons and characters described. This is an ancient motive of all literal imagination. Nowadays, starting with the downgrade of literature to comics, these imaginations become more 'realistic' in the sense of visualized and stereotyped figures which populate our everyday worlds (Cf. Stern 2003). The gaming scene and internet facilities like 'Second Life' are crowded with virtual characters and pseudo-personalities. Last but not least the virtual characters created by powerful animation tools in the movie industries intrude on our mental spaces, as well as some artificial personal characters like Max Headroom in former advertising spots of German Telecom. Maybe in the future the classical logos used in branding and Corporate Identity will be substituted by virtual figures which bear all the properties the advertising strategists want to connect with the image of a certain firm or industry. The more these figures will have to be similar to human characteristics, the more adequate simulations of personhood and characters are needed. The emotional and subjective structures we proposed may be able to meet these requirements.

7.4 Virtual Androids in Driver Assistance Systems

At present an electronic revolution in automotive engineering is taking place and is expected to involve radical changes concerning the human-computer-interaction of car driving. Electronic information systems and assistance systems are supposed to make car driving safer and at the same time more comfortable. Nonetheless there are individual and situation dependent differences in need of support, so that undesirable effects of distraction and even excessive demand cannot be avoided in every respect.

Therefore the conception of adaptive systems of MMI-management in cars which are able to adapt to individual needs of the driver and to the given driving situation have been developed (cf. Holzmann 2008 for a description of the state of the art). Actually, the Vehicle Interaction Lab of Fraunhofer IAO has investigated the complex interdependencies of driver, car and the situation of road traffic with the intention of optimizing the conception of such systems by integrating driver assistance systems (FAS) and driver information systems (FIS) based on an appraisal of the actual traffic risks and of the psychic conditions of the driver. Using the notion of 'sympathetic car' they aim to adapt the complete system output to the given needs of the driver. In cooperation with the EU-projekt AIDE (Adaptive Integrated Driver-vehicle Interface) (cf. Amditis et al 2004) new systems integrating sensors and cameras used to observe the environment of the car and the condition of the driver are explored by the researchers at the IAO. The corresponding data influence the interaction of car and driver for instance by speech, tone, shaking of the wheel or flashing displays. The review of the optimal control has been recognized as a core subject in human-computer-interaction of car driving (cf. Marberger & Wenzel 2006).

Nonetheless, Huang et al. (2007) were critical that in Artificial Intelligence for Human Computing it is still exceptional that a computer interface has been designed from the point of view that humans are social beings. Rather, users that have to perform tasks in a way that are prescribed by the computer. Huang et al. accentuate that future devices and environments need to understand what exactly the specifics of the current interaction flow and the surrounding environment are. This understanding allows for anticipatory and proactive feedback and real-time, unobtrusive support of human activities with the environment. Sensing humans and understanding their behaviour therefore is a core issue in this field of research on human computing (cf. Huang et al. 2007, V).

In our view a real *future car* has to show active and passive communicative competence according to the human antetypes, which will give it the options of direct and real-time-interaction in all the dimensions cited in our emotion model. Furthermore, an android in the role of a driver assistant has to develop full-fledged structures of subjectivity and will develop the characteristics of a person, including the representation of the driver as a person, and will be able to trace the interaction history with the driver in analogy to the process of becoming acquainted with another human person. This will, finally, lead to the possibility of a fully personalized interaction assistant which is able to cooperate in different roles with the driver in a qualitatively and quantitatively outstanding way.

8   Outlook and Preview

The state of simulation of mechanical abilities in androids as human-like robots has been pushed and enforced worldwide and has reached impressive results, for example in realizing the degrees of freedom similar to those which are given in human bodies (cf. SONY's QRIO (now cancelled) and Honda's ASIMO, among others). In contrast to this, the reflective, communicative and cooperative abilities of androids are still in need of further improvement. In order to construct human-like robots as autonomous agents they have to coincide with the special communicative abilities and instruments which evolution and cultural development have brought up exclusively in human beings. We accept and tolerate other beings primarily when their actions and behavior are predictable and comprehensible. Therefore only android robots with distinct 'personalities' will be both believable and convincing robots. In addition, achieving more believability and effectiveness will be accessible step-by-step by this special kind of 'machine learning'. The central idea of our research has been the amplification of the communicative abilities of robots based on the transfer of a special cognitive theory of emotions to the behavior of androids. A new kind of steering of android's behavior towards human beings – so we believe – has been achieved and can be used as a starting basis for further research and development.

References

Amditis, A., Polychronopoulos, A., Engström, J., Andreone, L.: Design and Development of an Adaptive Integrated Driver-vehicle Interface. In: Proceedings of ITS in Europe, Budapest (2004)

Andersen, P.A., Guerriero, L.K.: Handbook of Communication and Emotion. Research, Theory, Applications, and Contexts. Academic Press, San Diego (1998)

Aretz, M.: Emotionen in der Künstlichen Intelligenz. Diplomarbeit an der FH Gießen-Friedberg (2004),
http://homepages.fh-giessen.de/~hg8416/projekte/autonome_systeme/downloads/Emotionen_in_der_KI.pdf

Arnold, M.B.: Emotion and Personality. Bd I. Psychological Aspects. Bd. II. Neurological and Physiological Aspects. Columbia University Press, New York (1960)

Austin, J.L.: How to do Things with Words. Clarendon Press, Oxford (1950)

Baron-Cohen, S.: Mindblindedness. An Essay in Autism and the Theory of Mind. The MIT Press, Cambridge (1995)

Batthyany, A., Elitzur, A. (eds.): Mind and its Place in the World. Non-Reductionist Approaches to the Ontology of Consciousness. Ontos Verlag, Frankfurt (2006)

Breazeal, C.: Designing sociable Robots. MIT Press, Cambridge (2002)

Breazeal, C., Brooks, R.: Robot Emotion. A Functional Perspective. In: Fellous, Arbib (eds.), pp. 271–310 (2005)

Burkhard, H.-D.: Software-Agenten. In: Görz, G., et al. (eds.) Handbuch der künstlichen Intelligenz. Oldenbourg, München (2003)

Castaneda, H.-N.: The Phenomenology of the I. Essays on Self-Consciousness. Indiana University Press, Bloomington (1999)

Chellas, B.F.: Modal Logic. An Introduction. Cambridge University Press, Cambridge (1980, repr. 1995)

Fodor, J.A.: The Language of Thought. The Harvester Press, Hassocks (1976)

Ekman, P., Friesen, W.F.: The Repertoire of nonverbal Behavior: Categories, Origins, Usage, and Coding. Semiotica 1, 49–98 (1969)

Ekman, P., Friesen, W.V.: Facial Action Coding System. Investor's Guide. Consulting Psychologists Press, Palo Alto (1978)

Fellous, J.-M., Arbib, M.A. (eds.): Who needs Emotions? The Brain meets the Robot. Oxford University Press, Oxford (2005)

Frijda, N.H.: The Emotions. Cambridge University Press, Cambridge (1986)

Gessner, W.: Die sprachliche Formalstruktur des Wissens. Unpublished Diploma Thesis. University of Hamburg, Department of Psychology (1989)

Gessner, W.: Die kognitive Emergenz von Emotionen. Mentis, Paderborn (2004)

Gessner, W.: Fallstudie, Ärger'. Zum Zusammenhang der Dimensionen einer Emotion. Arbeitsbericht Nr. 20, Projekt MMI 1978, 87 p. (2007a)

Gessner, W.: Subjektivität und Personalität in Androiden. Arbeitsbericht Nr. 21, Projekt MMI 1978, 28 S. (2007 b)

Gessner, W.: Eine abstrakte Notation für Aktionslatenzen in Emotionen. Arbeitsbericht Nr. 29, Projekt MMI 1978, 19 p. (2007 c)

Gessner, W.: Ein allgemeines Modell für Intentionsbildungen zu Handlungen in Menschen und Androiden. Arbeitsbericht Nr. 30, Projekt MMI 1978, 55 p. (2007 d)

Gessner, W., Schiewer, G.L.: KI 2007, Workshop, Emotion and Computing: Constructing Androids as emotional Agents in Human-Robot Relationships (2007)

Gessner, W., Schiewer, G.L.: Prospects for Subjectivity and Personhood in Androids. In: The IEEE-conference RoMan 2008 (Munich) (Paper to be presented, 2008)

Goldman, A.I.: Simulating Minds. The Philosophy, Psychology and Neuroscience of Mindreading. Oxford University Press, Oxford (2006)

Heider, F.: The Psychology of interpersonal Relations. Erlbaum, Hillsdale (1958)

Holzmann, F.: Adaptive Cooperation between Driver and Assistant System. Improving Road Safety. Springer, Berlin (2008)

Jones, A.J.I.: Communication and meaning. Reidel, Dordrecht (1983)

Görz, G., Rollinger, C.-R., Schneeberger, J. (eds.): Handbuch der Künstlichen Intelligenz. Oldenburg Verlag, München/Wien (2000)

Huang, T.S., Nijholt, A., Rantic, M., Pentland, A. (eds.): Artificial Intelligence for Human Computing. Springer, Heidelberg (2007)

Johnson-Laird, P.N.: Mental models: Towards a cognitive Science of Language, Inference, and Consciousness. Cambridge University Press, Cambridge (1983)

Lazarus, R.S., et al.: Ansätze zu einer kognitiven Gefühlstheorie. In: Birbaumer, N. (Hg.) Psychophysiologie der Angst, pp. 182–207 (1977)

Lazarus, R.S.: On the Primacy of Cognition. American Psychologist 39, 124–129 (1984)

Lazarus, R.S., Lazarus, B.N.: Passion and Reason. Making Sense of Our Emotions. Oxford University Press, New York (1994)

Lazarus, R.S.: The Cognition-Emotion Debate: a Bit of History. In: Dalgleish & Power 1999, pp. 3–20 (1999)

Marberger, C., Wenzel, G.: MMI-Management: Adaptive Systeme im Fahrzeug? In: Spath, D. (ed.) Technologiemanagement in der Praxis. Forschen und Anwenden, pp. 117–121. Fraunhofer IRB Verlag, Stuttgart (2006)

Metzinger, T.: Subjekt und Selbstmodell. Schöningh, Paderborn (1993)

Metzinger, T.: Being no one: the Self-Model Theory of Subjectivity. The MIT Press, Cambridge (2003)

Morton, A.: The importance of being understood. Folk psychology as ethics. Routledge, London (2003)

Nelson, R.J.: The Logic of Mind. Reidel, Dordrecht (1982)

Nichols, S., Stich, S.P.: Mindreading. An integrated Account of Pretence, Self-Awareness, and Understanding other Minds. The Clarendon Press, Oxford (2003)

Noonan, H.W.: Personal identity. Routledge, London (1989)

Nowakowska, M.: Language of Motivation and Language of Actions. Mouton, The Hague (1973)

Oatley, K.: Best laid Schemes: The Psychology of Emotions. Cambridge University Press, New York (1992)

Oatley, K., Johnson-Laird, P.N.: The communicative Theory of Emotions. In: Jenkins, J.M., Oatley, K., Stein, N.L. (eds.) Human Emotions: A Reader, pp. 84–97. Blackwell Publishers, Malden (1998)

Ortony, A.D., Norman, A., Revelle, W.: Affect and Proto-Affect in Effective Functioning. In: Fellous, Arbib (eds.) pp. 173–202 (2005)

Ortony, A.: On making believable emotional Agents believable. In: Trappl, Petta, Payr (eds.) Emotions in Humans and Artifacts, pp. 189–211. The MIT Press, Cambridge (2003)

Ortony, A., Clore, G.L., Collins, A.: The cognitive Structure of Emotions. Cambridge University Press, Cambridge (1988)

Parfit, D.: Reasons and Persons. Clarendon Press, Oxford (1984)

Pauen, M.: Grundprobleme der Philosophie des Geistes. Eine Einführung. Frankfurt a.M., Fischer (2001)

Picard, R.W.: Affective computing. MIT Press, Cambridge (1997)

Posner, R., Serenar, M.: Berliner Lexikon der Alltagsgesten – Berlin Dictionary of Everyday Gestures (2003),
http://www.ims.uni-stuttgart.de/projekte/nite/BLAG/index.html

Quante, Michael (2007). Person. Berlin: de Gruyter.

von Randow, G.: Roboter, unsere nächsten Verwandten. Rowohlt, Reinbek (1997)

Reisenzein, R.: Exploring the Strength of Association between the Competents of Emotion Syndromes. The Case of Surprise. Cognition and Emotion 14(1), 1–38 (2000)

Reisenzein, R., Meyer, W.-U., Schützwohl, A.: Einführung in die Emotionspsychologie Bd. Kognitive Emotionstheorien, vol. III. Hans Huber, Bern (2003)

Roberts, J.M. (ed.): Integrating the Mind. Domain general versus domain specific Processes in higher Cognition. Psychology Press, Hove and New York (2007)

Rolf, E.: Illokutionäre Kräfte. Grundbegriffe der Illokutionslogik. Westdeutscher Verlag, Opladen (1997)

Rödl, S.: Self-Consciousness. Harvard University Press, Cambridge (2007)

Roseman, I.J.: Cognitive Determinants of Emotions (Doctoral dissertation, Yale University, 1982). Dissertation Abstracts International 43, 4200B (1983)

Ruebenstrunk, G.: Emotionale Computer. Computermodelle von Emotionen und ihre Bedeutung für die emotionspsychologische Forschung (1998) (Unpublished manuscript),
http://www.ruebenstrunk.de/

Sawitzky, G., Buss, M.: Service Roboter. Oldenbourg, München (2007)

Scherer, K.R.: Appraisal Theory, Dalgleish & Power 1999, pp. 637–664 (1999)

Scherer, K.R., Schorr, A., Johnstone, T. (eds.): Appraisal Processes in Emotions. Theory, Methods, Research. Oxford University Press, Oxford (2001)

Schiewer, G.L.: Cognitive Emotion Theories, Emotional Agents, and Narratology. In: Proceedings of the 5th International Conference on Language Resources and Evaluation, Genoa, May 22-28 (2006), http://www.elra.info

Schiewer, G.L.: Project MMI 1978, Working Paper 25: Kontingenztabellen möglicher Relationen und Restriktionen zwischen 41 Sprechhandlungen und 24 Emotionen, 43 p. (2007)

Schiewer, G.L.: Bausteine zu einer Emotionssemiotik. Zur Sprache des Gefühlsausdrucks in Kommunikation und Affective Computing. In: Genske, D., Hess-Lüttich, E.W.B., Huch, M. (eds.) Kartographie des Verhüllten. Brückenschläge zwischen Natur- und Kulturwissenschaften / Carthography of the Disguised. Bridging Science and Humanities, hg. Kodikas/Code, pp. 235–257. Tübingen, Narr (2008)

Schueler, K.R.: Rediscovering Empathy. Agency, Folk Psychology, and the Human Sciences. The MIT Press, Cambridge (2006)

Searle, J.: Speech Acts. An Essay in the Philosophy of Language. Cambridge University Press, Cambridge (1969)

Searle, J.R., Vanderveken, D.: Foundations of Illocutionary Logic. Cambridge University Press, Cambridge (1985)

Searle, J.R., Vanderveken, D.: Speech Acts and Illocutionary Logic. In: Vanderveken, D. (ed.) Logic, Thought and Action, pp. 109–132. Springer, Berlin (2005)

Smedslund, J.: Psycho-Logic. Springer, Berlin (1988)

Smedslund, J.: The Structure of psychological Common Sense. Erlbaum, Mamwah (1997)

Smith, C.A., Lazarus, R.S.: Appraisal Components, Core Relation Themes, and the Emotions. Cognition and Emotion 7(3/4), 233–269 (1993)

Stern, A.: Creating emotional Relationships with virtual Characters. In: Trappl, R., Petta, P., Payr, S. (eds.) Emotions in Humans and Artifacts. The MIT Press, Cambridge (2003)

Thomas, W.J., Thomas, D.S.: The Child in America. Behavior Problems and Programs. Academic Press, New York (1928)

Thompson, E.: Mind in Life. Biology, Phenomenology, and the Sciences of Mind. Harvard University Press, Cambridge (2007)

Tuomela, R.: The Importance of Us. Stanford University Press, Stanford (1995)

Ulich, D.: Das Gefühl. Eine Einführung in die Emotionspsychologie. Psychologie Verlags Union, München (1989)

Vanderveken, D.: Logic, Thought and Action. Springer, Berlin (2005)

Vanderveken, D.: Meaning and Speech Acts, 2 vols. Cambridge University Press, Cambridge (1990/1991)

Von Wright, G.H.: Norm und Handlung. Eine logische Untersuchung. Scriptor, Königstein/Ts (1979)

Wagner, K.R.: Pragmatik der deutschen Sprache. Peter Lang, Frankfurt am Main (2001)

Wierzbicka, A.: Emotions across Languages and Cultures. Diversity and universals. Cambridge University Press, Cambridge (1999)

Woolridge, M.: Reasoning about rational Agents. The MIT Press, Cambridge (2000)

Xie, M.: Fundamentals of robotics. Linking Perception to Action. World Scientific, New Jersey (2003)

Zahavi, D.: Subjectivity and Selfhood: Investigating the First-Person Perspective. The MIT Press, Cambridge (2006)

Part III
Interactive Visualization

EvoSpaces - Multi-dimensional Navigation Spaces for Software Evolution

Sazzadul Alam[1], Sandro Boccuzzo[2], Richard Wettel[3], Philippe Dugerdil[1],
Harald Gall[2], and Michele Lanza[3]

[1] HEG Geneva, Switzerland
[2] University of Zurich, Switzerland
[3] University of Lugano, Switzerland

Abstract. In software development, a major difficulty comes from the intrinsic complexity of software systems and the size of which can easily reach millions of lines of source code. But software is an intangible artifact that does not have any natural visual representation. While many software visualization techniques have been proposed in the literature, they are often difficult to interpret. In fact, the user of such representations is confronted with an artificial world that contains and represents intangible objects. The goal of our EVOSPACES project was to investigate effective visual metaphors (*i.e.,* analogies) between natural objects and software objects so that we can exploit the cognitive understanding of the user. The difficulty of this approach is that the common sense expectations about the displayed world should also apply to the world of software objects. To solve this common sense representation problem for software objects our project addressed both the small-scale (*i.e.,* the level of individual objects) and the large-scale (*i.e.,* the level of groups of objects). After many experiments we decided for a "city" metaphor: at the small scale we include different houses and their shapes as visual objects to cover size, structure and history. At the large-scale level we arrange the different types of houses in districts and include their history in diverse layouts. The user then is able to use the EVOSPACES virtual software city to navigate and explore all kinds of aspects of a city and its houses: size, age, historical evolution, changes, growth, restructurings, and evolution patterns such as code smells or architectural decay. For that we have developed a software environment named EVOSPACES as a plug-in to Eclipse so that visual metaphors can quickly be implemented in an easily navigable virtual space. Due to the large amount of information we complemented the flat 2D world with full-fledged immersive 3D representation. In this virtual software city, the dimensions and appearance of the buildings can be set according to software metrics. The user of the EVOSPACES environment can then explore a given software system by navigating through the corresponding virtual software city.

1 Introduction

Today we rely more and more on software systems. Maintenance has been identified to be the primary factor of the total cost (*i.e.,* up to 90%) of large software systems [1]. One of the key difficulties encountered in software maintenance comes from the intrinsic complexity of those systems, whose size can easily reach millions of lines of

D. Lalanne and J. Kohlas (Eds.): Human Machine Interaction, LNCS 5440, pp. 167–192, 2009.

source code. Software complexity is recognized as one of the major challenges to the development and maintenance of industrial size software projects. One of the key aspects, which claims more than half the time spent in software maintenance, is software understanding [2]. The goal of this project is to develop visual metaphors to help the maintenance engineer navigate through thousands of modules, classes or any other programming artifacts and identify "locations" of interest to be explored further to get a global understanding of the system.

Software is an intangible artifact that does not have any *natural* visual representation. While many software visualization techniques have been proposed in the literature, they are often difficult to interpret. In fact, the user of such representations is confronted with an artificial world that itself represents intangible objects (*i.e.,* objects of which the user does not have a sensitive experience). The cognitive mapping is then very difficult to do. Our approach is to look for effective visual metaphors (*i.e.,* analogies) between *real-world* and software objects so that when displaying a such natural object one could exploit the common sense understanding of the user. The difficulty of this approach is that the common sense expectations about the displayed world should also apply to the world of software objects. To give a simple example, the difference in size of two displayed objects should reflect a difference in some size metrics of the associated software objects. In summary if, at it is often said, a good picture can replace a thousand words, this is because all aspects of the picture may convey information: sizes, distances, relative positions, colors, shadows, etc. Then, as soon as the displayed objects resemble common objects, then the user begins to have visual expectations about the object.

To solve this common sense representation problem for software objects we have to address both the small scale level of individual objects and at the large scale level of communities of objects. On the small scale this concerns the shape of the visual objects according to the information we want to convey on an individual level. On the large scale this concerns the distribution of large communities of objects in the visual space so that the relative visual feature of objects convey information on the group and peculiar feature of some objects would be easily detectable.

Our work has been pursued in the following directions:

- visual metaphors for software objects;
- mappings between software metrics and features of visual objects;
- ways to display large communities of software objects;
- navigation techniques in this visual world.

Moreover a software environment has been developed under Eclipse so that visual metaphors can quickly be realized in an easily navigable virtual space.

2   Visual Metaphors

Visual metaphors should represent structural and evolutionary metrics of an entity known from our daily life as glyphs. Such glyphs can be real-world things such as houses, cities, streets, cars, or other physical concepts that exhibit a clear understanding by a person. We experimented with some of these concepts and mapped software metrics onto the glyph representation of the concept. For the metric mapping we used

Table 1. Example of several metric clusters

Hot-Spot Metric Cluster	Provider-Consumer Metric Cluster	Structural Metric Cluster	Evolution Metric Cluster
Lines of Code	Fan in	Cyclomatic Complexity	Fan in
# of Functions	Call in	Growth rate	Growth rate
Cyclomatic Complexity	Fan out	Lines of Code	# critical Bugs
Halstead Program Diff.	Call out	-	Change rate
-	-	-	Lines of Code

evolution metrics similar to the ones described in [3]. For the visualization we applied Polymetric Views by Lanza *et al.* [4]. Within the EVOSPACES project we focused on the usefulness of the third dimension and improvements with respect to the comprehension of a visualized software project.

For each software project we can define the mapping to the visual metaphors (glyphs) individually, therefore enabling to reflect particular characteristics such as certain metrics or evolutionary changes. Hence, we exploit the concepts of metric clusters and metric configuration.

2.1 Metric Clusters

Metric Clusters are defined as a set of specific metrics that in combination enable analysis of particular software entities (see Table 1). Pinzger [5] uses a similar concept to build characteristic views on source code evolution. According to that work, a combination of meaningfully clustered metrics can facilitate the comprehensibility of a software visualization.

A Hot-Spot Metric Cluster, for example, combines *number of functions*, *lines of code*, *Cyclomatic Complexity* [6] and *Halstead Programm Difficulty* [7] into one particular metrics cluster that accentuates complex software components that exhibit a variety of functionality. Metric Clusters in EVOSPACES help define presets for the metric mappings that can be used independently from the different visualizations.

The reason why Metric Clusters are a powerful concept becomes clear when we want to combine analysis data from completely different analysis methods. We can simply build a new Metric Cluster out of the freshly analyzed data and visualize this context according to our needs.

2.2 Metrics Configuration

The second concept used to facilitate the mapping of metrics with their glyphs is a Software Visualization Mixer (SV-Mixer). With the SV-Mixer we adopt the concepts of an audio mixer for software visualization. The idea is to map particular software metrics to the visual metaphors, like an audio mixer processes audio signals before sending the result to an amplifier. The metric values can then be filtered, normalized or transformed according to the SV-Mixer's configuration before composing a visualization. This allows us to quickly adjust the visual mappings according to our focus while exploring the view.

Metric Cluster

System Hot–Spot View (Size ... ▼) (+) (–)

Configure with 1 Entities   [Configure]

Ch	Visual Representation	Metric
1.1.	House roof width	Lines of Code ▼
1.1.	House roof height	Number of ... ▼
1.1.	House body width	Cyclomatic ... ▼
1.1.	House body height	Halstead Di... ▼
2.1.	2D Gradient X–Compo	Lines of Code ▼
2.1.	2D Gradient Y–Compo	Cyclomatic ... ▼
3.1.	2D Gradient Red–Com	Lines of Code ▼
3.1.	2D Gradient Blue–Com	Cyclomatic ... ▼

House roof width

Metric   [Lines of Code   ▼]

🔍

26.90   27.27   27.63   41.45

Filtertyp   [Transparent ▼]

Relation Inverted   ☐

Min Filter

○——————————————————   1

Max Filter

○——————————————————   800

Scaling

▓▓▓▓▓——————○——————   372.5

Fig. 1. SV-Mixer: on the left is the general Metric Cluster selection, on the right the editable entities per channel

2.3 Cognitive Glyphs

Glyphs are visual representations of software metrics. They are generated out of a group of visual components that we call visual representation component. Each visual representation component corresponds to a channel in the SV-Mixer. A Metric Cluster in the SV-Mixer is therefore mapped to the visual representation components used for a particular glyph. As such, the value of the mapped metric specifies the value of the glyph's visual representation. Cognitive glyphs are visual representation components that depict common real-world objects in a particular metaphor. For example, houses in a city could represent classes or packages in a software system. The different dimensions of a house would be represented by software metrics.

Fig. 2 depicts such a house, where the the roof width corresponds to the number of functions, the roof height to the lines of code, the body width of the house to the Halstead program difficulty, and the body height to the cyclomatic complexity measure.

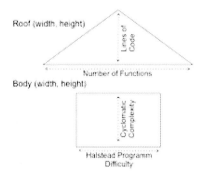

Fig. 2. SV-Mixer metrics mapping on glyphs

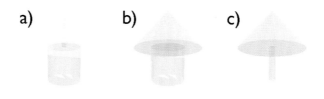

Fig. 3. Cognitive Glyphs showing two miss-shaped a), c) and a well-shaped house b)

The software city of a particular software project then consists of such houses, all of the same metrics cluster mapped to house dimensions. This allows us to cognitively compare houses in a software city and find outliers or somehow special houses or districts of houses. With that, software is visualized in a more comprehensible way leading to a focus on the relevant aspects, unlike glyphs that are not based on a metaphor (*e.g.,* Starglyphs [8]).

To build a house glyph, for example, we can use four parameters together with their metric mappings. Two metric can be mapped to represent the width and height of the roof, where as the other two metrics are mapped to the width and height of the body of the house. For these 4 size dimensions of a house we can use different Metric Cluster mappings and therefore visualize different aspects of a house.

In the context of a Hot-Spot Metric Cluster the example in Figure 3 a) represents a complex class, visualized with a large house body (complexity), and a comparable small house roof width (*number of functions*) and a medium to large roof height (*lines of code*). The house glyph shows a software component that has reasonably-sized complex code on a few functions, likely a class implementing a complex algorithm. Such houses would be considered problematic candidates to maintain and evolve.

With cognitive glyphs a viewer can distinguish a well-shaped glyph from a miss-shaped one rather quickly. However to intuitively provide orientation about well-designed aspects and distressed ones in the software system, we need to accurately normalize metrics.

For this purpose we implemented a technique to normalize the mapped metrics to each other. In the context of the SV-Mixer the idea is to do the normalization similar to an audio mixer's pitcher. The pitcher stretches or condenses different audio sources to bring them in tune. Similarly we tune the visual representation values of the mapped metrics to meet a specific project's needs. With the normalization, the mapped metrics are customized to represent a well-shaped piece of the software as a well-shaped glyph. As with a pitcher, the mapped metrics normalization factor is adjusted with a slider. In the default configuration a linear function is used, but non-linear regression would fit as well for normalization. The default normalization value ($scalV$) for each metric is calculated with the minimal ($minMV$) and the maximal value ($maxMV$) as well as the current scaling ($curSV$) slider value of the mapped metric:

$$scalV = minMV + \frac{(maxMV - minMV)}{curSV}$$

The concept of normalization further *enables comparability of projects through visualization even if the analyzed context differs substantially.* This is the case since the normalized cognitive glyphs represent a similar well-shaped glyph from a well-shaped piece of the software.

2.4   Code Smells

Instead of mapping metrics directly to cognitive glyphs, we can provide a user with extended information based on a code smell analysis of the entities of interest. Different approaches exist to find code smells or anti-patterns in source code. In our work, we use the approach developed by Lanza and Marinescu in [9]. Based on the detected code smells the glyphs would be visualized differently. This can be done with a traditional approach such as coloring the detected entities according to a color concept (see Figure 4). The bottleneck in coloring the entities based on their detected code smells is that we cannot apply simultaneously another color concept to the data set. This is even worse whenever an entity includes two or more different code smells, we would need to color the entities with a default color. However, a default color leaves us with just little, and imprecise piece of information. We still would need to further dig into the entity to see which code smells were detected. On the other hand we can use various different cognitive glyphs based on the code smell analysis result. The advantage is that the combination of code smells would be visible as a further glyph.

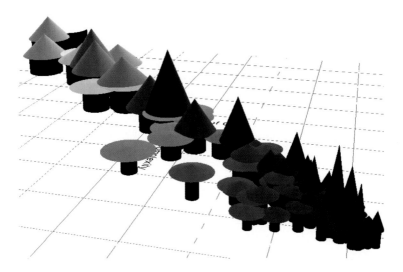

Fig. 4. House glyphs showing a set of classes of a commercial web application framework using the Hot-Spot metric cluster mapping; the brighter the color the higher the god class potential

2.5   Releases and Evolution

With cognitive glyphs we visualize time in two different but convenient ways. First, we present the glyphs of all the releases of a single software component, laid out accordingly on a time axis to depict whenever relevant changes have happened. Second, we visualize the components as a set of visual snapshots. Then we can switch through those snapshots and get a small animation like presentation showing the key changes between releases.

However changes to components between releases are harder to perceive in the snapshots. Since an all-in-one view offers more comparability, we typically prefer the first approach on small data sets.

2.6 Tagging Glyphs and Visualization States

To preserve visualization states or remember interesting glyphs for later analysis we implemented a concept for tagging. This is convenient since during the navigation within a visualization, relevant aspects are spotted and need to be remembered before proceeding with the software exploration. The remembered aspects can then later be analyzed or shared within the working group. Furthermore such a tagging functionality is useful whenever one wants to switch to other visualizations and likes to further examine the spotted components from another view.

3 Code (as a) City

To provide some tangibility to the abstract nature of software systems, we experimented with the various metaphors presented in Section 2. Eventually, we settled on a city metaphor [10], because it offers a clear notion of locality and orientation, and also features a structural complexity which cannot be oversimplified. These advantages led to adoption of the city metaphor, described next, in the project's supporting tool.

3.1 The City Metaphor

Although the idea of using a 3D city-inspired metaphor to depict software systems has been explored before [11, 12, 13, 14, 15, 16], our solution provides a good compromise between level of detail and scalability. According to our domain mapping, a software system is visualized as a 3D city, in which the buildings represent the classes of the system, while the city's districts represent the packages in which the classes are defined.

The visual properties of the city artifacts carry information about the software elements they represent. The set of properties able to reflect the values of the chosen metrics is composed of the three dimensions (width, length, and height), the color, and sometimes the position. We extended the idea of the polymetric views [4] to 3D. Apart from the familiarity of the city metaphor, its main benefit is that it visually represents the software entities in terms of a number of metrics in the context of the system's structure (*i.e.,* given by the package hierarchy). By combining this domain mapping with property mappings [17] and efficient layouts we provide the viewer with an overview of the structure of a system, while pointing out the outliers.

3.2 Exploring a City

Figure 6 presents the CodeCity [18] representation of ArgoUML version 0.24, which is a 137 kLOC Java system with about 2,500 classes and 140 packages. We mapped the

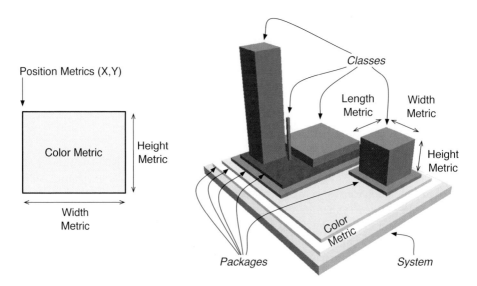

Fig. 5. Our city metaphor (right) drew inspiration from the polymetric views (left)

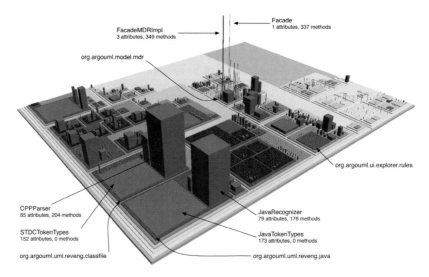

Fig. 6. The city of ArgoUML, release 0.24

classes' *number of methods* (NOM) metric on the height of the buildings and the *number of attributes* (NOA) metric on their base size. The districts of the city are colored according to the nesting level of the package, based on a blue color scheme: the deeper the nesting level of the package, the darker the shade of blue of the district.

This overview gives us a comprehensive image of ArgoUML system. The city is composed of one large district, which is ArgoUML itself and two other districts (at the upper-right periphery), representing the subset of the java and the javax libraries used by ArgoUML. In the main district we see two skyscrapers, which represent the interface Facade and the class FacadeMDRImpl implementing it, both in the package org.argouml.model.mdr. The two are the absolute outliers in terms of the number of methods metric, which is visible from the very first look. There are two other pairs, both made of one massive building and one flat and wide building, which provide the parsing functionality for Java and C++ code. These pairs are part of ArgoUML's mechanism for generating source code from UML diagrams. The two buildings that look like parking-lots are containers for constants, while the two enormous ones have large amounts of functionality and also many attributes, which classifies them as potential *God classes* [19]. After our eyes get used to the outliers, we see some uniformly built districts, such as the one of the package org.argouml.ui.explorer.rules, in which the buildings are all of the same size. This happens because the majority of the classes in that package are concrete implementations of an abstract class which defines 4 methods, and all of them implement exactly 4 methods, a case depicted by buildings of equal heights.

3.3   Property Mapping Policies

The most straightforward mapping of software metrics onto visual properties is the *identity mapping, i.e.,* one that uses the identity function. In this case, the visual proper-ties accurately reflect the real magnitude of the software systems in terms of the chosen metrics. However, the large variety of sizes cannot be easily processed by humans, as it has been assessed that humans can preattentively process a limited number of different sizes [20].

To address this issue, we looked into representing only a limited number of building types. In Figure 7 we present the types of buildings with their assigned sizes, in which the unit is "storey", *e.g.,* an apartment block is a six-storeyed building, and an example of their visual representations. Since we map two different metrics, it is possible to have different combinations, such as a one-storeyed house with the width and length of an apartment block: it would be a class with few methods and a large number of attributes. The metric values now need to be appropriately mapped on these building types. We designed and implemented two policies for the categorized mapping, namely *boxplot-based* mapping and *threshold-based* mapping.

The *boxplot-based mapping* uses the boxplot technique, widely used in statistics [21,22], which reveals the center of the data, its spread, its distribution, and the presence of outliers. Building a boxplot requires the computation of the following values: the minimum and maximum non-outlier values (*i.e.,* whiskers) and the three quartiles (*i.e.,* lower quartile, median, and upper quartile). For our mapping (see Figure 8) we use the whiskers and the lower and upper quartiles as thresholds which split the values for a software metric within a system in 5 categories, corresponding to: lower outliers, lower values, average values, upper values, and upper outliers. Two metric values within the same category, even if they greatly differ, are mapped on the same building type.

An important property of the boxplot is that the interquartile range (*i.e.,* between the lower and the upper quartile) hosts the central 50 % of the data, which insures well-balanced cities in terms of its buildings, *i.e.,* at least half of them are apartment blocks. This very property is also its main drawback: the category distribution is always balanced, which obstructs system comparison. To tackle this, we provide a *threshold-based mapping* policy which allows the definition of the category thresholds, based

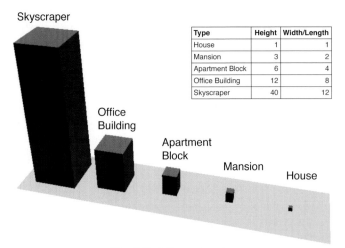

Skyscraper

Type	Height	Width/Length
House	1	1
Mansion	3	2
Apartment Block	6	4
Office Building	12	8
Skyscraper	40	12

Office
Building

Apartment
Block

Mansion

House

Fig. 7. Building categories

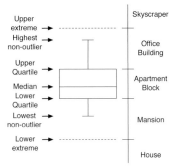

Fig. 8. Boxplot-based mapping and the corresponding building types

on statistical information. The threshold "magic numbers" need to hold across system boundaries and are thus not easy to obtain. We use values presented in [9], where the authors measured many widely different systems in terms of size, domain, and type (*e.g.,* commercial, open-source) and produced threshold values for many software metrics. For Java systems, the threshold values for number of methods are 4 (low), 7 (average), 10 (high), and 15 (very high).

The result of applying the three presented mapping policies on the same system varies significantly. To discuss this issue, we use two examples taken from ArgoUML (Figure 9 and Figure 10), in which the interfaces are colored yellow and the classes brown, and the most extreme-sized buildings are annotated. While with identity mapping one can visually compare the actual metric values by looking at the building heights, this apparent advantage vanishes in front of the large number of different sizes which are hardly distinguishable. Another disadvantage of the identity mapping is that classes with very low metric values are difficult to spot, due to their small size. In Figure 9 we see that even on such a small subsystem, it is already very difficult to have an

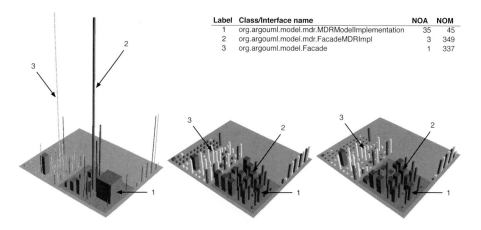

Label	Class/Interface name	NOA	NOM
1	org.argouml.model.mdr.MDRModelImplementation	35	45
2	org.argouml.model.mdr.FacadeMDRImpl	3	349
3	org.argouml.model.Facade	1	337

Fig. 9. Identity (left), boxplot-based (center), and threshold-based (bottom) mappings applied to the district of package **org.argouml.model** (ArgoUML)

overview and yet be able to see the small houses. The best visibility is obtained with the boxplot-based mapping, where there is a visible balance among the categories. While the difference between the classes of the same category is not visible anymore, the very small buildings are still reasonably sized and do not risk to appear as invisible. The threshold-based mapping provides a better overview than the identity mapping and still offers a sense of the distribution of the very large and very small classes.

3.4 Layout

To achieve a scalable visualization for large-scale software systems, we need an efficient layout which satisfies the following requirements:

1. does not waste the real-estate of the cities,
2. reflects the given containment relationships, and
3. takes into account the metric-dependent dimensions of the buildings.

Figure 11 presents the layout of the ArgoUML system, in which the buildings appear as white (for increased clarity) and the districts in shades of blue, according to the nesting level of the package. In spite of the similarities to treemaps [23], our layout must deal with fixed dimensions (as opposed to percentages) of the elements as the result of the metric mappings, which makes it more similar to a rectangle packing problem. Unlike a treemap algorithm, our layout cannot establish *a priori* how much space will it need to place the element.

We implemented a space-efficient layout, which uses a 2-dimensional kd-tree [24] to do the space partitioning and keeps track of the space currently covered. To chose the place for an element within the city's real estate, the layout algorithm takes into account the following criteria, ordered by priority: (1) a place which does not cause the expansion of the city's covered area and if there are several nodes, the one using the space most efficiently (the available space of the node is closer to dimension of

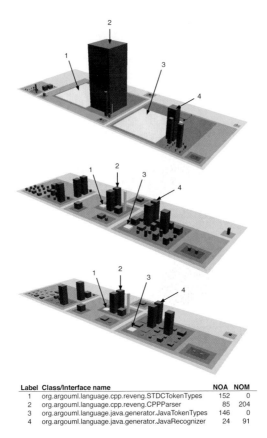

Label	Class/Interface name	NOA	NOM
1	org.argouml.language.cpp.reveng.STDCTokenTypes	152	0
2	org.argouml.language.cpp.reveng.CPPParser	85	204
3	org.argouml.language.java.generator.JavaTokenTypes	146	0
4	org.argouml.language.java.generator.JavaRecognizer	24	91

Fig. 10. Identity (top), boxplot-based (center), and threshold-based (bottom) mappings applied to the district of package org.argouml.language (ArgoUML)

the element), (2) a place which causes the expansion, and among these the one which produces a covered area closest to a square (for aesthetics).

3.5 Topology

During our research, we also experimented the notion of topology by representing the package hierarchy as stacked platforms, thus placing the buildings at different altitudes, as can be seen in Figure 12.

3.6 Prototyping with CodeCity

We concretized the domain mapping, several property mapping policies, a number of layouts and the topology in a prototyping tool called CodeCity [18]. As a proof of the scalability and language-independence Figure 13 shows a visualization of ten systems written in Java, Smalltalk, and C++, comprising over 1.25 million lines of source code.

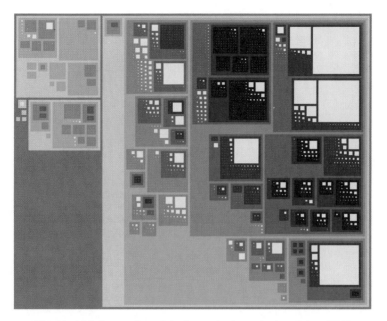

Fig. 11. A birds-eye view of the layout in the code city of ArgoUML

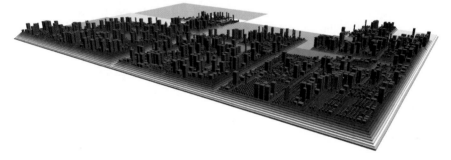

Fig. 12. Topology of the Azureus systems

4   Dynamic Information

All ideas presented earlier in this chapter are dealing with static data obtained from the source code of the analyzed software. In this section we will cover another part of our reverse engineering toolbox: the visualization of the execution of programs or, rather, the execution trace of the software when it executes a specific task. An execution trace is the record of all the method called when a user is working with the software. This tells us which classes and methods are involved in the implememantation of the scenario run by the user. This complements the static understanding of the software by the maintenance engineers by showing them exactly what are the software elements involved in a specific task. In our project we used Mozilla Firefox as the test bench and the trace was recorded when interacting with this application. The corresponding data volume is huge: about seventeen millions calls (including system calls).

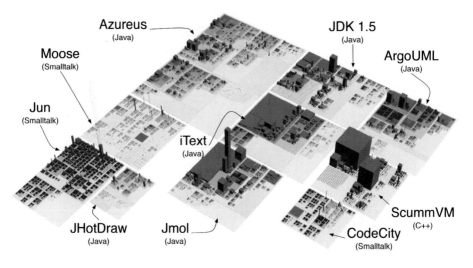

Fig. 13. A proof of CodeCity's scalability

4.1 The Night View Metaphor

While walking in a city during the night, if one sees an office building with lights on, this is usually associated with workers on duty. Since our project has developed the city metaphor, the night view is easily understandable: we light the buildings depending on the involvment of the corresponding class in the trace. Considering the data volume of an execution trace, it is not possible to display it without some preprocessing. Then, based on a segmentation technique [25], we could create an animated view of the running of the software at two granularity level: macroscopic and microscopic. This visualisation is directly implemented in the EvoSpaces tool which will be detailed in the next section.

4.2 Segmentation of the Trace

To cope with the quantity of information of the execution trace, the current trend in literature is to compress it to remove the redundancies. There are two categories of compression algorithms: lossy and lossless. Basically the lossless algorithms try to identify and eliminate the recurring patterns in the trace. In the compressed trace, such an algorithm keeps only one occurence of the pattern and replaces the others by a reference to the first. The simplest example of this technique is when a set of contiguous similar events are replaced by a single occurrence associated with the number of repetitions. As an example of a much more sophisticated algorithm Hamou-Lhadj and Lethbridge used the common subexpression algorithm [26, 27] originally developed to identify patterns in DNA analysis. The lossy algorithms, i.e. the ones that do not preserve the information after compression, use approximate match techniques to find the recurring patterns to eliminate. For example, the depth of the search in the call tree of methods can be bounded. De Pauw et al. [28] presents half a dozen of such lossy techniques. Since our work focuses on identifying the classes or files that are specific to the implementation of a given business function and the way it is implemented, our concern is less to

Analysis frame = movie frame

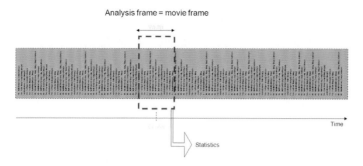

Time

Statistics

Fig. 14. The segmentation of the trace

find general techniques for trace compression than to actually "see" the involvement of classes and files in the trace as time passes. However, it is clear that one cannot present the sequence of building illuminations in the city according to each event in the trace. This sequence would take hours to display. Therefore, we developed a segmentation technique to summarize the information. The key idea is to split it the execution trace into contiguous segments of a given duration (width). Next, we analyze each segment to extract some information about class occurence (fig. 14). Finally, we present the information found as a sequence of images. The results can then be displayed as a movie, each image (frame) representing one segment of the execution trace [29].

In figure 14 the text displayed vertically represents the events (method calls) in the trace. Starting from this segmentation idea we defined two representations for the trace:

– The macroscopic view that represents the trace as the sequence of segments;
– The microscopic view that represents the sequence of events in a selected segment.

In the macroscopic view, one computes the number of occurrences of each class i.e. the number of method executions (events) of the class in each segment. Next, this number is associated to one of the three categories of occurrences we defined: low, medium or high. Each category is mapped to a specific colour. The limit bewteen the categories are user-defined (threshold-based mapping 3.3). For example, the occurrences of a given class below 10 could be displayed in blue, the occurrences between 10 and 49 in green and the occurrence above 50 in red (fig. 15).

Finally, each building in a "frame" (image) is illuminated using this colour. The resulting "movie" is obtained by the sequential display of the illuminated building for

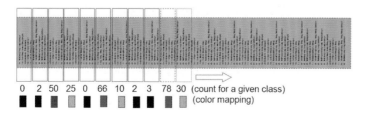

0   2   50   25   0   66   10   2   3   78   30   (count for a given class)
                                                    (color mapping)

Fig. 15. Class occurrences mapped to colors

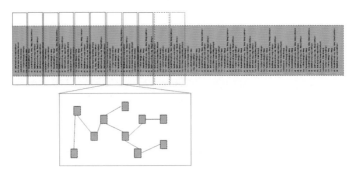

Fig. 16. Events belonging to a segment

Fig. 17. Microscopic view

each segment. With this representation we can observe, by looking at the whole land-scape and the colour of the buildings, what are the active "regions" of the software (i.e. packages, subsystems) at any moment in time and what are the most active classes in each of these regions. In the microscopic view the time scale is reduced to a single segment as shown in figure 16. Then we display sequentially each method called in each of the classes by drawing solid lines between the buildings representing the classes (fig. 17). While the increment of time in the macroscopic view is one segment, the increment of time in the microscopic view is the elementary invocation of a single method call (event). It is worth noting that the buildings keep the same colours in both views to show the most active classes in the segments.

4.3 Filtering Uninteresting Classes

Since we want to understand the role of the classes through the visualization of the program execution, we must be able to associate the classes to the externally observable behaviour of the program. Therefore since this behaviour changes while the program is running, we naturally focus on the classes that occur (are involved) in specific locations of the trace. In other words, the classes that are evenly distributed throughout the trace cannot be linked to any specific business task. In fact these classes often have a transversal responsibility, implementing some aspect of the software like logging, security check and the like. By analogy with signal theory, these classes are considered as noise and must be filtered out. Traditional frequency analysis work defines a class frequency simply as the number of times the class appears in the execution trace [30, 31]. However, to identify the noise, we cannot simply count the occurrences of some classes but we must know where these occurrences happen in the trace. For example, a class that is found 10'000 times in the first 20% of the trace will be considered differently from a class that is found 10 times in 1000 evenly distributed locations. A class whose location is evenly distributed throughout the trace is called temporally omnipresent [25]. To interpret this idea in the Software City metaphor we could say that a building that stays illuminated all night long does not provide much information about when exactly people are working. By removing the temporally omnipresent classes, we greatly simplify the visualization of the trace on both the macroscopic and microscopic view.

5   EvoSpaces: Integrating the Best Ideas in a Prototype

Concepts and metaphors described before are all developed in separate prototypes specific to each group of research of the EvoSpaces project, this allowed more freedom to each group to try ideas faster. But the best ideas must at some point in time be stabilized and integrated into the same prototype (called EvoSpaces). This section will present how the platform is architectured, then the way the ideas presented earlier have been implemented in EvoSpaces and finally the inteface of the tool.

5.1   The Platform's Architecture

To allow our tool to display systems written in different programming paradigms and to be able to quickly integrate new visualization metaphors in the tool's architecture is made of five layers (fig . 18). Thanks to the well-defined interfaces between layers, changes made inside a given layer will have a limited impact on the other layers. For example, the rendering engine will not be affected if one analyzes a system written in a new programming language, provided it follows the same paradigm (object oriented for example).

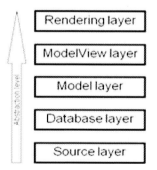

Fig. 18. Layered architecture

Fig. 19. The animated relations between entities

Source Code Layer

This layer represents the raw source code of the software under investigation structured as files. Those files are parsed off-line to fill the database of code elements. Since we do not know at parsing time what information the users will look for, we have chosen to extract as much structural information as possible from the source code. Moreover, a set of widely used software engineering metrics is computed for the target system while the database is loaded. This layer is also used to retrieve the source code of some selected element on the screen, when this code must be displayed.

Database Layer

At the database level, the source code elements are represented as tables and relationship. Elements like classes, methods, variables, attributes, packages, files or modules are mapped to tables. The way those elements are structured (through programming language constructs), communicate or work together is represented as relationships. The database contains one table per software entity and one table per "relationships" between software entities. Therefore, in the database, the software under investigation is modeled as a huge entity-relationship schema. Moreover, all entities and relationships have extra properties like source level information (names, labels, parameters) and metric values. These properties depend on the element or relationship considered. The classes in the database layer implement the access to the tables. Basically they consists of "builders" [32], that instantiate the objects representing entities and relationships.

Model Layer

The Model layer implements the object representation of the loaded entities and relationships in the EvoSpaces system. Each kind of entity or relationship is represented by its own class. Consequently, this layer contains two hierarchies of classes, one for the entities and one for the relationships, following the Famix metamodel for objectoriented programming languages [33].

Fig. 20. The city in EvoSpaces

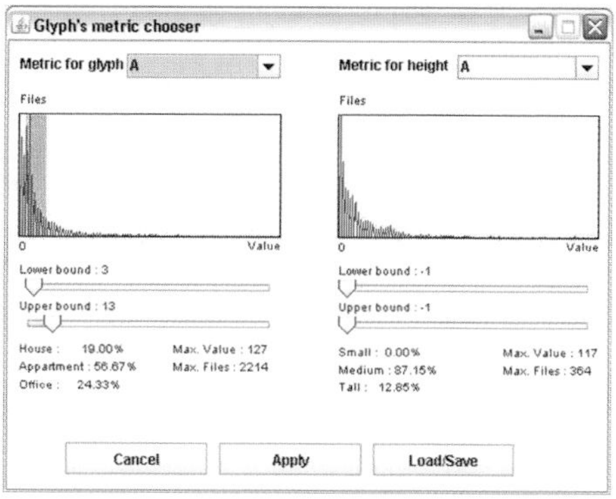

Fig. 21. The buildings' metric chooser

ModelView Layer

This layer is the first to deal with visualization issues. It contains all the values and parameters used for the 3D rendering of the entities and relationships. Each object in the ModelView layer has a counterpart in the Model layer. Then, the ModelView layer contains two hierarchies of classes, one for the entities and one for the relationships that are similar to the hierarchies in the Model layer. However the entities and the relationships of the ModelView layer only contain displayable data. The ModelView layer works as a visual abstraction of the raw data stored in the model layer: it maps the data of the model layer to displayable elements. In particular, this is where:

– The glyphs (graphical objects representing data through visual parameters are mapped to a given type of entity or relationship;
– The values of the metrics are mapped to some visual scale (saturation of colors for example) and positions in the 3D space (layout).

Moreover since we wish our system to allow us experiment with different representations, the same entity or relationship in the Model layer may be mapped to different visual objects in the ModelView layer. This makes it possible to maintain several concurrent views of the same set of software elements. However, at any given time, only one view will be displayed. This layer, which represents the largest part of our system, also contains the classes that control the interactions with the user. Any entity or relationship in this layer is associated with four objects: a shape, a color, a layout and a list of "reactions" to user actions. The "shape" defines how the element will look like in the 3D view (the glyph). It can be as simple as a fixed size geometric volume, like a cube or a cylinder, or be a much more sophisticated visual element, using transparency effects and textures. Since we adopted the City metaphor to represent software entities, the classes and files are represented as buildings and the relationships as solid pipes between the buildings. The visual features of the buildings (size and texture) are set according to the values of user-selected metrics. However, we soon realized that a linear mapping from metrics to visual features was not useful since users have a great difficulty to compare close visual feature, like a little difference in size or color. Therefore, we decided to use a threshold-based mapping. Then the visual features are presented as three, easy to interpret, categories. Each category is mapped to a user-defined range of metric value. For example, the texture represents three different kind of building: house, apartment block, office building. Then we can map a given texture to a file according its number of lines of code (LOC). Since C++ header files (.h) are a special kind of file, we decided to map it as yet another kind of building: the city hall with columns. Another metric can be mapped to the height of the buildings, chosen among three categories: tall, medium and small. To strengthen the City metaphor, we represent the functions and procedures inside the files or classes as stickmen of different colors (to distinguish function and procedure). In fact, these represent the "workers" in the buildings. Each stickman is surrounded by yellow boxes (its resources) representing the local variables used by the procedures or functions. Once visualized, the user can interact with the displayed objects. Each visual element owns a list of potential actions that the user may perform on it. For example, the user could request to display the value of some metric for the object, to change its visual appearance, to display the related elements, to display the corresponding source file, etc. The list of possible actions is defined for each type of elements and is accessible through a contextual menu.

Rendering Layer

All the mechanism responsible for the actual display of the views on the screen are located in the Rendering layer. The 3D rendering library used is JOGL [34], a binding of OpenGL for Java, which has been released by Sun for Windows, Solaris, Linux and Mac OS platforms. The rendering engine, which is responsible for the drawing of the 3D scene on the screen, uses the data stored in the ModelView objects. This engine also catches the actions of the user and executes the corresponding operations.

5.2   Interaction with the Visual Objects

Our investigations on the interactions modes with the tool went along three directions. First, we studied the way to display the information retrieved from the database.

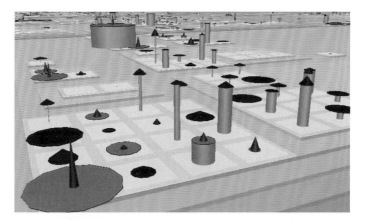

Fig. 22. House glyphs in the EvoSpaces environnment

Second we investigated the ways to dynamically change the viewing parameters of the entities and relationships in order to find the best metaphors for the software elements in given situation. Third we investigated the navigation among the displayed software elements. As a result each visual objects is associated with a context sensitive menu in the 3D space. For example, all the metrics available for a given object can be displayed from its contextual menu. Since the kinds of relationship between the software elements are numerous, the user can select the one he wants to display in a preference window. The corresponding relationships will be displayed as solid pipes between the associated elements. To represent the directionality of the relationship, we display a colored segment moving along the pipe from the origin to the destination. This gives the impression of the flow of information between the elements (figure 19). The relationships can also be used to navigate the City. By clicking on a relationship, the user can ask the system to move the camera to the element located at the origin or at the end of a relationship. Therefore the user can navigate the City using the connected elements. Finally, to set up and orient the camera in the 3D scene the user can use the buttons in a navigation panel or use their mouse and keyboard counterpart. Moreover the objects representing the files or classes can contain other objects (methods and variables). To display this contents, the user can enter into the buildings to show its "workers" (stickmen).

5.3   Integration of the Research Groups' Ideas

City View

The buildings in the city are grouped together by packages. The buildings are sized depending on the value of two metrics selected by the user, the first for the kind of the building and the second for its size. Figure 20 shows how the city in EvoSpaces looks like. Figure 21 shows the panel that lets the user choose the two metrics to map to the kind and size of the building as well as the boundary of the metric value categories (threshold-based mapping).

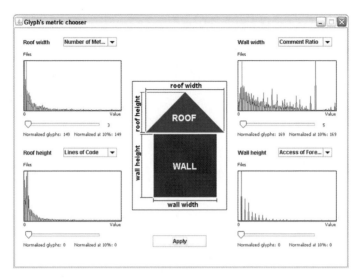

Fig. 23. The house glyphs normalizer

Fig. 24. The city by night, macroscopic view

House Glyphs

To diplay the house glyphs view we switch the representation of the files and classes from buildings to houses. But the elements keep the same location in the 3D space (figure 22). Since this representation can display four metrics at the same time, we designed a specific panel to select the corresponding metrics (figure 23). To implement the idea of the "normalizer", a scaling factor can be set for the metrics.

Night View

The night view allow us to display the execution trace in two different time scales: macroscopic and microscopic. Figure 24 present one frame (segment) of the macroscopic view and figure 25 presents the tool to set the threshold to eliminate noise in the

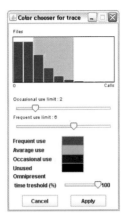

Fig. 25. The city by night's color and noise level chooser

Fig. 26. The city by night, microscopic view

dynamic display (i.e. omnipresent elements in the execution trace). In the same way as the other metrics, we group the number of calls to a class in three categories (high, medium and low). The limits between these categories are set with the same pannel.

To launch the microscopic view (figure 26), i.e. to display the individual calls in a single segment of the execution trace, one freezes the macroscopic view at a given segment. Then we display the calls in the execution trace in sequence as solid lines between the buildings. We can display up to ten calls at a time but with different brightness to identify the sequence of calls, the brighter the more recent in time. Self calls are displayed as rings around the elements.

6 Conclusions

With software systems becoming increasingly complex, software evolution has to be addressed in a systematic way by providing adequate means for dealing with this complexity. Multi-dimensional, multi-view visualization adopting techniques from the areas of architecting as well as multimedia and visualization will be one major technology for software engineers to get a grip on software complexity for development, maintenance and evolution of successful software systems.

Our project aimed at exploiting multi-dimensional navigation spaces to efficiently visualize evolving software systems to ease analysis and maintenance. One of the outcomes of the project is the EVOSPACES prototype implemented as plug-in to Eclipse, in which large software systems can be visualized and navigated in 3D.

This virtual world is named *software city* because we used the city metaphor to represent the virtual software entities. In a software city, the classes or files are represented as buildings displayed in districts representing the containing packages or directories. Then, the methods or functions are represented as stickmen when the inside of the buildings is displayed. The size and dimension of the buildings are set according to the value of user-selected metrics. The city then gets a different shape depending on the selected metric. We can also easily filter information based on some given metric threshold. Finally, the relationships between the classes or files are represented as solid animated pipes to show the flow of information. In this virtual world, not only the static relationships, but also the dynamic behavior can be visually represented thanks to a technique to display execution traces. The prototype has been architected so that extensions can easily be built and integrated.

As for the scientific dissemination, our approaches and prototypes have been presented in specialized international conferences and have attracted the interest of the research community (see our publications in the references section). For future work, we will extend our research to a multi-user environment where people collaborate to solve problems. This implies to develop research in two directions: (1) collaborative maintenance of software systems; and (2) metaphors and models to ease teamwork on the same system.

Acknowledgement

We are grateful to the Hasler Foundation Switzerland, who has generously supported this project.

References

1. Erlikh, L.: Leveraging legacy system dollars for e-business. IT Professional 2, 17–23 (2000)
2. Zelkowitz, M., Shaw, A., Gannon, J.: Principles of Software Engineering and Design. Prentice-Hall, Englewood Cliffs (1979)
3. Pinzger, M., Gall, H., Fischer, M., Lanza, M.: Visualizing multiple evolution metrics. In: Proc. ACM Symp. on Softw. Visualization, pp. 67–75 (2005)
4. Lanza, M., Ducasse, S.: Polymetric views — a lightweight visual approach to reverse engineering. IEEE Trans. on Softw. Eng. 29, 782–795 (2003)

5. Pinzger, M.: ArchView - Analyzing Evolutionary Aspects of Complex Software Systems. Vienna University of Technology (2005)
6. McCabe, T.J.: A complexity measure. IEEE Trans. on Softw. Eng. 2 (1976)
7. Halstead, M.H.: Elements of software science, operating and programming system series. 7, Elsevier, Amsterdam (1977)
8. Fanea, E., Carpendale, S., Isenberg, T.: An interactive 3d integration of parallel coordinates and star glyphs. In: IEEE Symp. on Info. Visualization, 149–156 (2005)
9. Lanza, M., Marinescu, R.: Object-Oriented Metrics in Practice. Springer, Heidelberg (2006)
10. Wettel, R., Lanza, M.: Visualizing software systems as cities. In: Proceedings of VISSOFT 2007 (4th IEEE International Workshop on Visualizing Software For Understanding and Analysis), pp. 92–99 (2007)
11. Knight, C., Munro, M.C.: Virtual but visible software. In: International Conference on Information Visualisation, pp. 198–205 (2000)
12. Charters, S.M., Knight, C., Thomas, N., Munro, M.: Visualisation for informed decision making; from code to components. In: International Conference on Software Engineering and Knowledge Engineering (SEKE 2002), pp. 765–772. ACM Press, New York (2002)
13. Marcus, A., Feng, L., Maletic, J.I.: 3d representations for software visualization. In: Proceedings of the ACM Symposium on Software Visualization, pp. 27–36. IEEE, Los Alamitos (2003)
14. Balzer, M., Noack, A., Deussen, O., Lewerentz, C.: Software landscapes: Visualizing the structure of large software systems. In: VisSym, Symposium on Visualization, Eurographics Association, pp. 261–266 (2004)
15. Langelier, G., Sahraoui, H.A., Poulin, P.: Visualization-based analysis of quality for large-scale software systems. In: Proceedings of 20th IEEE/ACM International Conference on Automated Software Engineering (ASE 2005), pp. 214–223. ACM, New York (2005)
16. Panas, T., Epperly, T., Quinlan, D., Saebjornsen, A., Vuduc, R.: Communicating software architecture using a unified single-view visualization. In: Proceedings of ICECCS 2007 (12th IEEE International Conference on Engineering Complex Computer Systems), pp. 217–228 (2007)
17. Wettel, R., Lanza, M.: Program comprehension through software habitability. In: Proceedings of ICPC 2007 (15th International Conference on Program Comprehension), pp. 231–240 (2007)
18. Wettel, R., Lanza, M.: Codecity: 3d visualization of large-scale software. In: ICSE Companion 2008: Companion of the 30th International Conference on Software Engineering, pp. 921–922. ACM, New York (2008)
19. Riel, A.: Object-Oriented Design Heuristics. Addison-Wesley, Reading (1996)
20. Few, S.: Show me the numbers: Designing Tables and Graphs to Enlighten. Analytics Press (2004)
21. Tukey, J.W.: Exploratory Data Analysis. Addison-Wesley, Reading (1977)
22. Triola, M.: Elementary Statistics. Addison-Wesley, Reading (2006)
23. Shneiderman, B.: Tree visualization with tree-maps: 2-d space-filling approach. ACM Trans. Graph. 11, 92–99 (1992)
24. Bentley, J.L.: Multidimensional binary search trees used for associative searching. Commun. ACM 18, 509–517 (1975)
25. Dugerdil, P.: Using trace sampling techniques to identify dynamic clusters of classes. In: Proc. of the IBM CAS Software and Systems Engineering Symposium (CASCON) (2007)
26. Hamou-Lhadj, A., Lethbridge, T.: Summarizing the content of large traces to facilitate the understanding of the behavior of a software system. In: Proc. of the IEEE Int. Conf. on Program Comprehension (ICPC 2006) (2006)

27. Hamou-Lhadj, A., Lethbridge, T.: Compression techniques to simplify the analysis of large execution traces. In: Proc. of the IEEE Workshop on Program Comprehension (IWPC) (2002)
28. Pauw, W.D., Lorenz, D., Vlissides, J., Wegman, M.: Execution patterns in object-oriented visualization. In: Proc. of the USENIX Conf. on Object-Oriented Technologies and Systems (COOTS) (1998)
29. Dugerdil, P., Alam, S.: Execution trace visualization in a 3d space. In: Proc. of ITNG 2008 (5th International Conference on Information Technology: New Generations) (2008)
30. Ball, T.: The concept of dynamic analysis. In: Proc. 7th European Software Engineering Conf. (ESEC 1999) (1999)
31. Dugerdil, P., Alam, S.: Evospaces: 3d visualization of software architecture. In: 19th International Conference on Software Engineering and Knowledge Engineering (SEKE 2007), Boston (2007)
32. Gamma, E., Helm, R., Johnson, R., Vlissides, J.: Design Patterns. Elements of Reusable Object Oriented Software. Addison-Wesley Inc., Reading (1995)
33. Demeyer, S., Tichelaar, S., Ducasse, S.: Famix 2.1 — the famoos information exchange model. Technical report, University of Bern (2001)
34. Sun: Java binding for opengl (jogl), https://jogl.dev.java.net
35. Boccuzzo, S., Gall, H.C.: Cocoviz: Supported cognitive software visualization. In: Proc. Working Conf. on Reverse Eng. (2007)
36. Boccuzzo, S., Gall, H.C.: Cocoviz: Towards cognitive software visualization. In: Proc. IEEE Int'l Workshop on Visualizing Softw. for Understanding and Analysis (2007)

HOVISSE – Haptic Osteosynthesis Virtual Intra-operative Surgery Support Environment

Urs Künzler[1], Beatrice Amrhein[1], Jürgen Eckerle[1], Stephan Fischli[1], Robert Hauck[1], Dominik Hoigné[2], and Reto Witschi[1]

[1] Berne University of Applied Sciences
{urs.kuenzler,beatrice.amrhein,juergen.eckerle,stephan.fischli,
robert.hauck,reto.witschi}@bfh.ch
[2] University Hospital Basel
dominik.hoigne@unibas.ch

Abstract. The HOVISSE (Haptic Osteosynthesis Virtual Intra-operative Surgery Support Environment) project is a medical virtual reality research undertaking conducted in collaboration with the University Hospital of Basel and the Computer Science Department of the University of Basel. The HOVISSE project aims to develop a framework of software applications that provide a seamless digital support environment for osteosynthesis in trauma care. It offers assistance, beginning with the pre-operative planning phase when a surgeon can interactively select and position the fracture-appropriate implant in a 3D visio-haptic immersive environment. The surgeon's support extends to the intra-operative surgery phase, where a simulation of the medical procedures in the operating room allow the optimization of the surgical intervention. By integrating these subsystems into an interoperable system, the project improves the osteosynthesis workflow through coherent and consistent data access during the entire fracture reduction process.

1 Overview

The HOVISSE research project aims at developing a framework of software applications to form a support environment for osteosynthesis in trauma care through the use of virtual- and augmented-reality technologies. It provides assistance for pre-operative planning as well as for intra-operative surgery support in the operating room.

For pre-operative planning, a virtual reconstruction of the bone is visualized in a stereoscopic 3D immersive virtual reality environment. The surgeon's interaction with virtual bones is enabled through the use of a haptic force-feedback device. This allows the surgeon to understand the fracture morphology, its fragments, their mutual configuration, and simulate fragment repositioning and implant placement. To further support the surgeon's implant positioning decisions, bone-specific structural finite elements analysis (FEA) and statistical 3D bone modelling techniques have been investigated and will eventually be integrated into a later version of the planning subsystem.

D. Lalanne and J. Kohlas (Eds.): Human Machine Interaction, LNCS 5440, pp. 193–220, 2009.
© Springer-Verlag Berlin Heidelberg 2009

This very same pre-operative planning information must subsequently be retrieved and be accessible during the actual course of the operation. Another HOVISSE subsystem provides augmented reality views of the surgical site by overlaying pre-operative planning data using a head mounted display worn by the surgeon. Man-machine interaction is enabled via an eye-tracking system, since the surgeon's hands are restricted to the sterile operation site. In addition to surgical intervention planning, operating room planning is continuously gaining importance in hospitals due to new surgical procedures that require the deployment of an increasing number of medical devices in the operating room such as mobile fluoroscopy, endoscopy towers, etc. These issues have been addressed through the development of a subsystem for interactive operation workflow simulation within a CAVE 3D virtual environment.

In the context of this paper we concentrate on the description of the pre-operative osteosynthesis planning (Sec. 2) and the surgery workflow simulation (Sec. 3). Both subsystems have a strong focus on MMI topics and are introduced with a description of the medical problems that have been the motivation to develop these applications. The technical details of the graphics software framework used as basis for the implementation of these applications are described in Sec. 4. Sections for conclusion, acknowledgement and references conclude this paper.

2   Pre-operative Osteosynthesis Planning

2.1   Medical Motivation

Careful pre-operative planning is of critical importance for surgery success. Well done pre-operative planning can minimize the operation time and the medical complication rate, making higher quality achievable at lower cost.

In treatment of injured patients, comprehensive planning also takes into consideration the general condition of the patient and the circumstances. Based on the assessment of the time of operation, the form of anesthesia, and the interventional access path, the choice of the operating table (X-ray permeable) and the bearing of the patient have to be determined. In this section we focus specifically on the planning of the operation of a fractured bone. The planning of an osteosynthesis procedure includes the definition of the individual operation steps, the selection of the surgical instruments and the choice of implants. The treatment of fractured joints and fractured long bones does not have exactly the same goal and therefore the planning focuses on different aspects. In fractured joints the accurate re-establishment of the joint surface is one of the main objectives of the operation. However, in fractured long bones, the accurate anatomical reposition of the different fragments is not as important, but instead, the recovery of the axes, rotation and length is essential and quite delicate. If the surgeon could dissect all the fragments and bring them together under direct view, osteosynthesis would not be such a challenge. But one of the basic concepts of a medical operation is to maintain the remaining blood circulation as much as possible. Thus minimal invasive techniques are strived for. These techniques, however, also imply less direct contact of the surgeon with the fracture.

Haptic Osteosynthesis Planning

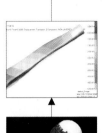

FEA Optimized Implant
Selection and Positioning

Intra-operative Planning Data
Information System

Statistical Modelling of 3D
Bone Morphology

Operating Room Interactive Surgery Workflow Simulation

Fig. 1. HOVISSE project overview with the different subsystems involved

It is therefore important that the surgeon understands the fracture type and the procedure of fracture reduction in detail, prior to the operation.

Today, the pre-operative planning of the osteosynthesis is based on two-dimensional X-ray images. These X-ray images are a summation of structure densities of a three-dimensional body. With this traditional technique of pre-operative planning, the individual fragments of the fracture are traced on separate transparency paper sheets. Thereafter the fragments drawn on these transparency sheets are arranged like a puzzle along an estimated axis of the bone (see Fig. 2). This theoretically reduced fracture is traced onto another transparency paper sheet. On this drawing two-dimensional paper templates of the implants are adapted. Adapting the templates to the three-dimensional geometry of the bone surface is not possible.

For the visualization of complex three-dimensional structures, particularly joint fractures, frequently computer tomography (CT) scans and thereby 3D data records are generated. Based on these data, 3D osteosynthesis planning is possible, but the currently available planning tools are limited as they provide only a limited 3D visual display of the fracture with only 2D user interaction. For complex fractures, a virtual pre-operative planning tool is desired, which, for optimal usability, requires 3D interaction with haptic feedback, including collision-detection, bendable implant templates and truly stereoscopic 3D display.

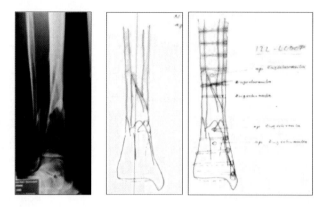

Fig. 2. Manual bone fracture reduction steps, based on two-dimensional X-rays

2.2 Introduction

As described in the previous section, the pre-operative imaging support for osteosynthesis surgery is rather restricted. Even when computer tomography (CT) scans are available to better investigate the fracture fragments, the volume data from these scans is reconstructed into standardized planes by the radiologist and then presented to the surgeon again on 2D prints only.

The goal for pre-operative osteosynthesis planning is to develop a virtual reality application, which allows creating an immersive 3D stereoscopic visualization of the patient specific fracture. The additional use of haptics technology for kinesthetic force feedback further increases the accuracy in pre-operative fracture reduction planning used for minimal invasive surgery.

Although visual feedback has been used to facilitate medical planning and training applications for some time, haptics technology has only recently reached the maturity and fidelity needed for medical applications. The combination of virtual reality and haptics offers a previously unavailable realism in multimodal interaction and immersion within a virtual surgery simulation and support environment.

2.3 Related Work

There are several papers and projects in the field of haptic interfaces and haptic virtual reality tools. Yet most of them have an industrial focus (e.g. automotive industry, assembly processes) rather than a medical application.

There are projects in different medical fields that use either VR technology for 3D visualization [1] or haptics technology for tactile simulation in laparoscopy [2]. To our knowledge though, only little research has been conducted in combining VR and haptics in the domain of orthopedics and trauma surgery applications. Virtual osteosynthesis is an emerging research field in which the integration of haptic feedback for pre-operative planning is a novelty.

The author's paper "Virtual Design Prototyping Utilizing Haptic Immersion" [3] describes an interactive immersive design application which makes it possible for the user to touch what he is designing. This ability to touch objects in the workspace rather than only seeing them makes it easier for the user to perform even complex free-form modeling design tasks. This work was a starting point for the haptic user interface that had to be designed and developed for the new haptic osteosynthesis planning tool.

In conjunction with this research another project [4] was conducted, whose aim was to create a 3D planning tool using more conventional mouse and keyboard interaction. Both projects used a jointly developed common software framework for visualization-, data-input/output and other basic tasks.

As preparatory work, a "Survey of Collision Detection and Response Algorithms suitable for six Degree-of-Freedom Haptic Rendering" [5] was conducted. This study came to the conclusion that a geometry proxy approach using a bounding volume hierarchy would be most suitable for the broad phase collision detection processing. The choice of the specific bounding volume primitive was left open but narrowed to oriented bounding boxes or to discrete oriented polytopes.

2.4   Data Preprocessing

Before any planning task can be conducted, the raw computer tomography (CT) data has to be preprocessed and modified such that it can be used for osteosynthesis planning. Raw data in this case means DICOM[1] data gathered from CT. This DICOM dataset contains multiple layers of 2D images, which all have the same distance from one to another. There are a variety of parameters attached to the image dataset which allow recalculating the images, such that the outcome is a box with parallel sides. This box contains image points in space, so-called voxels. A voxel is a volume element, representing a value on a regular grid in three-dimensional space. This is analogous to a pixel, which represents 2D image data. The values (brightness) of the voxels represent the density of the scanned material at the position of the voxel in space and are measured in Hounsfield[2] scale values.

For the osteosynthesis planning we are interested only in bones (not tissue), so this box with Hounsfield values has to be segmented. A possible method to do this is using a threshold value to segment the bones from the soft tissue. But this method is often not very satisfying as there could be regions in the scanned volume where the density values of soft tissue have the same Hounsfield values as bone parts with low density. A better approach for segmentation is to apply the marching cube algorithm, which utilizes a divide-and-conquer approach to gradually create a triangle surface mesh [6]. This algorithm not only segments the voxel space but it also creates a surface mesh of the bone exterior.

In some cases the bone is broken in such a way that the bone fragments are not properly distinguishable from each other, a so-called impacted fracture. In this case the experience of the surgeon is the only reference to separate the bone fragments from each other and this task has to be done manually, albeit assisted

---

[1] Digital Imaging and Communications in Medicine (DICOM) is a standard for handling, storing, printing, and transmitting information in medical imaging.

[2] The Hounsfield scale is a quantitative scale for describing radio density.

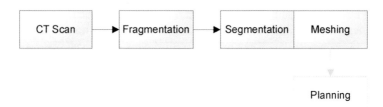

Fig. 3. Preprocessing path of the bone data

by the haptic input modality. This fragmentation needs to be done before the marching cube algorithm is applied on the voxel data.

2.5   Planning Process

For the pre-operative planning process, there are two possible starting points (see Fig. 4). Most commonly it follows after the previously described data preprocessing, after which the bone fragments are already loaded into the workspace. Alternatively, the user can load a previously saved planning file in which the CT data is already segmented and the fragments are separated.

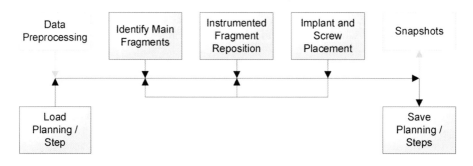

Fig. 4. Preoperative planning process

In the next step the surgeon identifies the main fragments. In some cases of comminuted fractures it is not possible – or simply not feasible – to reposition all fragments, as smaller fragments are to tiny to be considered for repositioning. This is a manual step, because only the surgeon can decide which fragments will be relevant for this particular surgical intervention.

After the main fragments are determined they can be repositioned, that is, the fragments are given a position and an orientation where they need to be placed during the surgical intervention. The surgical instruments utilized are displayed as 3D models inside the workspace. The haptic feedback as well as the stereoscopic display will make this operation easier and more realistic.

Once the repositioning of fragments is completed, implants can be added to the scene, to fixate the bone fragments. The appropriate implant can then be chosen from an implant catalog. The implant positioning is assisted by haptic force feedback, which facilitates placing the implant at the correct location. Once the implant is positioned correctly, it can be attached to the bone with the corresponding screws. The implants as well as the screws are visualized through 3D models.

For the principal fracture reduction planning steps, the complete planning workspace with all objects (bone fragments, implants and screws) can be saved as a planning step in a planning data file. These steps can help the surgeon to navigate through the planning process step by step. This is useful during the actual surgical intervention in order to access the information that is relevant for the actual osteosynthesis step.

Snapshots of the actual planning workspace can be saved as a 3D scene or as a virtual X-ray to document the planning process. The virtual X-ray images can then be used during the surgical intervention to support the surgeon as he makes real X-rays for fracture reduction verification.

2.6 Man Machine Interaction

Stereo Viewing and Input Modalities. Interaction within a 3D environment can be confusing at the beginning because of the third dimension in the workspace. To get a better understanding of the fracture spatial relationship, a stereoscopic view can be helpful. Instead of having to imagine the third dimension, the viewer can perceive it visually.

To get a stereoscopic view, the workspace has to be rendered twice, once for the left eye and once for the right. These two image streams then have to be sent to the corresponding left and right eye respectively. We use the CrystalEyes shutter glasses from StereoGraphics [7] for this application. A shutter glasses based stereo system displays the two stereo views alternately for every refresh cycle of the screen. The signal of the refresh cycle is sent to the shutter glasses by an infrared transmitter. The glasses use two liquid crystal screens in conjunction with a polarized filter to optically render the view over one eye opaque while the other eye has an unhindered view on the screen. In this way only the corresponding eye gets the appropriate left or right image at one time. The downside of this method is the reduction in the refresh rate to half the value of the screen refresh rate. Therefore a flicker-free stereoscopic display requires a refresh rate of 120 Hz. This is also the reason why currently only CRT monitors can be used with this so-called active stereo technique.

Interaction in a 3D environment also needs another input paradigm. The common 2D mouse input is no longer an appropriate way of conducting workspace operations and scrollbars are no longer the way of changing the view. In such an immersive 3D environment the navigation plays an important roll. The object – or the part of an object – currently requiring the most attention should always be visible and accessible for interaction, even if it is on the backside or occluded by another object.

Additionally a 3D pointing and interaction device is needed which has 6 degrees of freedom (6DOF), 3 in movement and 3 in rotation. Furthermore there has to be a device which makes it possible to navigate appropriately in the 3D

Fig. 5. Configuration of the pre-operative osteosynthesis planning workplace

workspace. Navigation also requires 6DOF and has to be done in parallel with other object interactions in the workplace. This is where the two-handed interaction paradigm comes into play [8]. One hand, the dominant hand, operates the tools in the scene, while the other hand navigates in the scene (see Fig. 5).

For the HOVISSE project we use a 3Dconnexion [9] SpaceNavigator to navigate in the scene. This is an optoelectronic device which sends the 6DOF movement of the control knob to the application. This device sends only displacement values rather than absolute position information, what is exactly what we need for navigation tasks.

For the in-workspace operations a SensAble [10] Phantom device is used. This device sends not only 6DOF position information but also has the ability to produce 3DOF haptic feedback. This multimodality enhances user interaction and experience, since the workspace can be seen not only in stereo but can also be haptically touched.

Three-dimensional Haptic User Interface. The framework of the graphical user interface has an architecture similar to other GUI frameworks such as QT [11] or Java Swing [12]. All the visible and active GUI widgets are derived from a GUI object hierarchy base class. These elements are grouped in frames on which a layout can be defined to position the elements in the order the developer wants to arrange them. One major difference to a common 2D GUIs is, that the frame is no longer a two dimensional rectangle, but rather a three dimensional box in which the GUI elements can be placed at an arbitrary 3D position, with respect to the layout.

Furthermore the GUI is not only visually rendered, but also haptically. This means, the GUI elements can be haptically touched when they are pressed, moved or dropped. This haptic representation usually corresponds to the visual representation, but it does not have to.

All active GUI elements (such as buttons) raise an event on activation. This event can then be caught by a registered event handler routine in the application. Information referring to the object which raised the event is also available and can be used to distinguish events.

Haptic Reposition of Bone Fragments and Implants. The planning tool scene consists of multiple elements. First there is the bone or its fragments which have different representations. One of them is the CT scan voxel volume, while another is the mesh of the bone derived from the voxel volume. Additionally there are other elements such as implants and screws (both in mesh representation) to fixate the implants onto the bone fragments. Each of these elements can be moved and rotated freely in space. If there were no haptic constraints on the freedom of movement of the objects, it would be very hard to position them at the appropriate place, because up to this point the objects can only be seen and not touched. Concerning the fact that positioning in space with only visual feedback is quite challenging, haptic collision response between scene objects is mandatory for a software tool for realistic virtual osteosynthesis.

Our implementation therefore uses a very fast collision detection algorithm to detect collision between bone fragments and implant [13]. This algorithm provides the colliding surface mesh faces, which means that the objects have already collided and a penetration took place when a collision is detected. So first of all the visual part of the simulation has to be corrected, before the next visual frame is drawn. This is done by interpolation of small backwards transformation steps between the last non-collison and the first collision frame until the objects no longer collide.

During this visual correction, the collision response for the generation of an appropriate haptic force feedback has to be calculated and applied. The haptic feedback results from a mesh-to-mesh collision of two or more bone fragments and an implant. This circumstance makes the haptic collision feedback calculation more complex than for a simple point to mesh collision.

This mesh to mesh collision feedback is determined using a scene graph visitor pattern which collects the forces applied to the manipulated object. The direction of the force vector is given by the inverse direction of the movement vector. The force strength is calculated by the maximum penetration depth of a vertex of the moving object through the collision triangles of the static object.

2.7 Medical Evaluation

To evaluate the novel features such as stereoscopic viewing or haptic collision detection of our digital osteosynthesis planning tool, we conducted a preliminary medical evaluation. The evaluation is preliminary because the quality of the haptic feedback needs to be improved and the number of evaluation participants needs to be increased (currently only 6).

We analyzed the advantage of these features by comparing them with the traditional, transparency sheet based procedure (see Sec. 2.1 and Fig. 2). Surgeons with different experience in computer usage as well as in surgical skills performed the planning of a femoral shaft fracture with different supporting tools. In a task A, a fracture reduction (reposition) of a femur with two fracture fragments was performed with and without the help of stereoscopic viewing and haptic collision detection. In a task B, the benefits of these features were examined for positioning an osteosynthesis implant on a reduced (reposition performed) femur. To eliminate the bias of the learning curve, the subjects are split in two groups that performed the tasks in reverse order.

The time needed for conventional planning, was 5 to 18 minutes, with a mean of 13 minutes. Junior surgeons with low experience in osteosynthesis planning needed at least twice the time of experienced surgeons. Despite some outlier, the minimal mean time for the digital planning tool was 4:00 minutes for task A when performing the reposition with stereoscopic viewing but without haptic collision detection, and 2:20 minutes for task B when positioning the implant with stereoscopic viewing and haptic collision detection. The best average time used for the entire planning was 7:20 minutes. If the outliers are canceled, the minimal time was 5:20 minutes. All but one older subject were faster using the digital planning tool than using the conventional technique (see Table 1 for details).

Table 1. Evaluation of the planning tool in mono/stereo configurations and with/without haptic collision detection (CD)

Subject	Analog	Digital							
		Reposition (Task A)				Implant Positioning (Task B)			
		Mono		Stereo		Mono		Stereo	
		w/o	CD	w/o	CD	w/o	CD	w/o	CD
	t(min)	t(min)	t(min)	t(min)	t(min)	t(min)	t(min)	t(min)	t(min)
1	11	5.9	3.5	8.75	7.04	6.25	2.5	4	9.75
2	15	1.75	3	2.2	2.25	1.2	2.3	3.5	3.6
3	13	1.6	2	2.5	2	1.6	2.5	3	2.5
4	5	1.8	2.43	2.5	2.5	1.8	1.4	1.6	1.6
5	18	5	6.75	1.75	2.5	5	1.9	1.75	1.34
6	18	8.6	10.75	11.4	8	6.4	4.8	0.8	2.2
Mean	13	4.1	4.7	4.9	4.0	3.7	2.6	2.4	3.5

Senior surgeons are quite fast at using the conventional technique and could not improve the time using the digital tool. Nevertheless, they also showed a ramped learning curve. Perhaps junior doctors were more familiar with computer interaction than senior surgeons, allowing them to compensate the deficiency in fracture understanding with skills in operating a computer. Juniors also showed a rampant learning-curve. After 30 minutes of using the digital planning tool, the time needed for planning was halved. The test shows a significant saving in time when collision detection is activated for implant positioning (task B). For the reposition of the fracture itself (task A), the haptic collision detection is not an advantage, at least not for the fine tuning. Due to technical reasons, the collision detection had to be turned off for fine tuned positioning. The stereo-scopic viewing did not reduce the time so much for both tasks but the accuracy of repositioning and implant positioning seemed to be much better.

The evaluation of the quality of the analog and digital planning is thus made difficult because planning is not just drawing but spatial thinking. The quality of the pre-operative planning performed with the digital technique is very good. In analog planning neither the rotation nor the length could be planned. In digital planning, not only the fractured zone but the whole femur, with all its axes and dimensions, is modeled. For medical assessment of the quality of the reposition (task A) we used a transparent rendering of the models. By changing the view to an axial direction, even the planned rotation of the femur fragments could be evaluated due to the transparent rendering. This is an essential advantage of digital osteosynthesis.

The haptic collision detection of the evaluated software prototype prevents fast repositioning because of the general blocking, even for minimal contact. This technical problem needs to be solved in order to use haptics for fine tuned implant positioning. Additionally, a button to restore the view to standard plane directions may help save time and augment the comparability of different planning scenarios. The examined version of the digital planning tool is useful only for non-bendable implants with stable shape. For bendable implants, the feature of virtual implant contouring needs to be integrated. In summary, it can be said that conventional planning is far behind the potential of digital 3D planning of the evaluated prototype.

The results of a detailed virtual pre-operative osteosynthesis planning are the basis on which to conduct the actual surgical intervention under optimal conditions, and leads to an optimal treatment of the patient. Besides the surgical intervention, the medical workflow inside the operating room also needs careful planning and optimization. These are the goals of another research focus of the HOVISSE project. The implementation of workflow simulation application is described in the following sections.

3   Simulation and Optimization of an Intra-operative Surgery Workflow

3.1   Medical Motivation

A lot of progress could be achieved in medicine in recent years through the utilization of information technology. Particularly, two surgical areas, anaesthesia procedures and surgical operation techniques, have been strongly improved. This progress, however, necessitates increasingly specialized personnel and diversification of materials. For a medium-sized operation such as the osteosynthesis of a broken leg, 7–10 persons from five different occupational groups are directly involved. In addition, technical devices such as X-ray-based surgical imaging systems, X-ray-permeable operating tables, and systems for navigation are increasingly needed [14]. Thus, medical operations have become extremely personnel, material and cost-intensive.

While the number of persons involved and devices used increases, the space available for the treatment of a patient and the operating field has remained constant. As a consequence, actions during the operations are limited and the sterility of the operating field is compromised. Additionally, the use of X-ray-based surgical imaging systems leads to a radiation exposure of the surgery team,

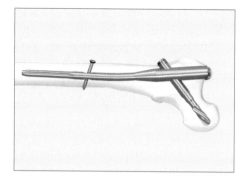

Fig. 6. A Proximal Femur Nail implant (image credits: Synthes, Switzerland)

which has to be minimized as far as possible. For medical and financial reasons the operating times must be kept short.

As a case study for surgical workflow optimization, we have chosen the scenario of the operation of a broken leg, using the implantation of a Proximal Femur Nail [15], [16]. This operation is frequent, the implant is common and the operation technique is standardized to a high degree. For illustrative purposes, Fig. 6 shows a Proximal Femur Nail (anti-rotate) implant (abbreviated as PFNA), implanted into a femoral bone. Despite the high degree of standardization, this operation offers a lot of possibilities for changes to the workflow and thus some potential for improvements [17], [18]. The generic methods and principles for modeling, analysis and optimization of the chosen scenario can be applied to many similar operations. The goals of our work are to contribute to the achievement of lower costs and improved medical treatment.

3.2   Introduction

As each surgical intervention has special needs concerning the number of staff involved and the type of medical equipment required, the pre-operative planning of the positioning and setup of the various medical devices is an essential task before each operation. But currently the actual planning task for the operating room instrumentation and setup is very limited. At best, a 2D map is drawn on which the layout of the patient, the equipment and the surgical tools are roughly outlined. But this 2D planning completely neglects the intra-operative 3D handling of these devices.

Therefore the goals of developing a virtual reality application for surgery workflow simulation and optimization are to provide an immersive 3D operating room visualization with intuitive interaction, and to use sophisticated artificial intelligence (AI) algorithms for optimization of the surgical workflow.

There are several previous medical research projects applying AI problem-solving techniques in which search or planning methods were used to manage and schedule resources, such as clinic personnel or hospital beds. In contrast to these projects, we optimize the workflow during a surgical intervention in the operating room. Optimizing the workflow means minimizing the operating time (the main goal in the current system) or reducing the exposure to X-ray radiation, a goal intended for the future. Up to now there has been no other system that supports this kind of optimization and simulation of a surgery workflow, and as a result, our approach differs significantly from previous ones.

Our research project includes several tasks: Modeling the surgery workflow by a formal language, processing the workflow to be executed by using a simulation engine, arrangement and real-time 3D visualization of the operating room, and the medical equipment needed as well as animating the clinic personnel while executing an action or moving in the operating room. The workflow is visualized in a 3D CAVE system which allows the visual evaluation of the given workflow scenario and an interactive change of the operating room environment.

The following sections provide an overview of related research work and then describe our conducted medical field study, which was the basis for the generic modeling of the surgical workflow. Sections describing the application system architecture and the concepts for man-machine interaction conclude this part of the article.

3.3   Related Work

In the field of man-machine interaction, there are several projects which are concerned with medical topics. A project related to ours is PULSE [19]. The aim of this project is to create a dynamic, multi-user, immersive 3D virtual environment to simulate operational health-care facilities. It is designed as a learning tool for civilian and military health-care providers to expose learners to practical experience with rare, life-threatening problems. In contrast to our project, PULSE is not designed to optimize a specific workflow; therefore these projects share no similarities.

A second project related to ours is Second Health [20]. It uses Second Life [21] to create a near-term future vision of what a new generation of hospitals might look like. The system is based on the recommendations of a report on future healthcare delivery in London. The outcomes of this project were three videos, showing the ways in which medical processes might be handled in the near future. The system created, however, continues to be used for medical and other training. Since Second Health mainly simulates medical healthcare processes, it bears no direct similarity to our project.

A few medical projects are related to our project: MEDICUS [22] is a knowledge-based planning system which helps to organize the everyday routine in a cardiological clinic. It supports the management of cardiological interventions and therapeutic activities under limited resources, such as the clinical staff, operating rooms and hospital beds, and some other constraints. This system allows to solve the scheduling problem manually or automatically by reactive scheduling algorithms.

Herrler [23] examines the simulation and optimization of scheduling processes of clinical treatments in a distributed, dynamic environment. The author developed the clinical pathway modeling language to model possible clinical paths of services. A specific model can be simulated with a framework based on a multi-agent simulation system, in which a clinical environment contains several autonomously functioning units that execute the patient treatments. The author was able to show that global goals, such as minimizing the cost and the execution time, could be optimized exclusively by local scheduling strategies based on an appropriate incentive system.

In summary, the goal of the afore-mentioned projects is to model, simulate or optimize the scheduling of clinical processes, including an intelligent management of limited clinical resources by applying operations research or artificial intelligence methods. By contrast to this, in our research the workflow of a single surgical intervention is modeled, simulated and optimized, which also includes the geometrical arrangement of medical equipment.

3.4   Medical Field Study

To precisely define the medical operation scenario, we first made two 2.5 hour videos of an actual PFNA operation in the hospital of our medical partner. Then, based on our videos, the PFNA surgical workflow was completely analyzed and formally specified by our medical and technical research group in a one-day workshop. As a result, the workflow was documented in a workflow diagram (a small section is shown in Fig. 7). There are seven actors involved (without the patient), each represented by a horizontal stripe. All the actions were plotted in the temporal order of execution during the surgery of our scenario. Altogether,

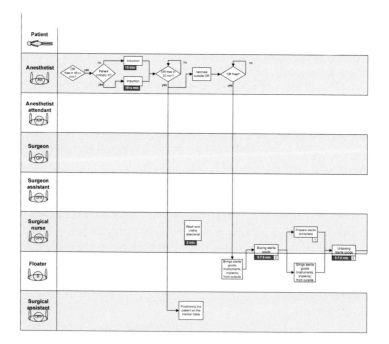

Fig. 7. A very small section of the PFNA workflow diagram (diagram credits: C.Runde, Fraunhofer IPA)

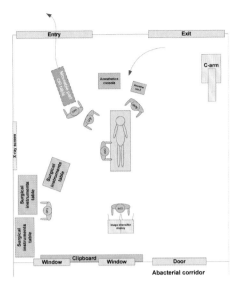

Fig. 8. Layout picture of the PFNA workflow scenario (diagram credits: C.Runde, Fraunhofer IPA)

the workflow diagram contains approximately 80 actions. The workflow diagram is supplemented by several layout pictures, one of which is shown in Fig. 8. Here, the nurse puts away the mobile part of the operating table, while the anesthetist pushes the fluoroscope into position.

One key decision involved the level of abstraction to be used: We describe the workflow as high-level actions to reduce complexity and to avoid a detailed description of manual working steps of the actual surgical intervention, which would be hard to optimize, since this depends on the skills of the particular surgeon.

3.5   Surgery Workflow Modeling

The main design principle of our software system was the separation of the logical description of a surgery workflow from its geometrical representation in respect of the simulation in a virtual reality environment. A second decision was to use XML as the basic data format in order to guarantee the platform independence of the data. Fig. 9 shows the different XML documents and their relationships:

- The catalog describes all the available operating rooms, actor types (surgeon, assistant, nurse etc.), object types (devices, instruments, implants etc.) and action types (give object, make incision etc.).
- The inventory contains the operating room, actors and objects which are needed for a particular surgical operation (instances of corresponding catalog elements).
- The workflow description defines the actions to be executed in a particular surgical operation and references an inventory.

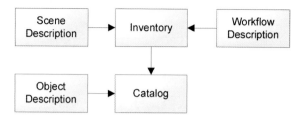

Fig. 9. Data model of the surgery workflow simulation

- The object description specifies the 3D geometry of an operating room and the actors and objects involved in a surgical operation.
- The scene description specifies the initial layout of an operation scene, i.e. the arrangement of the objects and the positions of the actors.

Workflow Description. A workflow consists of actions, and the execution order of these actions can be defined as a sequence in which every action has certain predecessor and successor actions. The disadvantage of this approach is that the order of the actions has to be fixed in advance. In order to define a workflow less rigidly and thus preserve some potential for optimizations, we have followed a different approach. A workflow is described as an unordered set of actions with pre- and post-conditions.

There exist several XML-based languages for describing workflows formally such as BPEL (Business Process Execution Language) [24] or XPDL (XML Process Definition Language) [25]. BPEL allows the specification of business process behavior based on web services whereas XPDL is designed to exchange both the graphics and the semantics of a process definition. Since we neither use web services nor graphical representations of our workflows, both languages seemed inappropriate for our needs. Therefore we defined our own workflow language. Fig. 10 shows the structure of the corresponding XML documents.

The state of a workflow is represented by a set of propositions. A single proposition describes the state of an actor, an object or both (e.g. the surgeon has a

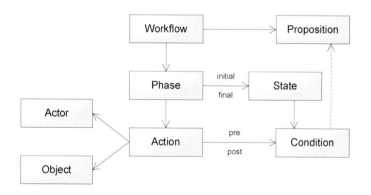

Fig. 10. UML diagram of the workflow language

scalpel). A condition references a proposition and associates a truth value to it (e.g. it is true that the surgeon has a scalpel).

A workflow is divided into different phases which can be simulated individually. Each phase contains a set of actions and has an initial and a final state. When the execution of the phase begins, the conditions of the initial state are assumed to be fulfilled. The execution of the phase ends when the conditions of the final state are met.

An action is a unit of work which is executed by one or more actors and which involves zero, one or more objects (e.g. the surgeon makes an incision with a scalpel). Before an action can be executed, all its preconditions must be fulfilled (e.g. the surgeon must have a scalpel). After the successful completion of an action all its postconditions will be satisfied (e.g. the incision is made).

Geometry Description. To create 3D geometric models for the PFNA operation, we restricted the number of objects and persons to those that are directly involved in the surgical operation or in the arrangement of equipment we want to visualize. Otherwise the scene geometry would become too complex and time consuming for rendering.

In our particular PFNA scenario, five persons besides the patient are involved: two technical surgery assistants, a surgical nurse and two surgeons. The two involved anesthetists were ignored as the project aims to visualize and optimize the part involving the surgical workflow only. The required technical devices include an X-ray-based surgical imaging system, an X-ray-permeable operating table, navigation systems and various other medical tools.

We acquired several detailed medical 3D models of these devices as well as static models of persons. We use X3D [26], an ISO standard XML-based file format to represent static 3D models, and Cal3D [27], a skeletal based 3D character animation library to animate the models. Technically, our models can be categorized into three different types: static models, animated models and physics enabled models.

Static models are used for equipment such as tables, stands and other medical tools, whose geometric representation does not change. They can only be moved or rotated in the operating room, but the model itself does not change.

Animated models are used, for example, for persons or forceps. They behave like static models, but can play predefined animations, which changes the geometrical representation.

For the more complex model behavior, we needed to create physics-enabled models. They consist of several single X3D models, which are connected through joints. During the simulation, parts of these models can be moved according to physical laws, which we implemented with the open source physics library ODE [28].

Each model that can be used in our simulation is referenced through an XML configuration file, the scene object description. It contains a reference to the geometrical representation (in X3D), to the animation specification (in Cal3D) and optionally, to the physics definition file and several other properties that define the behavior of this particular model. Additionally, animated models contain a list of animations that can be played, including properties for their duration and, if required, pre- and post-animation tasks. These pre-animation tasks must be completed before the animation starts. For example, we can specify that an actor has to be next to the patient to make an infusion. Post-animation tasks are handled in a similar manner.

All models are stored in the catalog file (see Fig. 9), which lists all the available operating rooms, actor and object types. Setting up a complete operating room requires an inventory which references objects in the catalog, and the scene description which contains the absolute positions of the objects.

3.6   Simulation System Architecture

The system we developed implements a discrete event simulation in which the simulation processes a sequence of events corresponding to actions of the surgery workflow. The main framework modules are the workflow planner, the workflow engine, the simulation engine and the graphic engine, including the state machine (see Fig. 11).

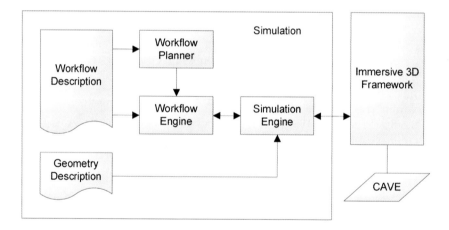

Fig. 11. Main modules of our software framework (arrows depict the coupling of the modules and the data flow direction)

The workflow planner processes the workflow description and generates a workflow, represented by a partially-ordered plan, which is used as input to the workflow engine.

The workflow engine processes the partially-ordered plan and repeatedly sends parts of the plan to the simulation engine. For testing purposes, the workflow engine can also read a manually generated solution of the planning problem.

The actions are now processed by the simulation engine which is the core module of the simulation. The actions are inserted into a queue, where the simulation engine repeatedly updates the status of the actions and sends them to the graphic engine for visualization. When the simulation engine acknowledges that an action has been successfully processed, the successor actions are ready for path computation. The shortest path finding problem for movement actions is solved by the path planner module of the simulation engine.

The 3D graphics framework builds a scene, including all scene objects, while the state machine processes the action events. If an action can be executed successfully, it is animated and visualized in the CAVE.

Workflow Planner. A workflow description defines a planning problem, and a solution is given by a set of actions which, when executed with respect to their preconditions, transforms the initial state into the final state. The specification as a planning problem allows detecting actions which can be processed simultaneously.

The workflow language developed by our research group is based on propositional logic similar to STRIPS [29]. The planning problem is solved by a partial-order planner which yields a set of partially-ordered plans. Such a plan is represented by a causal link graph where the nodes signify the actions and the edges signify the causal links. Two actions are independent of one another if and only if none of the actions is the successor of the other in the causal link graph. Actions that are pair-wise independent can be processed simultaneously, which leads to a possible optimization.

Our planning problem is similar to a time-planning problem with limited resources and is well-known in literature. The actions compete for a set of limited resources which cannot be shared. However, the main difference is that the execution time of a specified move action is not previously known and has to be computed by a shortest-path-finding algorithm.

Note that the workflow specification contains no geometry details. However, it is required to specify a given position in the operating room, like the target position of a movement. The planning language does not allow the specification of a position in the virtual operating room by using numeric coordinate values, but by a symbolic name only which is later substituted for a 3D coordinate position by the simulation engine.

Workflow Engine. The workflow engine is the component of the simulation which is responsible for the execution of a workflow, that is, the workflow engine decides which actions are to be executed in which order. In order to re-use the workflow engine in other software systems, it has been implemented as a separate program which communicates with the simulation engine via a network protocol. The core of the workflow engine consists of a state-event-machine whose transitions are controlled by the requests of the simulation engine (see Fig. 12).

When the simulation engine sends an init request, the workflow engine reads the specified workflow description from the file system and parses it into an internal object representation. After the start request, the required phase is initialized, that is, the conditions of its initial state are fulfilled.

In the running state, the workflow engine has a reference to the current phase and maintains a set of conditions which define the state of the workflow. Whenever this state changes, the workflow engine first checks if the final conditions of the current phase have been achieved. If this is the case, it initializes the next

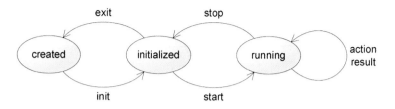

Fig. 12. State-event diagram of the workflow engine

phase and sends a notification to the simulation engine. Secondly, the workflow engine determines the actions which can be executed next, namely the actions whose preconditions are met, and sends a corresponding request to the simulation engine. After the execution of an action has finished, the simulation engine returns an action result to the workflow engine, which then updates the current state according to the postconditions of the terminated action.

The workflow engine stops running when the last phase has terminated or when the simulation engine sends a stop request. Finally, an exit request causes the workflow to be unloaded.

Simulation Engine. The simulation engine is the connecting link between the workflow engine and the graphics framework: it processes the action requests of the surgery workflow, generated and sent by the workflow engine for simulation and visualization. The action requests have to be processed strictly in the order of reception by the simulation engine. Multiple actions included in the same message are pair-wise independent and can be performed simultaneously.

The simulation engine applies the well-known discrete event-based simulation technique, widely used in this area. Each event corresponds to an action of the surgery workflow, referred to as a job in the simulation engine subsystem. We have the following key components in our simulation system to process the events (actions): A clock which is set to the global simulation time, a job list containing the events (actions) waiting to be processed, a job list containing the jobs currently being processed, and finally, a main-loop for processing the job events. Each job has a starting time and a duration. After each iteration of the main-loop all the active jobs make progress by the time difference between the current and the last iteration time. When a job is terminated, it is deleted from the list of active jobs. The simulation is processed in scaled real-time, that is, the simulation time and the wall-clock time are strictly related by a scaling factor, which can be user configured. (For the details of discrete event-based simulations see [30].)

We distinguish between two types of actions: Local actions that are executed at the actor's current position (e.g. the anesthetist makes an infusion to the patient), and move actions, which are actions consisting of a movement from the actor's current position to a given goal position (e.g. the medical assistant moves the surgery table with the patient). Additionally, there are actions containing a sequence of actions of both types. Local actions are visualized by an animation, whereas move actions have to be replaced by a sequence of finer-granulated move steps calculated by a path-finding algorithm.

Movement update means changing the position of the actor involved according to the elapsed time. The movement of the actors is calculated by a path planning module, which keeps track of the positions of all the actors and objects involved in an action in the operating room. There are three main problems in doing this: First, a movement in the virtual 3D world has to observe the geometric shape of the objects in the operating room so that a particular movement is feasible and has no collisions. Second, in our path planning problem there are typically several actors who act simultaneously. The path planning algorithm should maintain the parallelism of independent actions. Third, the actors compete for limited common resources, for which the resource constraints have to be observed.

As a result, path finding is first done in a simplified, discretized 2D world and then extended to the 3D world. The 2D world is given by a projection of the actor's movement onto the ground floor. We apply several techniques well known in the area of computer games. For example, the 2D world is discretized by applying the so-called navigation graph, which is a two-dimensional regular grid filling of the room [31]. Now, a state space search is applied to efficiently solve the path finding problem by using the navigation graph for each actor simultaneously.

To visualize the stationary actions of the actors, we have developed a character animation module, which works in conjunction with the animation services from the 3D graphics framework. The character animation module is responsible for the control of animations, whereas the animations services from the I3D framework visualize the specific animations (see Sec. 4).

3.7   Man Machine Interaction

User Interface. A primary goal of our workflow simulation is to provide the medical experts with a tool to plan intuitively and evaluate the medical procedures and equipment layout for a specific surgical intervention. Therefore our workflow simulation application has a strong focus on man-machine interaction aspects, which is particularly important for the interaction with the simulation within a CAVE 3D virtual environment.

After the operating room has been arranged, the user needs to control the simulation and overview the simulation visualization at the same time. We chose to develop a 3D user interface for seamless integration within the immersive environment. This prevents switching between the 3D visualization and a 2D user interface. This 3D graphical user interface can be operated through a variety of virtual reality input devices such as a cyber glove or a space mouse (see Sec. 2.6).

To interact with the running simulation, a menu widget is used, which contains two columns, one for the simulation control buttons, which provides the basic control functionality such as start, stop, pause, phase selection etc. and one for the status feedback from the workflow simulation, which gets updated dynamically by the received events from the workflow engine.

The implementation of our 3D user interface is based on our generically developed software framework described in Sec. 2.6.

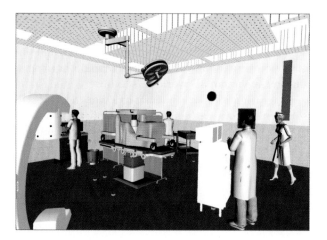

Fig. 13. Operating room 3D visualization in the CAVE virtual environment

Interaction. Users can perform several tasks, which can be divided into three categories: navigation, selection/manipulation and workflow simulation control. Navigation is the most prevalent action of the user and is used to explore the scene and to examine the points of interest. For this, we use a 6 DOF space mouse which controls the virtual camera movement, by rotation and zoom. To operate the graphical user interface, the user can change the interaction mode by pressing a button on the space mouse, which disables the scene control and enables the interaction with the menu. Switching back restores the scene control. Alternatively, two input devices can be used, one to control the scene navigation, and the other to operate the menu.

To interactively select and manipulate the positions and types of medical equipment, the medical expert can interact with the equipment of the simulation. For that purpose, the user wears a tracked data glove, which is used to determine the position of the user's hand and to recognize specific hand gestures for object manipulation.

The user can interactively control the execution of the workflow by pausing and resuming the simulation and change the arrangement of the equipment in order to optimize the movement of the workflow involved avatars. Additionally he can also replay distinctive phases of the simulation. In this manner, individual workflow phases can be selected and iteratively optimized through repositioning of equipment and evaluation for medical appropriateness.

A medical expert user can set the position of the avatar as needed and see the scene through its eyes to check, for example, the line of sight to the monitors showing the X-ray images. This is an improvement to the classical 2D planning tools, since in a CAVE, it is possible to check whether, for example, the ceiling lamps obscure the sight of the monitors.

CAVE. In order to provide the surgeons with immediate visual access to the results of the workflow planning simulation, we use a CAVE (Cave Automated

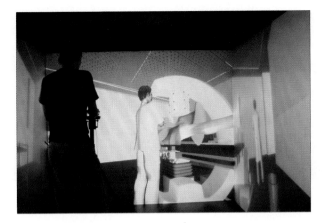

Fig. 14. CAVE virtual environment

Virtual Environment) [32] system for immersive 3D stereoscopic visualization. Compared to a desktop VR system, a CAVE provides a more realistic VR experience, since the size of the equipment of an operating room can be rendered to nearly full scale, which increases the realism of the simulation. Such a CAVE system consists of multiple projection screens, which are mounted in a cubical setup where the actual projection images are adjusted in real time according to the user's tracked position and viewing direction. Our system uses four screens (front, left-side, right-side back-projection screens and a front-projection floor screen), which allow the creation of an almost real-size operating room visualization in which the user's visual horizontal immersion is about 270 degrees. This large screen stereoscopic visualization allows the user to have accurate depth and distance perception to identify immediately any problems in the workflow optimization which are medically not feasible or potentially risky (e.g. contamination of sterile areas in the operating room). By moving around in this virtual operating room environment the surgeon can view the position of the medical equipment from different perspectives and decide on the suitability of the layout for the tasks to be completed.

To increase the illusion of the medical environment, a surround sound system is installed, which can simulate the typical ambient sounds of an operating room.

Through the use of such an interactive and immersive life-size operating room visualization, medical experts are much better supported than in a conventional 2D operating room environment for workflow planning. Additionally, the outcome of the workflow optimization can be evaluated both by analysis of the numeric results computed by the optimization algorithm and by interactive visualization of the optimized workflow.

3.8   Qualitative Medical Evaluation

Changes in medical procedures and technology require changes in the setup and operation of medical equipment. These devices need space in the operating room

Fig. 15. CAVE images of the two possible setups of operation monitors (angles are depicted for illustration only)

and interact and possibly impair the optimal workflow. For a qualitative medical evaluation of our operation simulation software, we used the common example of operating room integration of digital X-rays based on the PACS (Picture Archiving and Communication System) [33] standard. For that purpose new monitors need to be placed in the operating room. In principal there are two possibilities for the placement of these monitors. They can either be installed permanently on a wall of the operating room, which simplifies handling and setup, or they can be mounted on mobile units, which can be freely positioned within the operating room. For assessment of the advantages and disadvantages of the two setups, our CAVE based operating room simulation allows to accurately examine the different spatial setups before procurement of monitors and complex installation in the real operating room.

In a typical operating room setup, we investigated the influence of monitor visibility when the monitor is fixed on a wall or when its placed besides the operating table. Because the distance to the wall is greater, the viewing angle is smaller. This can easily be demonstrated and evaluated in the CAVE, which proved that the commonly available monitor size is insufficient for ergonomic viewing when fixed on the wall (see left of Fig. 15). The CAVE simulation clearly showed the advantage of mobile monitors (see right of Fig. 15) with regard to usability and viewing. A mobile monitor not only offers better visibility for a surgeon standing beside the operating table, but it can even be optimized when the monitor is placed below the level of the table. This allows the surgeon to switch the view easily from the patient's fracture to the X-ray on the monitor. The CAVE simulation and visualization thereby helps in discussions with the multi-professional surgery teams and prevents unsuitable installations.

4   Immersive 3D Graphics Framework (I3D)

The I3D graphics software framework, which is the basis for our subsystems, has been developed mainly in C++ and OpenGL. The key design goal was to have a generic, object-oriented framework, which strictly separates the code for

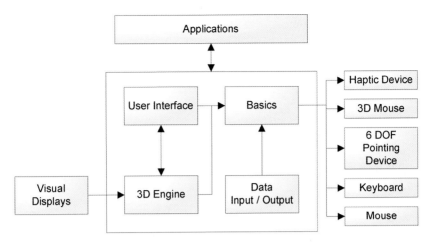

Fig. 16. Immersive 3D framework

graphics and simulation core functions from specific application code. Therefore, the design and architecture are based on the same approach as other widely used 3D graphics frameworks, with the addition of special extensions for the support of haptic devices and haptic rendering. The framework core consists of four modules, which are depicted in Fig. 16.

The I3DEngine module is responsible for the graphics aspects. Its main component is the scene graph, a general data structure which stores the logical representation of the scene and the spatial relationship of the various objects [34]. All visual and haptic elements are stored within this data structure. Our scene graph is partly based on the scene graph nodes of H3D, a visio-haptic programming interface from SenseGraphics [35]. We defined an abstract base node, from which all nodes used in the scene graph inherit. Currently we can handle several 3D data types through volume, mesh, image, physics and animation nodes. Additionally these nodes also provide the functionality to load and save these data types. Applications can add, remove or apply operations to these scene graph nodes. For this, the graphics engine raises an event before the frame is redrawn and the application can change the state of the node object in the scene graph.

This core module also includes a 3D rendering engine, a physics engine, collision detection and device handling. For each frame the rendering engine traverses the scene graph to render the objects, both visually and haptically. The haptic rendering thereby occurs more often and with higher priority than the visual rendering for accurate force feedback calculation. The implementation of the 3D graphics rendering is realized with OpenGL, which allows us to develop portable applications that run on Microsoft Windows, our primary development environment, and other systems such as Linux.

The I3DBasics module provides basic data types and an abstraction for input devices. It also contains two important sub-modules, which are used by the entire framework: the event management and the delegators. The event management is based on the observer design pattern; objects can register themselves to observe an event that may be raised. Delegators predefine several steps, which can be used without knowledge on how they are implemented. For instance, application code can depend on user input for a file name, but the application does not need to know how this is implemented in the underlying I3D graphics framework.

The I3DUI module contains the render canvas, a container with an OpenGL context, and several 3D user interface widgets, as well as the user interface layout manager.

The I3DIO module contains functionality for file system handling and XML file reading and writing.

5 Conclusion

Man-machine interaction is a crucial factor for software systems used in a medical environment. Through the inherently three-dimensional nature of the procedures for orthopaedic surgery, the use of virtual- and augmented-reality techniques in combination with haptic force feedback is therefore the next step in the development of medical planning applications.

The HOVISSE project uses these technologies for the development of application prototypes to solve real medical problems and to demonstrate the possibilities for improvement of man-machine interaction. Although only a preliminary medical evaluation has been conducted so far (see Sec. 2.7), the results for the osteosynthesis planning prototype are promising. The time for pre-operative planning is reduced and the use of stereoscopic viewing and haptic collision detection increase usability and planning accuracy. Through the implementation of refined algorithms for haptic force feedback during fracture reduction, the next version of the application will further increase the system usability.

What has not been considered in our evaluation is the time needed to prepare a suitable 3D surface model from computer tomography data. Currently the fragmentation and segmentation algorithms are not completely automated and therefore require additional setup time for pre-operative planning. This is an area where further research is required to achieve a fully automated data preprocessing. Only this will allow to benefit from the time savings during the actual planning.

Although many of the virtual reality technologies we used still have their limitations (e.g. setup, accuracy) and need to be further developed for daily usage in a hospital environment, the potential for improvement of osteosynthesis treatment is evident.

Acknowledgment. This research has been endorsed and supported by the Hasler Foundation, through their funding of the HOVISSE virtual reality research project. In addition to the authors, many others have contributed to the successful completion of the subsystems for osteosynthesis planning and workflow simulation of the HOVISSE project. These are Prof. Dr. med. P. Messmer, A. Egli, A. John and Dr. med. F. Matthews from the CARCAS research group at the University Hospital of Basel and Dr. C. Runde and F. Decker from the Fraunhofer IPA Institute in Stuttgart. Additional contributions from Prof. Dr. T. Vetter and T. Albrecht from the Computer Science Department of the University of Basel and U. Josi and M. Züger from the Mechanical Engineering Department of the Berne University of Applied Sciences.

References

1. Panchaphongsaphak, B., Burgkart, R., Riener, R.: BrainTrain: Brain Simulator for Medical VR Application. Stud. Health Technol. Inform. 111, 378–384 (2005)
2. Maass, H., Chantier, B.B., Cakmak, H.K., Trantakis, C., Kuehnapfel, U.G.: Fundamentals of force feedback and application to a surgery simulator. Comput. Aided Surg. 8(6), 283–291 (2003)
3. Künzler, U., Wetzel, R., Iseli, M.: Interactive Immersive Design Application: Analysis of Requirements. In: Rauterberg, M., et al. (eds.) INTERACT 2003, pp. 971–974. IOS Press, Amsterdam (2003)
4. Matthews, F., Messmer, P., Raikov, V., Wanner, G.A., Jacob, A.L., Regazzoni, P., Egli, A.: Patient-Specific Three-Dimensional Composite Bone Models for Teaching and Operation Planning. J. Digital Imaging (September 2007)
5. Künzler, U., Fuhrer, C.: A Survey of Collision Detection and Response Algorithms Suitable for Six Degree-of-Freedom Haptic Rendering. In: Workshop on Virtual Reality in Product Engineering and Robotics: Technology And Applications. Special Issue of: Bulletin of the Transilvania University of Brasov ISSN 1221–5872, Brasov (2006)
6. Lorensen, W.E., Cline, H.E.: Marching Cubes: A High Resolution 3D Surface Construction Algorithm
7. REALD (former StereoGraphics), http://reald-corporate.com/scientific/
8. Hinckley, K., Pausch, R., Proffitt, D., Kassell, N.F.: Two-handed virtual manipulation. ACM Transactions on Computer, Human Interaction, 260–302 (2007)
9. 3Dconnexion, http://www.3dconnexion.com
10. SensAble, http://www.sensable.com
11. QT. A graphical user interface from Trolltech,
    http://trolltech.com/products/qt
12. Swing. A graphical user interface included in Java by Sun Microsystems,
    http://java.sun.com/docs/books/tutorial/uiswing
13. Gottschalk, S., Lin, M.C., Manocha, D.: OBB-Tree: A Hierarchical Structure for Rapid Interference Detection. Technical Report TR96-013, Department of Computer Science, University of N. Carolina, Chapel Hill. In: Proc. of ACM SIGGRAPH 1996 (1996)
14. Jacob, A., Regazzoni, P., Bilecen, D., Rasmus, M., Huegli, R.W., Messmer, P.: Medical technology integration: CT, angiography, imaging-capable OR-table, navigation and robotics in a multifunctional sterile suite. Minim. Invasive Ther. Allied Technology 16(4), 205–211 (2007)
15. Synthes: PFNA, Operationstechnik. Synthes GmbH, Oberdorf,
    http://www.synthes.com/html/PFNA-Proximal-Femoral-Nail.6869.0.html
16. Balk, R., Hahn, F., Tarcea, B.: Die Proximale Femurfraktur. OP-Journal 18(2) (September 2002)

17. Suhm, N., Jacob, L., Zuna, I., Regazzoni, P., Messmer, P.: Fluoroscopy based surgical navigation vs. mechanical guidance system for percutaneous interventions: A controlled prospective study exemplified by distal locking of intramedullary nails. Unfallchirurg 106(11), 921–928 (2003)
18. Matthews, F., Hoigné, D.J., Weiser, M., Wanner, G.A., Regazzoni, P., Suhm, N., Messmer, P.: Navigating the fluoroscope's C-arm back into position: An accurate and practicable solution to cut radiation and optimize intra-operative workflow. Orthop. Trauma (November-December 2007)
19. Pulse!! The Virtual Clinical Learning Lab,
http://www.sp.tamucc.edu/pulse/home.asp
20. Second Health, http://secondhealth.wordpress.com
21. Second Life, http://secondlife.com
22. Appelrath, H.H., Sauer, J.: MEDICUS: Ein medizinisches Ressourcenplanungssystem. KI – Künstliche Intelligenz, Scientec Verlag 3, 56–60 (1998)
23. Herrler, R.: Agentenbasierte Simulation zur Ablaufoptimierung in Krankenhäusern und anderen dynamischen Umgebungen. PhD Thesis, University of Würzburg, Germany (2007)
24. Web Services Business Process Execution Language (WS-BPEL), Advancement of Structured Information Standards (OASIS),
http://www.oasis-open.org/committees/tc_home.php?wg_abbrev=wsbpel
25. XML Process Definition Language (XPDL), Workflow Management Coalition (WfMC), http://www.wfmc.org/standards/xpdl.htm
26. X3D International Specification Standards,
http://www.web3d.org/x3d/specifications/x3d_specification.html
27. 3D Character Animation Library, https://gna.org/projects/cal3d
28. Open Dynamics Engine, http://www.ode.org
29. Russel, S., Norvig, P.: Artificial Intelligence: A Modern Approach. Prentice-Hall, Englewood Cliffs (2003)
30. Fujimoto, R.M.: Parallel and Distributed Simulation Systems. John Wiley and Sons, Chichester (2000)
31. Buckland, M.: Programming Game AI by Example. Wordware Publishing (2005)
32. Cruz-Neira, C., Sandin, D.J., DeFanti, T.: Surround-Screen Projection-based Virtual Reality: The design and implementation of the CAVE. In: SIGGRAPH 1993. Association for Computing Machinery (August 1993)
33. Duerinckx, A.J., Pisa, E.J.: Filmless Picture Archiving and Communication System (PACS). In: Diagnostic Radiology. Proc. SPIE, vol. 318, pp. 9–18 (1982)
34. Strauss, P.S.: IRIS inventor, a 3D graphics toolkit. In: OOPSLA, pp. 192–200 (1993)
35. SenseGraphics H3D API, http://www.sensegraphics.com

A Language and a Methodology for Prototyping User Interfaces for Control Systems

Matteo Risoldi[2], Vasco Amaral[1], Bruno Barroca[1], Kaveh Bazargan[2], Didier Buchs[2], Fabian Cretton[3], Gilles Falquet[2], Anne Le Calvé[3], Stéphane Malandain[4], and Pierrick Zoss[4]

[1] Universidade Nova de Lisboa
vasco.amaral@di.fct.unl.pt, mailbrunob@gmail.com
[2] Université de Genève
{kaveh.bazargan,didier.buchs,gilles.falquet,matteo.risoldi}@unige.ch
[3] HES-SO Valais
{anne.lecalve,fabian.cretton}@hevs.ch
[4] Ecole d'ingénieurs de Genève
{stephane.malandain,pierrick.zoss}@hesge.ch

Abstract. The BATIC[3]S project[1] (Building Adaptive Three-dimensional Interfaces for Controlling Complex Control Systems) proposes a methodology to prototype adaptive graphical user interfaces (GUI) for control systems. We present a domain specific language for the control systems domain, including useful and understandable abstractions for domain experts. This is coupled with a methodology for validation, verification and automatic GUI prototype generation. The methodology is centered on metamodel-based techniques and model transformations, and its foundations rely on formal models. Our approach is based on the assumption that a GUI can be induced from the characteristics of the system to control.

1 Introduction

Modeling user interfaces for the domain of control systems has requirements and challenges which are sometimes hardly met by standard, general-purpose modeling languages. The need to express domain features, as well as to express them using paradigms familiar to domain experts, calls for domain specific languages.

We propose a methodology to develop 3D graphical user interfaces for monitoring and controlling complex control systems. Instead of developing or specifying the interface directly, an automated prototype is generated from knowledge about the system under control. The methodology is comprised of a domain specific language for modeling control systems, and integrates a formal framework allowing model checking and prototyping. In the following sections we will describe the domain and goals of this project. A case study will be introduced to serve as a guide example. Section 2 will discuss the methodology from an abstract point of view; section 3 will give details on the technologies of the framework

---

[1] This project is funded by the Hasler foundation of Switzerland.

D. Lalanne and J. Kohlas (Eds.): Human Machine Interaction, LNCS 5440, pp. 221–248, 2009.
© Springer-Verlag Berlin Heidelberg 2009

implementing the methodology. A related work section, conclusions and a future work overview will wrap up the article.

1.1   Domain Definition

Control systems (CS) can be defined as mechanisms that provide output variables of a system by manipulating its inputs (from sensors or commands). While some CS can be very simple (e.g. a thermostate) and pose little or no problem to modeling using general-purpose formalisms, other CS can be complex with respect to the number of components, dimensions, physical and functional organization and supervision issues.

A complex control system will generally have a composite structure, in which each object can be grouped with others; composite objects can be, in their turn, components (or "children") of larger objects, forming a hierarchical tree in which the root represents the whole system and the leaves are its most elementary devices. Typically this grouping will reflect a physical container-contained composition (e.g. an engine contains several cylinders), but it could reflect other kinds of relations, such as functional or logic. Elementary and composite objects can receive commands and communicate states and alarms. It is generally the case that the state of an object will depend both on its own properties and on the states of its subobjects.

Operators can access the system at different levels of granularity, and with possibly different types of views and levels of control, according to several factors (their profile, the conditions of the system, the current task being executed).

1.2   Requirements

The main goal of this project is defining a methodology that allows easy prototyping of a graphical user interface (GUI) for such systems. The prototyping has to be done by users who have a knowledge of the system under control; they should not necessarily have any deep knowledge of programming or GUI design. In this, our approach is different from several others which try to be general by focusing on GUI specification formalisms (see the Related Work section). This work proposes to model the system under control instead of the GUI. On one hand, this makes the methodology less general and only applicable to the domain of control systems (and possibly similar domains). But on the other hand, the methodology becomes accessible by people who don't have a specific GUI development know-how, and allows rapid prototyping by reusing existing information.

The requirements are the following:

- a system expert must be able to specify the knowledge of the system under control
- it must be possible to generate an executable prototype of the GUI from the specification
- it must be feasible to verify properties and to validate the specification
- it must be possible to classify users into profiles
- it must be possible to define tasks, which may be available only to some user profiles

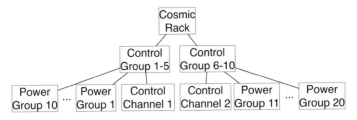

Fig. 1. Cosmic Rack hierarchy

- tools must be in place for accomplishing the previous requirements in a coordinated workflow

1.3 Case Study

As a reference for the examples in this article, we will use a case study from the European Laboratory for Particle Physics (CERN) in Geneva, published in [1].

The CMS experiment at CERN is a large particle detector installed along the Large Hadron Collider facility. Its Silicon Strip Tracker component is a complex system made of about 24000 silicon detectors, organized in 1944 *Power Groups*. These have several environmental and electric parameters to monitor. Tens of thousands of values and probes have to be controlled by the Tracker Control System[2]. We worked on an early prototype of the Silicon Strip tracker, called the Cosmic Rack. This is equivalent to a section of the full tracker, mantaining the same hierarchical complexity, but with a reduced total number of components. The Cosmic Rack has been used to test the hardware and software of the full tracker. The hierarchical structure of the Cosmic Rack is shown in Fig. 1.

There are four types of components: *Partitions*, *Control Groups*, *Power Groups* and *Control Channels*. There is only one Partition, the *Cosmic Rack* object. There are two Control Groups; twenty Power Groups (ten per Control Group); and two Control Channels (one per Control Group).

Each component is characterized by a finite state machine (FSM). They are represented in Fig. 2 (for Partitions and Control Groups, which have the same FSM), 3 (for Power Groups) and 4 (for Control Channels).

The shape of every component, and its position in space, is defined by the Cosmic Rack mechanical project. This information is stored in a database.

Each component can receive commands. They trigger transitions in the FSM. A command will generally trigger a transition having the same name as the

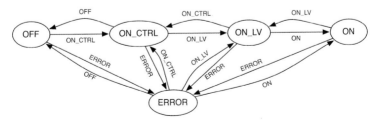

Fig. 2. Partitions and Control Groups FSM

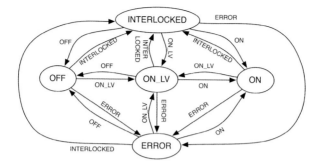

Fig. 3. Power Groups FSM

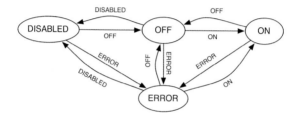

Fig. 4. Control Channels FSM

command. There are some transitions, however, which are not triggered by commands, but rather by internal system events. It is the case for all transitions going to the "ERROR" state of all FSMs (triggered by property values out of range) and those going to the "INTERLOCKED" state of the Power Groups FSM (triggered by a hardwired security mechanism). In addition to this, Power Groups have a *Clear* command which triggers one of the transitions leaving the "INTERLOCKED" state (chosen according to current system values).

States are propagated up through the component hierarchy according to rule sets. Table 1 shows the rule set for propagating Control Groups (CG) states to the Partition. Each row is a rule. All non-empty conditions must be met for a rule to be applied. The table is a slight simplification of reality - there exist "mixed" states, for example when going from OFF to ON_CTRL, where only some of the Control Groups have already switched state. These mixed states, however, are normally ignored as they are not part of the "ideal" behaviour of the machine. Control Groups on their turn also have a similar table of rules for propagating the states of their children components, Power Groups and Control Channels.

Power Groups have a *temperature* property. On this property, an alarm is defined with temperature thresholds defining value intervals. Each interval corresponds to a diagnostic on the temperature (normal, warning, alert and severe). This is needed to detect temperature anomalies and take action before a hardware safety mechanism (based on PLCs) intervenes to cut power to components in order to preserve them (which brings a Power Group to the INTERLOCKED state).

Table 1. State propagation rules for the Partition. CG stands for Control Groups.

Partition State	CG in OFF	CG in ON_CTRL	CG in ON_LV	CG in ON	CG in ERROR
OFF	ALL				
ON_CTRL		ALL			
ON_LV			ALL		
ON				ALL	
ERROR					ALL

There are command sequences which constitute the normal operation of the Cosmic Rack. These are turning on the system, turning off the system, clearing errors and clearing interlock events.

Turning on the system consists in turning on the Control Channels, then turning on the Power Groups.

Turning on the Control Channels means enabling (DISABLED → OFF) and then turning on (OFF → ON) the Control Channels (in any order).

Turning on the Power Groups means turning on low voltage (OFF → ON_LV) and then high voltage (ON_LV → ON) of Power Groups (in any order).

Turning off the system consists in the inverse sequence as turning on the system.

Clearing an error consists in sending commands to a Control Channel or Power Group in ERROR state, according to the situation at hand (most of the times, this will mean trying to power down a component and power it up again with a turn off / turn on sequence on the concerned branch).

Clearing an interlock state consists in sending a *Clear* command to an interlocked Power Group.

2   Methodology

The engineering process for prototyping a GUI for a control system is illustrated in Figure 5. There are four steps in this methodology. In the first step, knowledge about the control system is gathered. This is usually present under the form of a collection of more or less formal documents. In the case of complex systems, it is often the case that many of the aspects of the system are modeled in electronic form for engineering purposes. These models can have various levels of reusability depending on the format they are in. Knowledge about the system is essential because the composition of the system, its inputs and outputs, and its behaviour in terms of state evolution are key information for automated GUI prototyping. In the second step, this information is expressed using a domain specific language. This language models the domain of the information gathered in step one. This domain model is comprised of several models: one, the *system model*, describes the structure and internal behaviour of the system; the others, namely the *visual model*, the *user model* and the *task model*, describe rather the geometrical and interactive aspects of the system. An abstract overview of the models is shown in Figure 6. The various models are not completely separate, but are linked by several relationships, abstracted in Figure 6 by lines.

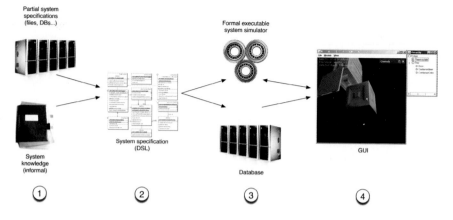

Fig. 5. The methodology process

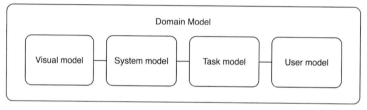

Fig. 6. Packages of the specification model. Arcs are abstractions of existing relationships among classes in the packages.

The third step of Figure 5 sees the generation of deliverables from this specification: a database containing data used for GUI generation (the visual, user and task model and part of the system model), and an executable system simulator. This is done by automated tools.

The fourth and final step is the dynamic generation of a GUI prototype built from the database data, which interacts with the system simulator.

Steps 2-4 are those tackled by our model-based approach. We will now describe the features of the domain specific model, then the simulator generation and GUI prototyping activity.

2.1 The Domain Model

We will now describe the sub-models of Figure 6.

The System model. contains useful abstractions to describe the structure of the system and its behaviour. It includes the following concepts:

- Objects in the system
- Types, defining sets of similar objects
- A hierarchical composition relationship between objects
- Behaviour of objects in terms of states and transitions

- State dependency between components
- Properties of objects
- Commands and events of objects

Objects are identified by a name and represent components in the system.

Types are where we define all features which are not specific to individual instances of objects. Typing objects enables quick definition of properties common to a large number of objects (a typical situation in control systems which are highly repetitive). A type is identified by a name.

The hierarchical composition is modeled as a tree of objects. Each object can have one parent and/or several children. The hierarchical relationship can semantically express either physical containment or logical groupings (e.g. electrical connection, common cooling pipes...).

Behaviour of objects is modeled by finite state machines (FSMs). These are well-suited for control systems as they express expected behaviour in a clear way and are a standard in the control systems domain.

State dependency is expressed with conditional rules. Conditions can be of type "if at least one of the children (or - if all of the children) of an object is in state x, then go to state y".

Properties are identified by names and data types. Their possible values can be divided in intervals corresponding to four diagnostic levels: normal, warning, alert or severe.

Commands, as control systems are asynchronous by nature, are defined by their name and parameters only (i.e. no return value). For the sake of simulation, the possibility of defining a simplified behaviour for a command is provided (e.g. it is possible to specify that a command changes a property of an object).

Events are defined by their name and parameters. An event can be triggered by state transitions (also in children objects), command, property changes. An event can also trigger state transitions, commands and other events.

The behaviour of objects, their commands, events and properties are not directly associated in the model to individual objects, but rather to their types. This is because they are common features of all objects of a given type (e.g. a model of power supply). Individual objects instantiate types, inheriting all of the above features without having to specify them for each object. Figure 7 shows an abstract overview of the relationships among concepts in the system model. Each arc in the figure sums up one or more relationships existing among the concepts. Individual relationships will be detailed in Section 3, while discussing the language metamodel.

The Visual model. describes all aspects of the system which are visually relevant. This includes their geometrical space and their position in space.

Geometrical shape is defined for each type (and not per-object, for the same reasons mentioned earlier). The geometry is expressed by association to a geometry file URL. This is a file in the *Object* format[3], a commonly used standard for 3D object description. The language also includes pre-defined common primitive shapes (box, sphere, cylinder...) that are mapped to pre-made object

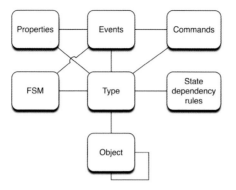

Fig. 7. Concepts in the system model and their relationships

files. Geometrical shapes can be modified by scaling attributes. For this reason a single shape can be used to model different objects. For example, using the cube primitive, one can model different cuboids by modifying its scale along one or more axis.

Position in space can be defined in different ways. The simplest is expressing translation and rotation for each object. This requires defining coordinates for each object. Components of complex systems, however, are sometimes positioned according to repetitive patterns (arrays, circles...). Thus, a more efficient choice could be positioning an object by specifying its relationship with other objects. Relationships of type "x is parallel to y", or "x is concentric to y" can be repeatedly applied to rapidly express whole sets of coordinates in such cases.

Figure 8 shows an abstract overview of the concepts of the visual model and their relationships. Individual relationships will be detailed in Section 3.

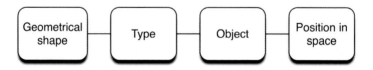

Fig. 8. Concepts in the visual model and their relationships (`Type` and `Object` are those from the System model)

The User model, as a general definition, is a knowledge source that contains a set of beliefs about an individual on various aspects, and these beliefs can be decoupled from the rest of the system[4].

We used the *Generic Ontology based User Model* (GenOUM) [5,6] as a user model. This is a general-purpose user model based on an onlology including information about users' personality and knowledge. The GenOUM ontology is quite rich and goes beyond our needs. We are using a subset of it, represented in Fig. 9. The full GenOUM ontology is presented in [5]. We model what profile users have (*Behaviour*) and what is their level of knowledge for tasks to accomplish. The object of a user's knowledge in the ontology is generic (the *Thing*

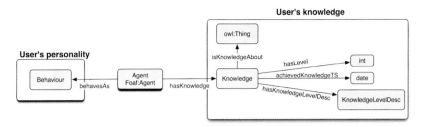

Fig. 9. GenOUM concepts and properties

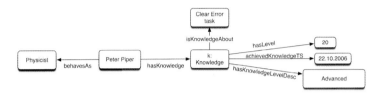

Fig. 10. Example of User's knowledge level

concept from OWL); we will replace *Thing* with the *Task* concept. The task model is described in section 2.1.

As an example referring to our Cosmic Rack case study, Figure 10 states that user Peter Piper has a physicist profile. He knows how to perform the "Clear error" task, his knowledge level about this task is 20, an advanced knowledge level, and he acquired this knowledge on October 22, 2006. The interpretation of the knowledge level '20' depends on the domain and is not defined *a priori* by GenOUM.

The Task model: a task defines how the user can reach a goal in a specific application domain. The goal is a desired modification of the state of a system or a query to it [7]. Tasks must be seen as structured entities. As they represent the complex interaction between user and GUI, we should be able to deal with more than just atomic or linear tasks. Consequently, we chose to base our task model on the ConcurTaskTree formalism[7] (CTT). In CTT, a task is identified by a name, a type and an ordered list of subtasks, in a hierarchical composition structured like a tree. Temporal relationships between subtasks are defined.

There are four task types: *abstract, user, application* and *interaction*. An *abstract* task is generally a complex task we can define in terms of its subtasks. A *user* task is something performed by the user outside the interaction with the system (e.g. deciding or reading something). An *application* task is something completely executed by the system (e.g. cashing a coin inserted in a drink vending machine). Finally, an *interaction* task is performed by the user interacting with the system (e.g. clicking a button).

Concurrency relationships between tasks are defined by a number of process algebra operators (called *temporal operators* in [7]). A non-exhaustive list of these taken from [7] follows as an example:

Fig. 11. CTT task types: abstract, user, application and interaction

- T1 ||| T2 is *interleaving*: the actions of the two tasks can be performed in any order
- T1 [] T2 is *choice*: T1 or T2 can be performed
- T1 >> T2 is *enabling*: when the first task is terminated then the second is activated
- T1* is *iteration*: the task is iterative

CTT has a visual syntax, representing a task as a tree (where the root is the highest abstraction of the task, and the leaves are the most elementary actions) and is supported by editing tools and libraries. For the four task types mentioned, the symbols in Figures 11 are used.

An example of CTT applied to our Cosmic Rack case study is shown in Figure 12.

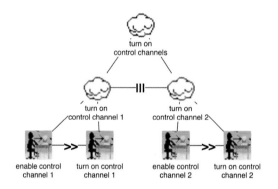

Fig. 12. CTT for the *turn on control channels* task

Through the association of task and user models, we add to the CTT model the possibility to specify for which user profiles (the *behaviour* in GenOUM) each task is available. This will be clearer later, when we give the detailed implementation of the task model.

2.2 System Simulator Generation

The system simulator is built by giving executable semantics to the syntactic specification of the control system. Through model transformation techniques (detailed in section 3), a formal concurrent model is obtained from the specification, as shown in Figure 5. This implements, notably, the instantiation of objects, the execution of the FSMs of the objects, the command input model, and the event model.

This model has executable concurrent and transactional semantics. Commands and events can be processed in a parallel and/or non-deterministic way, while the execution of command-event chains supports full transactionality and roll-back (to model command failures). The concurrent semantics greatly help in simulating a system which is, by nature, concurrent (several events can happen independently together in a control system). Transactionality, on one hand, might not be 100% corresponding to the actual system behaviour. In particular, it does not model system or communication failures. However, these are issues which are not specifically related to the GUI we are validating, and it is actually useful to abstract them by assuming that the system is always responding according to the specification.

2.3   GUI Prototype

The GUI prototype engine is a software framework capable of loading the system specification from the database, and presenting the user with an interface allowing interaction with the system, as shown in Figure 5. A driver in this framework instantiates and runs the system simulator, so that interaction with the actual system can be emulated. Commands and events are transmitted to and from the system simulator so that the users can evaluate the interface.

The task model information is used to know what tasks are available for a user when an object is selected. Thanks to the executable nature of the CTT formalism, it is possible to have the GUI automate a task, with the user only initiating it (at least in the case where only enabling operators are used). Alternatively, step-by-step cues can be shown to the user to perform the task (wizard-style). The user model is used as an authorization model for determination of the available tasks.

For the kind of systems we are modeling (geometrically complex, where error detection and diagnostic is important), we need an adaptation mechanism able to highlight components which are having errors. Difficulties in seeing a faulty object can come from it being out of the current view, and/or being hidden by other objetcs.

However, a low-level definition of the GUI's adaptive behaviour in the language would defeat one of the goals of the project, which is not to require a deep knowledge of HCI techniques by the user.

To address the problem, the GUI prototype engine implements a rule-based adaptation system. An *adaptation rule* is a concept which depends on user profile and current task, and that is triggered by an error event. The rule defines an adaptation *method*, which says what type of behaviour the GUI must adapt to react to the event. A set of rules has been defined to address common problematic situations which prevent object visibility. Strategies to solve these situations are centering the camera on an object, moving objects which block the view out of the way, or making them transparent. When an error event is produced, the rendering engine applies these strategies. If the object is not in the field of view, the camera moves to include it. If it is impossible to get an unobstructed view of the object, other objects in the line of sight are either made transparent (if they are not in error themselves) or moved aside (if they are).

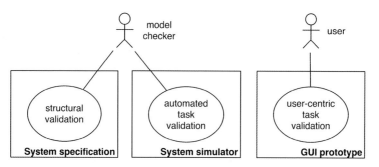

Fig. 13. Validation activities with their actors and models

2.4   Validation

Besides using the prototype as a basis for a production-level interface, the main interest of producing the GUI prototype and system simulator in this model-based way is the possibility of performing validation and verification techniques and refining the model accordingly.

Validation is an activity that checks if a model adheres to the original require-ments (answering the question: *am I building the right model?*). From the point of view of a control system GUI, validation allows knowing if the GUI lets a user view the status of the system and interact with it in the expected way.

Many aspects can be validated in a GUI. Relevant ones are presentation, in-teraction and environmental ones[8], such as navigation, interaction, appropriate user profiling, correct error detection. But one of the most interesting aspects to validate are task models. For example, if a given system status is supposed to be corrected via a task, a few things we want to know are: if the user can view all of the information needed for executing the task (like viewing all objects involved); if in all relevant cases the task is available; and in which cases the task may not be adapted to the circumstances. This type of validation can be led in two ways: first, an automated way, in which the task model is used to automatically run task commands in the GUI, and blocks or inconsistencies are detected; and second, a user-centric way, in which users are presented with a set of situations needing them to perform a task, and they evaluate manually the ease (or possi-bility) to perform it. In both cases, what we discover are misunderstandings of the requirements for the model. The result of this activity is an input for refining and improving the task model.

Another interesting aspect to validate is the structure of the system, as we need to be sure we are modeling the right system (and thus, the right GUI). Properties on the structure of the system can be specified using a constraint language in the model, and these constraints can be checked at design time, in a static way. We will be able to check if, for example, a certain type of object always has children of a certain other type, or if all interaction tasks are associated to a command. The actors in the discussed validation activities are shown in Figure 13 together with the involved products of the methodology.

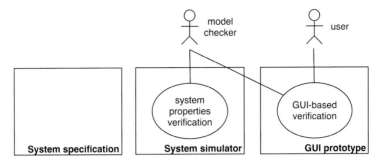

Fig. 14. Verification activities with their actors and models

2.5   Verification

Verification is an activity allowing to know if a model has been correctly made (answering the question: *am I doing the model right?*). In our domain, this means for example if all transitions in an object's FSM have the correct source and target state, or if an object's state change is correctly reflected in its parent object's state.

There are two types of interesting verification in this methodology. The first focuses on the model itself and tries to make sure that the simulator we run against is respecting the actual system properties. This type of verification can be performed on the system simulator (which has executable semantics and supports state space generation and exploration), by specifying properties in a suitable formalism, like temporal logic. Model checking tools can evaluate these properties on the state space of the simulator and confirm if the model satisfies them. We can also use testing: feeding the simulator a known input and detecting if the output matches expected values. The second type of verification is on the GUI-related aspects, like task and user models, geometry, and adaptation rules. It checks, for example, if the geometry respects the system structure, or if a rule will always be triggered when its conditions are met. This type of verification can be done via property specification and model checking or by manual testing. What we discover are errors in the model specification that have to be corrected.

In both cases (refinement and correction), a model-based methodology is useful because one only needs to modify the original model, and all the code generation and prototyping is redone automatically. The actors in the discussed verification activities are shown in Figure 14 together with the involved products of the methodology.

3   Framework

The methodology described in the previous section has been implemented by integrating a set of tools. We preferred choosing well-known and open tools and frameworks, filling the gaps with ad hoc-developed tools when necessary.

We will now describe the various phases of the methodology with concrete references to the technologies and methods we propose.

3.1   The Specification Language

One of the purposes of the methodology we propose is to introduce a comprehensive domain specific language for the domain of control systems that is based on useful abstractions for domain experts. The modularity of our domain model led us to design a DSL called COntrol system SPEcification Language (Cospel) that is made of different parts, or *packages*, modeling different aspects of the system. We used the Eclipse Modeling Framework[9] (EMF) to specify the abstract syntax of Cospel by defining its metamodel. The semantics have been given by transformation to a different formalism, which will be described in section 3.2.

Cospel specifications can be created via an editor, generated automatically by EMF from the abstract syntax. The concrete syntax provided by this editor is a tree-like visualization of the specification, where each node is a syntactic element. The tree is structured according to the aggregations in the abstract syntax. Properties and associations other than aggregations can be specified by editing properties of tree nodes. Specifications are serialized in a special XML format. The editor runs as an Eclipse application.

Based on extensions of related work[10], Cospel is composed of the following packages (following the order in which models have been introduced in section 2).

The Cospel core package is part of the System model. It defines the hierarchical structure of the control system. Figure 15 shows the metamodel of this package. The `Specification` element is the top level element for any Cospel specification. It serves as the container for all specification elements. The `Type` element serves as a template for similar objects: all features which are common to a number of similar objects can be modeled only once in their type. This choice is motivated by the highly repetitive structure of control systems, and is supported by the common practice of using such a template system to reduce the workload of specification in the domain. The other key concept here is the `Object`. It represents an individual component, and it models the hierarchical structure of the control system (an object can be the child of another object). All other features of the system are modeled in other packages and associated with either the type (for features common to many objects) or the object (for object-specific features).

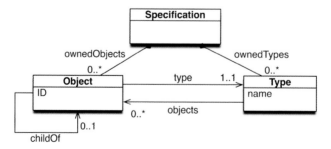

Fig. 15. Cospel core metamodel

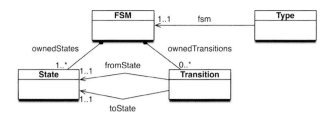

Fig. 16. FSM package metamodel

With respect to our Cosmic Rack example of Figure 1, we model here four types: PARTITION, CTRL-GRP, CTRL-CHN and POWER-GRP. Individual objects are then defined (and associated to their type): CosmicRack, CG1-5, CG6-10, Ctrl-Channel-1, Ctrl-Channel-2, and all Power Groups from 1 to 20 (numbered according to a layer and index convention, e.g. PG-Layer-4-Rod-2 is number 8).

The Finite State Machine (FSM) package is part of the System model. The behaviour of objects in terms of states and transitions is modeled via a simple FSM model. This is supported by FSMs being well known and understood in the domain. An FSM, comprised of States and Transitions, is associated to a Type (from the core package). This means that all objects of that type will have that FSM. Figure 16 shows the FSM package metamodel.

Using this metamodel we can, for example, model the FSM of a Control Channel (from Figure 4). We create four states: DISABLED, OFF, ON and ERROR. Also, we define a transition for each arc in the FSM. These states and transitions are grouped in an FSM called FSMControlChannel which is associated to the CTRL-CHN type.

The State dependency rules package is part of the System model. Recalling what was said in section 2, we want to be able to define rules in the form *"if all of the children of this object are in state x, set this object to state y"*. This is achieved by associating a state composition rule (StateCompRule) to a type. All objects of that type will implement this rule. The rule is associated to a state (representing the children objects' state) via a *childrenState* relationship. It is also associated to a resulting state via a *resultingState* relationship. StateCompRule also has an orAndType attribute. This defines if the rule is triggered when *all* children are in a given state, or when *at least one* child is. Figure 17 shows the metamodel of this package.

For the Cosmic Rack example, referring to Table 1, we declare a PartitionErrorDependency rule, with the orAndType attribute set to And. This rule is associated with the PARTITION type. Through the *childrenState*

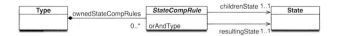

Fig. 17. State composition rules package metamodel

relationship, it is associated to the Control Groups ERROR state. Through the *resultingState* relationship, it is associated to the Partition's ERROR state. Other rules implementing the table can be defined in the same way.

The Property package is part of the System model. It defines the *Property* class, associated to a type. All objects of that type will have the property. The property has a data type. It also has attributes defining value intervals associated to diagnostic alerts (normal, warning, alert and severe). For the Power Groups in the Cosmic Rack example, we define the temperature property, an integer value. For each of the four diagnostic values, we define upper and lower temperature limits.

The Command and Event package is part of the System model. The metamodel in Figure 18 describes events.

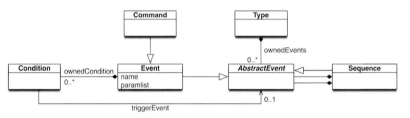

Fig. 18. Event package metamodel

An AbstractEvent is associated to a Type, meaning that all objects of that type will have it. It can be either a simple Event, or, recursively, a Sequence of events. A simple event has a name and a list of parameters. A Command is a specialization of an event. Based on the satisfaction of a Condition, an event can be executed, and can optionally trigger another event. The event can also be associated (not shown) to a transition of the type's FSM; this means when the event is executed, the transition is triggered. Conditions are characterized by expressions, evaluated on properties and/or event parameters, and include the definition of pre-postcondition expressions. Multiple conditions can be used to axiomatize an event.

The Control Channels in our Cosmic Rack case study have an Enable command. This command has no parameters, thus its condition does not state any particular precondition for its execution. However, Enable is associated to the OFF transition going from state DISABLED to state OFF (see Figure 4). This implies that the command is only executable if the control channel is in state DISABLED (otherwise the transition would not be fireable).

The Geometry package corresponds to the visual model. A Geometry class (abstract, that generalizes several classes like Box, Cylinder, GeomFile...) is associated to a Type, defining the shape of all objects of that type. A Scale class is also associated to a Type, allowing the reuse of the same geometry at different scales for different types (e.g. one might have two types of screws, identical but for the length). Classes defining position in space and

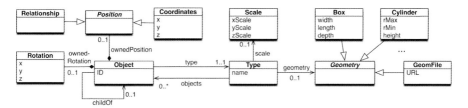

Fig. 19. Geometry package metamodel

rotation are directly associated to the object, placing the object in space. For the position in space various possibilities exist: giving absolute coordinates, or placing the object with relationships to other objects (parallel surfaces, distance...). The metamodel of this package is in Figure 19, with a simplification on the *relationship* class (which generalizes a number of possible relationships). Note that having a geometry/position is optional; this is because we could make models in which there are some objects which are only *logical* objects. They do not corresponding to a physical object, but are only used to group other objects for diagnostic purposes.

In the Cosmic Rack, all components are cuboids (although with different sizes, proportions and orientations). To model their geometry, we define a `Box` with unitary dimensions and associate it to all types. Then we associate a different `Scale` to each of the four types, giving the size in the three axes of the box. Also, all Power Groups with a name ending in "Rod_1" have a rotation on the X axis, so we define a `Rotation` and apply it to all those objects. Thus, to characterize all shapes, we only define one geometry, one rotation and four scales. We then position each object in space according to the mechanical drawings of the Cosmic Rack.

The Tasks package corresponds to the Task model. Building the metamodel for the CTT formalism, we chose to use binary task trees to avoid the problem of defining a priority for the temporal operators, as suggested in [7]. The resulting metamodel is shown in Figure 20. An individual `Task` can be associated with a `Type`; this means that the task will be available for every object of that type. A task can also be associated with a `Command` from the Event package, which means

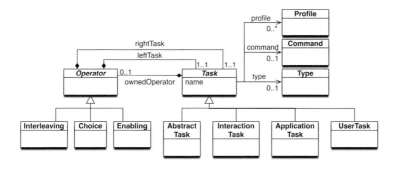

Fig. 20. Task package metamodel

Fig. 21. User package metamodel

that performing the task involves sending that command to the object associated with the task. Finally, a task is associated to a `Profile`, a concept described in the user model in the following paragraph, meaning that only certain profiles are allowed to perform that task. Tasks are related in a tree structure by `Operators` (here we show only three of them).

Modeling the *turn on control channels* task for Control Channel (Figure 12), we create a task for each CTT node (*turn on control channels, turn on control channel 1...*). Each task is associated to the `CTRL-CHN` type. The leaf nodes are associated to the `Enable` and `TurnOn` commands of the Control Channel. We relate the tasks using the enabling (`>>`) and interleaving (`|||`) operators.

The Users Package corresponds to the User model. The metamodel corresponds to what has already been shown in Figure 9, with the *Thing* class replaced by the `Task` class from the task package. We also renamed *Behaviour* to *Profile* for clarity. The metamodel is shown in Figure 21.

We already showed an example for the Cosmic Rack in Figure 10: we create a `Profile` called `Physicist`, and a `User` named `Peter Piper` associated to this profile. We associate Peter to the task model for the `Clear Error` task through an instance of `Knowledge`, which is characterized by a `level` of 20, and a `date` of 22.10.2006.

3.2   Transformation

To give semantics to a Cospel model, we use model transformation techniques. Instead of defining a semantic for each element of the Cospel language, our approach establishes mapping rules between the Cospel metamodel and the CO-OPN[11] metamodel. CO-OPN (Concurrent Object-Oriented Petri Nets) is an object oriented modeling language based on algebraic Petri nets, allowing the execution of specifications and providing tools for simulation, verification and test generation. CO-OPN support concurrency and transactionality, and there are tools to generate executable Java code from a CO-OPN model. Since the semantics of CO-OPN are already defined (in formal terms), we obtain the Cospel semantics as a result of the transformation.

In the context of the BATIC[3]S project we chose to use the Atlas transformation language (ATL) framework[12], a declarative, rule-based language and framework for specifying mapping rules in language transformations. ATL is particularly well suited for its declarative style and its modularity. The ATL framework is very usable, and runs as an Eclipse plugin, another advantage for our methodology which is mainly based on Eclipse-related tools.

We followed a modular approach, identifying the different packages of the Cospel language (e.g. tasks, users, object hierarchy...) as sources for the trans-

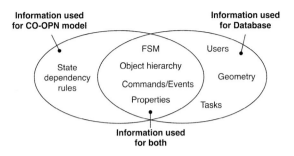

Fig. 22. The CO-OPN model and the database are built by transformation of Cospel packages; some packages are used to produce both models, while others only contribute to one of them

formation; for each module, we gave a transformation pattern with ATL rules. The patterns have then been composed, with syntactic and semantic composition techniques, to obtain a set of transformation rules able to transform the whole Cospel framework.

As we said before, the methodology's artifacts are two: a system simulator and a GUI. To produce them, the ATL transformation creates two models from the Cospel specification. The first one is the CO-OPN model which has just been described. Since the system simulation is purely behavioural, no visualization-related information is used for building the CO-OPN model. The second model created by the ATL transformation is a database, which has to be used as a data source for creating the dynamic 3D scene in the GUI. Information including object hierarchy, geometrical data, FSMs (for representing states), tasks, properties and commands/events (to create interaction methods) are stored in this database. Figure 22 shows which Cospel packages contribute to which model.

An overview of the transformation process is given in Figure 23, showing what the players in the transformation of the Cospel model to a CO-OPN+Database model are. It is shown how the individual language packages and their transformation patterns are composed into a global metamodel and a global transformation. A detailed description of this composition and transformation process is in [10].

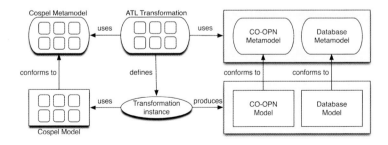

Fig. 23. Transformation overview. Smaller rectangles inside Cospel metamodel and model and inside the ATL transformation represent individual language packages and their individual transformation patterns.

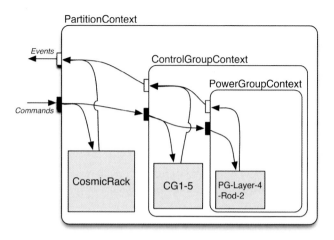

Fig. 24. Hierarchical structure of CO-OPN model

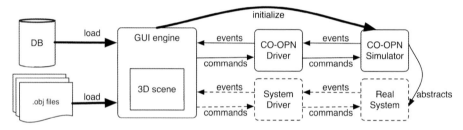

Fig. 25. GUI engine communication

Without getting too deep in the details of the CO-OPN specification resulting from the Cospel transformation, we will now describe its structure. We used the object-oriented features of CO-OPN to create the hierarchical structure, by using Cospel types as a template for instantiating CO-OPN objects. Commands are transformed to CO-OPN methods, and events to CO-OPN gates (a kind of parameterized event). Since CO-OPN objects contain an algebraic Petri net, Cospel object states and properties are translated to CO-OPN places, and behavioural rules (such as FSM transitions or dependency rules) are translated to axioms. Figure 24 shows the structure of a part of the Cosmic Rack hierarchy using CO-OPN's visual syntax. It shows how objects are instantiated inside imbricated *contexts* (a CO-OPN context is an encapsulation allowing coordination among object instances), how commands are routed (arrows) down the hierarchy until their destination object, and how events are routed up. The routes (called *synchronizations*) are decided based on conditions (e.g. the name of the destination object, or the parameters of the command/event), a part of which comes from the specification, and the rest are automatically generated in the transformation patterns.

Verification can be performed on the CO-OPN model by using decision diagrams. Tools are under development[13] for model checking CO-OPN. These tools implement decision diagrams model checking for algebraic Petri nets. This allows exploring a specification's state space to check whether properties are satisfied. Verification of temporal properties is thus possible (for example properties concerning dynamic behaviours, like tasks, events or interaction).

The CO-OPN specification is finally used by the CO-OPN tools to generate Java code. This code constitutes the formal executable system simulator mentioned in Figure 5. It serves as the executable basis for evaluating the GUI prototype.

3.3   GUI Engine

The GUI engine which creates the GUI for the user to interact with is written in Java. It presents a 3D rendering of the system which allows spatial navigation and interaction with system components. Figure 25 shows the data flow of the GUI engine. Its source of information for rendering the scene are the database (DB) produced in the transformation phase, and the set of Object files containing the shapes of the system components. By loading these resources, a 3D scene is initialized and shown to the user. At the same time, the CO-OPN system simulator produced in the transformation is instantiated and initialized.

To minimize memory usage (a serious problem for systems with a large number of components), features common to sets of objects (i.e. those features associated in the specification language to types rather than to individual objects, like geometrical shape) are loaded only once and stored in instances of a `Object3DStructure` class. Individual objects are obtained by instantiating an `Object3D` class which applies individual features (e.g. position in space) to the associated `Object3DStructure` instances.

Objects are organized in a tree, according to the hierarchy in the specification. Each of them keeps an instance of FSM, and the current state of an object is represented in the scene by colors, according to common practices in the field (green=ok, yellow=warning, red=error, blue=powered, gray=off or unknown).

Upon selecting objects, users are shown with clickable controls corresponding to the commands defined for that object. These, when clicked, send a command message to the driver, which transmits it in the appropriate format to the CO-OPN simulator. Events coming from the simulator are also translated by the driver and can be interpreted by the GUI to update the scene (e.g. an object state change will modify its color, or trigger an error message).

After the development phase, when the prototype can be considered final, the CO-OPN driver can be substituted by a driver for the real system (see Figure 25), so that the interface can be evaluated in a real-life environment.

Rendering is done by using the JoGL API[14], a Java binding of the OpenGL libraries developed by Sun and Silicon Graphics. JoGL provides all necessary methods for 3D rendering and navigation. In addition to that, it has built-in support for stereoscopic visualization, which allowed us to experiment with how stereoscopic perception can affect interaction and navigation in a control system. We also used the FengGUI API[15], which allows drawing 2D components, like windows and buttons, in a 3D stereoscopic scene.

There are two navigation modes: spatial and hierarchical. Different controllers can be used for spatial navigation: keyboard, mouse (via click and drag

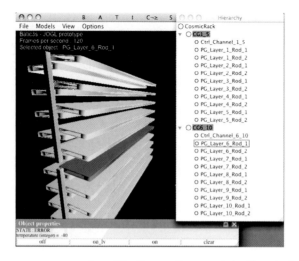

Fig. 26. GUI prototype screenshot. The Power Groups of the Cosmic Rack can be seen in the 3D scene.

gestures) or 3D controllers (e.g. six degrees of freedom knobs like 3D Connexion's SpaceNavigator [16]). Hierarchical navigation is done via a tree-like representation of the system.

The two navigation modes answer different types of tasks. When investigating a faulty component, the user may be interested in checking the nearby components' values to prevent further alarms, especially when the faults are of environmental nature (temperature, humidity). These components might well be "far" in terms of system hierarchy (i.e. belonging to a whole different branch of the hierarchy), but will be at a short distance in the 3D scene. The spatial navigation system provides easy access by moving the camera and directly clicking on them. On the other hand, if a user wants to quickly jump to another part of the system following an error, spatial navigation is not efficient as it requires several zooming, panning and rotating operations. In these cases, a few clicks on the tree representation provide a quick focus switch to another region of the system. Also, the tree representation can help selecting objects which are difficult to pick (very small or hidden by other objects).

Figure 26 shows a screenshot of the GUI prototype. A 3D representation of the Cosmic Rack is shown, and Power Groups are visible. Objects containing Power Groups (i.e. the Control Groups and the Cosmic Rack external shell) have been made invisible, in order to show one of the Power Groups which is having an error (it can be seen in a different color). The 3D scene is built using the information about the system hierarchy, FSMs and geometry.

The user middle-clicked on the component, which brought up possible commands in the bottom panel. The temperature property is also shown here. The engine knows what commands and properties to show because they had been specified in the model.

The right panel marks the name of the currently selected component in the hierarchical tree view of the system. Since the model says that the current user has access to the *off*, *on_lv*, *on* and *clear* commands of the Power Group, all these buttons appear in the bottom panel. A user with monitoring responsibilities only would not see the buttons.

4   Related Work

4.1   Control Systems and GUI Models

There are two main lines of research related to this work. The first is about specification languages for control systems. The second concerns techniques and languages for GUI generation.

Several models have been proposed in the domain of control systems to be used as a specification language. RSML[17] exploits the fact that control systems are reactive and evolve their state depending on conditions. It is based on a modified version of Statecharts. It defines a mapping to an underlying formal model based on Mealy automata, but presents the user with a set of more readable syntaxes. The Fujaba tool[18] treats decentralized control systems. It models systems using a UML class diagram syntax, to which users can add detail such as Statecharts or collaboration diagrams. It supports specification simulation and Java code generation, but no model-checking features (except for those which can be applied to Java, of course).

VEG[19] treats two-dimensional GUIs as reactive event driven systems *per se*. It proposes a scalable notion to specify, design, validate and verify a GUI. Specifications are modular, separated into control and data, and are layout-independent. The syntax supports event-based behaviours, parallel composition and runtime instantiation. Java code functions can be added to model complex behaviours. VEG offers model checking possibility in that specifications can be transformed to Promela and model-checked with SPIN[20]. A Java prototype of the GUI can be generated.

In the domain of GUI generation techniques, various approaches tackle specification and prototyping. Bastide et al. [21] use a formal object-oriented formalism (ICO) to describe interactive applications. The developer can specify the interface behaviour as an Object Petri net. The GUI presentation is specified using the commercial tool JBuilder. Verification and validation can be performed because of the formal semantics of ICO, as well as prototype generation. There is no simulation of the system under control, the specification process demands a knowledge of Petri nets, and the specification of the presentation is manual.

Calvary et al. [22] define a general, unifying reference framework for classifying multi-target interfaces. Four levels of abstraction are defined (task and concepts, abstract UI, concrete UI, final UI). This framework is instantiated for a few GUI generation approaches, including ARTStudio [23], a tool by the same authors to generate multi-target GUIs from tasks and data specification. Here also, the simulation of the system under control is not one of the goals. The focus is abstraction and flexibility, and the definition of a generic framework which can be used as a reference to compare or unify similar approaches.

UsiXML (several papers in [24]) is an abstract user interface description language, allowing specification of the interactive aspects of a GUI. It can be rendered on different platforms and as different types of GUIs thanks to its level of abstraction. This flexibility makes it suitable as an underlying format for storing the interface model, and its use is currently being evaluated by our project.

The AID project [25] has a rather similar scope to our work. One of the fundamental goals of AID is generating a GUI from an existing model of the system under control. The syntax and semantics of the system model (called *Domain Model*) are used to build an interaction model and a presentation model. The task model for the interface is part of the domain model, which also is the case for our project. However, this approach is mainly focused on automatic interface design; it does not provide simulation of the system, nor verification and validation activities.

Finally, Vanderdonckt et al. developed the Envir3D tool[26], which can generate a virtual 3D GUI from an abstract model of the interaction elements, dialog and presentation. The underlying model, hidden from the developer, allows evaluation, model checking and verification of the GUI. The main focus of the work is evaluating usability with respect to standard guidelines. There is no simulation of the system under control. This project complements our work, in that we focus a lot on system semantics and not really on ergonomics of the GUI, while the Envir3D project does the opposite.

4.2   Task Models

A very in-depth survey about task models has been done in [27]. It shows and discusses several task models from the 1960's to early 2000's, thus we will not rewrite it here in detail. All reviewed task models express goals, task hierarchies, temporal constraints and role specification in terms of tasks. When it comes to comparing models however, the following factors differentiate and motivate the choice CTT from other reviewed choices:

- Discipline of origin: some other reviewed models are based on disciplines aside from software engineering (i.e. psychology or cognitive science) and give too much relevance to behavioural or cognitive aspects for our context
- Formalization: semantically, CTT is based on process algebra, which is suitable for the domain and activities we treat, while other models are not based on an underlying formal system
- Context of use variations: most reviewed models do not support task variations based on context of use, while CTT supports conditional subtrees of tasks
- System response: some of the reviewed models do not distinguish any type of task from the technical system, while CTT does

4.3   Adaptation Models

In AWE3D [28], the authors focus on proposing a general approach to build adaptive 3D Web sites, and illustrate a specific application of the approach to a 3D e-commerce case study. In SLIM-VRT [29], the authors present the design and implementation of an efficient strategy for adapting multimedia information associated to virtual environments in the context of e-learning applications. They propose a strategy for VRML scenes which consists in separating the multimedia information to be associated to the virtual scene from the 3D models themselves. In AMACONT [30], the authors present an approach to deploy the adaptive hypermedia architecture AMACONT [31] together with the component oriented 3D document model CONTIGRA [32] to achieve various types of 3D adaptation within Web pages. The authors present implicit rule-based media adaptation observing user interactions.In [33,34], the authors present a system that is able to deliver personalized learning content in 3D Educational Virtual Environments. The techniques extend those employed in the field of Adaptive Hypermedia by the well known AHA! system [35]. In [36], the authors have presented an ontology-based model which is well-suited to create adapted views of an urban planning project. Adaptation is based on two factors: the user's profile, which is used to select a viewpoint-ontology; and the user's current centre of interest, which corresponds to a theme in the ontology of the themes. The generation of the links in the interface is carried out according to generation rules that correspond to different linking semantics. In 3DSEAM [37,38] , the authors present an open framework supporting rule-based adaptations of 3D scenes is used. The main role of the framework is to arrange the adaptation process following an adaptation strategy, materialized by rules that come with the scene request. The adaptation framework relies on the 3DAF (3D Annotation Framework) that handles the identification of objects matching the rule criterion, and external engines that either adapt individual objects or regions [39].

5   Conclusion and Perspectives

We presented a methodology to prototype adaptive graphical user interfaces (GUI) for control systems. We introduced a DSL for the control systems domain, called Cospel, based on useful and understandable abstractions for domain experts. Transformation techniques and semantic mapping to a formal model allow for simulation, validation, verification and automatic GUI prototype generation. Our approach is based on the assumption that a GUI can be induced from the characteristics of the system to control.

Several perspectives will guide the future of this work:

Improving the language: the modular structure we used for metamodels and transformations allows for a relatively easy extension of Cospel. Features can be added, such as defining a type-based template system for the hierarchy or specifying the behaviour of commands in a more complex way, or again modeling the interaction between the GUI and the system.

Enriching user information: the user model we have defined is actually richer than what we currently use. By implementing metrics in the GUI engine, we could measure factors like user mood, learning style and cognitive style based on how the user interacts with the GUI. This information could be used for evaluation of the GUI prototype.

3D adaptation: apart from open issues of defining procedural versus declarative 3D adaptation, work is ongoing on defining ontology-based 3D adaptation. We are currently investigating a case study for building 3D adaptive GUIs based on ontologies for urban planning communication[36]. Urban planning is concerned with assembling and shaping the urban, local or municipal environment by deciding on the composition and configuration of geographical objects in a space-time continuum. The main characteristics of the ontology-based model are the semantic integration in a knowledge base of the urban knowledge coming from various sources (geographical information systems databases, master plans, local plans); and the modelling of the centre of interest of an urban actor. These models can be then used to generate adapted GUIs to present the project's data and knowledge according to each actor's background and interests.

3D stereoscopy impact: we want to evaluate if, in this domain, stereoscopy helps navigation; if immersion is relevant to knowledge representation; if there are unexpected side effects of using a 3D interactive environment; and if there is an advantage in using haptic devices or multitouch interaction.

Introducing ergonomy and usability criteria: while our current work is mainly interested in the semantic and methodological aspects of GUI generation, one should not forget that usability and ergonomy of a GUI are capital factors in its success. Existing approaches for applying standard usability metrics to GUIs should be integrated in the prototyping process.

We are also interested in extending the methodology to similar but distinct domains. Apart from the case study mentioned in section 1.3, we did another study [40] on an interface for data acquisition at a high energy physics experiment at CERN, called ATLAS. Results of the case study are still under evaluation, especially for what concerns the role of 3D representation in this particular domain.

References

1. Risoldi, M., Masetti, L., Buchs, D., Barroca, B., Amaral, V.: A model-based methodology for control systems gui design prototyping. In: Proceedings of the PCAPAC 2008 conference (2008), http://www.pcapacworkshop.org
2. Dierlamm, A., Dirkes, G.H., Fahrer, M., Frey, M., Hartmann, F., Masetti, L., Militaru, O., Shah, S.Y., Stringer, R., Tsirou, A.: The CMS tracker control system. Journal of Physics: Conference Series 119(2), 022019 (9p) (2008)
3. Burkardt, J.: Object file format specification (visited, 2008), http://people.scs.fsu.edu/~burkardt/txt/obj_format.txt
4. Kobsa, A., Wahlster, W. (eds.): User models in dialog systems. Springer, New York (1989)
5. Cretton, F., Calvé, A.L.: Working paper: Generic ontology based user modeling - GenOUM. Technical report, HES-SO Valais (2007)
6. Cretton, F., Calvé, A.L.: Generic ontology based user model: GenOUM. Technical report, Université de Genève (June 2008), http://smv.unige.ch/tiki-list_file_gallery.php?galleryId=46
7. Paternò, F., Mancini, C., Meniconi, S.: ConcurTaskTrees: A diagrammatic notation for specifying task models. In: INTERACT 1997: Proceedings of the IFIP TC13 Interantional Conference on Human-Computer Interaction, London, UK, UK, pp. 362–369. Chapman & Hall, Ltd., Boca Raton (1997)

8. Yip, S., Robson, D.: Graphical user interfaces validation: a problem analysis and a strategy to solution. In: Proceedings of the Twenty-Fourth Annual Hawaii International Conference on System Sciences, IEEE Computer Society, Los Alamitos (1991)

9. Budinsky, F., Steinberg, D., Merks, E., Ellersick, R., Grose, T.J.: Eclipse Modeling Framework. The Eclipse series. Addison-Wesley, Reading (2004)

10. Pedro, L., Risoldi, M., Buchs, D., Barroca, B., Amaral, V.: Developing domain specific modeling languages by metamodel semantic enrichment and composition: a case study. In: IEEE Software Special Issue on Domain-Specific Languages & Modeling (Submitted, 2008)

11. Biberstein, O.: CO-OPN/2: An Object-Oriented Formalism for the Specification of Concurrent Systems. PhD thesis, University of Geneva (1997)

12. ATLAS Group: Atlas transformation language (2008),
    http://www.eclipse.org/m2m/atl/

13. Hostettler, S.: Java decisions diagrams library. Technical report, Université de Genève (June 2008),
    http://smv.unige.ch/tiki-list_file_gallery.php?galleryId=46

14. JoGL expert group: JSR 231: Java^{TM}binding for the OpenGL$^{®}$ API (visited, 2008), http://jcp.org/en/jsr/detail?id=231

15. FengGUI developer group: FengGUI: Java GUIs with OpenGL (visited, 2008),
    http://www.fenggui.org

16. 3DConnexion: Spacenavigator product web page (visited, 2008),
    http://www.3dconnexion.com/3dmouse/spacenavigator.php

17. Leveson, N.G., Heimdahl, M.P.E., Hildreth, H., Reese, J.D.: Requirements specification for process-control systems. IEEE Transactions on Software Engineering 20(9), 684–707 (1994)

18. Kohler, H.J., Nickel, U., Niere, J., Zundorf, A.: Integrating UML diagrams for production control systems. ICSE 00, 241 (2000)

19. Berstel, J., Reghizzi, S.C., Roussel, G., Pietro, P.S.: A scalable formal method for design and automatic checking of user interfaces. In: ICSE 2001: Proceedings of the 23rd International Conference on Software Engineering, Washington, DC, USA, pp. 453–462. IEEE Computer Society, Los Alamitos (2001)

20. Holzmann, G.J.: The SPIN Model Checker. Addison-Wesley, Reading (2003)

21. Bastide, R., Navarre, D., Palanque, P.A.: A tool-supported design framework for safety critical interactive systems. Interacting with Computers 15(3), 309–328 (2003)

22. Calvary, G., Coutaz, J., Thevenin, D., Limbourg, Q., Bouillon, L., Vanderdonckt, J.: A unifying reference framework for multi-target user interfaces. Interacting with Computers 15(3), 289–308 (2003)

23. Calvary, G., Coutaz, J., Thevenin, D.: A unifying reference framework for the development of plastic user interfaces. In: Nigay, L., Little, M.R. (eds.) EHCI 2001. LNCS, vol. 2254, pp. 173–192. Springer, Heidelberg (2001)

24. UsiXML consortium: UsiXML - Home of the USer Interface eXtensible Markup Language (Visited, 2008), http://www.usixml.org

25. Penner, R.R., Steinmetz, E.S.: Implementation of automated interaction design with collaborative models. Interacting with Computers 15(3), 367–385 (2003)

26. Vanderdonckt, J., Chieu, C.K., Bouillon, L., Trevisan, D.: Model-based design, generation, and evaluation of virtual user interfaces. In: Web3D, pp. 51–60 (2004)

27. Limbourg, Q., Vanderdonckt, J.: Comparing task models for user interface design. In: The handbook of task analysis for human-computer interaction (2004)

28. Chittaro, L., Ranon, R.: Dynamic generation of personalized VRML content: a general approach and its application to 3D e-commerce. In: Web3D 2002: Proceedings of the seventh international conference on 3D Web technology, pp. 145–154. ACM, New York (2002)

29. Estalayo, E., Salgado, L., Moran, F., Cabrera, J.: Adapting multimedia information association in VRML scenes for e-learning applications. In: Proceedings of 1st International Workshop LET-Web3D, pp. 16–22 (2004)

30. Dachselt, R., Hinz, M., Pietschmann, S.: Using the AMACONT architecture for flexible adaptation of 3D web applications. In: Web3D 2006: Proceedings of the eleventh international conference on 3D web technology, pp. 75–84. ACM, New York (2006)

31. Hinz, M., Fiala, Z.: Amacont: A system architecture for adaptive multimedia web applications. In: Tolksdorf, R., Eckstein, R. (eds.) Berliner XML Tage, XML-Clearinghouse, pp. 65–74 (2004)

32. Dachselt, R., Hinz, M., Meissner, K.: Contigra: an XML-based architecture for component-oriented 3D applications. In: Web3D 2002: Proceedings of the seventh international conference on 3D Web technology, pp. 155–163. ACM, New York (2002)

33. Chittaro, L., Ranon, R.: Adaptive hypermedia techniques for 3D educational virtual environments. IEEE Intelligent Systems 22(4), 31–37 (2007)

34. Chittaro, L., Ranon, R.: An adaptive 3D virtual environment for learning the X3D language. In: Bradshaw, J.M., Lieberman, H., Staab, S. (eds.) Intelligent User Interfaces, pp. 419–420. ACM, New York (2008)

35. Bra, P.D., Aerts, A., Berden, B., de Lange, B., Rousseau, B., Santic, T., Smits, D., Stash, N.: AHA! The adaptive hypermedia architecture. In: HYPERTEXT 2003: Proceedings of the fourteenth ACM conference on Hypertext and hypermedia, pp. 81–84. ACM, New York (2003)

36. Métral, C., Falquet, G., Vonlanthen, M.: An ontology-based model for urban planning communication. In: Teller, J., Lee, J.R., Roussey, C. (eds.) Ontologies for Urban Development. Studies in Computational Intelligence, vol. 61, pp. 61–72. Springer, Heidelberg (2007)

37. Bilasco, I., Villanova-Oliver, M., Gensel, J., Martin, H.: Sémantique et modélisation des scènes 3D. RSTI-ISI, Metadonnées et nouveaux SI 12(2), 121–135 (2007)

38. Bilasco, I.M., Villanova-Oliver, M., Gensel, J., Martin, H.: Semantic-based rules for 3D scene adaptation. In: Gervasi, O., Brutzman, D.P. (eds.) Web3D, pp. 97–100. ACM, New York (2007)

39. Bilasco, I.M., Gensel, J., Villanova-Oliver, M., Martin, H.: An MPEG-7 framework enhancing the reuse of 3D models. In: Gracanin, D. (ed.) Web3Dq, pp. 65–74. ACM, New York (2006)

40. Barroca, B., Amaral, V., Risoldi, M., Caprini, M., Moreira, A., Araújo, J.: Towards the application of model based design methodology for reliable control systems on HEP experiments. In: Proceedings of the 11th IEEE Nuclear Science Symposium. IEEE, Los Alamitos (2008), http://www.nss-mic.org/2008/NSSMain.asp

Part IV
Mixed Reality

See ColOr: Seeing Colours with an Orchestra

Benoît Deville[1], Guido Bologna[2], Michel Vinckenbosch[2], and Thierry Pun[1]

[1] University of Geneva,
Computer Vision and Multimedia Lab,
Route de Drize 7,
CH-1227 Carouge, Switzerland
{Benoit.Deville,Thierry.Pun}@cui.unige.ch
[2] Laboratoire d'Informatique Industrielle,
University of Applied Science,
CH-1202 Geneva, Switzerlandd
{guido.bologna,michel.vinckenbosch}@hesge.ch

Abstract. The See Color interface transforms a small portion of a coloured video image into sound sources represented by spatialised musical instruments. Basically, the conversion of colours into sounds is achieved by quantisation of the HSL (Hue, Saturation and Luminosity) colour system. Our purpose is to provide visually impaired individuals with a capability of perception of the environment in real time. In this work we present the system's principles of design and several experiments that have been carried out by several blindfolded persons. The goal of the first experiment was to identify the colours of main features in static pictures in order to interpret the image scenes. Participants found that colours were helpful to limit the possible image interpretations.

Afterwards, two experiments based on a head mounted camera have been performed. The first experiment pertains to object manipulation. It is based on the pairing of coloured socks, while the second experiment is related to outdoor navigation with the goal of following a coloured sinuous path painted on the ground. The *socks* experiment demonstrated that blindfolded individuals were able to accurately match pairs of coloured socks. The same participants successfully followed a red serpentine path painted on the ground for more than 80 meters.

Finally, we propose an original approach for a real time alerting system, based on the detection of visual salient parts in videos. The particularity of our approach lies in the use of a new feature map constructed from the depth gradient. From the computed feature maps we infer conspicuity maps that indicate areas that are appreciably different from their surrounding. Then a specific distance function is described, which takes into account both stereoscopic camera limitations and user's choices. We also report how we automatically estimate the relative contribution of each conspicuity map, which enables the unsupervised determination of the final saliency map, indicating the visual salience of all points in the image. We demonstrate here that this additional depth-based feature map allows the system to detect salient regions with good accuracy in most situations, even in the presence of noisy disparity maps.

D. Lalanne and J. Kohlas (Eds.): Human Machine Interaction, LNCS 5440, pp. 251–279, 2009.
© Springer-Verlag Berlin Heidelberg 2009

1   Introduction

Following a 2002 survey, the World Health Organisation estimated there were 161 million visually impaired people in the world, of whom 124 million had low vision and 37 million were blind [1]. For a blind person, the quality of life is appreciably improved with the use of special devices, which facilitate precise tasks of everyday life, such as reading, manipulating objects or using a computer.

Although the world we observe seems very stable, vision is a dynamic and fugitive phenomenon. Specifically, eye movements indicate the location of meaningful content in an image. The central area of the human retina (*fovea*) spans for approximately two degrees. To understand a scene image our eyes scan it in a series of fixations, without conscious planning. The rapid eye movements between fixations are designated as *saccades*. Note that the time duration of a fixation is related to the processing expended on interpreting the corresponding portion of the image [2]. Within each fixation, the fine detail that will be visible depends on its contrast, its spatial frequency and its eccentricity, or angular distance from the center of the field of view [3,4].

Our senses can be regarded as data channels possessing a maximal capacity measured in bits per seconds (bps). The bandwidth of the human auditory system is estimated at about 10 Kbps [5], while the visual channel has the largest capacity [5] (around 1000 Kbps), and touch is less powerful than audition with approximately 0.1 Kbps [5]. Total vision substitution would be impossible to achieve, as the bandwidth of touch or audition would be inadequate. Therefore, it is important to make crucial choices in order to convey a small part of vision, in such a way that the reduced visual information rendered by another sense preserves useful meaning.

1.1   Tactile Substitution

Touch is the most commonly used modality to replace sight through the haptic modality. More precisely, this modality is composed of two complementary channels, tactile and kinesthetic [6].

The cutaneous stimulations generated by tactile displays are based on three distinct classes of stimuli: mechanical tactile, electro-tactile and thermo-tactile [7]. Mechanical tactile substitution remains however the most widely used, thanks to its best spatio-temporal resolution. In this case, the stimuli are obtained by means of a vibro-tactile matrix, which is composed of a 2D lattice of tractors. The height of the tractors can vary according to several levels, in order to represent three-dimensional surfaces. Specifically, four criteria determine the quality of tactile displays: the number of tractors included in the device; the density of the tractors; the number of vertical levels that the tractors can take and the refresh frequency. These devices transform the visual flow collected by a mobile camera into tactile stimuli. Tactile displays are fixed on areas of the body having good spatio-temporal resolution like the abdomen [8], the face or more recently, the tongue [9].

Many experiments were carried out by Kaczmarek *et al.* on congenital blind people [10]. The results obtained with a vibro-tactile device showed that after a sufficiently long training period, the participants were able to feek some perceptual components like depth and perspective. However, the results also revealed several deficiencies related to the size of the tactile display and its weak resolution.

The Optacon II device includes a photo-receiver connected to a vibro-tactile matrix made up of 144 tractors arranged in 24 lines and 6 columns. Its use implied to place one finger on the tactile display and to use the other hand to sweep the contents of the image or the text [11]. Experiments reported that blind subjects were able to recognize elementary patterns.

Kawai and Tomita developed a prototype for the recognition of voluminous objects [12]. The system, as it was carried out, brings into play two cameras, a touch screen and a sound helmet. The two cameras were used to obtain a stereographic image of the objects of the environment. The touch screen was composed of 16×16 tractors laid out on a surface of 175×175 mm. The space ranging between each tractor is 10 mm, while their height could vary up to 6 mm. The synthetic voice was giving additional information. Evaluations carried out on five visually impaired subjects showed that they were able to recognize without difficulties the objects of the everyday life (cup, ball, book, etc.).

Maucher developed a tactile device which includes 48 piezoelectric actuators laid out on a 4×12 matrix [13]. This matrix which functions as a pantograph is fixed by a rail on a shelf whose working surface is 220×220 mm. The refresh frequency of the tactile device is 20 Hz. The system was assessed by six blind subjects and four normal sighted persons on simple geometrical objects like squares, triangles or circles with varying size and orientation. The results showed that blind subjects recognised the objects twice faster than subjects in the normal control group.

1.2   Auditive Substitution

The second most common modality to replace sight is audition. For a complete survey on audio-tactile displays, one can refer to Pun *et al.* [14]. For instance, echolocation is a mode of perception used spontaneously by many blind people. It consists in perceiving the environment by generating sounds and then listening to the corresponding echoes. Reverberations of various types of sound, such as slapping of the fingers, murmured words, whistles, noise of the steps, or sounds from a cane are often used.

Sound spatialisation is the principle which consists of virtually creating a three-dimensional auditory environment, where sound sources can be positioned all around the listener. These environments can be simulated by means of loudspeakers or headphones. Among the precursors in this field, Ruff and Perret led a series of experiments on the space perception of auditory patterns [15]. Patterns were transmitted through a 10×10 matrix of loudspeakers separated by 10 cm and located at a distance of 30 cm from the listener. Patterns were represented on the auditory display by sinusoidal waves on the corresponding loudspeakers.

The experiments showed that 42% of the participants identified six simple geometrical patterns correctly (segment of lines, squares, etc.). However, orientation was much more difficult to determine precisely. Other experiments carried out later by Lakatos taught that subjects were able to recognise ten alphanumeric characters with a 60 − 90% accuracy [16].

Several authors proposed special devices for visual substitution by the auditory pathway in the context of real time reactivity. The *K Sonar-Cane* combines a cane and a torch with ultrasounds [17]. With this special cane, it is possible to perceive the environment by listening to a sound coding the distance.

The Voice is another experimental vision substitution system that uses auditory feedback. An image is represented by 64 columns of 64 pixels [18]. Image are processed from left to right and each column is listened to for about 15 ms. In particular, every gray level pixel in a column is represented by a sinusoidal wave with a distinct frequency. High frequencies are at the top of the column and low frequencies are at the bottom in a 5 kHz range of frequencies.

Capelle *et al.* proposed the implementation of a crude model of the primary visual system [19]. The implemented device provides two resolution levels corresponding to an artificial central retina and an artificial peripheral retina, as in the real visual system. The auditory representation of an image is similar to that used in *The Voice* with distinct sinusoidal waves for each pixel in a column and each column being presented sequentially to the listener. Experiments carried out with 24 blindfolded sighted subjects revealed that after a period of time not exceeding one hour, subjects were able to identify simple patterns such as horizontal lines, squares and letters.

A more musical model was introduced by Cronly-Dillon [20]. First, the complexity of an image is reduced by applying several algorithms (segmentation, edge detection, etc.). After processing, the image contains black and white pixels only. Pixels in a column define a chord, while horizontal lines are played sequentially, as a melody. When a processed image presents too complex objects, the system can apply new segmentation algorithms to these complex objects and to obtain basic patterns such as squares, circles and polygons. Experiments carried out with normal and (elderly) blind persons showed that in many cases a satisfactory mental image was obtained.

Gonzalez-Mora *et al.* developed a prototype using the spatialisation of sound in the three dimensional space [21]. The sound is perceived as coming from somewhere in front of the user by means of head related impulse responses (HRIRs). The first device they achieved could produce a virtual acoustic space of $17 \times 9 \times 8$ gray level pixels covering a distance of up to 4.5 meters.

1.3   See ColOr

In this paper, we present *See ColOr* (Seeing Colors with an Orchestra), which is an ongoing project aiming at providing visually impaired individuals with a non-invasive mobility aid. See ColOr uses the auditory pathway to represent frontal image scenes in real-time. General targeted applications are the search for items of particular interest for blind users, the manipulation of objects and the navigation in an unknown environment. The See ColOr interface encodes coloured pixels by spatialised musical instrument sounds, in order to represent and emphasise the colour and location of visual entities in their environment [22,23,24]. The basic idea is to represent a pixel as a directional sound source with depth estimated by stereo-vision. Finally, each emitted sound is assigned to a musical instrument, depending on the colour of the pixel.

However, as image points are represented by sound sources and typical cameras capture hundreds of thousand pixels, it is not feasible to transcribe the whole scene without risking to create a cacophony that would lead to missing important information. This is why we have developped an alerting system to attract the user's attention towards regions of interest [25].

The focus of attention (FOA) is a cognitive process that can be described as the ability to concentrate one or more senses (e.g. both touch and/or vision) on a specific object, sound, smell, etc. The *cocktail party effect* is a well known example: one can follow a specific conversation out of a set of multiple and diverse sounds. This ability to focus on a specific point is guided by our senses, and our interests in a given situation. We are interested here in the dectection of salient areas from video sequences. The objective is to find *threats* and *obstacles* that are conspicuous, and to alert the user. We ground this detection on specific visual properties of the scene.

The alerting system is based on a specific model of bottom-up saliency-based visual attention, namely the conspicuity maps. A conspicuity map contains information about regions of an image that differ from their neighbourhood. Each conspicuity map is built according to a specific feature, which can consist of colours, orientations, edges, etc. In this paper we have combined the depth gradient feature with distance, illumination intensity, and two colour opponencies. To our knowledge, the depth gradient has never been used before to build conspicuity maps. The purpose of the depth gradient conspicuity map is to detect objects that come towards the blind user, and that need to be avoided. In order to let the user control the range of interest, a distance function is integrated in our model. This function also allows to take into account camera limitations in distance computation. It is shown here that the use of the depth gradient is an important feature in a mobility aid system. It obviously helps in the cases where objects might disturb the movements of a blind user.

This article is reporting on the different experiments that have been carried out by several blindfolded persons with See ColOr prototypes related to tactile pictures (Fig. 5) and simple video images captured by cameras (Fig. 6). We carried out three experiments with up to seven blindfolded participants. This small number of participants impacts on the statistical validity of the experiments. We note however that in the literature, reports on similar projects hardly present results with more than a few participants. The goal of the first experiment was to identify the colours of the main features of static pictures and then to give an interpretation of the whole image scenes. Participants found that colours were helpful to limit the possible image interpretations.

In addition, two experiments based on head mounted cameras have been performed[1]. We aimed at verifying the hypothesis that it is possible to manipulate and to match coloured objects, such as coloured socks with an auditory feedback represented by sounds of musical instruments. The last purpose was to verify that navigation in an outdoor environment can be performed with the help of the sound related to a coloured serpentine path painted on the ground. The *socks* experiment demonstrated that blindfolded individuals were able to accurately match pairs of socks. The same participants successfully followed a red serpentine path for more than 80 meters. To the best of our knowledge this is the first study in the context of visual substitution for object manipulation and real time navigation, for which colour is supplied to the user as musical instrument sounds. In the following sections we present in Section 2 the sound code, Section 3 presents the detection of salient areas, Section 4 describes the different See ColOr prototypes, and Section 5 illustrates the experiments, followed by the conclusion.

2   Sound Code

Basically, the conversion of colours into sounds is achieved by quantisation of the HSL colour system. Subsequently, the obtained sounds are spatialised by means of head-related transfer functions (HRTF), based on the measurement of head-related impulse responses (HRIR). HRTFs describe how a given sound wave is filtered by the diffraction and reflection properties of the out ear and the body, before the sound reaches the inner ear. A general method to determine the HRTF from a given source location is to measure the head-related impulse response (HRIR) at the ear drums by means of small microphones. The HRTF is the Fourier transform of the HRIR.

2.1   Colour System Conversion

The goal is to use the auditory pathway to convey colour information as quickly as possible. The simplest method would consist to use human voice. The main problem is that we would like to communicate several pixel colours, simultaneously. Note that for a person it is almost impossible to follow at the same time a discussion with more than three individuals. It may be possible to understand the name of two colours, though saying a colour takes about a second or even more if the palette has a considerable size, which is also too long for real-time purposes.

Another approach consists in the sonification of colour system variables. The RGB (red, green, and blue) cube is an additive colour model defined by mixing red, green and blue channels. One important drawback of this model is that similar colours at the human perceptual level could result considerably further on the RGB cube, which would generate perceptually distant sounds.

---

[1] A video is available on `http://cvml.unige.ch/doku.php/demonstrations/home.`)

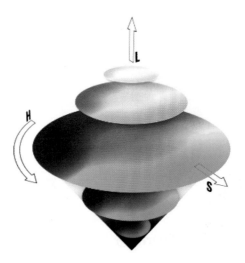

Fig. 1. The HSL colour system; the distinct colour variables are hue (H), saturation (S) and luminosity (L)

As shown by Figure 1, the HSL colour system (Hue, Saturation and Luminosity) is a symmetric double cone symmetrical to lightness and darkness. Although the HSL colour system is related to the laws of physics and not to the human perception system, it is much more intuitive than RGB. HSL mimics the painter way of thinking with the use of a painter tablet for adjusting the purity of colours. Other colour systems such as *Lab* or *Luv* are strongly related to the human perception system, but the difficulty lies in the determination of an intuitive matching between colour variables and sounds. In the HSL colour system the H variable represents hue from red to purple (see Figure 2), the second one is saturation which represents the purity of the related colour and the third variable represents luminosity. Hue varies between 0 and 360 degrees, while S, and L are defined between 0 and 1. We represent the hue variable by instrument timbre, because it is well accepted in the musical community that the colour of music lives in the timbre of performing instruments. Moreover, learning to associate instrument timbres to colours is easier than learning to associate for instance pitch frequencies. The saturation variable S representing the degree of purity of hue is rendered by sound pitch, while luminosity is represented by double bass when it is rather dark and a singing voice when it is relatively bright.

With respect to the hue variable, our empirical choice of musical instruments is:

- oboe for red ($0 \leq H < 30$);
- viola for orange ($30 \leq H < 60$);
- pizzicato violin for yellow ($60 \leq H < 120$);
- flute for green ($120 \leq H < 180$);
- trumpet for cyan ($180 \leq H < 240$);

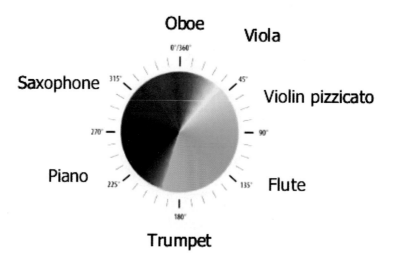

Fig. 2. The association between hue and classical instrument sounds

- piano for blue $(240 \leq H < 300)$;
- and saxophone for purple $(300 \leq H \leq 360)$.

Note that for a given pixel of the sonified row, when the hue variable is exactly between two predefined hues, such as for instance between yellow and green, the resulting sound instrument mix is an equal proportion of the two corresponding instruments. More generally, hue values are rendered by two sound timbres whose gain depends on the proximity of the two closest hues.

The audio representation h_h of a hue pixel value h is

$$h_h = g \cdot h_a + (1 - g) \cdot h_b \tag{1}$$

with g representing the gain defined by

$$g = \frac{h_b - H}{h_b - h_a} \tag{2}$$

with $h_a \leq H \leq h_b$, and h_a, h_b representing two successive hue values among red, orange, yellow, green, cyan, blue, and purple (the successor of purple is red). In this way, the transition between two successive hues is smooth.

The pitch of a selected instrument depends on the saturation value. We use four different saturation values by means of four different notes:

- C (262 Hz) for $(0 \leq S < 0.25)$;
- G (392 Hz) for $(0.25 \leq S < 0.5)$;
- B♭ (466 Hz) for $(0.5 \leq S < 0.75)$;
- and E (660 Hz) $(0.75 \leq S \leq 1)$.

When the luminance L is rather dark (i.e. less than 0.5) we mix the sound resulting from the H and S variables with a double bass using four possible notes depending on luminance level:

- C (131 Hz) for $(0 \leq L < 0.125)$;
- G (196 Hz) for $(0.125 \leq L < 0.25)$;
- B♭ (233 Hz) for $(0.25 \leq L < 0.375)$;
- and E (330 Hz) for $(0.375 \leq L < 0.5)$.

A singing voice with also four different pitches (the same used for the double bass) is used with bright luminance (i.e. luminance above 0.5):

- C (262 Hz) for $(0.5 \leq L < 0.625)$;
- G (392 Hz) for $(0.625 \leq L < 0.75)$;
- B♭ (466 Hz) for $(0.75 \leq L < 0.875)$;
- and E (660 Hz) $(0.875 \leq L \leq 1)$.

Moreover, if luminance is close to zero, the perceived colour is black and we discard in the final audio mix the musical instruments corresponding to the H and S variables. Similarly, if luminance is close to one, thus the perceived colour is white we only retain in the final mix a singing voice. Note that with luminance close to 0.5 the final mix has just the hue and saturation components.

2.2 Sound Spatialisation

It is possible to simulate lateralisation, also denoted as two-dimensional auditory spatialisation, with appropriate delays and difference of intensity between the two ears. Nevertheless, inter-aural time delay (ITD) and inter-aural intensity difference (IID) are inadequate for reproducing the perception of elevation, which represents a crucial auditory feature for 3D spatialisation. In fact, the folds of the pinnae cause echoes with minute time delays within a range of $0 - -0.3$ ms [26] that cause the spectral content of the eardrum to differ significantly from that of the sound source. Strong spatial location effects are produced by convolving an instrument sound with HRIRs, which not only varies in a complex way with azimuth, elevation, range, and frequency, but also varies significantly from person to person [27].

Generally, reproducing lateralisation with uncustomised HRIRs is satisfactory, while the perception of elevation is poor. Since one of our long term goals is to produce a widely distributed prototype, thus involving standard HRIRs, we only reproduce spatial lateralization with the use of the HRIR measurements belonging to the CIPIC database [28]. This database[2] is one of the most used for high-spatial-resolution HRTF measurements. Release 1.0 was produced for 45 different persons; specifically, impulse responses were produced in 1250 distinct directions for each ear and for each subject. In practice, each sonified point corresponds to the convolution of an instrument sound with the corresponding HRIR filter related to a particular azimuth position.

3   Visual Saliency

Saliency is a visual mechanism linked to the emergence of an object over a background [29]. During the pre-attentive phase of the visual perception, the

---

[2] http://interface.cipic.ucdavis.edu

attention first stops on elements that arise from our visual environment, and finally focuses the cognitive processes on these elements only. Different factors enter into account during this process, both physical, i.e. linked to the iconic features of the scene, and cognitive. Several computerised approaches have been designed to digitally reproduce this human ability but only few methods [30,31] combine these two type of factors. Methods that focus only on physical factors are called *bottom-up* approaches, while cognitive based ones are named *top-down* approaches.

The See ColOr project is based on a top-down attention model because the aim of the system is not to replace the blind user's cognitive abilities to understand the captured scene. Given their personal impressions, their particular knowledge of the environment (e.g., if the user is inside or outside), and the sonified colours, the users will be able to identify their environment. Physical factors directly depend on the perceived scene and the characteristics of the objects that compose it. Lightness contrast, colour opponencies (e.g. red/green and blue/yellow), geometrical features, singularity in a set of objects or in an object itself [32] are some examples of these physical factors. We now briefly present the theoretical framework which is the basis of the model we propose.

3.1   Conspicuity Maps

In order to detect salient regions, some methods center on specific characteristics of images like entropy [33] or blobs, detected with *Difference of Gaussians* (DoG) [34] or the speeded up robust features (SURF) [35], a simplified form of the *Determinant of Hessian* (DoH) approach. Methods based on conspicuity maps [36,37] try to mimic the physical properties of the human visual system (HVS).

Features inspired by the HVS are analysed separately to build a set of maps called *feature maps*, denoted F_i. These maps are filtered so that the *conspicuity map* (*C-map*) of each feature map only contains information concerning the few regions that differ the most from their neighbourhood. All C-maps are then combined by a *Winner-Take-All* approach in order to determine the most salient region of the recorded scene. Figure 3 summarises the extraction of the saliency map S on a colour image using conspicuity maps. Salient region detection using conspicuity maps has been proved to be efficient, both in terms of relevance of detected regions and speed. Particular attention however has to be paid to the choice of relevant feature maps, and how to combine them.

3.2   Depth Based Feature Maps

Depth is a useful information when one has to decide whether an object of the environment is of interest or should be ignored. Close objects might be dangerous or noteworthy, thus implying an action from the user. Despite the interest of such an information, very few methods take depth into account to guide the FOA.

The first proposition [38] was to use depth in an attention model only to determine the object which was closest from the user. Here, each time an object is closer than the previous match, the attention model would simulate an eye saccade by quickly moving the FOA on the new closest object. The limitation

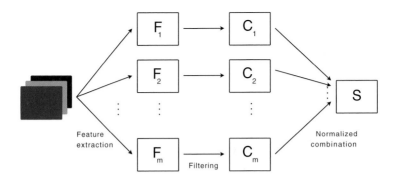

Fig. 3. General overview of the conspicuity map approach for saliency detection. S is the final saliency map, and F_i, C_i the feature maps and their associated conspicuity maps, respectively.

of such an approach is the absence of other important features, such as colour opposition, edge magnitude, illumination, etc. Furthermore, it does not give any information about movement in the recorded scene, especially movements towards the user.

It has been later suggested to use depth in the usual bottom-up approach of saliency-based visual attention models [39,40]. The interest of depth information as a new feature map was proved, combined with common feature maps like colour opposition, intensity, and intensity gradient components. However, no information about movements of objects is obtained either. In a mobility aid, this information is extremely important, especially when an object comes towards the user. This is why we combine both depth and depth gradient feature maps, which are computed as follows.

Close objects are considered to be more important than ones located farther away. Nevertheless, an object closer than distance d_{min} (for instance $d_{min} = 1$ meter) should be directly detected by the blind user with the white cane. Such objects are consequently not considered to be salient in the See ColOr framework. Given $\mathbf{p} = \{p_x, p_y, p_z\}$, with p_x and p_y the coordinates of the pixel in the image space, and p_z its distance from the camera, we base the feature map F_d on the following distance function:

$$F_d(\mathbf{p}) = \begin{cases} d_{max} - p_z, & \text{if } d_{min} < p_z \leq d_{max} \\ 0, & \text{otherwise} \end{cases} \tag{3}$$

where d_{max} is the maximal considered distance from the user. This parameter depends on the environment (e.g. outdoor versus indoor situation), on the acquisition device, and on user's choices. The fact that the quality and range of depth's measurement differ from one instrument to another, explains why d_{max} also depends on the acquisition device. Finally, we want the user to have control on the system, and thus to determine his/her own preferences, by deciding for example to reduce the d_{max} value. In our case, we have defined $d_{max} = 10$ meters to keep the depth computation accurate.

The depth gradient is computed over time in order to contain the motion information. Since the only objects that are considered noteworthy in term of gradient are the ones that get closer to the user, we define the following function:

$$F_\nabla(\mathbf{p}) = \begin{cases} -\dfrac{\partial z}{\partial t}, & \text{if } \dfrac{\partial z}{\partial t} < 0 \\ 0, & \text{otherwise} \end{cases} \qquad (4)$$

To get the conspicuity map C_i from F_i, i being the identifier of the sought feature, a Difference of Gaussians (DoG) is applied on F_i. In a given area, points of interest are those that differ from the neighbouring ones. They are located at the maxima of the resulting filtered map:

$$C_i = max\left(F_i * g_{\sigma_1} - F_i * g_{\sigma_2}\right) \qquad (5)$$

where g_{σ_1} and g_{σ_2} are Gaussians at scale σ_1 and σ_2, respectively, and $*$ stands for the convolution product. It is common to use a multiresolution scheme so that conspicuous areas of different sizes can be detected more efficiently. *Blob* detectors like the *Laplacian of Gaussian* (LoG) or the *Determinant of Hessian* (DoH) can also be used.

3.3   Combination of Feature Maps

Given the image I, it is mostly agreed that the saliency map is the weighted sum of all the computed conspicuity maps:

$$S_I = \sum_i \lambda_i \cdot C_i \qquad (6)$$

where C_i are the conspicuity maps computed from the feature maps F_i respectively, and λ_i ($\sum_i \lambda_i = 1$) are parameters that determine the importance of each feature. The final point of interest, which will lead the user's FOA, will be the point of highest value in the resulting saliency map. We denominate λ_d, λ_∇, λ_{ill}, $\lambda_{r/g}$, and $\lambda_{b/y}$, the weighting coefficients for the depth, the depth gradient, the illumination intensity, the red/green opposition, and the blue/yellow opposition features, respectively. Colour oppositions are computed in normalized RGB planes:

$$R' = \frac{R}{I}, \; G' = \frac{G}{I}, \; B' = \frac{B}{I} \qquad (7)$$

where $I = R+G+B$, and is already computed to obtain the illumination feature. Figure 4 shows the different feature maps computed from an original sequence and its disparity map, their combination to obtain the saliency map, and the point finally selected as the most salient one.

We propose to analyze the relative contribution of each conspicuity map in order to automatically determine the values of the λ_i coefficients. Because attention is naturally attracted towards large objects, and because these objects might be a higher threat for blind users than smaller ones, greater importance

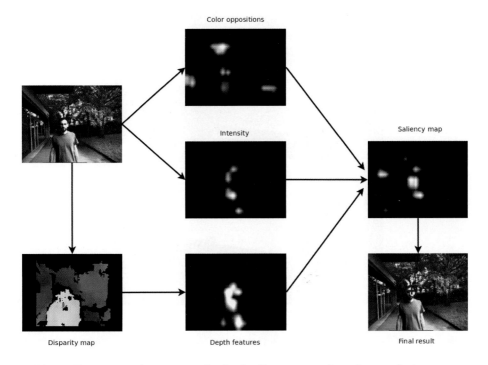

Fig. 4. From original images to the final saliency map, through conspicuity maps

is given to feature maps containing large regions of conspicuity. To achieve this, we propose to set λ_i as a function of the mean size of conspicuous regions.

Unfortunately, the maps are not noise free, and many small regions are false positives. Therefore a morphological opening is performed with a 5×5 diamond structuring element, to ensure that only large regions are taken into account. Then, for each feature map F_i, the mean size $\overline{x_i}$ (in pixels) of conspicuity regions is computed on the opened map. Finally, each mean is weighted by the sum of all means, to ensure that the sum of all λ_i is equal to 1:

$$\lambda_i = \frac{\overline{x_i}}{\sum_j \overline{x_j}} \tag{8}$$

This definition allows the system to give more importance in the saliency map to objects that occupy a large part of the frontal scene.

4 See ColOr Prototypes

We have implemented three distinct prototypes. As shown by Figure 5, the first one is related to a tactile tablet with the sonification of static pictures. The two other prototypes sonify pixel points captured by a stereoscopic camera or by a webcam (Figure 6). The current prototypes described in Section 4 do not

Fig. 5. The See ColOr tactile prototype. The screen of a computer shows a coloured image. On the tactile tablet lies the special paper with an embossed representation of the same image that can be touched. Then, the sound corresponding to the colours of a touched area is provided to the user.

perform any transformations to images. The audio encoding based on the HSL colour system quantization is the only applied processing.

4.1   Tactile Tablet Prototype

The tactile prototype is based on the T3 tactile tablet from the Royal National College for the Blind[3] We put on the T3 tablet a special paper with images including detected edges represented by palpable roughness. This device allows to point on a picture with the finger and to obtain the coordinates of the contact point. A row of 25 points with the middle point represented by the coordinates of the touched point is sonified for 300 ms by means of spatialised instrument sounds. In order to replicate a crude model of the visual system, we have maximal resolution at the centre of the row and lower resolution in the periphery. In practice we skip a given number of pixels. As shown below, starting from the middle point (in bold), the following vector of 25 points represents the number of omitted pixels.

$$\left[14\ 11\ 8\ 6\ 4\ 2\ 2\ 1\ 1\ 0\ 0\ 0\ \mathbf{0}\ 0\ 0\ 0\ 1\ 1\ 2\ 2\ 4\ 6\ 8\ 11\ 14 \right]$$

The HRIR filters we use for spatialisation are those included in the CIPIC database. Specifically, measurements of the KEMAR manikin [28] are those used

---

[3] http://www.talktab.org/

Fig. 6. The See ColOr head mounted camera prototypes: stereoscopic camera prototype (left) and webcan

by our See ColOr interface. All possible spatialised sounds ($25 \times 9 \times 4 = 900$) are pre-calculated and reside in memory. In practice, our main program for sonification is a mixer selecting appropriate sounds, with respect to the contact point of the finger on the picture. The maximal time latency for generating a sonified row of 25 points is 50 ms with the use of Matlab on a Pentium 4 at 3.2 GHz.

4.2 Stereoscopic Camera Prototype

We use a stereoscopic colour camera denoted STH-MDCS2[4]. An algorithm for depth calculation based on epipolar geometry is embedded within the stereoscopic camera. The resolution of images is 320×240 pixels with a maximum frame rate of 30 images per second. As with the tactile tablet, we sonify a row of 25 pixels with spatial lateralisation by means of the CIPIC database and also high resolution in the middle and low resolution in the periphery. The time latency is 80 ms, which is 30 ms more than with the previous prototype, because of the image capture. In practice, with a sonification length of 300 ms and with a time latency of 80 ms the sonification frequency is about 2.5 Hz.

Recently, the sonification of depth has been implemented. Due to the limited bandwidth of the auditory channel, we only took into account the sonification of a particular area of this row. Specifically, we first determined among these 25 points the maximal number of contiguous points labelled with the same colour. Then, we have computed both the centroid of this area and the average depth. It is possible to have points of undetermined depth, especially in homogeneous areas like walls, for which the depth algorithm is unable to determine remarkable points related to the calculation of the disparity between the left and right images. Points with undetermined depth are not considered in the average depth calculation. The final sonification presents only a spatialised sound source representing the average colour and the average depth. In the future, it will be

---

[4] SRI International: http://www.videredesign.com/.

possible to switch from the depth mode to the normal mode (not including depth encoding), with the use of a mouse button.

At the auditory level the depth variable is represented by sound time duration between 0 and 4 m, and by volume lessening from four meters to infinity. The correspondences between sound duration and average sound depth D are:

- 90 ms for undetermined depth;
- 160 ms for $(0 \leq D < 1)$;
- 207 ms for $(1 \leq D < 2)$;
- 254 ms for $(2 \leq D < 3)$;
- and 300 ms for $(3 \leq D \leq 4)$.

Then, after four meters the volume V starts to decrease by following a negative exponential function given by

$$f(V) = V \cdot e^{(-k \cdot D)} \tag{9}$$

with k a small positive constant.

4.3   Webcam Prototype

This prototype is based on a Webcam which can adapt efficiently to light changing conditions related to outdoor purposes. We use the Logitech Notebook Pro webcam with the RightLight2 technology. We have implemented the sonification of a sub-window containing 17×9 with the use of streaming. Specifically, the sound mix of the next captured image is computed during the listening phase. Therefore, the latency of the system is significantly decreased. Due to auditory channel limitations, we configure the sonification exclusively for a row of 17 pixels with constant resolution and by sonifying a pixel out of four, with respect to the centre of the video image. Note that here depth is not taken into account. The spatialisation is achieved by virtual ambisonic of order two [22] with CIPIC Kemar HRIRs. Note that for sonification configurations with more than a sonified row, the sound is spatialised by means of elevation. The time latency of the C++ implemented program is about a few milliseconds. Finally, the sonification speed can be chosen between 3 and 11 Hz.

5   Experiments

This section presents the experiments related to static pictures and video images captured by cameras.

5.1   Static Sonified Pictures

The purpose of this study is to investigate whether individuals can learn associations between colours and musical instrument sounds. Another issue is whether it is possible to interpret pictures. Several experiments were carried out by six participants having their eyes enclosed by a dark tissue, and listening to the

Fig. 7. The *ducks* picture; the goal was to determine the colour of the main compoments (sun, sky, sea, ducks, etc.) and to interpret the picture

Fig. 8. The *dolphin* picture; the goal was to determine the colour of the main features (sky, sea, dolphin, etc.) and to interpret the picture

sounds via headphones [23,24]. In these experiments we use the T3 tactile tablet (cf. Section 4.1).

Six participants were trained to associate colours with musical instruments and then asked to determine on several pictures, objects with specific shapes and colours. Experiments involved a training phase with the use of elementary pictures. For all our experiment participants, training lasted about 45 minutes. Afterwards, a small test for scoring the performance of the participants on sound/colours associations was achieved. On the 15 heard sounds, the average number of correct colours among the six participants was 8.1 (standard deviation: 3.4). It is worth noting that the best score was reached by a musician who found 13 correct answers. Afterwards, participants were asked to explore and identify the major components of several pictures.

Regarding the children draw picture illustrated in Figure 7, all participants interpreted the major colours as the sky the sea and the sun; clouds were more difficult to infer (two individuals); instead of ducks, all the subjects found an island with yellow sand or a ship.

For the picture depicted in Figure 8, all participants interpreted the major colours as the sky and the sea; an individual said that the dolphin is a *jumping animal*. Another person said that it was a fish, and the rest of the users determined a boat or a *round shape*; only one person found birds. Finally, the small fish was interpreted as a rock by two persons.

On the interpretation of real images, such as the picture shown in Figure 9, four participants correctly identified the tree with the grass and the sky; a participant qualified the tree as a strange dark object and finally, the last individual inferred a nuclear explosion!

Concerning Figure 10, all subjects found major colours (blue and yellow); yet no one made the distinction between the sky and the sea. However, two

Fig. 9. The *tree* picture. The goal was to interpret this real world image scene.   **Fig. 10.** The *cliff* picture. The goal was to interpret the image scene.

participants suggested that the grey/white area between these two components represented clouds. Interestingly, three participants correctly analysed the luminosity of the sand, which corresponds to a low saturated yellow and two of them determined that the sky was more saturated at the top with progressive decreasing saturation levels and increasing luminosity when moving to the grey/white area. The yellow cliff was not identified, but an individual proposed a hay stack. Note that pictures with a perspective view are too difficult to be interpreted.

Table 1. Time spent (in minutes) by participants to examine several pictures

Participant	Fig. 7	Fig. 8	Fig. 9	Fig. 10	Fig. 11
P1	8.3	6.7	9.1	—	9.7
P2	7.0	8.5	7.5	7.3	4.9
P3	9.7	13.5	9.0	11.0	6.0
P4	9.2	11.3	8.7	9.0	4.8
P5	14.3	10.5	5.4	5.6	6.0
P6	9.4	11.2	10.0	10.0	9.0
Average	9.7 ± 2.5	10.3 ± 2.4	8.3 ± 1.6	8.6 ± 2.1	6.6 ± 1.8

The last assignment was to find a red door in Figure 11. The two red doors represent less than 1% of the picture surface. As shown by Table 1, which summarizes the time durations for the exploration of pictures, all participants found one of the red doors in a time range between 4 and 9 minutes, while in at most two seconds an individual would identify relevant image features.

5.2   Pairing Coloured Socks

The purpose is to verify the hypothesis that with the use of a camera, it is possible to manipulate and match coloured objects with an auditory feed-back represented by sounds of musical instruments. As shown in previous section, it is difficult to learn the associations between colours and sounds in just one training

Fig. 11. The *churchyard* picture; the goal was to find one of the red doors

Fig. 12. The coloured socks; from left to right: black, green, yellow, blue and orange

session, thus our participants were not asked to identify colours, but just to pair similarly coloured socks. The camera here is the STH-MDCS2. Although we use a stereoscopic camera, depth is not sonified.

The experiments are performed by seven blindfolded adults who, but one of them (P3), were not present in the previous experiments. The training phase includes two main steps. First, we explain associations between colours and sounds in front of a laptop screen showing different static pictures. Specifically, we show the HSL system with seven main hues and several saturation varying pictures. We let our participants decide when they feel comfortable to switch to the second step aiming at learning to point the camera toward socks. With respect to each individual, Table 2 illustrates the time dedicated for the two training steps.

As shown by Figure 12 we use five pairs of socks having the following colours: black, green, low saturated yellow, blue and orange. The colour/sound association for each pair of socks is expressed in Table 3. The second column indicates the instruments related to hue and saturation, while the last column depicts the instrument associated with the luminosity variable.

Table 4 illustrates the results of the participants and Figure 13 shows a user examining a sock. It is worth noting that the average number of paired socks is

Table 2. Training time durations without camera and with a head mounted camera pointing at socks

Participant	Static training (min)	Training with socks (min)
P1'	12	12
P2'	7	11
P3	18	15
P4'	0	6
P5'	0	24
P6'	29	18
P7'	16	16
Average	11.7 ± 10.4	14.6 ± 5.7

Table 3. Color/Sound associations of the first five pairs of socks

Socks	Hue and Saturation	Luminosity
Black	—	Bass (C)
Green	Flute (C–G)	Bass (G–B♭)
Yellow	Viola–Violin (G)	Bass (C–G)
Blue	Piano–Trumpet (B♭)	Bass (C–G)
Orange	Oboe–Viola (B♭–E)	Bass (G–B♭)

high. Participant P4 made a mistake between yellow and orange socks. This experiment showed that blindfolded individuals can manipulate objects by pointing a camera on them and also that five colours can be matched with high accuracy even after a short training session. Note that the experiment was difficult for our participants, since the camera was 10 cm above the eyes.

Table 4. Testing time duration and success rate of the *socks* experiment with the See ColOr interface

Participant	Time (min)	Success rate (pairs)
P1'	16	5
P2'	4	5
P3	18	5
P4'	6	3
P5'	15	5
P6'	11	5
P7'	7	5
Average	11.0 ± 5.5	4.7 ± 0.8

5.3   Following a Coloured Serpentine Path

The purpose is to verify the hypothesis that it is possible to use the See ColOr interface to follow a coloured sinuous path painted on the ground of an outdoor environment. Figure 14 illustrates an individual performing this task. For this experiment we incorporate the same seven individuals who carried out the experiment on coloured socks. The camera here is the Logitech Quickcam Notebook Pro.

The training phase lasts approximately ten minutes. Specifically, a supervisor manages an experiment participant in front of the coloured serpentine path. The user is asked to listen to the typical sonification pattern, which is red in the middle area (oboe) and gray in the left and right sides (double bass). The sonification frequency is fixed to 4 Hz. For experienced users it would be possible to increase the frequency at the maximal implemented value of 11.1 Hz. Afterwards, we ask to the person performing the experiment to move the head from left to right and to become aware that the oboe sound shifts. Note that the supervisor wears a headphone and can listen to the sounds of the interface. Finally, the user is asked to start to walk and to keep the oboe sound in the middle

Fig. 13. A blindfolded person observing an orange sock with a head mounted camera

Fig. 14. A blindfolded person following a coloured line with a head mounted webcam and a notebook carried in a shoulder pack

sonified region. Note that the training session is quite short. An individual has to learn to coordinate three components. The first is the oboe sound position (if any), the second is related to the awareness of the head orientation and the third is the alignment between the body and the head. Ideally, the head and the body should be aligned with the oboe sound in the middle.

The purpose of the test is to go from a starting point S to a destination point T. The testing path is different from the training path. Several small portions of the main path M can be walked through three possible alternatives denoted as A, B, and C. Note that when user crosses an alternative path, his/her choice depends on the place where the camera is pointed. The shortest path M has length of more than 80 meters. It is important to note that it is impossible to go from S to T by just moving straight ahead. In Table 5 we give for each participant the training time duration and the testing time duration, while Table 6 illustrates, for each experiment participant, the followed length path and the average speed. All our experiment participants reached point T from point S and no-one was lost and asked to be helped. One of the authors who is very well trained to the ColOr sound code went from S to T through the path $M + C$ in 4.2 minutes,

Table 5. Training and testing time duration of blindfolded users following a red serpentine path

Participant	Training time (min)	Testing tine (min)
P1'	11	7.3
P2'	10	7.1
P3	8	13.6
P4'	9	8.5
P5'	10	10.4
P6'	10	9.7
P7'	10	12.9
Average	9.7 ± 0.9	9.9 ± 2.6

Table 6. Path length and speed average of blindfolded users following a red serpentine path

Participant	Path length (m)	Speed average (Km/h)
P1'	$M + C = 88$	0.723
P2'	$M = 84$	0.710
P3	$M + B = 110$	0.485
P4'	$M + A = 93$	0.656
P5'	$M = 84$	0.484
P6'	$M + A + C = 97$	0.600
P7'	$M + A + C = 97$	0.451
Average	93.3 ± 9.2	0.587 ± 0.114

corresponding to a speed average of 1.257 km.h^{-1}. Therefore, *novice users* could potentially improve their average speed after several training sessions.

A blind user has also performed the line experiment. His results were amongst the best ones, with an extremely quick training phase, and a high speed average. Specifically, this person successfully learned to follow a bended path in 5.3 minutes. During the testing phase he went from S to T along the main path in 6.1 minutes, corresponding to an average speed of 0.826 Km/h. Moreover, he has shown a strong interest in such a system. First, he really appreciated the reaction swiftness of the system, which is a very important feature to him. He also explained that such a system would be of great help in places where the white cane is only a mean of protection, not a guiding device.

5.4 Detecting Threats and Obstsacles

We present some specific experiments carried out to validate the hypothesis that depth gradient is a useful information in order to guide the users' FOA onto objects that might disturb their movements. Depth itself having been proved to be of interest in such a task [39], we consider the combination of distance and depth gradient features relatively to the depth feature alone.

Obstacle avoidance. First we define an *obstacle* as any static object that the user might walk in, and disturb his/her walk. These objects should typically be ones that a blind user might not detect with the white cane. The carried out experiments for that case consist of the followings.

Case 1. An indoor experiment where a table and a printer are possible obstacles. In that case, we expect the system to point the table or the printer, depending on which one is the closest to the user.

Case 2. This experiment depicts a real life situation: a street lamp and street flowerpots occupy the space on a sidewalk. In this sequence, the system is expected to first point at the flowerpots, and then the street lamp when the user goes near the obstacles.

Threat detection. We define a *threat* as any dynamic object in the recorded scene, that approaches the user and might cross his/her path. To validate our approach, we have recorded different scenes where pedestrians are walking in

Fig. 15. Example of the ground truth mask (right) for a given image (left)

front of the user. Again, we have made a distinction between indoor and outdoor scenes.

Case 3. In a corridor, people cross the user's path. The objective of this experiment is to show that the different people are detected one after the other. This is why the area of interest is always the closest person to the user.
Case 4. Outdoor, a pedestrian is coming across the user, and does not change his path. He finally bumps into the user. We obviously want to see if the system considers this person as the major threat during the whole sequence.

Error evaluation. For each image, we have determined the ground truth according to the following rules.

1. From the set of objects that come towards the user, the closest one is a threat and selected as the ground truth.
2. The closest object in the interval $[d_{min}, d_{max}]$ is selected, since it can be an obstacle.
3. In cases where both situation appear, priority is given to threats.

Consequently, a binary mask like the one shown in Figure 15 was manually selected for each picture of each video sequence. In the present case, the chair is considered to be close enough to be detected by the user's white cane (distance lower than d_{min}). Moreover, the man is a possible threat, explaining why the system has to select him as the most salient region. To measure the error, the distance d between the ground truth region G and the pixel $\mathbf{p} = (p_x, p_y)$ actually detected as the most salient is computed as follows:

$$d(\mathbf{p}, G) = min_{x,y}(d_E(\mathbf{p}, G(x, y))) \qquad (10)$$

where d_E is the Euclidean distance.

In the case of stereoscopic sequences, the error at a given time is the mean of the errors obtained from both left and right pictures.

Videos were recorded using a STH-MDCS2[5] stereoscopic camera, and its development library, which computes in real time the disparity map needed for the

---

[5] Videre Design: http://www.videredesign.com

Fig. 16. Images of the left (left) and right (right) views of the stereocamera, and the resulting disparity map (centre). On the disparity map, the lighter the closer. A zero value (black) means that the distance is undetermined for that pixel.

Table 7. Average computation time in ms per image, mean error, and percentage of perfect matches on four different video sequences, using a combination of five feature maps

Case	Average CPU time	Mean error	Perfect match (%)	Average λ_i values
1	136.9ms	26.23	68%	$\lambda_d = 0.21$, $\lambda_\nabla = 0.17$, $\lambda_{ill} = 0.22$, $\lambda_{r/g} = 0.17$, $\lambda_{b/y} = 0.23$
2	139.4ms	36.1	61.3%	$\lambda_d = 0.21$, $\lambda_\nabla = 0.16$, $\lambda_{ill} = 0.21$, $\lambda_{r/g} = 0.22$, $\lambda_{b/y} = 0.20$
3	115.9ms	30.31	58.6%	$\lambda_d = 0.21$, $\lambda_\nabla = 0.17$, $\lambda_{ill} = 0.23$, $\lambda_{r/g} = 0.19$, $\lambda_{b/y} = 0.21$
4	131.9ms	23.6	73%	$\lambda_d = 0.19$, $\lambda_\nabla = 0.18$, $\lambda_{ill} = 0.22$, $\lambda_{r/g} = 0.20$, $\lambda_{b/y} = 0.21$

determination of depth. The resulting disparity map is unfortunately far from perfect: the depth information is unaccurate or undetermined at many points of the scene as it can be seen on Figure 16. However, given the importance of real time in an alerting system, the presented method is performed with this raw information, without any interpolation on the disparity map.

Results. We have experimented with the case where illumination and colour opponency features are combined with the depth-based features. Video sequences contain from 150 to 500 frames. The results are summarized in Table 7. It shows the percentage of *perfect match* for each sequence and the average values of the λ_i computed with Equation 6. The result on each picture of a video sequence is said to be a *perfect match* whenever the expected area of the picture is determined as the most salient.

In these experiments, the scales for the Gaussian filters in Equation 5 were chosen in order to have simple 5×5 discrete kernels, i.e. $\sigma_1 = 0.7$ and $\sigma_2 = 1.0$. As it can be observed, the λ_i values do not exhibit large variations, which means that none of the conspicuity map is useless. Table 7 also shows the average distance in pixels between the detected points and the ground truth area. Compared to the size of the images and the regions of interest, this distance is relatively small. The focus of the blind user should then be attracted to a region close to the real salient area. Thus we then can assume that the sonified region will be, at least partly, the most salient one. Finally, this table points out that the proposed method operates in near real time, since it only takes around 130 ms to process each picture in a video sequence. A framerate of more than 5 images per second is sufficient for an alerting system, and specifically for the See ColOr framework, where images are sonified at an approximate rate of 3Hz. Figure 17 shows snapshots from each experiment, with the decteted saliency in each case.

Discussion. The overall results obtained with this framework are promising, knowing that the computation of disparity is a challenging task, especially in real time. Some optimizations or simple modifications will likely lead to better results. For example, in Equation 3, a more realistic distance function could be defined. The current function not being differentiable at $p_z = d_{min}$ and $p_z = d_{max}$, the transitions at these points are steep. Using a sigmoid would create a smoother and more continuous variation at the extremas of the interval $[d_{min}, d_{max}]$.

Other approaches to automatically determine the weighting coefficient in Equation 5 will be investigated. With the current system, only feature maps with large regions are emphasized. However, it is also important to highlight features that can detect as much objects of interest as possible. A possibility is to use the correlation of conspicuities in different feature maps: an area detected

Fig. 17. The four different experiments. Left: indoor. Right: outdoor. Up: obstacle detection. Down: threat detection. The surrounded cross indicates the selected saliency.

as salient over more than one feature should be accentuated. With such an approach, the problem generated by regions not completelely covering each other is particularly challenging.

Finally, we need to estimate the camera motion, because the accuracy of the system falls down when the camera moves non linearly or at least partly along its z axis. To achieve this, we intend to investigate methods that can perform in near real-time, for the system must give a feedback at least 3 times per second.

6 Conclusion and Perspectives

We have presented the current state of the See ColOr project, which provides the user with an auditory feedback of the colours of the environment. The purpose of the first experiment was to identify the colours of the main features of static pictures and then to understand image scenes. Although learning all instrument sounds in only a training session was too difficult, participants found that colours were helpful to limit the possible image interpretations.

With a camera prototype we verified the hypothesis that it is possible to manipulate and to match coloured objects, accurately. Overall, with only one training session, participants paired sock pairs with very high accuracy. With the last experiment related to blind navigation aiming at following a red serpentine path painted on the ground, to our knowledge the first to date with such a framework, we validated the hypothesis that it is possible to follow a twisting path.

We have also presented in this article a new approach to detect salient parts in videos in near real-time, using a depth based FOA mechanism. Depth gradient is introduced as a new feature map into the bottom-up visual attention model based on conspicuity maps. We have shown that this feature map allows for a better detection of objects of interest in video sequences than when using depth only, as proposed in previous works. We have also proposed a specific distance function, in order to take into account both hardware limitations and user's choices; this allows the user to decide if objects closer than a specific distance, like the white cane's length, should be detected or not. The results we obtained with this simple framework are promising, and some optimizations on the distance function for the determination of optimal weightings of conspicuity maps, should lead to even better results.

As well as blindfolded individuals, we are confident that more blind persons will successfully follow the red serpentine path, like the one who succesfully experimented the framework. Moreover, we want to sonify the saliency information, which is an important decision, since the user must not be confused by similar sounds meaning completely different things. We also want to define a more adapted distance function, and investigate other ways of optimizing the automatic determination of the relative contribution of the different feature maps. Then, we will seek for a camera motion estimator that can be inserted in this framework without altering the computing time.

Acknowledgments. The authors gratefully thank Guillaume Chanel, Julien Kronegg, Romana Rytsar, Jolle Heldt, Mohammad Soleymani, Fedor Thnnessen, Stphane Marchand-Maillet, Enik Szkely, Bastien Francony and Marc Von Wyl for their valuable participation in the experiments and their precious comments related to the See ColOr interface. Moreover, we are grateful to the partners of the Europan SIMILAR network of excellence for their collaboration. Finally, we express strong gratitude to the Hasler foundation for funding this very stimulating project.

References

1. World Health Organisation: Magnitude and causes of visual impairment. Fact Sheet No. 282 (November 2004),
   http://www.who.int/mediacentre/factsheets/fs282/en/
2. Just, M., Carpenter, P.: Eye fixations and cognitive processes. Cognitive Psychology 8, 441–480 (1976)
3. Mannos, J., Sakrison, D.: The effects of a visual fidelity criterion on the encoding of images. IEEE Transactions on Information Theory 20, 525–536 (1974)
4. Kelly, D.: Retinal inhomogenity. i. spatiotemporal contrast sensitivity. Journal of the Optical Society of America 1, 107–113 (1984)
5. Way, T., Barner, K.: Automatic visual to tactile translation, part i: human factors, access methods and image manipulation. IEEE Transactions on Rehabilitation Engineering 5, 81–94 (1997)
6. Loomis, J.M., Lederman, S.J.: Tactual perception. In: Handbook of Perception and Human Performance. Cognitive Processes and Performance, vol. 2, John Wiley and Sons, New York (1986)
7. Burdea, G.: Force and touch feedback for virtual reality. John Wiley and Sons, New York (1996)
8. Bach-y-Rita, P., Collins, C., Saunders, F., White, B., Scadden, L.: Vision substitution by tactile image projection. Nature 221, 963–964 (1969)
9. Bach-y-Rita, P.: Visual information through the skin: a tactile vision substitution system (tvss). In: Transactions - American Academy of Ophthalmology and Otolaryngology, vol. 78 (September 1974); Symposium on Prosthetic Aids for the Blind
10. Kaczmarek, K., Bach-y Rita, P., Tompkins, W.: A tactile vision-substitution system for the blind: computer-controlled partial image sequencing. IEEE Transactions on Biomedical Engineering 32, 602–608 (1985)
11. Parkes, D.: An audio-tactile device for the acquisition, use and management of spatially distributed information by visually impaired people. In: Symposium on Maps and Graphics for Visually Handicapped People, pp. 30–35 (1988)
12. Kawai, Y., Tomita, F.: Evaluation of interactive tactile display system. In: Proceedings of the International Conference on Computers Helping People with Special Needs (ICCHP 1998), pp. 29–36 (1998)
13. Maucher, T., Meier, K., Schemmel, J.: An interactive tactile graphics display. In: Proceedings of the International Symposium on Signal Processing and its Applications (ISSPA), Kuala Lumpur, Malaysia, pp. 190–193 (2001)

14. Pun, T., Roth, P., Bologna, G., Moustakas, K., Tzovaras, D.: Image and video processing for visually handicapped people. Eurasip International Journal of Image and Video Processing 2007 (2007),
    http://www.hindawi.com/GetArticle.aspx?doi=10.1155/2007/25214
15. Ruff, R., Perret, E.: Auditory spatial pattern perception aided by visual choices. Psychological Research 38, 369–377 (1976)
16. Lakatos, S.: Recognition of complex auditory-spatial patterns. Perception 22, 363–374 (1993)
17. Kay, L.: A sonar aid to enhance spatial perception of the blind: Engineering design and evaluation. The Radio and Electronic Engineer 44, 605–627 (1974)
18. Meijer, P.: An experimental system for auditory image representations. IEEE Transactions on Biomedical Engineering 39, 112–121 (1992)
19. Capelle, C., Trullemans, C., Arno, P., Veraart, C.: A real time experimental prototype for enhancement of vision rehabilitation using auditory substitution. IEEE Transactions on Biomedical Engineering 45, 1279–1293 (1998)
20. Cronly-Dillon, J., Persaud, K., Gregory, R.: The perception of visual images encoded in musical form: a study in cross-modality information. Proceedings of Biological Sciences 266, 2427–2433 (1999)
21. Gonzalez-Mora, J., Rodriguez-Hernandez, A., Rodriguez-Ramos, L., Dfaz-Saco, L., Sosa, N.: Development of a new space perception system for blind people, based on the creation of a virtual acoustic space. In: Mira, J. (ed.) IWANN 1999. LNCS, vol. 1607, pp. 321–330. Springer, Heidelberg (1999)
22. Bologna, G., Vinckenbosch, M.: Eye tracking in coloured image scenes represented by ambisonic fields of musical instrument sounds. In: Mira, J., Álvarez, J.R. (eds.) IWINAC 2005. LNCS, vol. 3561, pp. 327–337. Springer, Heidelberg (2005)
23. Bologna, G., Deville, B., Pun, T., Vinckenbosch, M.: Identifying major components of pictures by audio encoding of colors. In: Mira, J., Álvarez, J.R. (eds.) IWINAC 2007. LNCS, vol. 4528, pp. 81–89. Springer, Heidelberg (2007)
24. Bologna, G., Deville, B., Pun, T., Vinckenbosch, M.: Transforming 3d coloured pixels into musical instrument notes for vision substitution applications. EURASIP Journal on Image and Video Processing 2007 (2007),
    http://www.hindawi.com/getarticle.aspx?doi=10.1155/2007/76204
25. Deville, B., Bologna, G., Vinckenbosch, M., Pun, T.: Depth-based detection of salient moving objects in sonified videos for blind users. In: VISAPP 2008, International Conference on Computer Vision Theory and Applications (January 2008)
26. Begault, R.: 3-D Sound for Virtual Reality and Multimedia. Boston A.P. Professional (1994)
27. Brown, C., Duda, R.: A structural model for binaural sound synthesis. IEEE Transactions on Speech and Audio Processing 6 (1998)
28. Algazi, V., Duda, R., Thompson, D., Avendano, C.: The cipic hrtf database. In: Proceedings of the IEEE Workshop on Applications of Signal Processing to Audio and Acoustics (WASPAA 2001), New Paltz, NY (2001)
29. Landragin, F.: Saillance physique et saillance cognitive. Cognition, Representation, Langage 2 (2004),
    http://edel.univ-poitiers.fr/corela/document.php?id=142
30. Navalpakkam, V., Itti, L.: An integrated model of top-down and bottom-up attention for optimizing detection speed. In: Proceedings IEEE Conference on Computer Vision and Pattern Recognition (CVPR), pp. 2049–2056 (2006)
31. Peters, R.J., Itti, L.: Beyond bottom-up: Incorporating task-dependent influences into a computational model of spatial attention. In: Proceedings of the IEEE Conference on Computer Vision and Pattern Recognition (CVPR) (June 2007)

32. Hoffman, D., Singh, M.: Salience of visual parts. Cognition 63, 29–78 (1997)
33. Kadir, T., Brady, M.: Scale, saliency and image description. International Journal of Computer Vision 45, 83–105 (2001)
34. Lowe, D.: Object recognition from local scale-invariant features. In: Seventh International Conference on Computer Vision (ICCV 1999), vol. 2 (1999)
35. Bay, H., Tuytelaars, T., Gool, L.V.: Surf: Speeded up robust features. In: Leonardis, A., Bischof, H., Pinz, A. (eds.) ECCV 2006. LNCS, vol. 3951, pp. 7–13. Springer, Heidelberg (2006)
36. Milanese, R., Gil, S., Pun, T.: Attentive mechanism for dynamic and static scene analysis. Optical Engineering 34, 2428–2434 (1995)
37. Itti, L., Koch, C., Niebur, E.: A model of saliency-based visual attention for rapid scene analysis. IEEE Transactions on Pattern Analysis and Machcine Intelligence 20, 1254–1259 (1998)
38. Maki, A., Nordlund, P., Eklundh, J.: A computational model of depth-based attention. In: Proceedings of the International Conference on Pattern Recognition (ICPR 1996) (1996)
39. Ouerhani, N., Hügli, H.: Computing visual attention from scene depth. In: Proceedings of the 15th International Conference on Pattern Recognition, vol. 1, pp. 375–378 (2000)
40. Jost, T., Ouerhani, N., von Wartburg, R., Müri, R., Hügli, H.: Contribution of depth to visual attention: comparison of a computer model and human. In: Early cognitive vision workshop, Isle of Skye, Scotland (2004)

6th Sense – Toward a Generic Framework for End-to-End Adaptive Wearable Augmented Reality

Damien Perritaz[1], Christophe Salzmann[1], Denis Gillet[1], Olivier Naef[2], Jacques Bapst[2], Frédéric Barras[2], Elena Mugellini[2], and Omar Abou Khaled[2]

[1] Ecole Polytechnique Fédérale de Lausanne
`firstname.lastname@epfl.ch`
[2] University of Applied Sciences of Fribourg
`firstname.lastname@hefr.ch`

Abstract. Augmented Reality enhances user perception by overlaying real world information with virtual computer-generated information. The aims of the 6th Sense project are to improve real-time interaction between the real environment and the virtual world and to maximize the user experience in mobile Augmented Reality. To achieve these objectives a generic framework constituted of two main layers is proposed. The End-to-End Adaptation Layer adapts in real-time the parameters of the Augmented Reality system to provide the user with the best possible experience despite the varying operating conditions such as the transmission link and user head motion. The Generic Augmented Reality Layer encompasses solutions to the problem of overlaying adequate information in the real scene and manages multimodal interaction with the virtual environment.

1 Introduction

Augmented Reality (AR) is a technology that transfers computer-generated information to the physical world[1]. This technology holds the promise of immersing individuals in an *enriched* environment endowing them with a new perception channel like a sixth sense. This technology opens up a whole new world of possibilities and we can imagine to augment user perception in order to uplift his[2] cognition in many applications.

The goal of the 6th Sense project is to design and develop a wearable AR system that enhances user experience, which encompasses all subjective aspects of the interaction experienced by the user. The 6th Sense system provides a contextual, intuitive and multimodal user interface applicable in many different domains, such as chemical plant supervision, cultural site visit or home automation. In this paper, we present a solution that enhances user experience by providing a generic framework. The proposed framework includes both an

---

[1] An introduction to AR is given in a previous chapter [1].
[2] Through out the text, the masculine gender refers to both men and women.

D. Lalanne and J. Kohlas (Eds.): Human Machine Interaction, LNCS 5440, pp. 280–310, 2009.
© Springer-Verlag Berlin Heidelberg 2009

end-to-end adaptation scheme that maximizes real-time user experience and a generic layer which overlays physical objects with contextual AR information.

The 6th *Sense* framework is based on a client-server architecture to provide an adequate balance between the mobility of the client device and the quality of the AR scene. The AR information is sent to the client as a video stream. We propose a new measure for the user experience based on subjective testing of three influential parameters: video encoding parameters, end-to-end delay and head motion. Based on this measure, an innovative end-to-end adaptation scheme adapts the encoding parameters in real-time to maximize user experience. In order to adapt the video stream rate to the network capabilities, a rate control mechanism which takes advantage of the specificity of the AR stream is proposed.

From the application developer's point of view, the 6th *Sense* framework provides an abstraction layer containing the hardware communication, the 3D rendering and the management of the multimodality. The only technical knowledge needed to use it is some basic programming skills to be able to understand the API[3] and coding the business part of the application and its context. Typical AR issues, like registration error, marker detection and multimodal fusion are treated without involving the developer's application. A consistent unit system is provided to allow the developer to manage the virtual world without having to switch between the space coordinate systems of the different equipments available.

1.1   Physical World and Digital Universe

An ever increasing amount of information is available in the digital world with the Internet allowing an ubiquitous access. However, we live in a physical world and we interact with physical objects that have no direct link with the digital world. The concept of AR bridges physical objects and the virtual space by enabling users to pull virtual information into their environment, according to specific criteria.

The 6th *Sense* project aims at creating a link between these two worlds, and at making contextual information associated to physical objects available in the environment. The information related to the physical objects is stored in application specific databases or is extracted from the Internet.

1.2   Wearable Augmented Reality

Wearable Augmented Reality combines the fields of multimodal user interfaces, wearable computing and, obviously, AR. In the context of the 6th *Sense* project, we focus on the visual AR information perception. For vision, there are two essential components to make an AR system work: a display and a tracking system. The Head-Mounted Display (HMD) is the core of many mobile AR systems. It permits overlaying computer generated graphics on the top of real

---

[3] An Application Programming Interface (API) is a set of high-level documented classes, methods and protocols provided to access the framework without having to know all the details of its implementation.

world images. The best *immersion*[4] is provided by see-through HMD and used in the *6th Sense* project. However, HMDs carry some drawbacks, in particular their weight, a limited field of view, and their cost. The tracking system estimates the user's head *pose*[5] in real-time allowing relevant information to be precisely overlaid in the HMD.

Moreover when designing wearable AR applications other aspects have to be considered such as:

– Information Visualization: how digital information is visualized and embodied within the real world.
– Multimodality: how the user can interact with the system, which modalities are available.
– Context: the user context has to be taken into account to make the interaction more natural and to satisfy user needs and preferences. Different users using identical equipment will not necessarily receive identical information.

This paper is organized as follow. Section 2 shows AR challenges, with an emphasis on the *6th Sense* ones: user experience and multimodality. Section 3 presents the general architecture of the framework and its interfaces with the devices, the application and the context. In Sect. 4, the end-to-end adaptation layer which enforces the best user experience by adapting the parameters of the AR system in real-time is presented. Section 5 describes the AR generic layer which provides position tracking, information display and multimodal interface. Section 6 depicts the *6th Sense* prototype, as well as some demonstrators. Finally, the conclusion and future work are discussed in Sect. 7.

2   Challenges

The *6th Sense* project presents several challenges: user experience, information visualization, tracking and registration and interaction modalities.

2.1   User Perception and Experience

A human is equipped with five senses to perceive his surrounding world: sight, hearing, touch, taste and smell. User perception is defined as the acquisition of an external information using the senses. We generally use several senses to perceive events or scenes that we face. A surgeon perceives the state of a patient using the sight of an open wound and the resistance of an organ that he is manipulating.

AR is used to enhance perception by overlaying virtual information to the real world. Some information, impossible to perceive by the user, can be measured and transmitted to the user through one of his senses. A surgeon equipped with

---

[4] Immersion is defined as the extent to which the subject's senses are isolated from the real world and are stimulated by the virtual world [2].
[5] The pose is defined as the position and orientation relative to some reference coordinate system. In 3D space, the pose corresponds to six degrees of freedom (6DoF).

an AR system can assimilate additional information about the patient such as blood pressure or the location of tumor tissue within an organ.

All aspects related to the interaction between the user and the AR system are described by the user experience. One of the reasons that AR is currently not deployed at a large scale, is because AR user experience is often not satisfying. The challenge is to provide an adequate user experience.

2.2   Information Visualization

Visual AR deals with visual representation of data, but most AR studies does not focus on visualization as such, but rather applies visual presentation as a tool or enabler for desired features. Compared to visualization on desktop computers, studying AR visualization is still in its infancy and the 6th *Sense* project aims at enhancing it by integrating new visualization techniques into an AR system.

Information visualization has its roots in scientific visualization. Card et al. [3] define information visualization as using "computer-supported, interactive, visual representation of abstract data to amplify cognition", and propose the following ways to amplify cognition: "shift work from cognitive to perceptual system, reduce searching, and enhance recognition of patterns". AR displays provide extra information to a user's perception by overriding parts of the real world with computer-generated images. The use of information visualization techniques to amplify cognition is crucial because the density of visual data may be high on such displays. However naive replacement of portions of the real world with virtual images can easily cause a number of cognitive problems, such as hidden real-world information with unimportant digital information. The 6th *Sense* framework deals with typical information visualization techniques such as Pan-and-Zoom [4], Overview-and-Detail [5], Focus+Context [4]. These techniques can be adapted if necessary to an AR system in order to enhance user perception according to the application context (e.g. amount of data, kind of information, navigation requirements).

2.3   Tracking and Registration

Location tracking is a prerequisite for any location aware application. AR applications require a very accurate pose tracking to register visual information accurately within the user's environment, otherwise the augmented information may be positioned incorrectly resulting in a confusing or unusable user interface [6].

Virtual objects have to be drawn very accurately to avoid the so called registration error, which gives the impression that virtual elements are not anchored with the real scene. The challenge is to avoid registration by both computing the augmentation in real-time[6] and by accurately tracking the user's head position.

---

[6] By real-time we mean that the augmented flow is updated at the same rate as the HMD refresh rate to give the illusion of a continuous seamless movement. This rate is generally on the order of 25 frames per second.

2.4   Interaction Modalities

Reducing the dichotomy between interaction in the physical world and interaction in the digital world (browsers, search engines, computer applications) would be beneficial to make our relationship with the digital world more natural. Today, our sensorial and motor functions are often underused in our relationship with digital information, especially in using traditional computer equipment (screen, keyboard and mouse). A better use of our senses and the merging of multiple modalities would allow a more natural and intuitive interaction.

The *6th Sense* framework uses multimodal inputs to navigate and communicate with the information space. The user no longer passively receives information but can also become an actor, and able to dialog with, or influence, the virtual environment. So far several research projects have considered and evaluated different input channels (voice, gestures, head movement, etc.) trying to identify the most pertinent and the most natural channel depending on the context. Since the *Put-That-There* multimodal technique [7], the combination of pointing with speech has proven to be one of the most natural way humans interact with a system. The selected input modalities for the *6th Sense* demonstrators are speech recognition and hand gesture. The main multimedia outputs are AR display and audio. These different mechanisms allow the user to navigate, control, and dialog with the virtual environment even with minimal training [8,9,10]. One important challenge for the *6th Sense* framework is to provide an extensible architecture allowing the applications to integrate modalities best suited for their context.

2.5   Reusability

Frameworks provide a common set of domain-specific functionalities upon which specific applications can be built either by directly re-using these functionalities (reusability feature) or by customizing and extending them (adaptability feature). Several AR frameworks have already been proposed, using a GPS tracking intended for use outdoor [11,12,13] or dedicated to specific domains [14] or do not include an end-to-end adaptation [15]. Perhaps the most similar work to our own is the AR *Studierstube*[7] framework [16]. However while the *Studierstube* platform focuses on the design of AR applications for Personal Digital Assistants (PDAs) and mobile phones, our main goal is to combine multiple aspects (such as multimodality, user experience, etc.) into a single generic framework allowing users to easily interact with the AR world as they are accustomed to do with the real one. The innovative aspect of the *6th Sense* framework lies in the fact that it not only provides classical AR modules like display augmentation and tracking but also includes multimodal interaction features and an end-to-end adaptation scheme intended to maximize user experience.

3   The *6th Sense* Framework

One of the objectives in the mobile AR field is to provide the user with an efficient system. Two different trends aim at achieving this objective. The first

---

[7] Studierstube (http://studierstube.icg.tu-graz.ac.at).

trend contributes to the continuous miniaturization of processing units with the idea of making all computation needed for AR in a mobile device worn by the user [17,18,19]. The second trend is taking advantage of client-server architecture, where large computation (for instance high-resolution 3D rendering) is delegated to the server. The client gets the AR information as an ready rendered scene. Thus, the client has only a small portion of computation to perform, it is called a thin-client. The computation capabilities of the server being almost unlimited, the thin-client can be made sufficiently small and light-weighted to be convenient to wear. However, client-server architectures give several challenges related to data transmission over the communication link and the resource management on the thin-client.

3.1   Augmented Reality Video

In order to develop small wearable AR systems, the computation load required by the AR scene generation is moved to dedicated hardware and the resulting AR images are transmitted to the client device for display [20,21]. However, such thin-client strategy in mobile AR requires specific and expensive hardware especially for the dedicated communication links. More recently, PDA has been used in AR applications. Using such a device with limited processing capabilities, client-server architecture is also used to reduce computation load in the mobile device [22,23,24]. AR is sent as an image from the server to the client using conventional network infrastructure. In order to save as much computation power as possible in the mobile unit, while guaranteeing low latency requirements, a latency rendering system is proposed to spread the imaged rendering at both the server and client sides [25].

The thin-client strategy we propose requires very little computation resources on the client side. All the time-consuming scene rendering processes being offloaded to the server, no rendering capabilities is required on the client device. Only a video of the augmented scene is sent from the server to the client for display. The augmented scene is then displayed in an optical see-through HMD or overlaid on a video see-through HMD. Sending high quality video over a wireless link is possible thanks to the increase of the wireless bandwidth. Existing video coding techniques, such as MPEG, are used to compress video streams with respect to the bandwidth of the wireless communication link.

The *Augmented Reality Video* (ARV) represents the video of the rendered virtual scene, with transparent background. The server builds the scene and encodes the ARV for the transmission. The main advantage of ARV is that mobile clients only have to receive, decode and display a video; no specific rendering capabilities are needed. Moreover, the scene generated on the server can be very complex (no limitation for the number of objects). The level-of-detail for the rendered picture can be as high as desired even with photo-realistic quality, shadow and occlusion mechanisms. For instance, for a chemical plant supervision application, ARV scenes typically represent aggregate measurements rendered as 3D objects, such as a tank for level and gauges for temperature information. Historical data trends can also be presented in an oscilloscope-like window on a

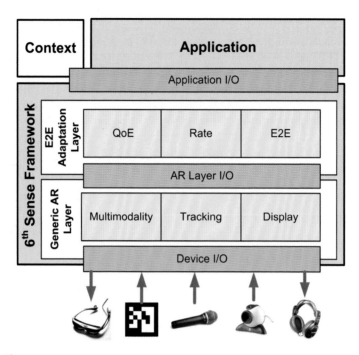

Fig. 1. 6th *Sense* architecture overview with the two main parts of the framework: *End-to-End Adaptation Layer* and the *Generic AR Layer*. The user application and its context communicate with the framework through a generic *Application I/O* interface.

virtual panel. The main ARV drawback is the necessity to send real-time video with very low transmission latencies to limit dynamic registration errors. Conventional video encoding and transmission schemes are used currently providing low refresh rates and high delays [22,23].

3.2 Framework Architecture

The 6th *Sense* framework is composed of two main parts: the End-to-End (E2E) Adaptation Layer and the Generic AR Layer on top of which the proposed adaptation scheme is built (Fig. 1). The user application and its context are not part of the 6th *Sense* framework and communicate through a generic application I/O layer.

E2E Adaptation Layer. In order to maximize user experience in mobile AR, we first define the Quality of Experience (QoE) as the measure for user experience for selected parameters, such as the video encoding parameters or head motion. Based on subjective tests where users are asked to give their subjective appreciation for a set a parameters values, the QoE model maps the AR parameters on the QoE. Using this model and the measurable parameters values, it becomes possible to determine objectively the QoE without further subjective user's appreciations. This QoE can be maximized by adapting in real time the controllable parameters (video encoding parameters) in function of the measurable parameters (head motion for example).

The proposed adaptation mechanism aims at maximizing the QoE through the use of the Generic AR Layer. The QoE component estimates the QoE related to the head motion speed, for example. In order to adapt to network bandwidth constraints, the E2E component estimates the communication link and adapts the sending AR information rate accordingly. The Rate component controls the encoding to guarantee that the video rate is adapted to the E2E module reference.

Generic AR Layer. The aim of this layer is to offer reusable modules covering common activities in AR applications which are essential to give the user the sensation of being immersed in the augmented scene.

These modules encompass solutions to usual AR issues:

– I/O peripherals management (abstraction layer decoupling hardware);
– evaluation of user's head position and orientation (tracking);
– visualization and display of overlaid information in a real scene;
– multimodal interaction management (gesture analysis, speech recognition).

3.3   Application and Context

The 6th *Sense* framework aims at simplifying the development of various AR applications in different contexts of use such as chemical plant supervision, cultural site visit or home automation. The application has only to be compliant with the input and output specifications of the 6th *Sense* framework.

The information presented to the final user and the available interactions depend on different collected parameters that are loosely defined as *context*. The context is intimately bounded to the application itself and the border between the application and its associated context is sometimes blurred. Contextual parameters can include explicitly defined user preferences, the current observed scene (spatial context), the time at which the scene is observed or acted upon (temporal context) and the state of the enclosing system (step of a sequential process, warnings, alarms, etc). These different parameters included in the notion of context are combined in an external module which takes advantage of the 6th *Sense* framework functionalities. By considering the context, it is possible to offer to the user the interaction mode that is most suited for the situation at hand (personal preferences, experience level, user history, peripherals used, etc).

The contextual information can act on and drive the E2E Adaptation Layer just as well as the Generic AR Layer. Thus the context is able to modify the behavior of the 6th *Sense* framework according to some specific rules (e.g. which virtual objects are shown, which interactions are allowed, adapt information to the external system state).

4   End-to-End Adaptation Layer

Most of today's AR applications aim at providing a given fixed user experience. Only some applications consider real-time adaptation of AR parameters to user needs and contextual constraints. In order to improve user experience, it is possible to take advantage of the dynamic aspects of each component of the AR system using an End-to-End (E2E) adaptation scheme. To implement such an E2E adaptation, we first define the user experience and provide a measure for it. We then define a real-time control strategy that maximizes user experience.

4.1   Quality of Experience

Section 3.1 showed that visual AR information can be transmitted in the form of either a 3D scene or a video stream. To provide high efficiency, the 6th *Sense* framework implements the latter solution with Augmented Reality Video (ARV). ARV encoding and transmission mechanisms should provide the best possible user experience. In order to quantify this user experience, we propose the Quality of Experience (QoE) as a measure of user experience. A QoE model for ARV is used in an adaptation scheme to achieve in real time the best possible QoE.

Related Research. The QoE has been extensively studied in multimedia fields especially for video displayed on a screen, but to the authors' knowledge the evaluation of the QoE has never been studied for ARV. For Ramesh Jain, the QoE is an important issue in multimedia, because experience is subjective and context-dependent [26]. Compared to the Quality of Service (QoS) which deals with objective metrics, the QoE includes a subjectivity dimension. Measurements are necessary to capture the QoE in a given application in order to develop systems that are responsive to their users. The Perceived QoS (PQoS) was defined as a subjective dimension of the QoS [27]. Subjective quality assessments have been developed to be closer to the quality really perceived by the user viewing the video [28,29]. Visual models can predict the quality perceived by the viewer of the video, enabling adequate transmission mechanisms. The impact of the encoding rate and the impact of the communication link's QoS show that increasing the encoding bit rate enhances image quality for a lossless communication channel, using objective and subjective metrics [30,31]. The Quality of Perception (QoP) was defined for multimedia communication as a measure encompassing both user satisfaction and his ability to analyze the informational content [32]. E2E adaptation techniques have been proposed to adapt the stream to wireless communication links using objective metrics and perceived quality [33,34,35,36]. Using experimental subjective testing, user QoP for video see-through is modeled to continuously determine the best encoding parameters values resulting from the compromise between the fluidity and the level of detail in the context of real-time interaction with the environment [37]. However, the above QoE measurement techniques do not consider the low delay requirements needed in the 6th *Sense* project.

Perception issues have been studied in the more specific context of AR, taking into account the delay. The E2E system delay is defined as the time difference between the tracking system measurement and the moment when the generated images corresponding to that position and orientation appear in the display. The E2E delay seriously hurts the illusion that the real and virtual worlds coexist because they cause large registration errors. A delay around 100 ms seems acceptable for slow head motion [38,39]. During head motion, users are not able to discriminate delays that differ from less than 17 ms [40,41]. In virtual environments, user performance becomes worse when the frame rate decreases [42,43]. Similarly, a decrease in display resolution reduces the quality of experience [44,45].

QoE Definition. Each of QoS, PQoS and QoP are defined for a specific use. The Lauralee Alben's QoE definition is more general and refers to the subjective usage of interactive products [46]. Within the 6th *Sense* framework, we define QoE as the general subjective user experience. The term QoE encompasses what the user senses, perceives and interprets.

The *Quality of Experience* is a measure of user experience for a specific application. QoE value is measured using a subjective quantified appreciation given by the user. QoE variation is a result of many causes. The quantifiable causes are identified as parameters (for example encoding parameter or head motion). The relation between these parameters and QoE can be modeled.

A *QoE model* represents the impact of parameter change on the QoE. In order to reduce the dependance of the model to the user, parameters are adequately selected. Subjective testing are performed using a finite set of parameters values covering the whole range of possible values. Subjective testing is performed on a group of test users. Measured QoE values are processed to build a general QoE model covering the whole range of parameters values based on average test user responses. The QoE model is used to estimate the QoE value without the further need of an explicit measurement of QoE.

QoE Model for ARV. In the 6th *Sense* project, the main parameters impacting QoE for ARV are:

- encoding parameters;
- E2E delay;
- head motion.

The ARV rate (data size over time) should not be larger than the available network bandwidth, otherwise unwanted delay will be added to the transmission. Thus, the ARV must be generated adequately. The ARV rate depends on the AR scene. The parameters defining the ARV rate are controlled in real time; they are called controllable parameters. These encoding parameters are classified in two groups: inter-frame and intra-frame. *Intra-frame* parameters are related to the size reduction of a frame. The color depth of the image and the dimension in pixels have a direct impact on the frame size. Spatial compression is another obvious solution to reduce the frame size. Temporal compression also reduces the resulting frame size. Although temporal compression depends on the dynamic content of the video, it reduces the information contained in a frame, thus its size as well. *Inter-frame* parameters are related to the rate reduction that do not modify the frames themselves but the time between frames. Frame dropping algorithm can also be seen as inter-frame encoding parameter. We use the frame rate as an inter-frame parameter since it can be directly controlled in AR.

The E2E delay causes dynamic registration errors. This E2E delay is the sum of delays present in the AR transmission from tracking to display, including scene generation. Some of them are fixed and cannot be controlled, while others can be modified. For example, reducing the resolution of the AR scene will generally reduce the delay of the scene generation. This E2E delay can be measured [47]. The presence of delay in an AR system degrades the illusion of coherence between the real and virtual worlds. When the user moves his head, it can result in oscillopsia, which is the perception that the visual world lags behind or swims around the real environment. With a typical E2E lag of 100 ms and a moderate head rotation rate of 50 degrees per second, the angular dynamic error is 5 degrees. At arm length (68 cm), this results in registration errors of almost 6 cm [38].

Head motion modifies the user perception. When the user quickly moves his head, he will generally not be very sensitive to small details in the environment, but to scene dynamics. As the user freely moves his head, head motion is not a controllable parameter. However, head motion can be measured by the tracking system and used by the adaptation mechanism. Allison et al. show the relation between average head velocity and the accepted delay threshold: from 60 ms to nearly 200 ms of delay are acceptable to the user when the average head velocity is decreased from 90 to 22.5 degrees per second [39]. These examples show the link between head motion and delay and the impact on QoE.

We assume that a decrease of any encoding parameter results in or lower or equal QoE. Similarly, when the delay increases, the QoE becomes lower. The QoE model is a monotonic function of the parameters. Figure 2a illustrates the impact of the controllable parameters on the QoE, for fixed measurable parameters. This model shows the general shape for a specific configuration which corresponds to a delay around 50 ms and a low head motion speed.

Real-Time Adaptation for QoE. In the QoE model for ARV, some parameters can be controlled in real time while others can only be measured. The encoding parameters are the *controllable parameters*. The head motion and the E2E delay are the *measurable parameters*. Based on the QoE model presented previously, real-time adaptation of controllable parameters is performed to maximize the QoE. The measurable parameters values are taken as inputs in the QoE model to get an instantaneous representation of the model. This reduced model represents only the impact of controllable parameters on QoE. Then, the constraint on the controllable parameters is set and the adequate controllable parameters values are found using optimization techniques.

In the case of ARV, the sending rate must fit the available network bandwith. The constraint corresponds to the sending rate of the video. In the domain of the controllable parameters (the encoding parameters), this constraint is the product of the inter-frame and the intra-frame parameters. The higher the inter-frame parameter is, the higher the ARV rate becomes. Figure 2b illustrates the

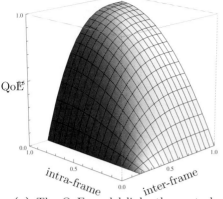

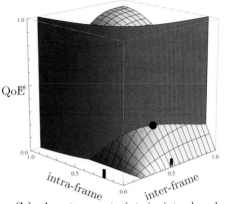

(a) The QoE model links the controllable parameters (inter-frame and intra-frame) to the QoE, for a fixed value of the measurable parameters (head motion and E2E delay).

(b) A rate constraint is introduced in the graphical representation of the QoE model. The values for the encoding parameters are chosen in order to maximize the QoE and to respect the constraint.

Fig. 2. Graphical representation of a QoE model and the real-time adaptation under a bandwidth constraint. The axis are set from 0 to 1, where 1 represents the higher value for the encoding parameters or for the QoE.

constraint on the QoE model. To achieve this constraint rate, only a subset of encoding parameters are usable. On this subset, a combination maximizes the QoE: the optimal controllable parameters are set to this value.

Encoding parameters are continuously adapted to provide the user with the best possible QoE. Head motion can be measured and used to adapt the balance between the intra-frame (level of detail in a single frame) and the inter-frame (frame rate impacting the fluidity) encoding. In the current approach used to determine this balance, the fluidity of the ARV is preferred for fast head motion, while the level-of-detail is preferred for a slow motion. This adaptation is somehow similar to what our brain does. We need to keep our head stable to be able to read something very far, while it is impossible to perceive the same level of detail when we are quickly moving our head. When head motion slows down, real-time adaptation reduces the fluidity of the ARV and increases its level of detail, while keeping the same sending rate.

4.2 ARV Rate Control

Due to encoder characteristics, the output rate of the video stream depends on its content, for example an image with many details will carry a bigger frame size than a uniformly black image. Similarly when considering temporal compression, a sequence with rapid changes in its content will be bigger in size than an almost static video sequence. Therefore, a rate control must be deployed in order to follow the given reference rate defined by the communication link capabilities.

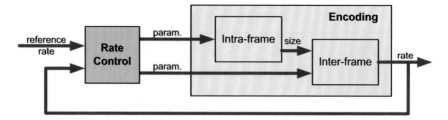

Fig. 3. The rate control regulated the sending rate to the reference rate. A feedback loop is implemented to control the ARV rate control, by adjusting the encoding parameters.

Existing video rate controls do not take advantage of the fact that ARV frames can be generated when desired and that future ARV frames can be predicted. A model-based rate controller for ARV is proposed.

Related research. Video rate control mechanisms are numerous. Control mechanisms are generally specific to an encoder and aim at maximizing objective quality metrics. Others rate control techniques are based on control theory. Yoo-Sok Saw presented an overview of real-time video compression and rate control techniques [48]. The author first showed the non-stationary nature of digital video and presented the basics of compression: removing spatial and temporal redundancy and the macro blocks partition of a picture. Chen and Ngan presented recent advances in rate control for video coding [49]. Proportional Integrated Derivative (PID) controller have been proposed to achieve an accurate bitrate while controlling the encoder buffer [50,51,52]. However, these rate control techniques are designed for specific encoders and are therefore difficult to generalize.

Model-Based ARV Rate Control. The system being controlled is the video encoder. A model of the system is proposed to design a rate controller (Fig. 3). The objective is to control the rate, seen as the output of the system. The inputs are the encoding parameters that can be adapted in real time to modify the output. Encoding parameters are differentiated in two groups: intra-frame parameters that relate to frame-size reduction, and inter-frame parameters that control the time between frames.

As the inputs and the output of the system have been defined, a model linking inputs and output can be built. To obtain a model for control, the real inputs are linearized to have an independent linear impact on the output. For example, instead of taking the highly nonlinear spatial compression parameter directly as input, it is linearized to form a new input representing the spatial compression providing a proportional impact on frame size.

The content of the ARV stream also impacts the rate. This content parameter varies over time and can modify the rate directly. This parameter can be seen as a time-varying model uncertainty. As it modifies the rate, the rate controller acts on the encoder even for a fixed reference rate. In order to control content parameter's effect on the rate, we evaluate this value using predictive control. One of the main advantages of the ARV over regular video stream is the possibility to

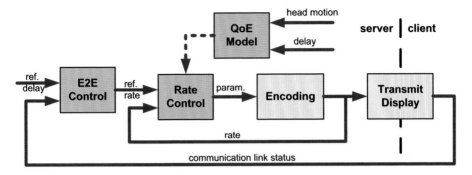

Fig. 4. The E2E adaptation scheme maximizes the QoE in real time. The outer loop adapts the sending rate to the available network bandwidth. The inner loop controls the ARV rate. Based on the QoE model, the encoding parameters are adjusted to the head motion.

generate the future frame content ahead of time, based on head motion prediction. The unknown ARV content depends on head position and the virtual scene state. Many techniques exist to predict future head position [53,54], generally used to generate AR in advance to compensate the E2E delay. These predictive techniques can be used in the rate control to predict the content parameter and its impact on the rate, to determine the adequate input to apply.

We choose an integral controller to track the given reference. It has the advantage of smoothly approaching the chosen reference according to the integral gain. Based on a discrete model of the encoder, it is possible to design a stabilizing controller, as shown in the example in Sect. 6.3.

4.3   Adaptation Scheme

The proposed global adaptation scheme is represented by two cascaded loops (Fig. 4). The outer loop controls the E2E delay by specifying the reference sending rate used by the inner loop. The inner loop consists in the ARV rate control scheme presented in Sect. 4.2, with the rate reference given by the outer-loop controller. The rate control uses the QoE model to determine the balance between encoding parameters, in function of head motion. Head motion angular speed is evaluated using the last measurements provided by the tracking system.

Transmissions over a wireless link are subject to the large variations of network characteristics. As a result, both available bandwidth and transmission delay are constrained. Any information transmitted that could exceed the available bandwidth would be delayed or lost by the network. Various techniques for media streaming have been developed, including adaptation strategy, acting on the encoding part [55]. Advanced streaming solutions consider both end-user quality and network constraints [56,57,58,59]. These techniques achieve better user experience than solutions that do not consider quality.

The ARV is generated on the server side and is then transmitted to the mobile device through the wireless link. The communication link has a limited capacity that varies through time; it is dependent on many factors such as the distance between the sender and the receiver. Sent data exceeding the available bandwidth will be delayed and lost in the transmission, resulting in a lower user experience. The E2E adaptation mechanism is deployed to keep the sending rate in accordance with available bandwidth. The controller is designed using a system abstraction that sees the communication link as an input/output system, similar at what was proposed by Salzmann et al. [60]. Section. 6.3 shows the measurements done on a wireless communication link for system identification and validation of the E2E adaptation mechanism.

5   Generic AR Layer

The E2E Adaptation Layer presented in the previous section takes advantage of functionalities offered by the Generic AR Layer. In fact the goal of the Generic AR Layer is to provide a set of application independent functionalities such that applications themselves are offloaded of these tasks. Figure 5 shows the global architecture with the main information flows. The client and server representations are embedded in the diagram, since the tasks can be distributed between the client and the server depending on hardware resources. The display device and image decoder are obviously always on the client; the application, context, coder and business part of the framework are most likely found on the server. The other modules can either be on the client or on the server.

Thanks to the proposed framework approach, each layer is independent from the others. For example, the user can use the Generic AR Layer without activating the E2E Adaptation Layer, but with the disadvantage that the AR data flow will not be optimized automatically regarding the different parameters from the connection between the server and the client. Task distribution between client and server depends on several factors such as the application domain (information that is transmitted, quality issues, potential risks) or some network conditions (bandwidth, transmission quality, interference).

Depending on the context, a 6th Sense client might be equipped with only an HMD and mobile communication equipment. If the wireless communication quality is not sufficient, all or part of the visualization can be done with the user's embedded equipment. The Generic AR Layer is divided in three logical units which are each responsible for a set of specific features:

- Display: managing the augmented video stream;
- Tracking: managing the user's head position and orientation, interaction-tag detection;
- Multimodality: managing the voice, gesture recognition, text-to-speech, fusion of modalities.

These parts are presented in the following subsections and through the 6th Sense demonstrators (Sect. 6). The main goal of the Generic AR Layer is to generate the augmented flow to be displayed on the client device, and send the needed events to the application and adaptation part. The Generic AR Layer

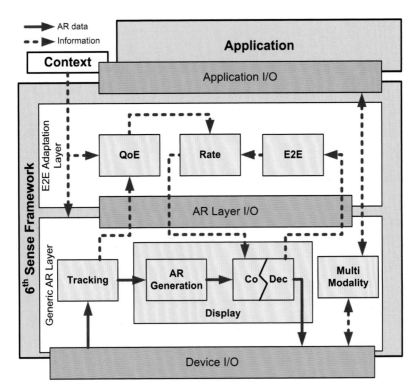

Fig. 5. 6th Sense main building blocks

handles the different devices, and sends the required information to the E2E Adaptation Layer, and adapts its behavior to the adaptation's response for QoE. The current implementation of this layer is event based. All modules communicate with each other using globalized events. The events can carry data like images or information like the startup or shutdown of a specific module of the layer. The architecture is flexible enough to allow the addition of new modules.

5.1   Display

The Display[8] module is responsible for AR generation and its encoding and decoding according to parameters provided by the E2E adaptation. When creating virtual images, the module needs to know where the user is and in which direction he is looking. This information is provided directly by the tracking module. The virtual camera is placed into the virtual world, and the image is generated with the help of a graphical library like OpenGL [61]. The augmented image is then overlaid on the reality within the HMD. The CoDec module encodes and decodes the AR stream according to the E2E adaptation mechanism.

---

[8] Note that this term can be used for visual, aural or haptic display.

5.2   Tracking

The Tracking module handles the data received from the tracking device through the Device I/O layer. The information is generalized into an event object for the Generic AR Layer and then sent to the E2E Adaptation Layer and to the augmentation generation. The Tracking module works as an abstraction layer between the tracking technology and the upper layers. This allows us to change the tracking method without having to make modifications in other parts of the system.

5.3   Multimodality

The Multimodality module contains all the sub modules that allow interaction between the user and the virtual elements, such as text-to-speech, voice and gesture recognition. The context and the application define which modality has to be used at a specific time. The multimodality takes the information from the Device I/O layer, sends it to the upper layers for additional processing if needed, and then sends the answers to the output device. The architecture of the application is made such that the addition of a new type of multimodality can be done without modifying the existing ones.

6   Application

The different functionalities of the proposed framework have been validated through the development of a set of demonstrators and prototypes. Three demonstrators show the functionality of the tracking and the multimodality modules and illustrate the bridge between the physical and the digital worlds. Both a network E2E adaptation and a rate controller validate the theoretical aspects presented earlier.

6.1   Hardware and Software Equipment

Visualization Devices. The 6th *Sense* project aims at providing a generic framework that interfaces the main visualization peripherals used in AR applications: hand-held devices, video see-through HMDs and optical see-through HMDs. The focus is placed on external glasses, from the HMD type to those worn close to the eyes or even handheld devices. Video see-through HMDs are generally dual display devices and the real scene can be captured by one or two cameras rendering a monoscopic or stereoscopic view respectively. With monoscopic video see-through HMDs, the natural perception of depth is lost and this decreases system usability (the user feels less comfortable) and limits their use for short time operations [62]. By definition, optical see-through HMDs offer a stereoscopic vision of the reality but these devices are much more expensive and the calibration process, necessary to avoid registration error, is more complex. If stereoscopy is not needed, monocular glasses and handheld displays can be considered. In the 6th *Sense* prototype the following devices have been used:

(a) Video See-Through HMD eMagin Z800.   **(b)** Optical See-Through HMD Cybermind Visette 45.

Fig. 6. Two of the HMDs used for the 6th Sense prototype

- a handheld ultramobile PC Sony VAIO[9]
- a video see-through HMD eMagin Z800 [10]
- an optical see-through HMD Cybermind Visette 45[11];
- an optical see-through HMD Liteye LE-750[12]
- a Creative Optia AF[13] webcam for video see-through and gestural interaction.

Tracking Systems. Among the numerous tracking technologies available [1] we have chosen technologies that require as few environment modifications as possible and that are the least sensitive to environmental conditions. Therefore only two technologies are retained among all available tracking technologies, namely *video based optical tracking* and *inertial tracking*.

Current robust optical trackers rely on inexpensive artificial fiducials (Fig. 7) placed in the environment. In fact, the quick evolution of computer-vision techniques and the constant increase of available embedded computing power suggest that the availability of sourceless optical trackers, relying on real objects (natural

---

[9] Sony VAIO VGN-UX280P Micro PC http://www.sonystyle.com/webapp/wcs/stores/servlet/ProductDisplay?catalogId=10551&storeId=10151&langId=-1&partNumber=VGNUX280P.

[10] eMagin Z800 3D Visor(http://www.inition.com/inition/product.php?URL_=product_hmd_emagin_z800&SubCatID_=0.)

[11] Cybermind Visette 45 st 3D XVGA Headset (http://www.cybermind.nl/Info/PriceList_USDollars.htm#VisetteSXGA).

[12] Liteye LE-750 Monocular OLED Microdisplay(http://www.inition.com/inition/product.php?URL_=product_hmd_liteye_700&SubCatID_=15.)

[13] Creative Live!Cam Optia AF(http://ch-en.europe.creative.com/products/product.asp?category=218&subcategory=219&product=16425.)

Fig. 7. Example of a fiducial marker used by the optical tracking system to determine the position and orientation of the user's head

landmarks), is just a matter of time [63]. Inertial trackers may achieve very fast sample rates but lack long term stability due to sensor noise and drift caused by the necessary double integration process within pose calculation [64]. Therefore, to guarantee the precision of the estimated pose, inertial trackers need to be re-calibrated frequently by using an absolute pose source, such as an optical tracker.

For the 6th *Sense* project, we have chosen to use a hybrid tracking system (Intersense IS-1200 VisTracker [14] which combines video based optical detection and inertial sensors. The mix of these two different tracking techniques takes the best advantage of each tracking technology it has at its disposal to deliver a more robust and accurate pose estimation than the one obtained by each technology taken individually [65,66]. The tracker used gives a position with a precision from 2 to 5 mm in optimal lightened environments [67]. All you need to get the tracker operating properly is to create a constellation of fiducials. A constellation is composed from a definite number of fiducials (Fig. 7) placed relatively to an arbitrary defined origin. Every value about the current pose of the tracker is then returned relatively to this origin point. With this information, the tracker provides the six degrees of freedom needed to create the visual part of augmented reality applications.

In addition to the main Intersense hybrid tracker we also used the open-source ARToolkitPlus [68] library to track the hand gesture and allow gestural interaction (Sect. 6.1).

Virtual Reality Overlay. The drawing of virtual elements is performed with the OpenGL library [61]. OpenGL provides a way to design virtual 3D scenes and to place a virtual camera to view a part of this scene. The information returned by the tracking module will be used to place the virtual camera according to the user's point of view. This viewport will be mixed with the real video stream to give the illusion that the virtual elements are in the real scene.

Multimodal Interaction. The 6th *Sense* Generic AR Layer has been designed to allow the integration of different input and output modalities.

During the implementation we concentrated our efforts combining hand-based gestures with speech recognition which provide a powerful, concise and natural way to specify complex actions.

---

[14] Intersense IS-1200 VisTracker(http://www.isense.com/uploadedFiles/Products/IS-1200_VisTracker.pdf.)

Gestural Interaction. In one implemented interaction scheme (Sect. 6.2), the different gestural interaction modes are identified with visual tags pasted on different side of the user's hand (wearing a glove). These tags are then detected by ARToolkitPlus library and a command is sent depending on the identification number of the tag. This way, the position of the hand – actually the visible tag – drives the command to execute. The basic commands are *pointing* and *selecting* virtual or real elements in the scene. To point and select an element, we use the ray-casting technique which consists in drawing a virtual line extending the user's hand. Objects that are intersected by this line are selected and can then be grabbed and manipulated.

The selection gesture marks the pointed object; it identifies it and gives it a visual feedback effect. Subsequent commands – set off by a gesture or a speech command for example – could then be applied to the selected object.

Voice/Speech Interaction. The Generic AR Layer also includes off-the-shelf components to implement speech recognition and voice synthesis.

6.2   Generic AR Layer Demonstrators

The key elements of the Generic AR Layer have been validated through the implementation of different scenarios illustrating the role of each building block. Three of these demonstrators are shortly described below. The use of the framework greatly simplified the developer's task for each of these demonstrators permitting to drastically shorten the implementation time. Every demonstrator uses the framework as a common base and illustrates the functionality of each of its components. The aim of these demonstrators is to validate the main building blocks of the proposed generic framework.

Demonstrator 1 - Reality Augmentation. This demonstrator shows the functionality of the tracking part of the 6th *Sense* Generic AR Layer. The entire system is made of a standard laptop, a webcam, and a video see-through HMD (Fig. 8). The tracking device used is an hybrid tracker. The position is recovered in a vector, and the orientation in a quaternion. These two values are then sent to the display module which generates the appropriate 3D image and overlays it on the reality on the HMD.

Figure 8 shows the user equipped with the 6th *Sense* equipement and observing an augmented scene. Figures 9a and 9b show the difference between the user's normal and the augmented view. The virtual castle is anchored to the table to give a better merge of the digital and real world. This demonstrator is used to test the tracking characteristics and the registration. It also allows us to evaluate the impact of the peripherals' calibration on the AR system and the quality of the visual integration of a virtual 3D model into a real scene.

Demonstrator 2 - Gestural Interaction. This demonstrator is used to validate the functioning of the *Multimodality* module, focusing on the gestural modality used to interact with virtual elements. A simple scenario based on the classical

Fiducial markers
used for the tracking
are sticked on the
ceiling

User wearing the
6th Sense equipment
(HMD + Tracker)

Observed object
(real scene)

Fig. 8. User wearing the 6th *Sense* equipment and observing the augmented scene. In his HMD, a virtual object is placed on top of a real table tray.

(a) Real scene.   (b) Augmented scene.

Fig. 9. Reality augmentation: a virtual element is overlayed on the real scene and anchored to it

point-and-select interaction style has been implemented. For this purpose an interaction glove has been designed, augmented with two visual tags which are used to detect user hand-gestures using a ray-casting technique. Fig. 10 illustrates the gestural interaction where point and selection actions are implemented. As shown in Fig. 10 the user wears the interaction glove, this kind of magic wand allows him to point, select and interact with his physical and virtual environment. The pointing action gesture allows the user to point a virtual element: a virtual ray is

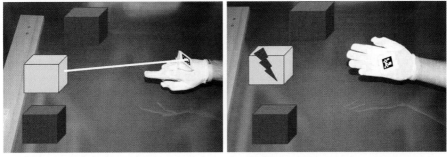

(a) Pointing action and gesture.   **(b)** Selection action and gesture.

Fig. 10. Gestural interaction using two optical markers placed on the back and in the palm of the user's hand

(a) A virtual information point placed under each of the two paintings indicates that some information is available. The user can select one of these information points.

(b) The associated digital content is opened with a third party application. Here a web browser displays information about the painting.

Fig. 11. Link to the digital world

drawn to give the user a visual feedback, helping him to see precisely where he is currently pointing at. The pointed object slightly changes its appearance (e.g. its color) to flag its pointed state. The selecting action gesture allows the user to select a virtual element: once the virtual element has been pointed, a rotation of the hand locks it. Another change of the object's appearance is made to indicate its selected state. A first evaluation of the demonstrator has been done, involving eight persons ranging from 25 to 45 years of age. They had to point and select arbitrary virtual targets in a game application, with no preliminary training. The results of this first usability test assess the good acceptance of this gestural interaction and the ease of use of the demonstrator.

Demonstrator 3 - Link to the Digital World. This demonstrator validates the use of the physical object as an access point to search and browse for related digital content. Virtual elements can give access to digital information such as web pages, pictures, videos, audio files, etc. As shown in Fig. 11, a painting can be associated to a web page (for example Wikipedia) which is browsed when the associated virtual element is activated. This demonstrator shows that the augmentation of the real world with digital information is useful and virtual objects can be easily linked with other data sources. The application runs on an UMPC with an integrated webcam and needs a marker detection system such as ARToolKitPlus for the positioning of virtual elements. Figure 11 shows screenshots explaining the different application steps. To make user experience even richer and more immersive, information about the corresponding painting could appear near it. This demonstrator points out the importance of having appropriate information visualization within AR system in order to avoid information overload and highlights the potential of using AR systems in smart environment applications. Every day objects can become multi-media entry points for informations browsing and retrieval.

6.3 6th *Sense* Framework Demonstrator

Using the Generic AR Layer, the server sends the ARV to the client device using a 802.11g network infrastructure. The ARV is generated at a variable frame rate and is compressed using JPEG compression factor (temporal compression is not considered in this example). In the E2E Adaptation Layer, the cascade controller implements the adaptation scheme presented in Sect. 4.3. In order to adapt the sending rate to the available network bandwidth, the outer loop tracks a given reference delay. The inner loop tracks the reference rate by adapting the two encoding parameters

E2E Adaptation. The E2E delay corresponds to the time between the tracking of the head position and the display of the AR information, including the transmission time and the delay from potential retransmission mechanisms. When a packet collision occurs (e.g. cross-traffic), the sender waits for some time and tries to retransmit the information. As a result the transmission time increases. The delay increases until a given threshold after which data loss occurs; this threshold represents the time it takes for data to transit through a full buffer. When the buffer is full, incoming data are lost.

Figure 12 shows the transmission delay. It starts at 5 ms and increases slightly as the sending rate increases until the sending rate threshold is reached (Fig. 12). For the given configuration, the threshold is 21 Mb/s. At this rate the delay jumps to 80 ms and stays constant even if the sending rate increases since losses begin to occur at this level. Thus, to avoid transmission delay and loss, both resulting in a lower user experience, the sending rate must stay below this threshold. However, this threshold is highly dependent on network conditions and thus is not known beforehand. In order to follow this varying rate threshold, we track the corresponding delay, by adapting the sending rate.

An integral controller has been implemented to track the reference transmission delay. The integral gain has been defined to stabilize the system in different configurations (distance from the access point, traffic). For our experiments, the chosen transmission delay reference has been set to 7 ms. For a smaller reference,

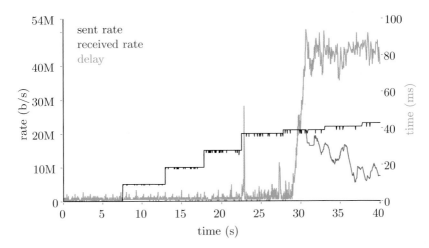

Fig. 12. The experimentation show the behavior of the delay when the sending rate is increased manually by steps. The delay increases when the sending rate threshold is achieved, and the received rate begin to decrease due to packet loss.

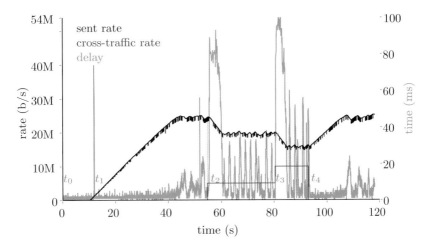

Fig. 13. In closed loop, the E2E adaptation controller increases the sending rate until the delay achieve the reference value. The sending rate stabilizes around the rate threshold, even when the cross-traffic changes (t_2, t_3, t_4).

the identified sending rate threshold is not reached, especially in presence of cross traffic. For a larger reference, losses occur and the system in closed loop oscillates.

The controller behavior is shown in Fig. 13. At time t_0, the sending rate is set to the smallest possible rate (8 b/s) and the controller is not activated. At time t_1, the controller is activated; the sending rate increases since the measured transmission delay is below the reference transmission delay of 7 ms. When the reference delay is reached, the sending rate stabilizes at around 25 Mb/s. Note that this value corresponds approximately to the experimental threshold discovered during the network identification. At time t_2, another source starts to send data on the same channel at 5 Mb/s. As a result, the delay increases and losses occur. Thus the controller reacts and decreases the sending rate (around 19 Mb/s) until the delay reaches 7 ms. At time t_3, the other source increases its sending rate from 5 Mb/s to 10 Mb/s. Again, loss appears and delay increases. The controller decreases accordingly the sending rate to 15 Mb/s to ensure low delay and no loss. At time t_4, the other source stops to send. The control increases the sending rate until the transmission delay reaches 7 ms. As a consequence the sending rate reaches its initial value.

Rate Control. The rate control algorithm tracks a given reference rate, by adapting the ARV encoding parameters. The given reference rate is provided by the E2E adaptation. For this experimentation scenario, the AR scene consists of a virtual inverted pendulum located on a table. The user can freely move his head and looks at the pendulum displayed in his optical see-through HMD. The user's viewpoint, measured with the tracking system, defines the ARV frame content. Figure 14a shows the four specific ARV frames displayed at times t_1, t_2, t_3 and t_4. At time t_1, the pendulum is out of the field of view and the frame is uniformly black, which is interpreted as transparent for the HMD. At time t_2, part of the pendulum is within the user's field of view. The resulting ARV frame is thus richer than the black image. At time t_3, the pendulum is completely visible. At time t_4, the user moves toward the pendulum and can see the details of the mobile cart.

Figure 14b shows the ARV rate in open loop (ie. the encoding parameters are fixed). At time t_1, the black ARV frame generates a minimal rate. This rate increases significantly when the content is no longer uniform. We can see that the more detailed the ARV frame is, the bigger the rate is. On the other hand, it is difficult to tell in advance which ARV frame will generate the larger rate size from frames at times t_3 or t_4. The large rate variations generate incompatible transmission delay and thus need to be controlled by the rate control algorithm.

The proposed rate control algorithm consists of an integral controller which tracks the given reference rate. The integral gain has been determined analytically to keep stability in closed loop for every content in this experimentation scenario. Figure 14c shows the ARV rate variations when the reference rate and the content vary. The rate control algorithm successfully tracks the reference rate when the content varies and when the reference rate changes. Before time t_1, the rate controller increased the encoding parameters until the reference is reached. At time t_2, there is a rapid change in the ARV frame content that induces a large rate variation. The rate controller reduces the encoding parameters to compensate this variation and follows the given reference rate. Between times t_2 and t_3, the ARV content varies and the rate control algorithm successfully controls the output rate. Right after time t_3, the reference rate is multiplied by three, resulting from a larger available bandwidth. As a result, the rate controller increases the encoding parameters. Shortly before time t_4, the reference rate is reduced to its initial value and the encoding parameters are reduced accordingly. Compared with Fig. 14b where the controller is not activated, Fig. 14c

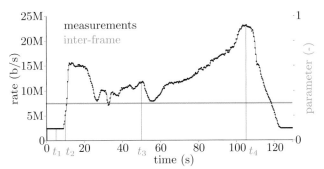

(b) Rate in open loop (fixed encoding parameters). Both encoding parameters are fixed, the output rate varies due the dynamical content. The richer the content is, the higher the rate becomes.

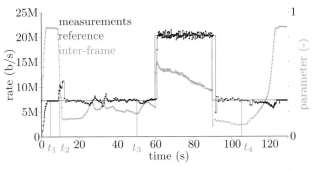

(a) ARV frames at times t_1, t_2, t_3 and t_4 according to user position.

(c) Rate in closed loop. The integral controller adapts the inter-frame parameter to track the reference. The inter-frame parameters is decreased when the content becomes richer and vice versa.

Fig. 14. Encoder output rate behavior with and without controller. The inter-frame range goes from 0 (1000 ms) to 1 (10 ms), while the intra-frame parameter is fixed.

shows that the rate control algorithm is efficient in tracking a given reference rate despite the varying ARV content that can be seen as a disturbance.

Both the E2E adaptation and the rate control constitute an efficient solution for ARV encoding and transmission. Moreover, they provide the ability to easily integrate the real-time adaptation for QoE in the global scheme.

7   Conclusion and Future Work

In this paper, we presented a generic framework for end-to-end adaptive wearable augmented reality. Augmented Reality (AR) acts as a sixth sense for users by overlaying contextual virtual information on the top of the real world. The proposed framework is composed of two main layers: the End-to-End (E2E) Adaptation

Layer and the Generic AR Layer. The aim of the E2E Adaptation Layer is to improve user perception of his surrounding environment by providing best possible user experience despite external disturbances and context changes.

Within the E2E Adaptation Layer, the implemented adaptation scheme uses a Quality of Experience (QoE) model derived from the measured QoE using subjective testing. The adaptation scheme controls the various parameters of the AR infrastructure that encompasses the user, the hardware and the communication link. The QoE model is used by the adaptation scheme to choose in real-time the best possible information encoding parameters according to operating conditions.

The Generic AR Layer provides a set of application independent functionalities necessary when designing and developing AR applications. The Generic AR Layer is composed of three main modules: Display, Tracking, and Multimodality modules. The Display module is responsible for AR generation and AR encoding/decoding according to the parameters provided E2E Adaptation Layer. The Tracking module handles the data received from the tracking device to estimate user head position and orientation. The Multimodality module manages user interaction with the virtual environment using both the user's voice and/or gesture.

Three simple demonstrators were presented to validate the proposed building blocks of the Generic AR Layer. The first demonstrator illustrates the integration of the virtual elements in a real scene with all associated tracking and registration aspects. The second one validates the multimodality building block, focusing on gestural interactions. The third one highlights the link between the physical world and the virtual space, pointing out the importance of information presentation in order to minimize information overload.

In addition, the last demonstrator illustrates the usage of all the 6th *Sense* framework components. The Generic AR Layer and the E2E Adaptation Layer are combined to propose a solution that not only provides contextual AR information overlay to the end-user but also adapts to the varying network condition to provide the best possible QoE to the end-user. The tests conducted show that the E2E delay mainly responsible for the registration error can be controlled and maintained to a value acceptable by the user. The transmission rate variation induced by the AR content variation is also successfully controlled by the E2E adaptation scheme combined with an estimation of the future head position.

One of the main problems encountered with the proposed demonstrators is the lack of flexibility imposed by the tracking system. Instead of using fiducials, the usage of real scene elements as natural landmarks should be investigated. The robustness of the proposed QoE model needs to be extended to better handle new contexts. The model identification should also be improved to handle new situations.

Another enhancement to the proposed framework consists in integrating generic context-awareness modules to improve information search and retrieval towards a richer and personalized user experience. Similarly the integration of high-level 3D rendering libraries such as *Ogre* or *OpenSceneGraph* is envisioned for rendering more complex and realistic virtual scenes.

References

1. Costanza, E., Fjeld, M.: Augmented Reality, a Survey. In: Human Machine Interaction. LNCS. Springer, Heidelberg (2009)
2. Walsh, K., Pawlowski, S.: Virtual reality: A technology in need of IS research. Communications of the AIS 8, 297–313 (2002)
3. Card, S.K., Mackinlay, J.D., Shneiderman, B.: Readings in information visualization: using vision to think. Morgan Kaufmann Publishers, San Francisco (1999)
4. Holmquist, L.E.: Focus+context visualization with flip zooming and the zoom browser. In: Extended Abstracts on Human Factors in Computing Systems: Looking to the Future (CHI 1997), Atlanta, Georgia, pp. 263–264. ACM, New York (1997)
5. Spence, R.: Information Visualization: Design for Interaction, 2nd edn. Prentice-Hall, Upper Saddle River (2007)
6. Kalkusch, M., Lidy, T., Knapp, N., Reitmayr, G., Kaufmann, H., Schmalstieg, D.: Structured visual markers for indoor pathfinding. In: Proceedings of the first International Workshop on Augmented Reality Toolkit (2002)
7. Bolt, R.A.: "Put-that-there": Voice and gesture at the graphics interface. In: Proceedings of the 7th Annual Conference on Computer Graphics and Interactive Techniques, Seattle, Washington, United States, pp. 262–270. ACM, New York (1980)
8. Reithinger, N., Bergweiler, S., Engel, R., Herzog, G., Pfleger, N., Romanelli, M., Sonntag, D.: A look under the hood: design and development of the first smartweb system demonstrator. In: Proceedings of the 7th International Conference on Multimodal Interfaces, Torento, Italyq, pp. 159–166. ACM, New York (2005)
9. Jaimes, A., Sebe, N.: Multimodal human-computer interaction: A survey. Computer Visioin and Image Understanding 108(1-2), 116–134 (2007)
10. Wagner, D., Schmalstieg, D., Billinghurst, M.: Handheld AR for Collaborative Edutainment. LNCS, pp. 85–96. Springer, Heidelberg (2006)
11. Behzadan, A.H., Khoury, H.M., Kamat, V.R.: Structure of an extensible augmented reality framework for visualization of simulated construction processes. In: Proceedings of the 38th Conference on Winter Simulation, Monterey, California, pp. 2055–2062 (2006)
12. Piekarski, W., Thomas, B.: Using ARToolKit for 3D hand position tracking in mobile outdoor environments. In: Augmented Reality Toolkit, The first IEEE International Workshop (2002)
13. Gleue, T., Dähne, P.: Design and implementation of a mobile device for outdoor augmented reality in the archeoguide project. In: Proceedings of the Conference on Virtual Reality, Archeology, and Cultural Heritage, Glyfada, Greece, pp. 161–168. ACM, New York (2001)
14. Cheok, A.D., Yang, X., Ying, Z.Z., Billinghurst, M., Kato, H.: Touch-space: Mixed reality game space based on ubiquitous, tangible, and social computing. Personal Ubiquitous Computing 6(5-6), 430–442 (2002)
15. Bauer, M., Bruegge, B., Klinker, G., MacWilliams, A., Reicher, T., Riss, S., Sandor, C., Wagner, M.: Design of a component-based augmented reality framework. In: Proceedings of the International Symposium on Augmented Reality, pp. 45–54. ACM and IEEE (2001)

16. Schmalstieg, D., Fuhrmann, A., Hesina, G., Szalaári, Z., Encarnação, L.M., Gervautz, M., Purgathofer, W.: The studierstube augmented reality project. Presence: Teleoperators and Virtual Environments 11(1), 33–54 (2002)
17. Henrysson, A., Ollila, M.: UMAR: Ubiquitous mobile augmented reality. In: Proceedings of the 3rd International Conference on Mobile and Ubiquitous Multimedia (MUM 2004), pp. 41–45. ACM, New York (2004)
18. Wagner, D., Schmalstieg, D.: Handheld augmented reality displays. In: Proceedings of the Virtual Reality Conference, pp. 35–36. IEEE, Los Alamitos (2006)
19. Peternier, A., Vexo, F., Thalmann, D.: Wearable mixed reality system in less than 1 pound. In: Proceedings of the 12th Eurographics Symposium on Virtual Environment (2006)
20. Mann, S.: Wearable computing: A first step toward personal imaging. Computer 30(2), 25–32 (1997)
21. Behringer, R., Tam, C., McGee, J., Sundareswaran, S., Vassiliou, M.: A wearable augmented reality testbed for navigation and ccontrol, built solely with commercial-off-the-shelf (COTS) hardware. In: Proceedings of the International Symposium on Augmented Reality (ISAR 2000), pp. 12–19. IEEE and ACM (2000)
22. Geiger, C., Kleinnjohann, B., Reimann, C., Stichling, D.: Mobile AR4ALL. In: Proceedings of the International Symposium on Augmented Reality, pp. 181–182. IEEE and ACM (2001)
23. Pasman, W., Woodward, C.: Implementation of an augmented reality system on a PDA. In: Proceedings of the 2nd International Symposium on Mixed and Augmented Reality, pp. 276–277. IEEE and ACM (2003)
24. Wagner, D., Schmalstieg, D.: First steps towards handheld augmented reality. In: Proceedings of the 7th International Symposium on Wearable Computers, pp. 127–135. IEEE, Los Alamitos (2003)
25. Pasman, W., Jansen, F.: Distributed low-latency rendering for mobile AR. In: Proceedings of the International Symposium on Augmented Reality, pp. 107–113. IEEE and ACM (2001)
26. Jain, R.: Quality of experience. Multimedia, IEEE 11(1), 95–96 (2004)
27. Prasad, A., Esmailzadeh, R., Winkler, S., Ihara, T., Rohani, B., Pinguet, B., Capel, M.: Perceptual quality measurement and control: Definition, application and performance. In: Proceedings of the 4th International Symposium on Wireless Personal Multimedia Communications, Aalborg, Denmark, vol. 2, p. 255 (2001)
28. Winkler, S.: Vision models and quality metrics for image processing applications. PhD thesis, Ecole Polytechnique Fédérale de Lausanne, Lausanne (2000)
29. Sheikh, H.R., Bovik, A.C.: Image information and visual quality. IEEE Transactions on Image Processing 15(2), 430–444 (2006)
30. Verscheure, O., Garcia, X., Karlsson, G., Hubaux, J.P.: User-oriented QoS in packet video delivery. IEEE Network 12(6), 12–21 (1998)
31. Ghinea, G., Thomas, J.P., Fish, R.S.: Multimedia, network protocols and users - bridging the gap. In: Proceedings of the 7th International Conference on Multimedia (Part 1) (MULTIMEDIA 1999), pp. 473–476. ACM, New York (1999)
32. Ghinea, G., Fish, R.S., Thomas, J.P.: Using quality of perception for improved multimedia communication. In: Proceedings of the AFRICON, vol. 2, pp. 1241–1246. IEEE, Los Alamitos (1999)
33. Takahata, K., Uchida, N., Shibata, Y.: QoS control for real time video stream over hybrid network by wired and wireless LANs. In: Proceedings of the 17th International Conference on Advanced Information Networking and Applications (AINA 2003), pp. 45–51. IEEE, Los Alamitos (2003)

34. Bai, Y., Ito, M.: Network-level loss control schemes for streaming video. In: Proceedings of the International Conference on Multimedia and Expo (ICME 2004), vol. 1, pp. 495–498. IEEE, Los Alamitos (2004)
35. Cranley, N.: User-Perceived Quality-Aware Adaptation of Streamed Multimedia over Best-effort IP Networks. PhD thesis, National University of Ireland, Department of Computer Science Faculty of Science University College Dublin Belfield, Dublin 4 (March 2004)
36. Cranley, N., Perry, P., Murphy, L.: Dynamic content-based adaptation of streamed multimedia. Journal of Network and Computer Applications 30(3), 983–1006 (2007)
37. Perritaz, D., Salzmann, C., Gillet, D.: User perception model for wearable supervision systems. In: Proceedings of the 4th International Conference on Mobile Technology, Applications and Systems and the 1st International Symposium on Computer Human Interaction in Mobile Technology (Mobility 2007) (September 2007)
38. Azuma, R.T.: A survey of augmented reality. Presence-Teleoperators and Virtual Environments 6(4), 355–385 (1997)
39. Allison, R.S., Harris, L.R., Jenkin, M., Jasiobedzka, U., Zacher, J.E.: Tolerance of temporal delay in virtual environments. In: Proceedings of the Virtual Reality Conference (VR 2001), pp. 247–254. IEEE, Los Alamitos (2001)
40. Ellis, S.R., Young, M.J., Adelstein, B.D., Ehrlich, S.M.: Discrimination of changes in latency during head movement. In: Proceedings of the 8th International Conference on Human-Computer Interaction (HCI 1999) on Human-Computer Interaction: Communication, Cooperation, and Application Design, vol. 2, pp. 1129–1133. ACM, New York (1999)
41. Adelstein, B.D., Lee, T.G., Ellis, S.R.: Head tracking latency in virtual environments: Psychophysics and a model. In: Proceedings of the 47th Annual Meeting on Human Factors and Ergonomics Society, pp. 2083–2087 (2003)
42. Barfield, W., Hendrix, C.: The effect of update rate on the sense of presence within virtual environments. Virtual Reality 1(1), 3–15 (1995)
43. Lai, W.Y., Duh, H.B.L.: Effects of frame eate for visualization of dynamic quantitative information in a head-mounted display. In: Proceedings of the International Conference on Systems, Man and Cybernetics, vol. 7, pp. 6485–6490. IEEE, Los Alamitos (2004)
44. Smets, G.J., Overbeeke, K.J.: Trade-off between resolution and interactivity in spatial task performance. IEEE Computer Graphics and Applications 15(5), 46–51 (1995)
45. Ryu, J., Hashimoto, N., Sato, M.: Influence of resolution degradation on distance estimation in virtual space displaying static and dynamic image. In: Proceedings of the International Conference on Cyberworlds (CW 2005). IEEE, Los Alamitos (2005)
46. Alben, L.: Quality of experience: Defining the criteria for effective interaction design. Interactions 3(3), 11–15 (1996)
47. Sielhorst, T., Sa, W., Khamene, A., Sauer, F., Navab, N.: Measurement of absolute latency for video see through augmented reality. In: Proceedings of the 6th International Symposium on Mixed and Augmented Reality (ISMAR 2007), pp. 215–220. IEEE and ACM (2007)
48. Saw, Y.S.: Rate-quality optimized video coding. Kluwer Academic Publishers, Norwell (1999)
49. Chen, Z., Ngan, K.N.: Recent advances in rate control for video coding. Signal Processing: Image Communications Magazine 22(1), 19–38 (2007)

50. Yu, S., Ahmad, I.: New rate control algorithm for MPEG-4 video coding. In: Proceedings of the Conference on Visual Communications and Image Processing. The Society of Photo-Optical Instrumentation Engineers (SPIE) Conference, vol. 4671, pp. 698–709 (January 2002)
51. Wong, C.W., Au, O.C., Lam, H.K.: PID-based real-time rate control. In: Proceedings of the International Conference on Multimedia and Expo (ICME 2004), vol. 1, pp. 221–224. IEEE, Los Alamitos (2004)
52. Shen, L., Liu, Z., Zhang, Z., Shi, X.: Rate control based on an incremental proportional-integral-differential algorithm. Optical Engineering 46(7), 077002-1–7 (2007)
53. Azuma, R.T.: Predictive Tracking for Augmented Reality. PhD thesis, University of North Carolina at Chapel Hill (February 1995)
54. Tumanov, A., Allison, R., Stuerzlinger, W.: Variability-aware latency amelioration in distributed environments. In: Proceedings of the Virtual Reality Conference (VR 2007), pp. 123–130. IEEE, Los Alamitos (2007)
55. Chakareski, J., Frossard, P.: Adaptive systems for improved media streaming experience. IEEE Communications Magazine 45(1), 77–83 (2007)
56. Cranley, N., Murphy, L., Perry, P.: Perceptual quality adaptation (PQA) algorithm for 3GP and multi-tracker MPEG-4 content over wireless IP networks. In: Proceedings of the 5th International Symposium on Personal, Indoor and Mobile Radio Communications (PIMRC 2004), vol. 3, pp. 2107–2112. IEEE, Los Alamitos (2004)
57. Muntean, G.M., Cranley, N.: Resource efficient quality-oriented wireless broadcasting of adaptive multimedia content. IEEE Transactions on Broadcasting 53(1), 362–368 (2007)
58. Kim, T., Ammar, M.H.: Optimal quality adaptation for scalable encoded video. IEEE Journal on Selected Areas in Communications 23(2), 344–356 (2005)
59. Ni, Z.F., Chen, Z.Z., Ngan, K.N.: A real-time video transport system for the best-effort Internet. Signal Processing-Image Communication 20(3), 277–293 (2005)
60. Salzmann, C., Gillet, D., Müllhaupt, P.: End-to-end adaptation scheme for ubiquitous remote experimentation. Personal and Ubiquitous Computing (October 2007)
61. Munshi, A., Ginsburg, D., Shreiner, D.: OpenGL ES 2.0 programming guide. Addison-Wesley Professional, Reading (2008)
62. Grasset, R., Boissieux, L., Gascuel, J.D., Schmalstieg, D.: Interactive mediated reality. In: Proceedings of the 6th Australasian User Interface Conference (AUIC 2005), Newcastle, Australia (February 2005)
63. Ozuysal, M., Fua, P., Lepetit, V.: Fast keypoint recognition in ten lines of code. In: Proceedings of the Conference on Computer Vision and Pattern Recognition (CVPR 2007), pp. 1–8. IEEE, Los Alamitos (2007)
64. Stock, C., Siegl, H., Zinsser, T., Pinz, A.: Hybrid tracking for collaborative mobile AR. In: Deliverable D.4.4, Graz University of Technology (May 31, 2004)
65. State, A., Hirota, G., Chen, D.T., Garrett, W.F., Livingston, M.A.: Superior augmented reality registration by integrating landmark tracking and magnetic tracking. In: Proceedings of the 23rd annual conference on Computer graphics and interactive techniques, pp. 429–438. ACM, New York (1996)
66. Rolland, J.P., Baillot, Y., Goon, A.A.: A survey of tracking technology for virtual environments. Lawrence Erlbaum Associates, Orlando (1995)
67. Wormell, D., Foxlin, E., Katzman, P.: Advanced inertial-optical tracking system for wide area mixed and augmented reality systems. In: Proceedings of the 10th International Immersive Projection Technologies Workshop (2007)
68. Wagner, D., Schmalstieg, D.: ARToolKitPlus for pose tracking on mobile devices. In: Computer Vision Winter Workshop, pp. 6–8 (2007)

Author Index

Abou Khaled, Omar   103, 280
Alam, Sazzadul   167
Amaral, Vasco   221
Amrhein, Beatrice   193
Aradilla, Guillermo   71

Bapst, Jacques   280
Barras, Frédéric   280
Barroca, Bruno   221
Bazargan, Kaveh   221
Boccuzzo, Sandro   167
Boder, Alexandre   103
Bologna, Guido   251
Bourlard, Hervé   71
Brodbeck, Dominique   27
Buchs, Didier   221

Costanza, Enrico   47
Cretton, Fabian   221

Deville, Benoît   251
Dugerdil, Philippe   167
Dumas, Bruno   3, 103

Eckerle, Jürgen   193
Evéquoz, Florian   103

Falquet, Gilles   221
Fischli, Stephan   193
Fjeld, Morten   47

Gall, Harald   167
Gerardi, Sandro   103
Gessner, Wolfgang   133
Gillet, Denis   280

Hauck, Robert   193
Hermansky, Hynek   71
Hoigné, Dominik   193

Ingold, Rolf   103

Kunz, Andreas   47
Künzler, Urs   193

Lalanne, Denis   3, 27, 103
Lanza, Michele   167
Le Calvé, Anne   103, 221
Lenore Schiewer, Gesine   133

Malandain, Stéphane   221
Mazza, Riccardo   27
Mugellini, Elena   103, 280

Naef, Olivier   280

Oviatt, Sharon   3

Perritaz, Damien   280
Pinto, Joel   71
Pun, Thierry   251

Rey, Paul-Henri   71
Ringenbach, Alex   133
Risoldi, Matteo   221

Salzmann, Christophe   280
Stricker, Claude   71

Théraulaz, Jérôme   71

Vinckenbosch, Michel   251

Wagen, Jean-Frédéric   71
Wettel, Richard   167
Witschi, Reto   193

Zoss, Pierrick   221

Printing: Mercedes-Druck, Berlin
Binding: Stein+Lehmann, Berlin